THE LIFE OF
LORENA HICKOK
E.R.'s Friend

THE LIFE OF
LORENA HICKOK

E.R.'s Friend

by
Doris Faber

WILLIAM MORROW AND COMPANY, INC.
New York   1980

We are grateful to the following publications for permission to quote from articles originally published by them:

The Bowdle *Pioneer*, the Ithaca *Journal-News*, the *Milwaukee Sentinel*, *The Minneapolis Star*, the *Minneapolis Tribune*, and *The New York Times*.

The excerpt on pages 158–159 reprinted by permission from TIME, the Weekly Newsmagazine; Copyright Time Inc. 1934

Selections from *Reluctant First Lady* by Lorena A. Hickok reprinted by permission of Dodd, Mead & Company, Inc. Copyright © 1962 by Lorena A. Hickok

Library of Congress Catalog Card Number 79-91302
ISBN 0-688-03631-7

Printed in the United States of America

First Edition

1 2 3 4 5 6 7 8 9 10

Book Design by Michael Mauceri

Preface

Lorena Alice Hickok died, at the age of seventy-five, on May 1, 1968. During the last decade of her life she had donated several cartons of letters to the Franklin D. Roosevelt Library in Hyde Park, New York. By the terms of her deed of gift nobody could inspect those cartons until ten years after her death, and then their contents were to be made available for virtually unlimited research. As the stipulated anniversary approached, the archival processing of The Papers of Lorena Hickok began.

On May 1, 1978, eighteen cardboard file boxes containing this new collection were routinely unlocked. In the boxes, along with many other letters and clippings, there were 2,336 letters from Eleanor Roosevelt to Lorena Hickok. About three quarters of these letters were written during the 1930's, starting in the autumn of 1932 just before the election that transformed a shy, ungainly woman of forty-eight into the nation's First Lady. The rest span another twenty years, ending in the autumn of 1962, when the internationally esteemed Mrs. Roosevelt died.

A few days after The Papers of Lorena Hickok were opened I received, purely by chance, an assignment to write a brief life of Eleanor Roosevelt. Thus I turned out to be the first person, apart from the F.D.R. Library's professional staff, to read a hitherto private correspondence that has irrevocably become part of our National Archives. It is a correspondence of extraordinary emotional impact, between a great woman and another woman who has been all but forgotten. Because of Eleanor Roosevelt's renown, their story belongs to history. I wish this were not so. In my Personal Note starting on page 329, I have described my own unavailing effort to postpone the inevitable disclosure.

But who was Lorena Hickok? To answer that question—and to

5

put her relationship with Eleanor Roosevelt into its proper context—has been the purpose of this book. I must emphasize here that
no fictional scenes will be found in the pages that follow; every
incident is based on evidence from documents or observers, and
every phrase that appears within quotation marks has been derived
from a source listed at the back of the book. Where I have been
unable to find reliable evidence I have preferred leaving the reader
to make his or her own surmises about what occurred, rather than
to weave unsupported presumptions into the record.

Also, I must add that I have chosen not to speculate about feelings alluded to only cryptically by either woman, or about the
attitudes of other people I could not consult. It would be interesting, of course, to know what Franklin Roosevelt really thought of
Lorena Hickok, but he was not a man who confided much regarding his private opinions. So on matters of this sort I have provided
just the clues that the newly opened correspondence contains, leaving each reader to arrive at any suppositions independently. Still,
the fact that I have read, and repeatedly reread, material not easily
accessible to the general public has imposed a special responsibility
that I have tried to meet. Therefore, at a few points in the story but
more fully in the notes starting on page 329, I have included some
of my own clearly labeled personal opinions.

I have not, however, in any way attempted a new biography of
perhaps the most eminent woman of modern times. Any reader
desiring more information about Eleanor Roosevelt's early life or
her public career than I have felt it appropriate to include should
consult her memoirs,° or Joseph P. Lash's masterly two volumes
based on thousands of boxes of her collected papers as well as on
extensive interviewing.† For I cannot stress too strongly that the
Eleanor Roosevelt who emerges in the Hickok Papers does not, to
any significant extent, differ from the First Lady of the World we
already know.

Unfortunately, the sensational tinge of the Hickok correspondence may, at least temporarily, eclipse its other aspects. Yet the
real importance of these letters lies in their spontaneous little
revelations illuminating the moods, the uncertainties, the inner ten-

---

° Eleanor Roosevelt's *This Is My Story* (Harper & Brothers, 1937); *This I Remember* (Harper, 1949); and *On My Own* (Harper, 1958).

† Joseph P. Lash's *Eleanor and Franklin* (W.W. Norton & Company, 1971); and
Eleanor: The Years Alone (Norton, 1972).

sions of a human being who came as close to true selflessness as anybody is likely to on this imperfect planet. It must be remembered, though, that the "Hick" to whom "E.R." wrote so candidly was the central figure in E.R.'s life just for a brief, if crucial, few years; it would do violence to the truth to imply otherwise. Thus I believe that a far more accurate perspective on their relationship can be attained by regarding it in Hick's frame of reference, because E.R. was for thirty years the central figure in Hick's life.

And what a life it was! Surely no one would ever have undertaken a biography of Lorena Hickok were it not for her connection with Eleanor Roosevelt. Nevertheless, it is not merely reflected glory that makes Hick fascinating. A South Dakota servant girl at fourteen, a star reporter in New York two decades later, a sub rosa White House resident during World War II, she merits attention in her own right. Now that the special problems confronting women have become the focus of widespread study, perhaps even men may be willing to read about an uncelebrated female who lacked physical beauty but who had a rare personal magnetism that especially attracted women, and who, in the breezy vernacular she always liked, was one hell of a writer.

Besides being the first journalist to recognize Eleanor Roosevelt's news-making potential, Lorena Hickok for three years early in the New Deal wrote confidential reports for Harry Hopkins, F.D.R.'s relief administrator. F.D.R. himself often asked to hear what Hick had been sending back to Washington from her fact-finding expeditions around the country. In 1935 Hopkins told the President's wife that posterity would consider these vivid Hickok reports the best available history of the Depression, and his prediction appears to have been not far from the mark. At any rate, the Hickok reports in The Papers of Harry Hopkins at Hyde Park have become a major source for scholars in the field of social welfare.

Thus it is not as strange as it might immediately seem that a branch of the United States National Archives accepted, sight unseen, the personal papers of Lorena Hickok. Then once the gift had been accepted, forces beyond any individual's control were irresistibly set in motion. For in recent years, as a result of Watergate and other upheavals, the archival profession has come under harsh criticism for suppressing too much—so the current trend is to be as open as a donor's stated wish permits. Even among archivists not otherwise given to Biblical citation, one text from St. John, chapter

8, verse 32, is now in high repute: *And ye shall know the truth and the truth shall make you free.*

Although I am not given to Biblical citation myself, I must add that the above words serve better than any I could possibly summon to explain why I have attempted to reconstruct the life of Lorena Hickok.

D.F.

Contents

Preface   5

Part I: "I'm going out and make a name for
myself . . ." 1893–1932   11

  1. Sadness in South Dakota   13

  2. Hired Girl   24

  3. Years of Loneliness   40

  4. Following Ferber into Journalism   47

  5. Hick's Front Page Days   58

  6. Success in New York   70

Part II: "I don't suppose anyone can ever stay so
happy . . ." 1932–1936   89

  7. Beginning a Very Special Friendship   91

  8. Hick Ceases to Be a Reporter   111

  9. The Depression: On the Road for Harry Hopkins   137

  10. Emotional Peaks and Valleys   153

  11. Learning to Let Go   172

  12. 1935: Year of Indecision   183

  13. War—or the World's Fair   200

Part III: "I'll be relieved when it's over . . ." 1937–1968   219

  14. Drifting Apart   221

  15. At Least Life Is Not Dull   240

  16. The 1940 Presidential Campaign   255

  17. Living at the White House   278

  18. Hick and Judge Harron   290

  19. Taking Refuge   302

  20. Hyde Park at Last   315

Afterword   326

A Personal Note and Some Acknowledgments   329

Notes on Sources   335

Index   377

PART I

"I'm going out and make a name for myself . . ."
1893–1932

1. Sadness in South Dakota

The town of Bowdle, in South Dakota, was celebrating its twentieth birthday in 1906. Already its wooden sidewalks were being replaced with cement, and electricity lit the streets and buildings. Such signs of progress gave the editor of the Bowdle *Pioneer* as much satisfaction as did the outdistancing of Satan implied by local support of four churches but only three saloons. Thus, in the issue of September 20, the piety of the following item:

SAD INDEED

A sad death occurred at 1 o'clock Sunday morning taking from the home—a mother—and what could be more sad than to leave a husband with three young girls in the home. Mrs. A. J. Hickok was taken violently ill Saturday evening a little after seven and the stroke of paralysis was so severe that she never spoke again. This sudden taking away was a very severe shock to the family and to the community and it was some time before it could be realized that she was dead. . . .

The bereaved ones have the sympathy of the whole community, for "what is home without a mother" and Mrs. Hickok was all the word means, a loving mother and a devoted wife.

Had the *Pioneer*'s editor been more familiar with the Hickok family, perhaps this obituary might have been phrased somewhat differently. But nobody in town knew much about the Hickoks, who had arrived less than a year earlier; and yet that hardly distinguished them, because so many of Bowdle's seven hundred residents were newcomers. Still it was suggestive of an even greater sadness than Bowdle suspected that Anna and Addison Hickok had never stayed anywhere long enough during the fifteen years of their marriage for their neighbors to become well acquainted with them.

It was Addison Hickok's temper that kept them on the move—his

13

terrible, ungovernable temper that lost him job after job. Possibly
Anna Waite's relatives had opposed the marriage because they perceived instability in this dour butter-maker who, like a rolling
stone, had turned up in the Wisconsin dairy area where they had
been farming ever since leaving western New York several decades
earlier. Or the opposition may have been based solely on the un-
suitability of the match between a spinster approaching her thirty-
seventh birthday, earning her keep as a seamstress, and a man who
certainly appeared to be some years her junior.

Nevertheless, Anna had run off with him to a nearby Congregational parsonage in the county seat of Elkhorn, where strangers
witnessed their ceremony. One month short of two years later, on
March 7, 1893, above a creamery in the leafy Wisconsin hamlet of
East Troy, Anna gave birth to her first child—Alice Lorena, who
would, as a schoolmate marveled decades afterward with no trace
of irony, "rise to the White House."

Lorena (very early the names on her birth certificate had been
reversed) was thirteen years old when her mother died. In a fragment of autobiography that she worked on when she was past fifty
but never seriously endeavored to publish, she was remarkably can-
did about some of the misery of her childhood. Devoting twenty
pages to the period preceding the sad event chronicled by the
Pioneer, she made her early emotions abundantly clear. Toward one
of her parents she felt mainly contempt, and the other she hated.

It was her mother who inspired increasingly bitter scorn. "I kept
wondering, all through those childhood years, why my mother, who
was a grown-up, too, and just as big as my father, let him do the
things he did," she wrote. And she added: "The first contact with a
human that I recall vividly was with my father. I had started biting
my finger nails. One day he thrust the tips of my fingers into my
mouth, and made me bite on them, holding my jaws together with
his big, strong hands, until the tears rolled down my cheeks."

In her maturity, Lorena still thought of her father as the most
undisciplined person she had ever encountered, but she attempted
to explain if not excuse his behavior. "I realize now that it was not
entirely his fault," she wrote. For he had had a frightful childhood,
being the son of a Civil War volunteer who had not returned and
who had left a wife and baby in extreme poverty. Then a brutal

stepfather had given her own father the worst possible example. "He was beaten when he was a child," Lorena wrote, "so I suppose it seemed right to him that I, too, should be beaten."

Lorena offered two other illustrations of her father's fierce temper. She recalled that once when she was about five her mother had suddenly drawn her into a bedroom, closing the door and the windows with a bang and, weeping, had held the child on her lap. "From without came whistling, crackling sounds and yelps of pain from my puppy. He had been chasing bicycles, and my father was beating him with a horsewhip." The other incident involved a tiny blue-eyed kitten named Tweezer. "One morning we children were slow getting dressed because we were playing with the kitten. My father strode into the room, seized the little thing by its hind paws, took it outside and dashed its brains against the barn. I saw its broken, bloody little body lying in the weeds when I went by on my way to school." That afternoon Lorena brushed away the flies, dug a hole, lined it with grass and leaves, and buried the remains of her pet.

It is notable that both of these incidents involved animals. For Lorena had decided, perhaps even before she could frame the idea consciously, that she liked animals better than people. Soft furry animals never flinched from her as if the mere sight of her in some way irritated them. But people did, or so she felt.

On the evidence of the one dim photograph of the Hickok family that has been preserved, the young Lorena, already taller than her mother, surely could not have been described as dainty. Yet she seems less plain than intractable, with a supercilious side-glance that nowadays might be considered appealing. Then, however, it marked her as a sullen troublemaker.

To read too much into a single old portrait is certainly risky, but to a surprising extent the five images depicted there fit the personalities that, more than forty years later, were attributed to them by the family's eldest daughter. Addison Hickok looks haunted; Anna, allowing for the distortion of her face by the reflection of her spectacles, harassed; Ruby, the middle daughter, appears to be a good and pretty girl; and Myrtle, the youngest, is glowering like the "bad egg" Lorena would call her many years afterward.

If one looks closely, though, at this family portrait, another shape emerges—a large furry creature placidly curled up on Anna Hickok's lap. Obviously it is a full-grown cat, so it cannot be the ill-fated Tweezer. But to infer from such mute testimony that Lorena exaggerated her childhood deprivation seems unjustified. Although independent testimony about the quality of this family's life no longer is available, Lorena's harsh account was at least indirectly corroborated in later years by Ruby, who refused to speak of her early years to her own closest friends.

Yet these children did have a pet, they were pampered to some extent with elegant clothing created by their seamstress mother, and they were given lessons on a parlor pipe organ. Lorena, implacably fair on many other occasions, at least tried to be fair to her father: "There must have been times when he was not angry—times when he was gay, affectionate, perhaps even indulgent with us children. But I do not remember them."

Such a lapse of memory could be accounted for by something else about her father that Lorena did not write. In her later years she would tell a few people that, on some unspecified occasion under circumstances she did not describe, besides being beaten by her father, she had also been raped.

Lorena did remember, rather unusually for a young female in those days, a public event that provided her with a personal hero. Late in the summer of 1901, Addison Hickok had left his wife and three daughters in the town where he and Anna had gotten married, while he went looking for work; they were living then in a dingy yellow cottage near the Elkhorn railroad tracks. Anna, ten years after defying her parents, had eight-year-old Lorena, four-year-old Ruby and two-year-old Myrtle to cope with alone that summer. Besides, she was taking care of her widowed mother who was seriously ill. Lorena was outside playing by herself one twilight when the telegraph operator ran from the station shouting a shocking message that had just come over the wire: President McKinley had been shot!

Lorena rushed inside to spread the news. But a local minister, having been summoned to comfort her grandmother, was just lifting his own voice. "Jesus, Savior, Pilot Me," he sang. The child was immediately hustled back outdoors and told to keep still. So Lorena paid more heed than she otherwise might have to the bulletins that the telegraph operator kept providing as William McKinley hovered at death's door for eight days, until he finally succumbed. Then a dauntless new President of the United States captured the heart of a very lonely young girl. His name was Theodore Roosevelt.

But it was not as unusual as it might seem for a child of eight and a half to become enthralled by a national figure in those pretelevision days. Teddy Roosevelt's exuberance, the excitement of having the nation's youngest chief executive dramatically installed in the White House with his irrepressible family of lively children—all of this, plus his previous celebrity as the colonel of "Roosevelt's Rough Riders" during the brief, glorious Spanish-American War, made a great splash in the newspapers, even those of a rural but literate Wisconsin county seat. And Lorena was a great reader.

Possibly, though, her full-blown hero worship of the then President Roosevelt did not flower quite as early as she would remember in later years. When her grandmother died shortly after President McKinley had, the Hickok family entered upon a two-year period of such constant upheaval that she needed stronger solace, which, fortunately, she found in Elgin, Illinois, not far from Chicago.

Using the hundred dollars Anna Hickok had inherited from her mother, Addison Hickok unaccountably rented a barber shop in Elgin. Conceivably he might have had some previous experience at the barber's trade, although almost any other occupation would have been safer for a man with his disposition. It does not seem that he assaulted any client, but he did not have much opportunity because he ran out of money after three or four months. Still it was during this period that Lorena's reading led to a memorable expansion of her private world.

She would always be sure that the first book she had ever read by herself was *Uncle Tom's Cabin*. Her mother had bought it from a traveling book agent, probably back in Elkhorn, and Lorena had started right in with the title page, wading patiently through an interminable preface about slavery, most of it far beyond the comprehension of an eight-year-old. But she never forgot her joy when she finally found herself embarked on the story itself. In the opening chapter, where Mr. Shelby, the kindly although financially embarrassed Kentucky master, bargains reluctantly with the slave trader for the sale of Uncle Tom and Eliza's little boy Harry, the two men sit in front of a fire eating oranges and sipping port wine. "For years," Lorena would write, "long before I knew what port tasted like, oranges and port wine represented to me the ultimate in luxurious living. I would sip a glass of water with my Christmas orange, pretending it was port."

Doubtless because Lorena's absorption in this book had not gone unnoticed, she was taken to see a stage performance of *Uncle Tom's Cabin* in Elgin. This was her first visit to any theater. For such an impressionable child, the experience had a not too surprising immediate effect. "I got so excited when little Eva, a child about my own age, with long, golden curls, went up to Heaven in her little white nightie, with the rose spotlight playing upon her, and all the slaves moaning in the background, that I became ill and had to be dragged out to the washroom."

Only years later, as a by-line reporter interviewing Mary Pickford, did Lorena discover that her reaction may have been so extreme because she had probably been carried away by the performance of that star at an early stage in her own career. But the young Lorena, seething beneath the sullen bluster with which she defensively surrounded herself, could not have helped coming under the spell of even a lesser talent. Already her world of books seemed far more bearable than the real world around her, and now she had found a grand new way of enjoying her fantasies.

Yet she could not do it alone. Moving so often—to a farm here, a town there, to a succession of shabby, cheerless houses—she had no friends, nor did she have the faintest idea of how to go about making any. Perhaps this was just as well during the increasingly unhappy post-Elgin years, when there was not too much that friends could have done to help her. What she needed was a victim.

And Lorena discovered the perfect victim for her purposes right at home in the person of her little sister, Ruby. Not quite four years younger than Lorena, Ruby had curly hair, then considered essential for feminine beauty, and it was as golden as Mary Pickford's. Lorena's hair, brown and straight, seemed the focal point of adult dismay about her appearance; once when the unkind comments had made her reckless, she snipped off several inches, but then she suffered even more because everybody snickered that she looked like a boy. Still the difference between these two sisters went deeper than anything that ribbons or bows could enhance. Ruby had the gift of getting along and Lorena did not. Indeed, Ruby was so determined to make even her big sister love her that Lorena, at first reluctantly, let Ruby into her own private world.

Soon Ruby was being trampled by Ben Hur's chariot or dragged seven times around the walls of ancient Troy; she was forced to clean the Augean stables; she was scalped at the Battle of the Little Big Horn. Everything Lorena read created a new role for poor Ruby, but it appears that Ruby did not mind playing the eternal victim. In later years, Ruby's tenacious amiability would often incense Lorena, but Ruby never ceased feeling that somehow she had to take care of her tremendously intelligent but hopelessly impractical older sister. For it went beyond Anna Hickok's powers to play her own maternal role after the family moved to South Dakota.

Lorena was ten when she descended from a day coach of the Milwaukee Railroad with her mother and two sisters at a dusty prairie town called Milbank. But Milbank in South Dakota was less forlorn than Summit a year later, where a cyclone blew away their barn while mother and girls huddled in terror in the cellar of their house. Bowdle, the following year, for all of its brave dreams of someday becoming a lesser Minneapolis, was still just another cluster of raw brick and frame structures, mostly one story high, lining five or six blocks on either side of the main street.

If you drove out in a buckboard, beyond the last house you could see the horizon in every direction. And there was nothing beneath that enormous sky to mark the presence of man except an occasional clump of cottonwood saplings planted as a windbreak near some settler's shanty. In 1903, Dakota east of the Missouri River was, Lorena would recall, "a vast, treeless prairie, round and flat, like an empty plate, white in winter, soft, grayish green in spring, golden in summer."

Instead of sturdy prairie grass, more and more of that gold was wheat. As recently as 1889, when North and South Dakota had been carved out of the legendary Dakota Territory, cattle ranching had been the area's sole lure to the intrepid easterner. This rough era still flavored the popular impression that Dakota was a paradise for menfolk. Indeed, all over the country it was part of Teddy Roosevelt's personal saga that, as a pallid city fellow, he had been infused by a new spirit hunting buffalo in Dakota; so the region credited with making a man of him naturally took a special interest in him.

Lorena certainly did in 1904, when T.R. won four more years in the White House. And it was on the next Saint Patrick's Day, ten days after Lorena's twelfth birthday, that the President attended a wedding which attracted more attention than it otherwise might have—the wedding of his twenty-year-old niece Eleanor.

Anna Eleanor Roosevelt had been born on October 11, 1884, in her maternal grandmother's mansion overlooking the Hudson River about a hundred miles north of New York City. She was the first child of a beautiful, high-minded society belle and a dashing polo player whose elder brother was named Theodore. It was not a happy marriage. For the dashing Elliott drank, and his weakness inflamed the chill religiosity that afflicted the former Miss Anna Hall to the extent that, after several increasingly tense years, she all but banished him. Only sporadically did their daughter see her adored father when she grew beyond the nursery stage.

She was not a beautiful child. Even so, the unreliable Elliott, nurturing righteous instincts that he himself could not live up to, cherished this solemn little girl far more than her mother did. Unfortunately, his strictures about proper behavior made her despair of justifying his love—even as he was forgetting her, under the stress of his own imperfection, for months at a time. Perhaps mercifully, allowing her to preserve a golden image of him, he died before her tenth birthday; two years earlier, the child's mother had succumbed to a mysterious fever. Thus it was Grandmother Hall who had charge of Eleanor and her younger brother, until Eleanor was sent to school in England.

There a gifted French schoolmistress recognized an exceptional sensitivity in this lonely adolescent and awakened a keen intelligence. When Eleanor returned to America to go through the tortures of a society debut, the same sensitivity and intelligence very much impressed her fifth cousin, once removed; possibly Franklin Roosevelt never made a more perceptive decision than when, still at Harvard, he asked Eleanor to marry him. It is also likely that they were deeply in love.

Out in Dakota, Lorena could hardly have been familiar with the romance of these peripheral young Roosevelts. Romantic as she was, her emotions were stirred by Dakota itself. As she would write decades later:

> New country it was, with everything in prospect, everything to be built, fortunes to be made. If you farmed, you could turn up a rich, black furrow as far as you wanted to. Not a stone, not a stump, nothing to halt the shining blade of your plow for miles and miles ahead! There was land for everybody . . . All you had to do was to stake out your claim, build some sort of shelter . . . and it was yours—acres and acres of it!

But, the mature Lorena added, that was the typically masculine attitude. For women, this bare, bright, windy Dakota was certainly no paradise:

> I think it must have fitted to perfection my mother's idea of hell. Most of the women were desperately homesick. They were always trying to save money, wistfully planning vacations "back East." My mother had lived until her middle forties in the beautiful Lake Geneva country in southern Wisconsin. She longed for trees, hills, water—more than anything else, lakes. In South Dakota there were a couple of rivers, the Missouri which in summer would be a wide bed of dirty gravel with a little trickle of water running down the center, and the "Big Jim," which wouldn't even have passed for a creek back in the land she loved. Near one of the little towns where we lived there was what was supposed to be a lake. They held Sunday school picnics there. That summer she persuaded my father to hire a team from the livery stable, and we went to the picnic. Instead of a lake, however, we found only a kind of mud hole filled with rushes and surrounded by a grove of dusty cottonwoods. Sitting there in the surrey, with the reins in her hands, she broke down and cried as though her heart were breaking.

Beyond this grief, and in addition to ceaseless domestic drudgery, Anna Hickok as she turned fifty also had to keep trying to maintain peace between her husband and the eldest of their three daughters. But even many years afterward, when Lorena herself had passed her fiftieth birthday, she could not restrain her bitterness over her mother's failure to protect her. "At times she tried," Lorena wrote, "but not very effectively."

Once when Lorena had been whipped with a stave out of a butter keg, and she had black and blue stripes all over her back and legs, she did hear her mother protest. Again, shortly before Anna died, the frenzied father had knocked his daughter down, and her mother did step between them, crying: "Do you want to kill the child?"

Yet Lorena could not accuse her father of ever having struck her mother, although she did mention "one bad time" when he hurled a chair after his wife as she ran weeping from the room. Then why did his eldest daughter arouse this man's frenzy? It could have been her defiance that provoked him. Lorena herself may have partly believed this when she wrote: "He used to shout, in paroxysms of anger, that he was going to break my temper. I wasn't afraid of him. I only resented him. Never once did he whip me—and the whippings grew progressively more severe as I grew older—when I didn't mutter, inaudibly behind my gritted teeth: 'You wouldn't dare do this to me if I were as big as you are.' "

But there was something else about Lorena that incited her father's ire. She could sing. And her voice was no childish soprano to harmonize, fairly effacingly, in any small church choir. Not only did she stand a few inches taller than any of her peers, either male or female, but she also sang a few octaves lower, in a throaty alto particularly suited to funeral music. So her father tried to force her to sing solo dirges at South Dakota funerals.

In those days coffins were always left open, and Lorena, like most children, was terrified of corpses. To stand in front of an audience on such an occasion was such torture for her that she refused to do it, which appears to have had severe repercussions. Pushed by his own demons, Addison whipped his daughter for refusing. Lorena, instead of giving in, extended her defiance to include solo performances of every description. Believing that she was hopelessly ugly, she had always detested singing or reciting before any sort of group, churchly or otherwise, but now her stubborn stand infuriated her father. "One of the worst whippings he ever gave me was inflicted because I refused to sing a solo one evening in church," she wrote.

But Lorena would not back down.

On Sunday evening, the sixteenth of September in 1906, Lorena Hickok was supposed to be on the program of the Christian Endeavor meeting scheduled by Bowdle's Congregational Church.

That much was noted in the *Pioneer* for the preceding Thursday, although no topic for her recitation was announced.

Half a century later, in her own account of her childhood treatment by her father, there was no mention of this recitation which, it must be assumed, did not occur as scheduled. For it was on the Saturday night before the meeting was to take place that Lorena's mother suddenly suffered the severe stroke of paralysis the paper lamented in its next edition. And early on the morning of the day the thirteen-year-old Lorena had been supposed to speak, her mother died.

2. Hired Girl

The housekeeper was a divorced woman, and she stayed all night at the Hickoks' after just a few weeks; so sympathy for the poor motherless girls soon was diluted with censure. Several times on the school playground Lorena noticed other children going off into huddles to whisper and giggle, giving her a most uneasy feeling. "It appeared that their parents were gossiping about us," she wrote dryly many years later.

What else she herself felt during the months immediately following her mother's death must be imagined, for her memoir swept past this period swiftly. Still, her sparse account did offer a few facts. Whether or not Addison Hickok had sought any assistance from his late wife's family, a diminutive, soft-voiced and lame relative of the departed Anna arrived within a few days.

Aunt Ella, Lorena had been taught to call her, but Ella Ellis actually was a cousin of her mother's so close in some ways that they had been more like sisters. To Lorena she meant even more. This gentle woman was, for a long period, the only person the troubled child really loved. "Rena," Aunt Ella called her.

If Lorena had lived nearer Chicago, or if Aunt Ella had been able to leave her own home more often during Lorena's early years—if Aunt Ella's influence could have been more pervasive—perhaps Lorena might have been spared much anguish. "Throughout those sullen, resentful, inarticulate years," Lorena wrote, "she was the only steadying influence." Unlike the child's harried mother, Aunt Ella never scolded her. Aunt Ella listened to her and seemed to understand her. "I now look back with astonished gratitude at her patience with me," the mature Lorena added.

Nobody can say precisely what Aunt Ella accomplished when she visited Bowdle right after Lorena's mother died, although she did bring boxes full of badly needed warm clothing. But the "steadying" Lorena referred to must have been much more urgently required. Also, merely by undertaking the journey, Aunt Ella demonstrated to Lorena that there was hope for her, and help for her, far beyond the limits of Bowdle. Yet Lorena made no move in the ensuing year, and then it was no impulse of her own that lifted her out of her vague drifting. She was pushed—by the woman she identified only as "the housekeeper."

Originally, Lorena could not have minded this woman's entrance into the household. She was no stranger; since landing in Bowdle, she had been giving music lessons, and it was from her that Lorena had learned the rudiments of pumping an organ. More to the point, Lorena had never liked to play house or, in real life, to cook and clean and sew and otherwise do for a family. Although some widowers might have expected a big girl of thirteen to take over, with the assistance of her two younger sisters, apparently Addison Hickok had quickly realized that he could not solve his problem so simply. Years later his eldest daughter noted, in a different connection, that she had never talked to her father if she could possibly avoid it. In this instance she did not have any difficulty in making her meaning clear.

So, as Lorena rather disdainfully admitted regarding the housekeeper: "For awhile after she came things seemed better. The house did not look as clean as it had when my mother took care of it, but at least we had regular meals." And her father's temper, she had to add, seemed to have been tamed. Indeed, at the insistence of the housekeeper her father quit his job as a butter-maker and became a traveling salesman for a feed concern. He wore a new tan suit, which looked too tight on him, a stiff white shirt and a brown derby. More important to Lorena, now he was away from home most of the time.

But soon the unnamed lady supposedly watching over the three daughters resumed other activities that kept her away, often until late at night. Then the children would gobble whatever they found in the pantry, and Lorena, turning fourteen, still at an almost total loss about how to make friends, would show up under one of the dusty, bug-shrouded streetlights suspended on wires in the centers of the intersections, wishing and dreading encounters with other girls and boys.

By now most of the other girls her age were frankly intent on attracting boys, as Lorena could not be because she judged the entire male sex by her own father. So the teasing and giggling, the boasting and strutting, did not truly engross her. "Oh, you kid!" her classmates unselfconsciously exclaimed. Mainly, Lorena just listened and observed.

The opportunities for other entertainment were slight in Bowdle. Not even the first flicker movies had opened yet in an empty store, and if they had, few would have been able to afford the price of admission. A runaway horse or a fire furnished diversion only sporadically, as did the sight of the banker's "autymobile"—a bright red vehicle that buttoned up in the back like a pony cart—being hauled ignominiously homeward by a team from the livery stable.

For Bowdle's girls, at any rate, the town's three saloons were only a source of wonder. In their sixth-grade physiology lesson they had seen the teacher cook the white of an egg by pouring alcohol over it in a glass, so they used to speculate about the stomach of the town drunkard. Did it ever come uncooked? If not, how did it digest any food? Or had he completely quit eating?

Thus the girls, in their sauntering, always speeded their pace and averted their eyes when passing the saloons, but they moved even faster near the dim hotel on one corner of the main street. As everybody was aware, a girl who had worked there had fallen in love with a married traveling man, and soon she had discovered that she was going to have a baby. And then she had swallowed carbolic acid.

Lorena, frozen in horror, had stood outside the town hall with some of her classmates on the afternoon when a cheap wooden coffin containing the young woman's body was carried out after a funeral attended only by the Methodist preacher and a few men. Thereafter, Lorena and the other girls used to run by the hotel—on the other side of the street.

If Lorena had attained even a tenuous acceptance in the year after the death of her mother, it was thanks to a carelessly kind-hearted girl with red braids and a wide grin, a girl named Lottie. Long afterward, Lorena would decide that an epithet popularized during World War II best described her own adolescent behavior. She was an "eager beaver," she judged herself. "I was too eager, showed off too much, laughed too loudly, tried too hard." Fortunately, Lottie liked her anyway, and Lottie was popular enough to be allowed this vagary. Lorena, consumed with her yearning to have a friend, secretly adored Lottie. But her only real joy still came from her haphazard reading.

Then one bright September morning in 1907, almost exactly a year following Anna Hickok's death, the housekeeper told Lorena at breakfast that her father was moving and she would need to find some other place to live. "You'd better see about it today," the woman said calmly. At least in hindsight, Lorena took the announcement as an undisguised blessing. "Perhaps I should have been dismayed," she wrote. "But I wasn't. I was actually relieved, exhilarated. Now I'd be free from my father's whippings and her nagging. I'd be on my own!" And she went off to school feeling grown up and important.

On the playground before the bell rang that morning, Lorena sought out Lottie and confided in her. Then these two fourteen-year-olds—quite naturally, given their environment—quickly arrived at a plan. "We decided," Lorena wrote, "that I had better find myself a job as a 'girl' working for my room and board."

Besides her cook and housemaid, plus a waitress when there were guests for dinner, the young Mrs. Franklin Roosevelt now employed a baby nurse; her first child, Anna, had been born the year Lorena's mother died, and the following year she gave birth to her son James. It was Eleanor's mother-in-law, however, who chose these servants and instructed them in their duties. Feeling woefully inexperienced, Eleanor allowed her husband's mother more or less to run her first home on East Thirty-sixth Street in the fashionable Murray Hill district of New York City, while Franklin finished law school and then embarked on a gentlemanly law practice. His legal work did not prevent frequent stays at his mother's Hyde Park estate, which he still considered home, or long sailing holidays up at the picturesque island of Campobello, off the coast of Maine, where his family had a summer place.

In Lorena's world there were just two categories of domestic servant, although the word "servant," with its toadying implications, was almost never used. She knew nothing then of the great houses of the wealthy, and their trained staff. Even in the moderately prosperous middle class, which Lorena had glimpsed while visiting Aunt Ella, most women managed their homes without any help at all, and the work was much harder as well as more time-consuming than vacuum cleaners and washing machines would later make it. Still, help was not unheard of—help in the shape of "a girl," or, more extravagantly, "a hired girl."

The former, of course, was usually a farm daughter who lived so far out into the country that getting back and forth to school posed a problem, especially in the winter. Thus, many a small-town family, not merely in South Dakota, was able to barter for a broad range of household assistance solely at the cost of the helper's food and shelter.

A hired girl, however, commanded the munificent wage of three or four dollars a week. But in a community like Bowdle, hardly anybody except the wife of the banker could aspire to the luxury of paid help on a regular basis. If someone was having a baby or there was a death in the family or, more happily, a wedding, a temporary arrangement might be made—for as short a period as possible. So Lorena had to recognize that her prospects in this direction were unpromising.

Lottie, practical as well as friendly, did more than just agree. During the morning recess she ran home to talk to her mother, returning, red and puffing, after the rest of the class had already taken their seats again. As soon as the teacher's back was turned, Lottie passed Lorena a note: Lottie's mother thought that young Mrs. O'Reilly, with a new baby as well as a toddler, might be interested.

At noon Lorena went down the street to see Mrs. O'Reilly, who gave her some cookies and milk—and a job. Six months after her fourteenth birthday, she thereby joined one of the least celebrated but most pervasive occupational groups in the United States around the turn of this century. Then, uncounted thousands of adolescent females, not just in rural areas, received their first and, not infrequently, their only experience of working outside of their own homes when they accepted such unpaid domestic servitude. Under the worst of circumstances they were subjected to abuses that would appall almost anybody, although probably just as often they were treated kindly. Lorena, during the next two years, in nine different jobs as "a girl" or "a hired girl," ran the gamut.

She worked in Bowdle as well as a couple of other dusty little Dakota towns, and also in the regional metropolis of Aberdeen, so big that its houses had street numbers. From four of her jobs she was fired, one she ran away from, one she just quit, and her father "removed" her from two. Her last employer, the most colorful of the lot, put her on a different path. Even the newer histories of this country, striving to illuminate everyday existence, can usually spare only a few words for a species of experience that affected a large number of American lives. Therefore Lorena's own account of her youthful thralldom may startle some young feminists.

Looking back four decades later, she would write that when school was dismissed on the afternoon of her lunchtime interview with Mrs. O'Reilly, she immediately went home to pack her possessions in a canvas satchel. She said goodbye to her sister Ruby, who was being sent to stay with the housekeeper's sister in the next town. And then she "proceeded, without regret or misgivings," to the O'Reillys'.

Only afterward did it occur to Lorena that Mrs. O'Reilly, a placid young woman with beautiful ash-blond hair, had showed no surprise at being approached for a job, nor had she asked any questions. Had Mrs. O'Reilly been more accustomed to the role of employer, Lorena might have faced an immediate rebuff, because the arrangement was not a great success. It was Lorena's own fault, she would concede decades later. Indeed, with her characteristic self-deprecation, she undoubtedly overstated her own shortcomings when she wrote:

> The O'Reillies had struck a poor bargain. What they got in return for their generosity was an overgrown, sleepy adolescent, inclined to be sullen and suspicious, too inarticulate even to thank them or let them know how much she liked them. Secretly I longed to be liked, had an intense craving for affection. But I seemed to be utterly incapable of doing anything about it.

That could not have been fully accurate, as Lorena herself indicated with a dash of the bravura that she also could claim, although she never seemed to believe it was something endearing. She persisted in feeling only children appreciated this part of her personality because only around little children could she be natural. Confident that they had not learned yet to despise her ill-favored exterior, any more than puppies or kittens did, she found it easy to entertain them, for "I was a good story-teller"—at any rate, good enough to have been able to beguile Ruby into doing the supper dishes alone by telling stories to her. But in a spurt of irrepressible candor Lorena had to add, "And I never saw the baby I could not startle out of a crying fit by reciting in a deep voice, with rolling r's and gestures:

> At midnight in his guarded tent
> The Turk lay dreaming of the hour
> When Greece, her knee in suppliance bent,
> Should tremble at his power-r-r!"

So it must be assumed that Lorena was of some help to Mrs. O'Reilly, at least with the babies. What else she contributed during her four months in this household is not nearly as material, however, as what she herself learned. On two subjects, her first job taught her more of lasting significance than anything she absorbed from the pink frame school she was still aimlessly attending.

Ever after, Lorena would recall that the O'Reillys were the first Catholics she had known intimately. Atypical as her upbringing had been in some respects, it had adhered to the Middle American norm of the early 1900's on the matter of religious bigotry; both of her parents had nourished a suspicion of Roman Catholicism amounting nearly to obsession:

> From the time I was in the first grade, eyebrows would go up and the word "Catholic" would be whispered whenever I mentioned the name of an Irish child at school. I vaguely resented it, even as a small child, partly because the Irish children always seemed more attractive to me than the others—they were so gay, not shy and awkward like me—and partly because I could not see that Catholics were any different from the rest of us.

Disposed as she was to resist parental precept, Lorena still observed the O'Reillys rather narrowly at the beginning. "That first night as we sat down to supper I noticed that both Mr. and Mrs. O'Reilly made some sort of fluttering gestures before their faces with their hands. Later I noticed that they always did this before eating." A harmless custom, Lorena decided. Then in her room she discovered only one picture, a small colored print of the Madonna and Child, hanging at the head of her bed. "I studied it a long time and decided I liked having it there." The fat little white candle she later found in the O'Reillys' bedroom, when she was helping to sweep up, struck her as rather cheerful and cozy. The only other

thing she noted about the O'Reillys' religion that made them different from Protestant families also seemed positive to her. It was the
fact that Mr. O'Reilly always went to church with his wife, every
single Sunday.

For the second lesson Lorena learned in those four months was
one that luckier girls absorbed from their own fathers. Until then,
her only firsthand awareness that a man could be lovable had come
from her maternal grandfather, who had died before her fifth birthday, and from Aunt Ella's husband, whose death a year later had
left her no male relative to admire, let alone love. So the sturdy
young Mr. O'Reilly with his laughing eyes was something new in
her experience. He used to putter around the house singing Irish
songs in a husky tenor and, if Lorena had only met the likes of him
sooner, her trust in the male portion of humankind might have
flowered naturally. As it was, he at least saved her from expecting
nothing but evil from all males.

Perhaps Lorena was right that this easygoing couple simply
lacked the meanness to fire a useless nuisance. However, they were
relieved of any such necessity by Addison Hickok who, around
Christmas of 1907, married the housekeeper. Then he made new
arrangements for two of his daughters: Ruby was sent, alone, by
train to some of her mother's relatives in Wisconsin, and Lorena he
put to work near his own residence in the South Dakota city of
Aberdeen, about forty miles eastward.

The job was in a boarding house. Lorena lived at the kitchen
sink, surrounded by mountains of dirty dishes, oceans of scummy
water and an endless succession of gray and damp and smelly dish
towels. Although Lorena was supposedly attending school, the
sharp-featured landlady forgot all about that. But after only a
month or so, Lorena had her revenge:

> The circumstances of my departure revolved around an old-
> fashioned oak sideboard that stood in the dining room. It had
> a space underneath that was designed for storing china, but
> was not used for that. After each meal all scraps of bread left
> on the table were tossed into this place. Once a week the
> accumulated scraps were swept out and made into dressing.
> House cleaning in the institution was most casual, and there
> were mice. Some of the boarders were suspicious. I verified
> their suspicions, at the rate of a nickel a head, on the days
> when we were going to have dressing. And I got fired.

Her next two jobs Lorena found for herself by answering want ads in the Aberdeen *News*. The first was such a change, into a neat and well-ordered household, that her own inadequacies doomed her. "Surly, sloppy savage that I was"—the worn-out soles of her shoes stuffed with wads of paper—"my new mistress let me go, and I don't blame her." Next, she landed down by the railroad tracks.

There a Mrs. Hagedorn ran a rooming house for railroad men, and Lorena "hired out" as a full-time maid for three dollars a week. Since it soon became obvious that no serious efforts at cleaning were ever made in this establishment—the sheets never were changed, as far as Lorena could discover—her time was occupied by running errands for her employer and listening to her.

> Mrs. Hagedorn—she may.have been under fifty, but I always thought of her as a very old woman—was scrawny and dirty, with stringy gray hair, bad teeth and a horrible breath. One of my chief duties was to keep her supplied with some powders that she took all the time. I never knew what the stuff was. I was only instructed to ask the druggist for Mrs. Hagedorn's medicine.

Upon taking some of the medicine, Mrs. Hagedorn was ready to talk. Sitting at a window, waving at the train crews as they shuttled back and forth past the house on switch engines, she would tell Lorena endless, detailed stories about what went on in "the houses." Bleakly side by side outside the city limits, "the houses" were a bungalow and a two-story frame dwelling comprising Aberdeen's official, protected red-light district. At that time Aberdeen was a railroad frontier town, for the Milwaukee line was extending out to the Pacific with tracks laid only about sixty miles beyond Mrs. Hagedorn's window. So it was to Aberdeen that the railroad construction men came to spend their money on weekends and have a good time.

Lorena, approaching her fifteenth birthday, was—how could she be otherwise?—extraordinarily reticent about matters sexual. Even when she was past fifty, she could not bring herself to say more about Mrs. Hagedorn's stories than:

> I do not know whether Mrs. Hagedorn had ever been inside "the houses" or not. Whether by imagination or experience, she was fascinated by them. Over and over again, until I knew the whole routine by heart—although a lot of it I did not

understand—she would tell me what happened at night, when hacks filled with men, their pockets bulging with money, went bumping across the railroad tracks and out the rutted road to "the houses," whose lights were visible from an upstairs window in Mrs. Hagedorn's rooming house. Suspecting her motives—as I didn't then, but do now—I wonder a little that Mrs. Hagedorn did not make more impression on me than she did with her tales. Sometimes I would go upstairs in the daytime and stare at "the houses," out across the railroad tracks and the sooty landscape, so lonely and dreary. What Mrs. Hagedorn did not know, of course, was that my hatred of my father made me dislike and distrust all men.

Indeed no girl could have needed a Mrs. Hagedorn less than Lorena did, or, in the bargain, the attention of one of Mrs. Hagedorn's boarders: ". . . One night one of the railroad men came staggering into the narrow closet off the kitchen where I slept. Wakened out of a sound sleep, I let out a good resounding yell, and he backed out. Thereafter I put a chair against the door, with its back firmly wedged under the knob."

Soon afterward Lorena answered another ad, this one for a girl to work in the bindery where an agricultural journal called *The Dakota Farmer* was produced. She was hired, but the binding machine defeated her. Even before being fired, though, one evening on her way back to the Hagedorn establishment where she was still staying, she bumped into her father, whom she had not heard from in months. Just a few days later he came to get her and reassert parental control.

Thus it was back to the kitchen for Lorena, at a new job in a domicile that this young reader of novels christened "the house of discord." Her employer here had a cousinly relationship with the woman who had become Lorena's stepmother, and that alone might have been enough to make the job unappealing even if Lorena, garbed in a new outfit suitable to her station, had not been obliged to give the whole of her three weekly dollars to her father, repaying him for the clothing he had bought.

But Mrs. Sharkey proved amply objectionable in her own right. A singer, she had dreamed of a concert career; instead, she found herself in Aberdeen, South Dakota, pregnant for the second time, furious at her husband and the whole world. "She would frequently go into fits of rage," Lorena wrote, "screaming and weeping and telling me—and any of the neighbors who cared to listen—that men should bear the children, and that, if they did, there wouldn't be so many brats in the world! When she wasn't screaming with anger, she coughed and whined. Soon after my arrival she and the existing baby, a pallid nervous fretful little thing, both came down with the whooping cough. She hoped she would lose the baby, but she hadn't when I left."

Lorena went next to an elderly widow who was taking care of a three-month-old granddaughter in a town near Bowdle. This job, again, was a referral from Lottie's mother, for Lorena had written her friend a long letter, pouring forth her troubles. As a result, she received railroad fare in the mail from a Mrs. Dodd, whose daughter had died in childbirth.

In her sixties, Mrs. Dodd was a patient, loving woman. "The first thing she did was to start cleaning me up!" Lorena marveled decades later. "But she went at it in such a tactful, kindly way. . . . She gave me scented soap for my bath and a can of cool, clean smelling talcum powder. She taught me how to shampoo my hair. . . . We began to do things about my clothes. . . . She even praised me when I did things right! I think I might have stayed on with Mrs. Dodd forever and might even have become an outstanding success as a housemaid, but one day there came a letter from her son-in-law in Wisconsin. He wanted her to bring the baby and make a home for him."

Then Lorena called upon a resource she had only just begun to appreciate. Back in the sixth or seventh grade, the county superintendent of schools had noticed her as one of his most promising scholars; now she wrote to him, having heard he was looking for someone to live with his aged mother. He came himself to tell her that his mother was a fussy old woman but Lorena should not mind—it would be a good home for the right girl. Once more she packed up her canvas satchel. The next day, in the buggy in which the superintendent traveled around the county on official business, he drove Lorena out across the golden prairie to his mother's farm.

Going west by train from Chicago to the Pacific coast [Lorena wrote in 1949] travelers may still see during long, dreary hours crossing the plains, homesteads not unlike that toward which we drove along an endless dirt road, straight as a tapeline, under the hot Dakota sun that August afternoon. First, a ragged cluster of cottonwood trees. Nearby, a forlorn huddle of shabby little buildings that look as though they had been dropped there years ago, with the idea of replacing with something better sometime in the future. And stretching away in every direction to the horizon, a vast, round, golden plate, dotted here and there with more lonesome little clusters of cottonwood trees. The wheat country.

It was dark when they arrived. Lorena's new mistress had not expected her—rural telephones were practically unheard of in Dakota then. It was immediately obvious that the superintendent's mother did not want Lorena. "Through faded, near-sighted eyes, she peered at me over a smoking lamp, muttered a curt greeting to her son." Since Lorena was there, it was grudgingly conceded she might as well stay. The threshers were coming tomorrow. They needed a cook.

At dusk the following evening the threshers moved in, a long train of dusty machinery and wagons. The crew consisted of about a dozen men, professional threshers, not neighbors coming to help as they had in Wisconsin when Lorena was a child. Their equipment included a kitchen on wheels, a kind of miniature caboose painted a dirty gray. Inside there was a big stove that burned soft coal, carried in an open wagon that tagged along behind. "I was shown the stove," Lorena wrote, "and supplies and cooking utensils." Then the old lady, who had hardly spoken to her all day, handed her an alarm clock set for three o'clock. Lorena was to get out the next morning and have breakfast ready for the entire crew by five o'clock.

> In the early morning darkness I staggered sleepily out, poured some kerosene into the stove, as I had been told to do, and tried to start a fire. It wouldn't start. The paper burned, and the flames licked the kerosene off the surface of the coal. That was all. I hauled out the hunks of oily black stuff, crammed in some more paper—there was no kindling—and tried again. I was still trying when one of the men appeared at daybreak and took over.

During the next three days, Lorena never did catch up. She felt like a squirrel in a sweltering cage, running round and round, never getting anywhere. Dripping perspiration, she struggled along in clouds of smoke that stung her eyes and caked on her skin, endlessly boiling, baking, frying, through bushels of grimy potato peelings, through sliding avalanches of dirty dishes, shoving hunk after hunk of soft coal into that stove that never got enough.

After supper on the third day the threshers finally departed.

Early on the following morning the old lady's hired man hitched up a team, and on the high seat of a lumber wagon Lorena rode to the nearest town, where she caught a train for Bowdle.

Entering a day coach, she glimpsed her father. Hastily Lorena slipped into the next car, but Addison Hickok had seen her and he followed her, sitting down on the seat beside her. He was wearing his town clothes and brown derby, although they did not look new anymore. In a tone of fury he berated Lorena as an ungrateful daughter, he said he could put her in jail for running away from the Searles', and he ought to because she was on the road to ruin. But no, he washed his hands of her.

Lorena had sensed something different even as he kept ranting, and at first she was puzzled. Then it came to her that his tirade could not hurt her now, that she was no longer a child to be cuffed about and worse. He would never touch her again. "I was grown up!" Lorena left the train at Bowdle but her father remained aboard. She never saw him again. Years later, when she was a star reporter, someone from out in Dakota sent word that he had committed suicide, and Ruby wanted her to join in wiring money for burial expenses. "Send him to the glue factory!" Lorena replied.

At fifteen and a half, Lorena still thought of herself as too big and awkward ever to be like other girls. But somehow from the experiences crammed into the past year, she had begun to acquire a sense of purpose. Or at least she knew that she did not want the kind of life she had, out of necessity, been leading. "I could not have put it into words at that time," she wrote forty years later, "but I think now that what I really wanted was self-respect. Lonely as I was, I did not expect love or affection from anyone. I just didn't know how to fit in with people. But at least I was not always going to be an under-dog. What I needed, I decided, was a better education."

So Lorena Hickok answered the roll call on the day that Bowdle High School resumed in September of 1908. Living with one of Bowdle's most prosperous families, doggedly scrubbing their clothes sometimes as late as midnight, she still managed to do whatever was expected by her teacher. But in the square pink building housing the town's entire educational establishment—the primary grades in one room, intermediate pupils in another, and the much smaller number of advanced scholars in a sort of alcove— there was not much breadth or depth to the high-school curriculum.

Lorena had been starting the eighth grade when her mother died, and she had begun the ninth while living with the O'Reillys. Since she had barely seen the inside of Aberdeen's more impressive academy, in effect she was a freshman again; but between the lines of her memoir it appears that, despite her domestic drudgery, she captured whatever prizes were offered that year to the handful in her class. After winning the February essay contest on the life of Abraham Lincoln, she was even selected to represent Bowdle at a regional declamatory contest.

Although she still dreaded standing up before an audience, Lorena had nerved herself to go through with her oration—a Civil War piece entitled "Music on the Rappahannock"—but the well-off wife for whom she was working refused to let her go on the Saturday of the contest. Instead of being relieved, Lorena quit. She quit her job, that is. Then, as her mind was inflexibly set on staying in that pink school, she went to see a woman her own mother would never have allowed in her house. Mrs. O'Malley was the outrageous wife of the owner of Bowdle's first saloon, but Mrs. O'Malley at times employed a hired girl. Unhesitatingly, she hired Lorena.

Under her purple satins, Mrs. O'Malley's heart could not have been warmer, a fact that Lorena already suspected because the old lady had once stopped her on the street, shortly after Lorena's mother died, to say a sympathetic word. At least seventy years old, Mrs. O'Malley rouged her cheeks a lurid crimson; when she remembered to eat, she ate just bacon and fried potatoes; and she drank. Yet she did something nobody else had ever done. She gave some serious thought to Lorena's future.

First Mrs. O'Malley, for all of her frayed peacock feathers a conventional person, invited a young fellow working on the railroad to supper in her cluttered cottage. After all, Lorena had turned sixteen and was large for her age. This potential swain obligingly did ask Lorena to go out with him the following evening, when, arrayed in one of her employer's lacy shirtwaists, Lorena accompanied him to the store where Bowdle's first movies were now being exhibited. After the show, they went with other young couples to the drugstore, which had recently adopted the innovation of serving conical scoops of vanilla ice cream in a saucer, with wafers on the side. While they sat eating there was a prolonged blast on a locomotive whistle down at the station, signaling an emergency somewhere along the line.

"With the others," Lorena wrote years later, "I went down to the station to see my beau off, and as he departed he suddenly grabbed me and kissed me. Whereupon I slapped him, with all my might. I did not see him again, nor could Mrs. O'Malley lure me into any more conversations with young men who worked on the railroad!"

Recognizing a setback that required a new strategy, Mrs. O'Malley plagued Lorena for information that Lorena was loath to provide. Had Lorena's mother not had any relatives who might be in a position to offer assistance? Aunt Ella had indeed written several times over the past year and a half, but Lorena, feeling unworthy, even fearing the loss of her independence, had not replied. Toward the end of that summer, though, Lorena could no longer keep her shell intact; she gave Mrs. O'Malley Aunt Ella's address. Then Mrs. O'Malley quite laboriously, because she was not accustomed to writing, wrote a letter. An answer came back immediately, enclosing railroad fare to Chicago. In Lorena's words:

Mrs. O'Malley accepted this challenge with joyous enthusiasm. The period of preparation for my departure was strenuous. More lace and ribbons and millinery were purchased, along with a dazzling pair of patent leather oxfords with ribbon ties about an inch wide. One day she announced she was going to do my hair for me. My braids, wound round my head Gretchen style, would never do in a big stylish place like Chicago. I emerged from her hand with a pompadour, heavily ratted underneath and sweeping down into a low dip over my forehead. Rouge and powder, applied with a chamois skin, she had insisted on almost from the day I entered her house.

It was decided that for traveling I would wear a light blue duck suit she had made for me, with a blouse consisting mostly of lace. The suit had been washed, and, under Mrs. O'Malley's ministrations, starched so stiff that the skirt would stand alone. The check Aunt Ella sent was undoubtedly ample to cover Pullman fare and meals in the diner, but neither Mrs. O'Malley nor I ever thought of such a thing. As a matter of fact, there were no Pullmans or diners on trains going through Bowdle. They were hooked on in Aberdeen. We assumed that I would make the entire trip in the day coach. And that I would need a packed lunch. One of the neighbors beheaded a hen, and it was duly fried and tucked in a big shoe box, along with other delicacies including some rather ripe bananas. And late one hot August afternoon, with what I took to be perspiration cutting furrows down through the cosmetics on her cheeks, Mrs. O'Malley kissed me goodbye on the bare sooty platform of the Bowdle railroad station.

One travels nowadays from Bowdle to Chicago in a few hours. It was not so in 1909. It took a whole night to get to Minneapolis—in a hot day coach, with the windows open and soot and cinders blowing in. A change of trains, involving a long wait, the following morning. Then a long, hot, sooty day in another day coach. By noon the contents of my lunch box had begun to smell so strongly that people were looking in my direction. So I regretfully tossed it out the window and bought cracker jack from the news butcher.

It was dusk in the big, crowded, busy Chicago station when a tiny woman, immaculate in a gray ensemble, limped forward to greet a tall, solemn, tongue-tied sixteen-year-old in a badly fitting, badly wrinkled light blue suit liberally smudged with soot, her face smeared with perspiration, powder and rouge, her tangled, matted hair dipping low on her forehead from one of the strangest hats ever turned out by Mrs. O'Malley.

The hands she held out in greeting were encased in spotless chamois gloves. It was the first time I had ever seen a pair of real chamois gloves.

3. Years of Loneliness

September, 1909, was a most auspicious month in which to begin attending high school in Battle Creek, Michigan. For this small city, named after a rivulet where a few Indians had been defeated in the 1830's, had just erected a grand new building of yellow brick and marble. And the handsome edifice was now ready to welcome its first students—a fact that may account for the local appearance of Miss Lorena Alice Hickok. Or perhaps her residence with relatives of her mother's, named Fish, had been arranged because Aunt Anne particularly needed domestic help.

Forty years later, the mature Lorena did not explain why she went to Battle Creek after just a brief stay in Chicago, but her silence must not be taken as a sign of any special reticence. Upon conjuring up those chamois gloves, she had actually completed the major portion of a task she had committed herself to with some reluctance. It had not been her own idea to write her autobiography; almost purely by chance she had agreed to submit a few chapters, plus a summary of the rest of her career, for a publisher's consideration. Thus her manuscript leapt past whole decades, until two subsequent adventures received detailed treatment. Still at every important juncture of her life as she lived it, there are other traces.

The very building where she earned her high-school diploma (expanded, half a century afterward, with a sleek new wing), yields evidence that Lorena Hickok was an outstanding student. During her first year she did so well that she gained firm status as a sophomore, despite the deficiencies of her preparation in Bowdle. Over a three-year period she took algebra and geometry, physics and physiology; she studied Latin, Greek and German, along with geography and drawing; also, she was exposed to some history and a good amount of English. Except for a B in physics and a B+ in drawing, she received straight A's.

Still it is *The Paean* that provides a better perspective, not merely in its edition celebrating her Class of 1912. If a visitor from some distant planet wished to see Middle America at its zenith, there could be no simpler means than perusing the yearbooks of Battle Creek High School from Lorena's era. What hopes this "hall of knowledge" inspired! What wholesome amusement did it foster! And yet, pictured among the Girls' Amateur Literary Society—the GALS, everybody called them—one does not find Lorena Hickok.

"Some of the others thought we were snobs," one of those members reminisced in 1978, with a slight chuckle. She felt sure, though, that Lorena must have been elected because Lorena had been so brilliant. But no, the picture reminded her; in addition to literary readings, the group had sponsored a "feed" once a month in somebody's house, really a social event, and Lorena could not have been interested.

Of course not. To see her plod along a school corridor with a lumpish gait that the cruel mimics among her classmates must surely have imitated—to see her, square of chin, taller, broader than most of her male classmates, obviously female only by her hair and her skirt and the ludicrous abundance swelling her shirtwaist—just to see her was deemed sufficient proof of her lack of interest.

Memory certainly can play strange little tricks after a lapse of sixty-six years, and a dainty old lady who had been one of Lorena's few friends in high school could not summon up the topic of Lorena's prize-winning senior oration. "I remember what she wore," this friend offered. "Her complexion was very reddish, and she was"—an apologetic smile—"a pretty good size, and she wore a red dress that was most unbecoming. I felt awfully sorry for her."

Nor were Lorena's relatives in Battle Creek any help. Uncle Will and Cousins Hartley and Herman ran the O.K. Laundry, across from the dairy. Aunt Anne, late in the spring of Lorena's senior year, "went sort of crazy," Lorena would tell Eleanor Roosevelt many years later.

In the year that Lorena had entered high school, Eleanor Roosevelt had given birth to—and less than eight months later had had to watch the burial of—her second son. This tragedy was at least dimmed by the birth of another healthy baby the following year, a boy named Elliott after her own father. Politics entered her life that winter. Dutifully she welcomed some quite uncouth callers when her husband, still under thirty, made his political debut in New York's state senate. But the young Mrs. Roosevelt rather enjoyed living up in Albany, away from her mother-in-law's constant prodding, even if she did have to move the three "chicks" to the third floor of their rented house after the nursery on the second floor, directly above the library, began reeking of cigars.

For Lorena in Battle Creek, one bright ray dispelled the darkness, and her gratitude remained fervent all the rest of her life. "The most gifted teacher I ever knew." That was how she referred to Miss Alicent Holt, a young instructor of Latin, Greek and English. Miss Holt surely devoted effort above the pedagogic norm to this pupil. They read poetry together. Lorena, starved for affection, must have adored her Latin teacher secretly, just as she had adored Lottie back in Bowdle. Yet in Lorena's junior and senior years, when her crush flowered, the relationship almost certainly was just as ingenuous as countless similar relationships have always been.

Still there were undercurrents. Alicent, less than ten years older than Lorena, was touched deeply by the trauma of a student so gifted, so sensitive, so subject to ridicule. It is not guesswork to suppose that she, too, had a sort of postadolescent crush; in 1935, when Lorena's work took her to Grand Rapids where Alicent was then teaching, after such a long gap the relationship between these two resumed on a somewhat different basis. As "Alix" and "Rena," they would grow much closer. But in Battle Creek, Alicent Holt's gift to Lorena Hickok was encouragement. Miss Holt gave Lorena the will to keep trying; it was Miss Holt who insisted that Lorena must make plans for going to college.

Lawrence University in Appleton, Wisconsin, was—and is—a fine small college, or more accurately, a cluster of very small colleges comprising a small university. Then and now, special training in music, for instance, has been a magnet for female students, giving Lawrence the distinction of having been one of America's first institutions to provide advanced instruction on a coeducational basis.

Even then, great oaks and elms shaded a campus regarded as exceptionally attractive. Furthermore, the thriving city of Appleton with its population of approximately seventeen thousand afforded—according to the Lawrence catalog in the year Lorena enrolled there—"the advantages of city life without the distractions and temptations of a great metropolis." But its principal attraction to Lorena at the age of nineteen could not have been readily apparent.

A year earlier, during her junior year in Battle Creek, a novel called *Dawn O'Hara* had introduced a new writer to American readers. Edna Ferber was still in her twenties; she was practically a local girl, having been born in nearby Kalamazoo; and she had started out, so bravely for a female at that time and place, as a newspaper reporter—on the Appleton *Crescent*. Indeed, the Dawn of her novelistic debut was a sob sister, beautiful and raven-tressed. Reading Dawn's adventures, Lorena forgot her own physical deficiencies; as a later generation would put it, she had found a role model.

So it was to Appleton that Lorena Hickok went with overflowing enthusiasm in the autumn of 1912. She had saved sixty dollars toward her expenses—"Average estimates of living expenses for women . . . $75 per semester"—and she expected to earn as she learned, possibly at the *Crescent* itself. That notion was not entirely farfetched; during the summer following her high school graduation, she had earned her nest egg writing social notes for the Battle Creek *News*. Should it prove out of the question, though, to get a part-time newspaper job, she was going to seek a position in some professor's home and work Saturdays in a store; she had it all figured out. Only if absolutely necessary, she might accept a little help from Aunt Ella, now living with a married daughter in Elgin.

Financially, Lorena could have managed. But what she had not counted on became sadly evident after she went out for the college literary magazine at the start of her freshman year, then wrote a story that it duly printed. Her tale was entitled "The Reward of Stuffing." It started:

> We had been living in Dakota only a short time, and, being a very egotistic maiden of thirteen, I had not yet outgrown my desire to demonstrate to my playmates the superiority of one who had lived in the East and had seen Chicago. At first my somewhat extravagant tales had been received with respect and admiration until, lured on by the successes, I had grown less and less adept in the art of "stuffing." My stories

had assumed proportions too great for the credulity of my hearers. . . .

At the age of nineteen, Lorena then proceeded to describe how she had erred six years earlier. On a cool morning in October, she related, "a number of us girls" were gathered about the steps of the salmon-colored schoolhouse they attended, discussing horsemanship. The others were all children of the plains, lithe as Indians, and perfectly justified in recounting with pride the varied adventures they had experienced upon the backs of the wiry little broncos they rode. But Lorena was not to be outdone by them.

"It is so exhilarating to feel oneself borne over hill and plain upon the back of a spirited steed!" she cried. And in her next breath, according to her later account, she launched into a wonderful fiction concerning the feats she had performed as a mere child riding her own thoroughbred. In fact, she had never ridden anything save her grandfather's plow horse—while her grandfather clung to the bridle—years ago in Wisconsin. Lorena talked on heedlessly, though, until the bell rang. Then as she started up the steps an older girl named Kate, whom Lorena particularly admired, approached her. "Say, Fatty," Kate said, "I heard you telling the girls just now how much you enjoy riding horseback, and I want you to go with me next Saturday at two o'clock. Will you? I know where I can get a mare you will like—she is very spirited."

It did not rain the following Saturday. "The day was warm, sunshiny and dusty," Lorena wrote. "A purple haze, which seemed to be filled with untold mystery, hung lazily over the distant horizon, blending equally well with brown plains and blue sky." But there was hardly any mystery about the probable outcome of the expedition, once Lorena beheld the horse Kate had procured for her. The beast was thin, with long legs, a stumpy tail and a tangled mane, as well as a pair of eyes flashing unrest. Her name was May.

Valiantly, Lorena edged toward the animal. After quite some difficulty, she found herself at last on May's back. But May declined to move—until Kate leaned over from her own steed, brandishing a strip of lath. And then May bolted. Lorena wrote:

She did not lope, she did not gallop, she did not even trot, she merely ran, and every time her hoofs would touch the ground I would bound up fully two feet into the air, only to come down again with the force of a thousand bricks. . . .

Finally, when I thought we had ridden at least six miles in this fashion, I jerked the reins frantically and shouted, "Whoa!"

The next thing Lorena knew, she was lying on the ground and Kate was crying in agonized tones into her ear: "Fatty, Fatty, are you killed? Please say something, please!"

Fortunately, Lorena seemed to have no broken bones. As soon as she was able they started home, with Kate riding one horse and leading the other while Lorena walked in the rear. For a few days afterward Kate was silent about the matter, restrained by remorse. "But," Lorena wrote, "the story was too good to keep, and so for weeks I was subjected to all the torture which youthful minds can invent."

In conclusion, when she was six years older and wiser, Lorena added: "It will suffice to say here that I never told any more yarns to that crowd." Also, she did not write any more yarns for her college magazine. Undone by her own skill in the use of the language, she must have been ragged more than she could bear after she herself had provided campus humorists with a marvelous opening—"Fatty, Fatty, are you killed?"

At first she undoubtedly joined the laughter. For everybody who knew Lorena, at any age, was struck by the way she enjoyed humor. She had her own notable laugh, notable not for its sound but for its accompaniment. Often the slightest joke provoked an almost silent shaking of her large shoulders, while tears streamed from her eyes. She always tried to brush away the tears with clenched-up knuckles. "Not a handkerchief," one of her Battle Creek friends would specify.

Much as Lorena may have felt like retreating from college after just a few months, she did not. She stuck out the year, going to classes only sporadically, working in a grocery to avoid dormitory meals, holing up at the Appleton Public Library to read Kipling instead of doing her Latin assignments. There was an inevitable impact on her grades, especially because of the rule that unexcused absences automatically reduced exam marks.

Under the circumstances it was amazing that her record was not worse. Only one failure, in Horace, marred a final report that would otherwise have brought no disgrace upon a lesser student: 83 in Milton, 80 in American Lit, 85 in Rhetoric but only 73 in Greek.

However, certain omissions gave a less favorable tinge to the summation that was sent to Aunt Ella at the beginning of June. Although Lawrence lacked the sectarian affiliation of so many small colleges then, it required not only daily attendance at chapel but also at least one classroom hour every week of religious studies. Lorena did not fulfill these requirements, nor did she meet another demand in a different department, implacably refusing to appear in bloomers for the compulsory four hours a week of physical training.

Replying to a letter from Aunt Ella asking why the report of Miss Lorena Hickok was not more satisfactory, Dr. Samuel Plantz, the president of Lawrence, wrote: "I would say that Miss Hickok is a very bright girl and could stand among the very best in college. She, however, is not a reliable student. . . ." Which impelled a touching letter from Aunt Ella that Lorena saved the rest of her life.

". . . Now my dear girlie you know my faith in you. I sincerely believe that next year you will rank among the very best in college. Oh how proud I would be of you, so let us work together. Whenever you need any advice go to Dr. Plantz . . . do not be discouraged for that which is yours will come to you." Then, after signing herself "Lovingly," two afterthoughts: "Do you need any more money now?" and "Please try *very very* hard to overcome getting angry that is the cause of many diseases."

More discouraged than angry, feeling like a hopeless misfit, Lorena left Appleton anyway at the age of twenty, in the summer of 1913.

4. Following Ferber into Journalism

Returning to Battle Creek made sense, after all, or so Lorena soon convinced herself. Boarding with the Browning family—Leta Browning had been nice to her all through high school—Lorena bounced back higher than ever because an idea that had occurred to her proved perfectly feasible. The father of Leta's closest friend was business manager of the Battle Creek *Journal*, and he put in the good word that got her hired as a cub reporter.

For seven dollars a week, Lorena had the pleasure of meeting the trains at the Michigan Central depot, and the pain of collecting countless silly little items about ice cream socials. Through that summer, autumn and winter, if the pleasure did not quite outweigh the pain, she still dreamed that it would. And her fantasies did have some foundation, owing to the extraordinary pull exerted by "the best advertised little old town of its size in the whole United States."

That was how Miss Daisy Buck, who ran the news stand in the railroad station, liked to describe Battle Creek, nor was she unduly boastful. Already the Brothers Kellogg, one purveying a whole new category of crinkly breakfast foods requiring no cooking, the other running an amazing establishment serving vast quantities of such delicacies as "Nuttolene with Cranberry Sauce"—already these gifted brothers were attracting hordes of visitors to this Michigan community with a population of only twenty-five thousand. In addition, Charles W. Post had already begun manufacturing Postum and Grape Nuts.

So not only drummers of the first convenience foods but also large numbers of people concerned about their own health were coming regularly to Battle Creek. At the "San"—Dr. Kellogg's domain, more formally the Battle Creek Sanitarium—there were *twelve hundred* rooms for individuals seeking relief from digestive disturbances. Originally most of the patients had been devout, unworldly Seventh Day Adventists, but in recent years members of Congress and even actresses had begun patronizing the establishment. So Lorena's dreams of encountering and interviewing somebody famous were not too unrealistic; unfortunately, though, the arriving sufferers she met proved to be merely ordinary citizens.

And her living arrangement, as much as her work, promoted dissatisfaction. Not that she had any cause for complaint at the Brownings' big frame house on Michigan Avenue. Indeed, she had never had a more comfortable room of her own or better meals, always served in the dining room with its handsome chandelier gleaming over the table. Always she was treated very kindly by Mrs. Browning and the Colonel, who was really a railroad man but who enjoyed the sound of his National Guard title.

The trouble was that Lorena had nothing of her own, nothing worth having. On the seventh of March in 1914, she marked an important birthday. She turned twenty-one, and although Mrs. Browning baked her a delicious cake, Lorena could not really enjoy it. She knew that she ought not to complain, but when she thought of both Browning girls and their prospects, how could she help feeling a little angry?

During that year Leta, who had graduated from high school with her, was off attending college in Ohio; Edna, three years behind them, was still home. Lorena got on with her easily enough, telling her on Sundays when they had to go to church, "Come on, Edna, let's go upstairs and get ready to appear before the public." But these girls, blessed with pretty faces and fine clothes, with loving parents to cushion their futures even if they failed to find a husband—how could they suspect her own inner turmoil?

Indeed all of the Brownings were quite surprised when Lorena blurted, "I'm going out and make a name for myself in the world!"

Bearing the name of an immensely popular ex-President, Franklin Roosevelt was in a remarkably precise way emulating his famous cousin. Theodore Roosevelt's first appearance on the national stage had been as Assistant Secretary of the Navy; now, by no coincidence, Franklin held this very position, thanks to his prescience in having become one of the first New Yorkers to think that New Jersey's Woodrow Wilson ought to be in the White House.

As the wife of the main deputy to a Cabinet member, Mrs. Franklin Roosevelt was among the most diligent payers of calls the capital had ever seen. She also, in 1914, gave birth to another son, christened Franklin junior, and the following year she became pregnant again.

Twenty-one-year-old Lorena returned to college in Appleton in September, 1914, but she left again after only one semester. When not a single sorority invited her to pledge she packed up swiftly, then boarded a train for the city where Edna Ferber had really begun her newspaper career.

Milwaukee in 1915 was a city of great charm on the edge of an emotional precipice. With the outbreak of Europe's war the preceding summer, this most German of American cities had begun to confront a problem of divided loyalties that would increasingly tear it, as American sympathies and then American soldiers were committed to the Allied cause. At twenty-one, Lorena took everything so intensely, from pastry to politics, that less than two years of Milwaukee exhausted her. But they were wonderful years.

For she was lucky enough, after just a brief period of floundering, to land a job on the Milwaukee *Sentinel*—as society editor. She was hired on her second or third try there because the woman who previously held the position had just offended a Mrs. Pabst. Apart from such hazards, society reporting was the only kind of reporting that Lorena knew she would detest, and it certainly did not fit her Ferber program whereby she would astound the city editor with her magic ways of turning routine assignments into page-one stories. Still, a few weeks of subsisting mostly on beans, while doing a part-time publicity job for a local college, had substantially altered her perspective.

Not that her new title meant that her money worries were over. Even in bigger cities than Milwaukee, with its population of nearly half a million, the standard pay for apprentice journalists, no matter what they covered, was then fifteen dollars a week. So Lorena remained at the YWCA, and the night before payday she still ate beans; most afternoons, though, she managed to stop by at Martini's.

In a city filled with beer gardens, it might not seem logical that the most popular newspaper hangout should be an inconspicuous coffee shop over on Water Street, run by a pair of Italianate Alsatians. But Edna Ferber, in lush paragraphs dripping adjectives, had told Lorena this was so, and neither the people nor the pastries that Lorena found there disappointed her. Since her cosmopolitan experience had been so limited, she was not even surprised that a type of flaky confection layered with custard, elsewhere called a Napoleon, appeared here as a Bismarck.

Years after Martini's had closed down its celestial oven, Lorena made one of her few statements of fact that might be open to question. "That's where I started to put on weight," she wrote to Eleanor Roosevelt in 1936. Yet it cannot be disputed that the process was encouraged by daily portions of plum or apricot or apple küchen, accompanying a cup of creamy hot chocolate she would always recall as even richer than that served at Rumpelmayer's in New York.

Still, if Lorena's bulk made her look older than her years, her surprising blue eyes were anything but stodgy. Lit with humor or the reverse, wistful, watchful, always wonderfully alive, they mirrored a range of feeling that usually struck other people as endearing. It was her eyes that people remembered, and the intense pink of pleasure or pain that so often suffused her whole face. Although Lorena would never believe it herself, she was really quite a handsome woman—or girl, then, for especially at Martini's Lorena was just beginning to enter adulthood.

Professionally, this European-style coffee house served Lorena in a very American way. It became her school of journalism. Sitting at one or another of the small, marble-topped tables in Martini's back room, she listened intently while reporters on the police beat expounded on the perils of taking any cop's word as gospel; she listened to City Hall reporters analyze the mayoralty prospects of the Socialist city attorney; she listened, day after day, to that boasting, crabbing, joking cacophony that constitutes newspaper shoptalk. Which is far more fascinating than any other kind of shoptalk, as every newspaper person will testify.

From it all, Lorena learned the nitty-gritty that the graduates of real schools of journalism still have to pick up on their own. And while she ground out her daily stream of wearisome wedding announcements she also kept dogging the city editor for a chance at something else. In less than a year a new passion led to her release from the nuptial drudgery that she detested even more than she had thought she would.

Music had always thrilled Lorena. Ever since she could remember, snatches of melody had run through her, somewhere in the back of her throat, vibrating soundlessly. Only soundlessly, because even though she had been able to carry a tune before she could talk, she never sang aloud anymore; her father had so effectively silenced her impulse by his efforts to make her sing at funerals that nobody back in Battle Creek had suspected her of any musical inclination. But in Milwaukee Lorena discovered opera.

Not only did the city boast a repertory company named for those omnipotent Pabsts. Milwaukee, with its large population of Germanic music-lovers, easily supported week-long visits by traveling troupes several times a year. At Martini's Lorena had made the acquaintance of a few local singers, and her most exciting reveries involved interviewing more famous visiting artists. So in November, 1915, when placards went up announcing several concerts by the most celebrated living diva—Geraldine Farrar—Lorena boldly asked for the assignment of interviewing her.

The city editor knew something Lorena did not know. Farrar's manager had relayed word that the prima donna was weary of being sought after by reporters tediously intent on asking the same questions she had already answered dozens of times. "No interviews" was her new policy. Perhaps the city editor felt a twinge of guilt when he muttered to Lorena that she could give it a try. More likely he thought the rebuff would be good for her.

Rarely had Lorena had cause to worry about what she should wear, but on this occasion she spent an entire week's pay for a new tailored suit, the skirt modishly trimmed at the hem with a thin band of monkey fur. So she thought she looked quite presentable when she set out to meet Geraldine Farrar. Unfortunately, the sky was cloudy and it had begun teeming by the time Lorena reached the depot near which the diva's private railroad car had been parked on a siding. But let Lorena, on page one of the next morning's *Sentinel,* tell what happened:

GERALDINE PROVES
SHE'S PRIMA DONNA

The Lady Reporter Charges Through
Mud to Private Car for Interview—
and Gets Her Feet Wet.

Miss Farrar Displeased

Diva in a Pout at Writers Who Ask
"Personal and Impudent Questions." So there.

By Lorena Lawrence

I always did admire prima donnas. Ever since I started in
the newspaper game I have wanted to interview one. Yes,
even though I know that genius is capricious. In the days
when I was a cub and not even a "struggling journalist,"
somebody told me that prima donnas were harder to reach
than kings, ladies in harems or murderers about to be hanged.
Now I believe it.

After splashing through exactly 163 puddles of water and
plowing through an acre or so of nice, rich mud, most of
which clung to my best shoes, I arrived at the private car of
the peerless Geraldine, only to learn first that she was indisposed; second, that she was "too tired to see reporters
tonight"; and lastly that she had become annoyed at the "personal and impudent questions which gentlemen and ladies of
the press had been asking her and therefore would submit to
no more newspaper interviews."

Wiggles Is Interviewed

. . . Even though I could not see Miss Farrar, I did have a
highly diverting and exciting interview with Wiggles, her pet
Boston Terrier, and her hairdresser, imported from Austria to
care for the prima donna's luxuriant black tresses. Wiggles
registered delight at making my acquaintance by attempting
to chew all the fur from my Sunday suit. He also kissed me—
oh, the thrill of it! To be kissed by Geraldine Farrar's dog!

"Down, Vee-gellssss! Kom hier!" hissed the hairdresser, who
waited with us in the cold damp vestibule. But Wiggles only
"wiggled" his sleek graceful brown body and made another
jump at my face. Very affectionate is Wiggles.

In the meantime, an Ethiopian gentleman informed us that Miss Farrar was "indisposed" and begged to be excused etc. etc. and would we wait to see her manager? We would. Upon his invitation we went into the car's living room . . .

Lorena managed to spin out this wonderful fluff of a nonstory for another six paragraphs, ending as she started back toward the depot: "Splash! More mud on my best shoes." She really had been angry, she would always add when she told the tale, as she did often in later years. "That dog ruined my new suit," she would grumble. Then, compulsively fair, she would have to mention that a thorough soaking in all of that rain had actually done worse, shrinking both skirt and jacket at least a full size.

So doubtless Lorena was quite a sight when she handed in her first nonsociety story, but that alone could not have accounted for the city editor's burst of laughter as he read it. What accounted for his penciling in "by Lorena Lawrence" before he flung it to the copy desk is somewhat less clear. In those days elegantly artificial nomenclature was often seen on the society page, which also printed syndicated columns with such headlines as: SEVERE WHITE STATIONERY PROPER FOR MATRON, BUT DEBU- TANTE MAY USE PINK. However, by-lines on news stories were a rarity then, and more likely Lorena herself romantically chose the euphonious alliteration.

In any case, Geraldine Farrar herself thought the story was funny and she sent a personal note to its author, along with an auto- graphed picture. Then her manager stopped by at the *Sentinel* to say Miss Farrar had changed her mind and now she would be happy to see Miss Lawrence. Lorena jutted forth her chin and said, "You can tell Miss Farrar for me to go to hell." Or at least that was how she told it later.

But thenceforth Lorena Lawrence diverted *Sentinel* readers every few weeks, often with an opus having some musical interest. When Ignace Paderewski played a benefit concert on behalf of a Polish war relief agency, his virtuoso performance was assessed by a music critic while Lorena wrote the adjacent feature story describ- ing the great ovation the famed pianist had received despite his insistence on having the hall heated to eighty degrees because he could not stand drafts.

She also met and interviewed the motherly Madame Ernestine

Schumann-Heink. Impulsively, that diva rewarded Lorena for a heartwarming story by removing a ring from her own finger and pressing it upon the young reporter; it was a sapphire ring with chips of diamond surrounding the stone. Aghast, Lorena protested that she could not accept such an expensive present. "Aw, shut up!" Madame Schumann-Heink complacently advised. So that was how Lorena Hickok would happen to have a sapphire ring available when she suddenly needed to bestow a symbolic gift of great splendor—in 1933.

But in 1916 the ring merely marked Lorena's promotion from the society page, for shortly after New Year's she moved ecstatically to covering general news on a regular basis. That did not mean a by-line a day, not then. Most days she anonymously told Milwaukee about a range of local events from school-board meetings to suffrage marches. At least in the case of the latter, she was too elated to mind the anonymity.

In her high school yearbook's class prophecy, Lorena herself had been envisioned as a suffrage orator. How much more exciting that, only four years later, she was actually interviewing the leader of the struggle for women's votes, Mrs. Carrie Chapman Catt! Indeed, the young reporter's newspaper writings clearly illuminate her inner yearning for contact with famous women; that her own mother had failed her so grievously must have disturbed her far more than the mature Lorena would allow most people to suspect. And perhaps the harrowing imperfection of her whole experience of family life also fed an inordinate need to glorify this country's closest approximation to royalty.

Lorena displayed this tendency with touching candor in a by-line story in February of 1916, just two months after the widowed President Wilson had married an attractive if not surpassingly lovely woman of forty-three. Lorena's opus was given the headline: FIRST LADY OF THE LAND WINS WAY INTO HEARTS OF THOUSANDS OF MILWAUKEANS BY PERSONAL CHARM. In the light of hindsight it makes arresting reading:

> I clasped the hand of the President of the United States but I was afraid to shake hands with his wife. Beautiful, smiling Edith Bolling Wilson inspired me with more awe and shyness than did her distinguished husband. I don't think that I could have been more nervous in the presence of anybody else in the whole wide world.

From the moment I learned that I was to "follow" Mrs. Wilson and interview her if possible, I experienced a sensation akin to panic. As the appointed time drew nigh and I approached the Hotel Pfister, I felt still more panicy [sic]. As I stepped from the elevator on the third floor I had that "gone feeling" in large doses. I waited with Mrs. C.B. Manville of New York who presented Mrs. Wilson with a large corsage of orchids.

Mrs. Manville, with her dignified silver hair and quiet grace, set me at ease somewhat, and I was listening interestedly to her explanation that she had had lilies of the valley put into the bouquet because Mrs. Wilson is a bride, when we heard cheering. It grew louder and louder as the President entered the lobby. There was the low rumble of the rising elevator, then a sharp click as the door slid open—and they came.

I stared at Mrs. Wilson—I seemed to have forgotten the existence of the President. She seemed above average height and rather slender. She appeared as stately as a duchess. My heart gave a sudden bound as I gazed at her exquisite features, and as her wonderful gray eyes rested on me for a moment I felt like kneeling. She was rather pale I thought and looked tired.

Mrs. Wilson was simply dressed . . .

Watching as that bouquet was presented, Lorena stood back and hoped she would be taken for a lady detective. Relieved then to be told no interviews would be allowed—"Had I been obliged to talk to Mrs. Wilson, I am sure that I should have collapsed from sheer terror"—the young reporter relaxed and gathered sufficient trivia to fill another half a column about the ceremonial activities during the rest of the day graced by "the loveliest woman I had ever met personally."

But such opportunities did not come often enough in Milwaukee to suit twenty-three-year-old Lorena, and she was always short of money. By the summer of 1916 she was so tired, so eager at the same time to make a bigger splash, that she quit. In nearby Chicago she had no luck. She did not care, though, for now her goal was New York.

It took her a year and a half to get there, and en route she stopped in Elgin. Not only Aunt Ella but also her sister Ruby was living there. Ruby, always so much more adept than Lorena at looking on the bright side, had finished high school from the home of Aunt Ella's daughter, quaintly named Eldora. As part of this household, out for a Sunday drive in the family's new automobile, Ruby had found an anchor that would steady her ever after if the going got rough. Rounding a corner rather too rapidly, Eldora's husband had caused Eldora to give a little shriek. "There goes mother!" she cried. Fortunately, Aunt Ella suffered no serious injury, and the incident became memorable merely from Ruby's lilting response thenceforth to any untoward circumstance. "There goes mo-ther!" she would cheerily chant.

Whether the third of the Hickok sisters ever rejoined the other two was something neither Ruby nor Lorena cared to discuss in later years. Most of their friends would never even know of Myrtle's existence, and she surfaced only once in Lorena's life after Bowdle, when she attempted during the 1930's to obtain a private interview with Eleanor Roosevelt. Myrtle's aim, apparently, was to tell the First Lady something about her older sister's childhood. "Blackmail," Lorena would tersely describe the effort. Mrs. Roosevelt found it impossible to see Myrtle.

Among Lorena's adventures on her way to New York was a short stint of press agenting for a Belgian actress. That left her stranded penniless, in a Minneapolis boardinghouse with bedbugs, on her twenty-fourth birthday. Her luck quickly turned, though, and she got a job on the Minneapolis *Tribune*. But in the spring of 1917 every newspaper was filled with war news, the United States was on the brink of joining the hostilities, and Lorena could not bear sitting out the excitement on the sidelines. Then she read a story from Russia headlined: KERENSKY AUTHORIZES WOMEN MARINES TO FIGHT ABOARD SHIPS. It gave her a thrilling idea. She would go immediately to New York, and from there she would somehow make her way across the Atlantic to become a war correspondent. Covering the Russian women's Legion of Death!

In New York she managed to get a job on the old *Tribune*. But the big city overwhelmed her, and in six weeks she was fired. Nobody would help her go to Russia. While she contemplated her next move, to pay her rent at a seedy boardinghouse on the West Side she swallowed her distaste and accepted work with an agency innocuously called the Commission on Training Camp Activities. In effect, Lorena became an auxiliary policewoman, patrolling River-side Drive near a Navy pier. Mission: separating girls from sailors. A few weeks of this was all she could endure. Then she decided she had better get herself a college education after all. Back Lorena went to Minneapolis, nearing the age of twenty-five, for a fresh start at the University of Minnesota.

Just about this time, in Washington, Eleanor Roosevelt was becoming nervous because of her husband's obvious attentions to her very attractive young social secretary, Lucy Mercer.

5. Hick's Front Page Days

Lorena's metamorphosis into a star reporter took another few years, but they were good ones. Of course, she had to support herself upon becoming a freshman again, but she got rehired by the Minneapolis *Tribune* with no difficulty because she willingly accepted that stimulating if tense category of newspaper work known as night rewrite.

That meant she spent from seven o'clock in the evening until at least three A.M. cradling the earpiece of an old-fashioned telephone with one hunched-up shoulder while she bent over a typewriter and clattered off paragraph after paragraph. Many of these were routine squibs phoned in by fellows covering police headquarters or listening to windy speeches at some testimonial dinner. But if there were a big fire or trolley accident, it would be up to her to put together a coherent story as quickly as possible from the fragmentary reports shouted into her ear by the man on the scene.

It was also expected, on night rewrite, that you could use your phone to rouse whoever might know all about whatever great event the night editor suddenly wanted covered right from the office. So it happened that Lorena, with a cigarette swirling smoke into her eyes—for now she smoked constantly—would speak over the telephone, night after night during the 1918 flu epidemic, with the president of the University of Minnesota. He had no idea, then, that the husky-voiced woman whose blasphemous banter enlivened his sleepless nights during this most distressing period when students were collapsing by the dozens—he had not the slightest idea that Miss Hickok of the *Tribune* was, during the daytime, a freshman at his own institution.

She was Miss Hickok to start with, but soon he and practically everybody else was calling her Hick. And "Hick" became more than just a nickname. It symbolized the emergence of a seemingly mature personality, a woman who had learned to relish her singularity. Not that Hick simply turned into one of the boys, although some of them surely thought so. Instead she combined two identities in a way that could not, despite the brash cheerfulness she generally exhibited, bring her happiness.

In the office, where a touch of outrageousness was appreciated, some nights she would light up a large cigar. Eventually she kept a pipe in her desk drawer, to puff at when the deadline pressure got too severe and her throat was too sore for her preferred Pall Malls. But if Hick was turning into a real character, she did not lack admirers. "As I remember Hick," a younger male colleague would reminisce a long time afterward, "she was endowed with a vast body, beautiful legs and a peaches-and-cream complexion. When she was pounding out a sob story, a tearjerker, we'd see tears streaming down her cheeks. When it was a humorous piece, her entire vast body rippled with merriment. And she could write both kinds—and the straight news variety, too—with an excellence few could surpass, then or now."

This was particularly noticed by the *Tribune*'s editor-in-chief, already a notable character himself. If Thomas J. Dillon sometimes acted as if he were trying to inspire a couple of stagestruck journalists to write a play called *The Front Page,* it was because he came from the same ripsnorting tradition that did inspire Ben Hecht and Charles MacArthur when they wrote their small masterpiece of city-room comedy. Yet the truth can be as dramatic as fiction, and Tom Dillon had once earned his own renown as a reporter by pitching his city editor into a wastebasket. Now that he was in charge, his tongue was his weapon. One day a beginning sportswriter confused the Boston Red Sox with the Cincinnati Reds. Roared Dillon: "Young man, you must know a hell of a lot about something because you know so goddam little about sports."

Built like a fullback himself, Dillon was snowy-haired by the time Hick came into his ken. She was not the only one who referred to him, when he was not around, as the O.M.—for Old Man. Although he was still in his early forties, he had covered a lot of newspaper territory already, from Kansas City to El Paso to Seattle, before returning to one of the scenes of his early journalistic triumphs. But despite his hard shell, Tom Dillon had a great big marshmallow for a heart. After observing Hick's production on night rewrite through one cold Minneapolis winter, when she was going to college from eight in the morning through noon, then doing a little homework, sleeping a couple of hours, and then producing topnotch copy all night long—he promoted her.

He made her Sunday editor at the beginning of the summer, just to give her a feel of how a newspaper's pages are made up. She was too good a writer to sit at a desk, Dillon reassured her. Quite often he and Hick crossed the street together to visit a convenient bar. "He taught me how to drink," Hick would brag on various occasions thereafter. Yet her implication must stand corrected; she rarely took more than two or three drinks. She sipped Prohibition poison (later, brandy would be her preference), she cherished the stage of feeling no pain but, to use one of her own favorite reverse constructions, no drinker was Hick.

Whether Tom Dillon influenced her in other respects to the extent that Hick would later claim must also be doubted. His wife, Clarissa—soon Hick was sufficiently well-acquainted with her to call her Ris—perhaps had almost as important an influence. For at the same time that Hick was becoming an outstanding reporter, the submerged Lorena was learning how to behave like a lady.

In this period, in Washington and then New York, Eleanor Roosevelt forgave, if not forgot, her husband's infidelity, and she began struggling to create for herself a life independent of him and of her domineering mother-in-law. Soon she was making use of the abilities she had been pleased to find she possessed during her strenuous plunge into volunteer activities connected with the war. Among the groups that began to rely on Mrs. Franklin Roosevelt for extremely efficient assistance were the League of Women Voters, the Women's Trade Union League and the women's division of the New York State Democratic Committee.

At the University of Minnesota where a twenty-five-year-old freshman enrolled as Alice L. Hickok, undoubtedly as a sort of alias, the new Hick materialized rather differently. No cigars demonstrated defiance here. But she did argue, vehemently, when the dean read to her from the book of rules, reminding her that all freshmen women were required to live in a dormitory. Nor was Hick's objection purely a matter of principle. After just a brief sufferance of meager boardinghouse existence upon her return to

Minneapolis, she had moved into the swank Leamington Hotel with a wonderful new friend.

Ella Morse—Ellie to her scores of friends—had such a sunny disposition that she never would discover how to feel sorry for herself. Other people, though, often pitied her as a "poor little rich girl." Little she certainly was, more than a head shorter than Hick, with such tiny feet that she had to have her shoes made to order. About the rich there was no question either, for her father had amassed a fortune from investments in wheat land and Minneapolis real estate; when he died, in 1925, he would leave her three quarters of a million dollars. But Ellie's mother had died in giving birth to her only baby, back in 1891. Thus Ellie, two years older than Hick, had been raised by a nurse and Grandmother Morse until the age of eleven.

A pale wisp of a child, by no stretch of anybody's imagination pretty, Ellie even then had a great gift for making friends. One of these, a girl named Bernice Barker, was so beautiful, so bright and sure of herself, that Ellie constantly asked her to visit. One day when Bernice's mother came to call for her daughter, Ellie introduced Mrs. Barker to her own father. Mrs. Barker was a widow. After she became Ellie's stepmother she never treated Ellie unkindly, but how could she help—perhaps only subconsciously—favoring her own lovely and talented Bernice?

So Ellie's life thereafter had been lived in Bernice's shadow. Bernice had numerous beaux, Ellie had none. Bernice, unfazed by snobby eastern college girls, made an outstanding record at Smith; Ellie, although she was one of the world's most dedicated appreciators of literature, flunked out after her first year. Twenty-seven when she met Hick, she was dabbling with English courses at the university and trying to write poetry, while she filled vacant hours with a lowly job in the *Tribune*'s society department.

Although Ellie's father frowned on her new idea of leaving the family mansion on Pillsbury Avenue, just as he had disapproved of her going to work, he did want her to be happy. So he not only provided the means for furnishing a three-room apartment at the Leamington in appropriate style, he also paid the rent. Surely it could not have occurred to him that he might thereby be subsidizing what the *Tribune* referred to in those straitlaced days, only if such a reference was absolutely unavoidable, as an "emotional aberration."

Some others who knew Ellie and Hick did wonder about them. To see that great big Hick, moony-eyed as she sat polishing Ellie's heavy sterling forks and spoons while little Ellie read aloud Shakespeare sonnets—to witness such domestic tableaux was, even in those days, grounds for an unspoken question. So was the embarrassing playfulness they often exhibited. "Hickey Doodles," Ellie would call Hick.

Still, the closest of their mutual friends then, a keen-eyed librarian who lived with her mother at the same hotel until she herself married, would shake her head half a century later when such questions were no longer unspoken. "I wondered about that," this extremely alert old lady would admit. "I don't think so. Some did, but on the whole I didn't." Another woman whose career exposed her to a sophistication far beyond Minneapolis of the 1920's would be more positive. "In all the years I knew Hick"—more than thirty years—"she never even raised the question in my mind."

If such testimony is inconclusive, the atmosphere of Minneapolis during the eight years Hick and Ellie lived there together must also be considered. The prevalent prudery did not even allow the newspaper for which Hick worked to use the word "resort" in describing any vacation area, on the grounds that the place might somehow be confused with another unmentionable kind of establishment. Of course, such ridiculous rules were the subject of constant jest in the irreverent news room, and no doubt Hick joined the laughter. But at the same time her extreme hankering for respectability must have modified any impulse toward the physical attachment that a less restrained society would assume from the loving dependence she and Ellie openly displayed.

On Ellie's side there was an additional inhibition. Despite repeated disappointments she still lived in hope of finding herself a man. Furthermore, neither Hick nor Ellie—in Minneapolis in the 1920's—could have known half as much about homosexuality as teenagers in much smaller communities could learn decades later merely by going to the movies. Hick, by far the worldlier, possibly recognized her own tendency in this direction. Even so, cherishing the ruby satin tea gown that Ellie bought for her, she had a strong inducement to keep that tendency suppressed.

Not that the Leamington Hick was a perfect lady, not at all. No more could Lorena Hickok stifle her prairie impulsiveness than a properly raised heiress like Ellie could appreciate feminine cigar-smoking. So even if what was then considered sinful was not attributed to them, they certainly struck everybody as an odd couple.

Ellie, with her talent for seeing the best in people of all description, had to learn to relish guests who would never have been welcomed at her family's home. Once when Hick went out of town to cover the trial of a girl accused of killing her lover, Hick turned up at the Leamington after the jury's verdict with a dazed young woman in tow. Ellie, greeting the stranger hospitably, exclaimed, "Oh, you got off, didn't you?"

Unlike as Hick and Ellie were in many ways, they created a team that eventually delighted even the mother of their librarian neighbor. At first Mrs. Welch had been rather startled by Hick's grumpy manners on arising around noon, but soon Mrs. Welch became her warm champion. That Hick had brought home a stray cat and named him François Villon enchanted her. When she tried, Hick could charm almost anybody.

So it was no wonder that Ellie purchased a Fannie Farmer cookbook and taught herself to cook artichokes as well as less exotic delicacies to please Hick. For Ellie's sake, Hick went to picnics where silly games were indulged in by the offspring of Twin City early settlers. Once Hick won great applause for balancing a broomstick on her nose. As far as their acquaintances could tell, they were serenely happy together. Hick even demonstrated her essential soundness by confessing to Ellie's respectable friends, now her friends, too, that she was falling madly in love with the leading candidate for mayor—a statement that would have provoked guffaws or stares of disbelief down at the office.

Hick wrote a few speeches for this candidate, and they must have been good ones, but right after he won, the new mayor married a light-headed flirt of a female who had spent the campaign embroidering handkerchiefs for him.

Hick still came to work just as usual in the sedate shirtwaists and brown or dark blue skirts that had become her standard office garb. A few tactful hints from Clarissa Dillon had taught her to shun more vivid attire, but otherwise Hick was far from inconspicuous. After her short stint as Sunday editor, her rise was meteoric.

College did not hamper her, for early in her sophomore year when the dean got insistent about dormitory living, Hick with few regrets bade her final adieu to higher education. Soon she was covering murder cases and interviewing a rather frowzy visiting Queen Marie of Roumania; she was the only woman reporter aboard the train upon which the French Marshal Foch traveled westward, thanking America for its wartime assistance to his country.

It was reserved for the *Tribune*'s political pundit to record the region's grief when Theodore Roosevelt died in 1919. The pages full of plaudits for a passing leader beloved throughout the area that still called itself the Northwest must have reimpressed Hick with presidential awe. In 1923, privileged to give Minneapolis its news about the passing of a much less heroic chief executive, she pulled out every stop in her story of the funeral train traversing nearby Iowa, bearing the coffin of Warren G. Harding.

IOWA VILLAGE WAITS ALL NIGHT FOR GLIMPSE AT FLEETING TRAIN

Citizens Bring Children to Pay Tribute to President as Cars Roar Away Into Dawn Carrying Body to National Capital.

by Lorena A. Hickok

Honey Creek, Iowa, Aug. 6 — Hurtling itself into the dawn at 50 miles an hour, the President's funeral train roared past Honey Creek at 4 a.m. today.

A blurred, agonizing glimpse into the dimly lighted observation car heaped to the ceiling with wreaths and flowers was all that Honey Creek got—and for this her 76 inhabitants had shivered on the dreary station platform for hours.

But in the words of H. L. Ham, station agent, postmaster and notary public, as he stared dazedly after the red tail lights dwindling away in the shadows, "Well, it was worth it, wasn't it?"

It was worth it. The long moaning whistle around the bend—the blinding shaft of light down the glittering rails—the roar and wind and trembling of the earth—the breathless wait for the rear car—the flashing vision of wreaths and flags and rigid figures in khaki—the red tail lights vanishing like pin points in the dark—yes, it was worth waiting for. . .

And so on, for nearly a column of strangely moving small talk, as a skilled writer depicted the biggest moment in a small hamlet's history. Could Hick really have felt such emotion about the passing of a nonentity whose sole distinction, after being elected by a populace weary of Wilson's high-minded internationalism, was that he had been the first President to ride to his inauguration in an automobile?

It was possible—in 1923—given Hick's remarkable urge toward presidential glorification. Of course, since Franklin Roosevelt had three years previously run for just the vice-presidency, and lost, Hick could not yet have such a special feeling about him. But as reporters must be indefatigable newspaper readers, she certainly was aware that during the summer after his defeat he had been stricken by a crippling attack of infantile paralysis, and that his political career had been at least temporarily halted while he struggled to regain the use of his legs. Out in Minnesota, though, Hick could hardly have heard how his wife, dutifully helping to keep his name before New York's Democratic faithful, was becoming increasingly involved with the women's division of New York State's Democratic Committee.

In any case, Hick's story about the Harding funeral train won her an award from the Associated Press, which every month singled out what its management considered the best examples of feature writing by reporters on its member newspapers all around the country. Such sentimentality was actually much in demand, and Tom Dillon himself wrote more than a few editorials that would cloy unbearably a few decades later, including one addressed to his long-deceased mother that started: "For the body you gave me, the bone and the sinew. . ."

To this hard-bitten Old Man, Hick's prizewinner about President Harding must have seemed like a sign from on high. Not only could she write, but now she had proved herself impervious to a certain disrespect that often disqualified good young reporters. Something he could not tolerate was a smart-aleck attitude about eternal verities, such as the Republican party. When a beginner handed in a piece possessing a dangerous potential, Dillon would grab it with a glint in his eye and demand: "Nothing smutty or subversive of revealed religion?" So the award inspired quite a gamble.

Clearly, Hick needed subject matter of sufficient magnitude to elicit a steady flow of front-page stories. For it was really wasting her to give her no larger scope than interviewing barbers and marcel-waving experts, irately contesting each other's rights to bob the hair of the city's flappers. Or as Thanksgiving approached, to let her play a little: "Now is the winter of Mr. T. Gobbler's disintegration . . ."

And in this period the *Tribune*'s page one badly needed some excitement, especially on Sundays in the autumn when a form of mass insanity was being covered only stodgily by specialists with a limited command of the language. One Saturday afternoon, Tom Dillon therefore assigned Lorena Hickok to do a "color" feature about the University of Minnesota Gophers.

It was at the height of the Big Ten football frenzy gripping the nation. For this was the era of the fabulous Red Grange of Illinois and of Notre Dame's legendary Four Horsemen. Particularly in the Middle West, in and around the home towns of the ten mighty teams, the mania had reached epidemic proportions, and professional football had not yet begun to offer sports fans an alternate stimulus to derangement.

On her first try Hick demonstrated the soundness of Tom Dillon's instinct. Being fresh from the classroom herself, she summoned up an authentic hero of American history—Oliver Hazard Perry, in the War of 1812—to help her write her lead. "We have met the enemy and he is ours," she proclaimed on the *Tribune*'s front page, taking the liberty of changing the enemy from plural to singular for good and sufficient reason, before proceeding:

> On his shield, with injuries that may put him out of the game for the rest of the season, we sent him back to Illinois Saturday night—"Red" Grange the Incomparable, football's hero of heroes.
>
> With him, and also with our respects to the whole sporting world, we dispatched his humble henchmen, the invincible Illini, trailing their proud banners in the dust.
>
> Forty thousand football fans, who gathered in the Memorial Stadium to see, not a football game but "Red" Grange in a track meet all by himself, got—with the exception of a thin wedge of Illinois rooters in the south stands—the glorious surprise of their lives Saturday afternoon. . . .

Nor could anyone object that she failed to mention the contest's final score, which happened to be 20–7, until the sixth paragraph. For just in case there might be a fan who was totally bereft of friends and lacked a radio, too, Dillon also ran a more conventional play-by-play account in tandem with Hick's football debut. Perhaps he was even a little concerned that the novelty of having a female describing a big game would not be appreciated by some of his readers, let alone some of his writers.

Dillon need not have worried. Hick, covering the Gophers Saturday after Saturday, inspired only affection. "She never stepped on anybody's toes," a Minneapolis sportswriter still turning out a weekly column more than half a century later would testify. Indeed, one day when she ran out to the end zone to hug a touchdown plunger, the burly Minnesota backfield's wittiest character jubilantly christened her "Miss Goofer."

As such, Hick appeared to be having the time of her life. Occasionally, though, she frightened Ellie by sinking into a ferocious mood in which she mercilessly flailed herself because she thought she had botched up a story or hurt somebody's feelings. Even Leta Browning back in Battle Creek had an inkling of the buried unhappiness. Once, after a game in Ann Arbor, Lorena paid her high-school friend an overnight visit, and before getting into bed she shocked Leta by moving a small table to a spot where it could easily be reached in the dark. She then set out cigarettes, matches, an ash tray. Lorena almost defiantly explained, "I wake up in the middle of the night."

But as far as most of her other friends or office cronies were concerned, Hick could not have been happier. Whenever the Gophers journeyed out of town, Miss Goofer rode the team's special train. She stayed at the same hotel and sat up absorbing the fine points of poker from her all-masculine colleagues. She even learned to squint knowledgeably from the sidelines during practice scrimmaging. But if she met none of the antagonism that would sometimes infuriate other feminine pioneers years afterward, undoubtedly it was because she did accept certain ground rules. She never even tried to get a place in the inviolately male press box; home or away, she watched from a grandstand seat purchased by the *Tribune* for her. And it probably never occurred to her to seek admission to the team locker room.

Not that Hick lacked feminist militancy. All on her own she had raised her consciousness to the point where, if she were assigned on a quiet day to cover something for the women's page, she would furiously grit her teeth. And the worst insult she could imagine professionally was to be asked by a hotel clerk if she was one of those Girl Scout ladies. Dammit, she was covering a serious news story!

Still, her antipathy marked what might be called an intermediate stage by feminist historians. During the 1920's women were just beginning to appear in appreciable numbers in newspaper news rooms, not just in those sequestered cubbyholes where columns of advice to the lovelorn and the like were produced. The same slow seepage was also happening in other fields. But, rather than call attention to the process, many of the pioneers preferred to consider themselves exceptionally able. Even decades later, no chauvinist male editor could match the disdain for traditionally women's news displayed by females who had managed to get hired as general reporters.

Yet Hick did see the total picture more clearly than any man could. Having become one of the area's best-known journalists, she was looked up to by beginners of both sexes, not only professionally. "I remember Hick as a friendly, casual, responsive woman," one of them would recall, "utterly unconscious of the fact that she was even then a personage." She was habitually amused, reassuring and sisterly, he would add. To her further amusement, student journalists would sometimes come to interview her. One such aspirant, in his subsequent essay, repeatedly qualified his praise for "the cleverest interviewer in this section of the country," sprinkling his copy with the phrase "this woman writer." That irritated Hick.

Not that it was easy for a woman to get a job on any newspaper, she told him. Oh, so she felt, then, that women lacked an equal opportunity with men in journalism? Damn right she did! "The best job in a newspaper office is, of course, the managing editorship," she added, "and you seldom see a woman getting a job like that." Still, if Hick nourished any desire to succeed Tom Dillon she kept it to herself.

As the 1920's advanced, though, something else was bothering her, something that the most amateur of psychiatrists might easily guess. Full as her life was in so many respects, Hick, approaching and then passing her thirtieth birthday, was consumed by a frustration that she may not have understood herself. Increasingly moody, prey to an awesome assortment of minor ailments—she had always suffered from the depredations of a category of indignity that she lumped under the heading of "abscesses," ear abscesses, throat abscesses, abscesses in unmentionable places—now she would find herself so utterly exhausted on occasion that she slept twenty, even thirty hours without feeling rested. At length, Ellie persuaded her to see a doctor.

It has not been medically proven that emotional unrest can trigger diabetes. But Hick, over several subsequent decades, would give ample cause for the pursuit of this line of research. By 1926 her elevated blood-sugar count did indicate incipient diabetes. Unmistakably, at thirty-three, she needed a good rest.

Ellie, a year earlier, had come into her inheritance. Loyally she proposed a plan that Hick gladly accepted. They would go to San Francisco, even then a mecca for artistic underachievers; Hick would take some time to try really to write. Had she not learned from interviewing Sinclair Lewis (WOULD'ST A NOVEL WRITER BE?) that writing the great American novel was a reasonable objective for someone with her skill at constructing a sentence? All she needed, she convinced herself, was sufficient leisure in a congenial environment. Then after a few months, the plan further proposed, she and Ellie would travel in the unhurried style of the prewar grand tour, over in Europe.

Toward autumn of 1926 Hick and Ellie therefore left the Leamington, ostensibly for just one year.

But in San Francisco, while Hick sat cursing and crumpling page after page, Ellie looked up some California cousins. Visiting them, she renewed her acquaintance with a small, dark, jolly former fellow-sufferer at dancing lessons in Minneapolis. Roy Dickinson had gone west, married, then been widowed; now he was running a country store out in the desert and he was delighted to bump into Ella Morse again. They eloped to Yuma, leaving Hick devastated. At thirty-three, her emotions churning fiercely, Lorena Hickok once more boarded a train for New York.

6. Success in New York

On Hick's second try she found New York less overwhelming, at least journalistically. Hired by the *Mirror*, with which William Randolph Hearst was trying to rival the snappy *Daily News*, she began by covering a sport that some prescient editor had conceived as a potential threat to football. But if Helen Wills and Helen Jacobs, playing tennis at Forest Hills, served as Hick's entree into the big time, after only a few months she advanced toward the front of the paper.

On January 12, 1928, the tawdry Snyder-Gray murder case ended in a flare of righteous retribution at the Sing Sing death chamber. Hick, lacking seniority, was spared having to describe the final hours of an adulterous corset salesman and his mistress, who had been convicted of killing her husband. Instead, Hick was thrown into the gap when the last stark headline had been eked from this pitiful affair. On January 13 all that actually happened was that a misunderstood freshman daughter of a stockbroker disappeared. Coincidentally, the young woman's last name was Smith and she was attending Smith College in Northampton, Massachusetts.

But Smith was also a name of political importance then. And William Randolph Hearst, with a powerful desire to win elective office, felt with some justification that he had been thwarted by New York's Governor Al Smith. It is immaterial whether Hearst himself gave orders to seize on the disappearance of Miss Frances St. John Smith, or whether it was one of his underlings who grasped the possibilities. The fact is that for the next several weeks the *Mirror* daily splashed in large black letters across its front page SMITH SCANDAL or SMITH HIGH JINKS or even SMITH TERROR. Was that not a slick way to embarrass the Governor?

So inventive were the Hearst minions, Hick included, that their competition was forced to play the same game. Rumors of kidnaping, of ransom, of orgies where college girls were drugged or worse, sent packs of reporters scurrying through the drifts of ordinarily sedate Northampton. Their efforts to enhance what should have been a fairly routine story of an eighteen-year-old runaway finally caused the president of Smith College to bar all strangers from the campus. So when Hick was invited to have dinner with a faculty member she had known at the University of Minnesota, she had to sneak after dark into Mary Ellen Chase's back door.

Shortly thereafter, Hick decided the *Mirror* was not for her. Then on August 8, 1928, *Variety,* the daily bible of show biz, disclosed that Dolores Del Rio had just arrived from Hollywood bringing seven servants and thirty-five wardrobe trunks. This was followed by: "Lorena Hickok, by-line sobbie on the *Mirror,* is going to the Associated Press."

Hick was then thirty-five, a woman of five feet and eight inches in height, weighing around one hundred and eighty-five pounds. That narrowing of her eyes, with which she had watched Gopher scrimmaging, had become second nature. Peering at whatever presented itself, her hands often clasped behind her back and her eyebrows slightly elevated as if some private joke were disposing her to a kinder assessment than might otherwise have struck her, she took the measure of any person or situation. For the benefit of those who sought to take her measure, she provided a few carefully studied clues: a slash of red lipstick to prove her modernity; dark, inconspicuous dress; and a whiff of perfume, a bright scarf, to counteract the mannish impression. But she wore flat-heeled oxfords because, dammit, her feet would not tolerate stylish shoes and she had to spend a helluva lot of hours striding around Manhattan. Take her or leave her, she had made it on sheer talent to the top of her profession, in the flagship New York bureau of the thoroughly respectable Associated Press.

Which did assign her, somewhat gingerly, to cover politics during that autumn of presidential electioneering. It was the year the Democrats finally gave Al Smith a shot at the White House despite his "Sidewalks of New York" accent and his Roman Catholic religion. The Republicans were offering that sound American, Herbert Hoover. Hick, as an apprenticeship, spent much of September running back and forth from the noisy AP news room on the sixth floor of 383 Madison Avenue to the General Motors Building on Broadway where the Democratic National Committee had its headquarters.

Besides picking up handouts and quizzing party spokesmen, Hick also made friends, as good reporters always do, among lesser potential sources. This impulse was not solely a calculated ploy. By the nature of their work, reporters find ordinary secretaries, for instance, rather boring, but a secretary in a position to hear political decision-making, discreet as she may be, makes a stimulating companion at lunch or over an off-duty drink. It would have been mainly at midday, at one or another of the nearby oases, where Hick's acquaintance with a stocky woman about her own age ripened into friendship. Outwardly pure New England, although really from the Bronx, Malvina Thompson at that period of her life went home every evening to cook dinner as Mrs. Frank Scheider, the wife of a high school industrial arts teacher.

That Malvina liked and trusted Hick soon became evident. A few days a week the brisk Miss Thompson did miscellaneous secretarial chores in the Democratic Committee's executive suite. The rest of the time she worked for its shy but awesomely efficient director of women's activities, who always said she much preferred remaining in the background. Nevertheless, one day in September of 1928 Malvina Thompson introduced Lorena Hickok to Eleanor Roosevelt.

It seems likely that Hick had asked Malvina to gratify her curiosity. For, of course, Hick already knew who Eleanor Roosevelt was.

From a limited celebrity as the wife of the unsuccessful candidate for the vice-presidency back in 1920, Mrs. Franklin D. Roosevelt was suddenly facing the limelight again. Her part in helping her husband to overcome the crippling effects of polio had yet to attract any widespread notice; her diligence behind the scenes in Democratic politics, reminding party loyalists about the potential availability of a most attractive candidate, had not yet impressed more than a small inner circle. But now this woman's husband, heeding Al Smith's pleas to give the national ticket a boost in New York State, had just emerged from his enforced retirement to run for governor.

Thus Hick, nodding affably while Mrs. Roosevelt answered a few

pro forma questions, was busy ticking off the lady's assets and liabilities as a political wife: on the plus side, that intangible as-
surance created only by money, and the clear intelligence radiating
from blue eyes of a surprising, luminous beauty; but what a pity
about those protruding teeth, not to mention the self-consciously
stiff posture that had to be expected when fate had further humili-
ated a homely woman by making her the tallest person in practically any gathering. Added to the liabilities inflicted upon her
were several self-imposed ones, starting with that terrible hairnet
drooping onto her high forehead, all too visibly advertising the
ineptitude of her hairdresser. In the bargain, her skirt was too long;
her blouse was a bilious green. Obviously she did not much care
how she looked.

Still, as Hick for the first time regarded the woman around whom
her own life would revolve for thirty years, she had just one personal thought. So this was Teddy Roosevelt's niece!

In the four years that remained before Hick was drawn into
Eleanor Roosevelt's orbit, they encountered each other only casually. But Hick herself would recall the dawn of her own special
interest as having occurred just a few days after their first meeting.
By chance, waiting for an elevator in the General Motors Building,
Hick saw Mrs. Roosevelt swinging off to an appointment that Malvina Thompson had mentioned—a luncheon debate with a witty
and chic Republican society matron. As Hick's eyes followed the
ungainly Democrat, she shook her head. You poor thing, she
thought, it will be murder for you at that luncheon. So she was
surprised to hear from Malvina that there had been no carnage and,
in fact, that when the Republican speaker had become rather
flustered because she had forgotten some figures she intended to
use, Mrs. Roosevelt had graciously supplied them.

Soon afterward Hick covered a Republican meeting where she
met one of Theodore Roosevelt's sisters. Personal as well as reportorial motives led her to ask Mrs. Douglas Robinson a question.
What was notable about her niece Eleanor besides her marriage to
a fifth cousin of the Democratic persuasion?

"Eleanor was my brother Ted's favorite niece," Corinne Robinson replied. "She is more like him than any of his own children."
That had to fascinate Hick.

As a result, she needed a little editorial chastening upon the occasion of her first actual interview with Eleanor Roosevelt. It took place on November 7, 1928, the day after Franklin Roosevelt's victory in his gubernatorial race—a narrow victory that provided no comfort for friends of Al Smith, who had lost his own state along with thirty-nine others to the seemingly safer Hoover. In those days, though, the proprieties forbade political comment by political wives, even if they did take a more than perfunctory role in their husbands' campaigning. Mrs. Roosevelt therefore made merely a few careful observations concerning the election returns.

Still, she captivated the submerged Lorena. For Mrs. Roosevelt served her tea in the drawing room of the Roosevelt town house on East Sixty-fifth Street. Wearing a lace-trimmed hostess gown considerably more becoming than anything she wore at the Democratic headquarters, she deftly poured from a handsome silver teapot that somehow called attention to her long, slender and amazingly graceful fingers. A little black Scottish terrier was curled up at her feet. All of this was like a dream to the seemingly composed reporter, who could scarcely believe that she was hearing her own voice ask politely about the dog, then about the Roosevelt children. Reticent as Mrs. Roosevelt was on other matters, Hick went back to the office and wrote a story ending: "The new mistress of the Executive Mansion in Albany is a very great lady." Her editor chopped off the sentence with his heavy black pencil. "Too editorial," he said.

For the next several years Hick made no real effort to further her acquaintance with Eleanor Roosevelt. Like most of the other women in her profession who had managed to escape the women's page—and the ratio of women to men covering general news was scarcely one in ten—she hated "women's page stuff" on principle; indeed if she ever did voice any lesser antipathy, she would be taking a chance on forfeiting the respect of her male colleagues. Instead, Hick gloried in her intermittent assignments to cover the governor, and only privately kept an eye on his wife.

Mrs. Roosevelt was always doing unexpected things, Hick noticed. Wouldn't her Uncle Ted have been proud of her when she boarded a little airplane in Albany in 1930, barely two years after Charles Lindbergh had flown the ocean? If Mrs. Roosevelt's aeronautic debut took her only as far as Poughkeepsie, still it was a bold venture for a matron of forty-five and Hick was much impressed by her daring. But when Mrs. Roosevelt was at Lake Placid with her husband to open the winter Olympics in February of 1932, and she accepted an invitation to ride the ice-sheathed bobsled run, the very idea sent chills through Hick. She only read about both of these exploits.

Every summer, though, when the governor and his wife took a trip around the state visiting prisons, hospitals and other institutions, Hick was part of the press crew accompanying them. Occasionally she did attempt a conversation with Mrs. Roosevelt, if only because they were the only women on those trips. While Mrs. Roosevelt was always courteous, she would offer no more than, "Isn't it a lovely day?" So Hick felt that she was being kept at arm's length—and those were extremely long arms. Her main picture of Eleanor Roosevelt during this period was just a vignette. In Hick's own words from a small book that she wrote three decades later:

> I can see her now riding beside her husband in the open car ahead—very erect, wearing a light printed silk summer dress and a hat considerably more becoming than some of those she had worn when I first met her. Someone said her daughter Anna had gone to work on her and persuaded her to spend a little more money on herself.
>
> But she still wore those hairnets!

During Eleanor Roosevelt's four years as the mistress of New York's Executive Mansion, Lorena Hickok moved steadily ahead professionally. While she did so, she drew emotional sustenance as best she could, and to the eyes of most beholders she seemed perfectly content with her Prinz.

He was a police dog, a pup who could appear ferocious. But on the Sundays when Hick had to take her turn watching the AP news ticker to make sure that nothing much was happening, and she brought him to the office, he meekly accompanied her up the freight elevator, then lay like a lamb beside her desk. It was not for protection that she counted on Prinz. In those days even a frail female could feel safe walking any street at almost any hour, and Hick, her voice so rich and robust that it certainly sounded as if she could sing Wagner, would readily agree that she was far from frail. However, for all of her humorous self-mockery, she still cringed at the implication that no one would dream of attacking her.

It cannot be doubted that Hick felt dreadfully lonely during these years. Indeed her inner fury over having *nothing* of her own, suppressed for so long, sometimes rose to the surface not too subtly disguised. One holiday season she sent out cards reproducing a sketch of Prinz that an artist acquaintance had made for her. Beneath this drawing were the words: "A Very Merry Christmas to You and Yours from Me and Mine."

Yet Prinz really was all she had, besides her work and a lot of mostly casual friends. Among these, the second woman hired by the AP in New York—all over the country, the agency employed only about a dozen females then—had fallen in love with a Chicago newspaperman who soon followed her east. At that time the sort of easy chatter about other people's emotional kinks that would become common decades later was hardly thought of, even by reporters who prided themselves on being several steps ahead of their readers. But Jane Eads did tuck away an impression regarding Hick and her Prinz that would not have escaped comment half a century afterward.

Jane, upon marrying, moved into an apartment only a couple of blocks from Hick's, and they often walked home together, usually stopping to pick up a few groceries. Then Jane might tarry briefly at Hick's place. "She'd open the door," Jane would recall, "and Prinz would be at her side instantly. She'd go absolutely ape over him. Talking as a mother to a loved, favorite child. And as soon as she would put her bags down Prinz, by then having leapt to the table, started slathering her with his long wet tongue all over her face! That was one thing that used to 'get' me! *She* loved it!"

But Jane marked it merely as a mild eccentricity. To her, and to the men she and Hick worked with, Hick preeminently was an outstanding reporter, a "pro" in every way. Everybody liked her, and the extent of their private reservation was that she reminded them, only in her appearance, of a police matron. With her heavy oxfords and plain skirts, her shirt sleeves rolled above her elbows, she could look forbidding while she was batting out a story. At ease, though, as the hostess at Sunday "brunch" time, serving up shakers full of pretty potent stingers to five or six of her colleagues, she was the life of her own party. What's more, being so fond of good eating, she had become a good cook. Indeed she generously loaned the newlywed Jane pots for her own parties and shared her favorite recipes, too. "She taught me how to bake thick huge steaks in the oven with catsup and A1 sauce on top. Sounds not so gourmet—but it was wonderful!"

The scene of Hick's Sunday get togethers was a handsome brick apartment house adjacent to the Beekman Tower Hotel in mid-Manhattan, very close to the East River. One floor above the lobby, she had a large living room with a sleeping alcove, a dressing room, a tiny kitchen, and what she delighted in calling her porch; it was a balcony just about big enough for Prinz to stretch out on, although the prevalence of dog hairs indoors proved that he had free run of the entire premises. Even so, the place was basically clean because Hick hated dirt. Just as with her clothing, though, her efforts at elegant simplicity tended to be defeated by circumstances beyond her control. After she had bought a striped cover to brighten her day bed, somehow she never found the time or money to do anything about the rest of the nondescript furniture the landlord had provided.

Still, Hick's yearning for status was soothed by the fashionable facade of her apartment at 10 Mitchell Place. Nevertheless, those who knew her could not ignore a disingenuous failing. "She had absolutely no idea of money at all," one of them would sum it up. Her own chilling opinion, volunteered several years later, was that only Prinz made her life worth living, and it was for his sake that she needed to be near the river. At any rate, she and her dog running together on an unused pier had become a neighborhood sight. It was just the limited sort of notoriety that she enjoyed.

But most of Hick's acquaintances had no idea how she managed to pay seventy-five dollars a month rent, plus another twenty dollars or so for the services of an auxiliary dog-walker, besides the additional expense of feeding such a large beast. For there was a reason why publishers liked to encourage glib reminiscence about "the newspaper game," spreading the notion of what fun it was; even at the height of the Hoover prosperity, at *The New York Times* the average pay for reporters was less than fifty dollars a week. As a by-line staffer on the AP, which did not preserve personnel records from this era, Hick probably made sixty. Improvident as she was, she very likely got into an acute financial bind every so often. There are reasons for believing that on at least a few occasions she was rescued by little Ellie, out in California.

Despite a hurt that never quite healed, that would always make Hick think of San Francisco as the place where Ellie had left her to marry Roy, Hick and Ellie wrote to each other religiously. Indeed their friendship never faded. Until Ellie's death in 1949 they met whenever they could, even though Ellie's husband and Hick could barely disguise their mutual hostility. Each thought the other was nothing but a fortune-hunter. Serene little Ellie loved them both, and if she did "bail out" Hick a few times after her marriage, as Roy would later maintain, the subsidizing had to stop soon because the Depression devoured Ellie's fortune.

Still, Hick kept digging into her purse whenever she heard a hard-luck story. Nobody could be more generous than she was, or more impulsive. Five-dollar bills that she really needed herself often went flying out of her hands to buy an extravagant toy for somebody's new baby, if not a couple of meals for a family suddenly deprived of its paycheck. And the same impulsiveness appears to have influenced her emotionally.

For some of Hick's activities away from her office probably did cross a line that frightened a substantial portion of the population. If she crossed it, she could only have done so in the anonymity of New York, where neither office friends nor her sister—for Ruby was now almost a neighbor—had to be aware of certain adventures.

Only happenstance made a confidante of a younger woman reporter who, half a century later, would insist on not being identified if her recollections were to be recorded; so she will be called Barbara Hanson. As a newcomer to high-pressure journalism, covering several assignments where she encountered the assured and established Lorena Hickok, Barbara was welcomed beyond perfunctory politeness. "Hanson," Hick would tell her, "I'm going to teach you how to play poker and swear—you might need it."

Even so, their acquaintance might not have progressed much further if they had not bumped into each other one afternoon when Barbara Hanson was carrying under her arm a controversial novel called *The Well of Loneliness,* treating in a sympathetic manner the previously taboo subject of lesbianism. Hick said, clearly on the spur of the moment, that she herself would not want to be seen with this book in the street or on the subway. That surprised young Barbara.

A few weeks later Hick and Barbara were both sent out of town on a story. As the only two females among the press crew, they shared a hotel room. Hick had not even stopped en route to pack a suitcase, but Barbara, already counting the months until she quit to get married, had taken the time to fill an overnight bag. Not atypically, Hick upon arriving felt symptoms of flu, and Barbara left their room rather late at night to purchase some aspirin and a toothbrush from the hotel's drugstore. When she returned, Hick, as Barbara would put it euphemistically so long afterward, "made for me."

Rebuffed by a terrified Barbara, Hick not only apologized, she also explained. "You were just so sweet to me," she said, "that it undid me." Then, as if it relieved her to talk, Hick proceeded to talk sadly and soberly for quite some time. She spoke of her miserable childhood, and she told Barbara about being raped by her father. Wryly she described the longing for respectability that still propelled her into such follies as buying English golfing shoes at Abercrombie's. She even poked fun at herself for her haste to seize her Minneapolis opportunity. But significantly, proving her loyalty to Ellie, she described Ellie as a girl from "Wel-les-ley," and yet Hick could not disguise the pleasure she herself had felt when she had gone to the theater with this "Wel-les-ley" socialite, and sat with her in a box.

By her own testimony that night, Hick, on arriving in New York after Ellie's defection, had said to herself, what the hell? For years she had been trying not to surrender to her "tendency," but why bother? "So she went off the deep end about various women," Barbara would recall, and "she also told me about some adventures with men. No, no, I don't think she ever lived with a man but she certainly experimented. After all, she had not been brought up like I was. Since she'd had that experience, why shouldn't she experiment with everything? Oh, yes! She told me about some adventure she had with some man, riding in one of those horse-drawn hansoms around Central Park."

Afterwards neither Hick nor Barbara referred to the subject again, although they remained friends until Barbara left New York to get married. Then they saw each other only a few times before losing touch, but there was one further remark by Hick in her long and shattering talk that Barbara would never forget. When "going off the deep end about various women" had been mentioned, Barbara had said, "I never knew what it was they did." Said Hick, abysmally grim, "You don't want to."

Still, those four years had happy moments. Opera at the Met, great theater, even prize fights—reporters could often cadge passes, and Hick did. Only rarely did she brood because, compared with Edna Ferber, she was still a nobody who merely read about that smart crowd who gathered at the Algonquin. Instead she relished sitting in speakeasies till the wee hours trading shoptalk with "the most interesting people," which was the way working reporters liked to describe themselves. Nursing her private misery, she developed a gift for listening to other people's troubles most consolingly. That made her feel useful, which she tried to believe was the most she could expect for herself.

Hick also operated as an outpost of Minneapolis, and sometimes it seemed as if that whole city aimed to look her up in the big town. For cherished friends like the Dillons, who came once a year to the newspaper editors' convention, she outdid herself, shepherding Ris on shopping expeditions, introducing the Old Man to her New York cronies. Mere acquaintances were accommodated, one after another, on Hick's day bed. Most hilarious, though, were reunions with visiting sportswriters. When they appeared somebody always gave a party to which Hick might bring her pup, because Prinz got lonesome spending so much time by himself. To see Hick striding with him through the lobby of a Times Square hotel around midnight was a memorable experience.

But Hick had only a thin layer of surface toughness hiding her soft core of unashamed sentiment. To her, the best thing about these years may have been Ruby's new proximity. During the war Ruby had taken nurse's training, courtesy of Uncle Sam, at the Walter Reed Army Hospital in Washington, but she had enough gumption to disdain the menial work for very little pay that was the common lot in the nursing profession then. So she, too, had gravitated toward New York and, at least financially, she had surpassed her sister. As the chief factotum for a prosperous surgeon who contributed frequent articles to medical journals, Ruby, his nurse-secretary, was earning a hundred dollars a week.

Of course that figure griped Hick. But if Ruby had made less, Hick would have worried about having to support her. The relationship between these loving sisters who also irritated each other, sometimes painfully, would baffle many people. Yet at this stage Hick surely appreciated the novelty of having family to feast with at Thanksgiving, to trim a tree with six weeks later. Her pleasure at the prospect of acquiring an amusing, dapper brother-in-law was a little diluted because Ruby's friend Julian seemed to work only intermittently at some sort of hospital fund-raising. But for the time being, Ruby and Julian filled a real need for the secretly suffering Hick.

Only Hick's work gave her increasing satisfaction. Just a few days after Herbert Hoover's electoral triumph in 1928, a disaster offered her a chance to prove her mettle. The steamship *Vestris*, wallowing in an autumnal storm off the Virginia Capes, sank with more than three hundred passengers and crew unaccounted for, and there was intense competition among newspapers and wire services to provide the true story of what had happened after the damaged vessel had begged aid by radio.

Hick not only managed to be present when the first rescue ship reached New York, she also beat everybody else into print. Her story, based on the accounts of survivors who had drifted twenty-two hours in lifeboats, was so graphic that *The New York Times*, despite its own staff's exploits, used what she wrote, verbatim, on its front page. That gave her the right to claim, at least technically, the glory of being the first female ever to have had her name appear above a page-one story in this illustrious journal.

The technicality was the fault of her own shop, which had insisted on having her do an as-told-to story. So her account went out over the wire with the by-line of a passenger: "By Paul A. Dana, As Told to Lorena A. Hickok, Associated Press Staff Writer." If such circumlocution struck Hick as a damn shame, at the AP headquarters they were jubilant. Although the agency ostensibly existed merely to serve its member newspapers, the cooperative spirit that had inspired its founding decades earlier had been replaced in recent years by cold-blooded competition, at least in the hearts of its top management. To them, getting any AP story printed prominently was all that mattered; had the *Times* seen fit to use a piece sent by that upstart United Press, Hick would certainly have heard disparaging remarks.

As it was, she got plaudits and plenty of opportunities. Since speed was so essential for an agency feeding news all over the country, to morning newspapers and afternoon newspapers with a range of deadlines that left little leeway for leisurely mulling, some AP staffers excelled in running to a telephone and dictating clear if undistinguished prose. When necessary, Hick did this. But when she had time to sit down at a typewriter, she could turn almost anything into a story that got her name—and those two important letters (AP)—into hundreds of dailies. For instance, in 1930 she wrote a crisp but tender-hearted interview with the old "general" who had led Coxey's Army to Washington in 1894 and was still promoting his own quirky plan for relieving unemployment. When Hick came to work a few mornings later, in her cubbyhole mailbox was an envelope from Minneapolis containing a ticker-machine copy of her Coxey opus, with two comments decisively penciled atop the first page. "A darn good feature," in the inimitable handwriting of Tom Dillon. "Seconded," by her former city editor. But if New York was less effusive, Hick's standing as the bureau's best reporter was usually acknowledged by her colleagues, and her bosses demonstrated their agreement in their own way by giving her the number one story most days, no matter that she happened to be a woman.

Thus she sat at the press table while New York's Mayor Jimmy Walker, famous everywhere for his playboy antics, tried to squirm out of charges that he was corrupt politically. She also went to Long Island with the pack that covered the mysterious drowning of a voluptuous "party girl" named Starr Faithfull. And in March, 1932, Hick went to a place called Hopewell in New Jersey, where she acquired her own personal collection of searing anecdotes about the Lindbergh kidnaping.

"I remember walking up Fifth Avenue the afternoon of March 2, on my way back to the office from some political pow-wow in Al Smith's office in the Empire State Building, cursing under my breath all the way and wondering if I would be justified in quitting the AP!" That was Hick, years afterward, recalling how she had felt because she was still in the city a full day after the first flash that the infant son of the famed aviator had been abducted. Not until the next morning was she taken off politics to join the AP team covering what appeared to be the story of the century.

The Lindbergh kidnaping certainly outdid any of her other journalistic experiences in sheer excitement and frustration. When she arrived at the crossroads hamlet below the secluded, and now tightly guarded, Lindbergh estate, hordes of newspaper people were already scrabbling the countryside for crumbs of information. Late that afternoon Hick and a photographer, having hired a car to pursue their own search for the missing baby, stopped to sip a beer at a rural speakeasy. There they overheard talk about an abandoned house nearby, hidden from the road amid tall trees.

They found it, and they also found muddy tracks that looked fresh. Hick seized a broken hockey stock atop a pile of debris, the photographer picked up a piece of lead pipe; they tiptoed from room to room, discovering nothing. Outside, they poked a few holes where the earth looked as though it had been recently disturbed, until darkness chased them. But neither her office nor the police seemed the least bit interested in following up her short piece about this eerie place near the Princeton highway. It would be two months later, after Hick was back on Madison Avenue, when the AP man based in Trenton phoned in the story for which he won a Pulitzer Prize. A truck driver, stopping along the same highway, had stumbled on a shallow little grave—diagonally across the road from Hick's abandoned house.

Yet the AP in New York pressed her fiercely for stories on its own tips while Hick was down in Hopewell. One night the news desk had somehow ascertained positively that the baby had just been returned. "Get on it!" Hick was ordered. It was snowing, she was no athlete, but she and a photographer practically crawled up a back route to the brow of the wind-swept hill upon which, as the journalistic prose of the era put it, "the Lone Eagle had built his nest."

While the photographer hung back amid some trees, aiming his camera just in case, Hick crept across the lawn alone, keeping her eyes on the police bastion in the brightly lit garage. Peering through several windows, she satisfied herself—if not her office—that nothing special was going on in that house that night.

For her trouble, she immediately got an acute case of laryngitis. And in after years the exploit would strike her as a perfect example of journalism at its prying worst; no matter that the AP's general manager piously announced that *his* people were not exceeding the bounds of taste and decency in their quest for Lindbergh leads, somebody sure as hell had given her the impression that she had better check out that rumor or look for another job.

But the police on the case were not having a happy time either. From five different jurisdictions, operating under five different commands, after days of snarling conflict they had tangled the investigation to the extent that one commissioner of public safety ordered his men home. To celebrate, although that was not really the right word, a party was scheduled in Trenton, and one of the AP men managed to get invited. Fearing for his own sobriety, he called Hick.

"Bill said I could bring you—I told him you were a good egg." So Hick fortified herself with a solitary steak before being summoned from her hotel room by a dour sergeant who escorted her to a corner suite where uniformed cops and plain-clothes men, desk lieutenants and motorcycle riders—but no other outsiders—were methodically getting drunk. By one in the morning the AP Trenton man was asleep on a sofa, while Hick, sliding every second glass underneath a chair, doggedly listened for some helpful hint. By four in the morning there was no one left in any shape to divulge a word—not that a tip of lesser magnitude than that the baby had been found could have justified such an ordeal—so Hick returned to her room and fell into bed.

Still, she would have hated to miss this experience, even after her perspective changed remarkably within the next several months. That process started the last day of June, on an occasion that was notable beyond any personal consideration.

By the summer of 1932 the United States was sunk deep into the worst Depression it had ever known, and no longer could pronouncements from Washington that prosperity was just around the corner mask the fearful truth. Tar-paper shacks where homeless men huddled in abject misery had sprung up all around the city. The emergency soup kitchens could not cope with the endless straggling lines of men, women and children.

Like almost everybody else, Hick had been trying to pretend it was all unreal, that it would somehow be solved on Wall Street where it had started or by a new quick stroke of magic in Washington. That she had even for an instant contemplated quitting her job early in March was a measure of her self-delusion, for there were no jobs in any field available then, especially for a woman only a year from her fortieth birthday. Indeed, like practically everybody who was still working, she had "cooperated" in averting more firings by accepting one pay cut of 10 percent; another was imminent. Also like everybody still being paid, she knew others who were not and who were getting desperate; without her sister Ruby, Julian would be starving.

At this most numbing crisis in America's history, the Democratic

party was convened in Chicago to choose its 1932 nominee for the
presidency. And in the garage adjoining the Executive Mansion at
Albany in upstate New York, Lorena Hickok waited with a cluster
of other reporters to hear the outcome of the Chicago balloting. If
things went as they expected, soon they would be surging across the
lawn to congratulate the winning candidate, who was listening
with his family to a radio upstairs in the mansion.

But there were numerous cross-currents swirling through that
Chicago convention, and it finally adjourned in full daylight the
next morning, following an inconclusive third ballot. All of the
other reporters drifted off before Hick and the head of the AP's
Albany bureau left the garage. As they emerged, Eleanor Roosevelt
had just come out on a screened side porch for breakfast. Upon
noticing the two stragglers, she went to the porch door and invited
them to join her.

Since all three of them were weary from their long vigil, nobody
spoke much during the meal. Hick observed, though, that Mrs.
Roosevelt seemed intensely preoccupied, almost to the point of
rudeness. As Hick thanked her on departing, she could hardly contain herself. The instant she felt it was safe she addressed her colleague: "That woman is unhappy about something." But to Elton
Fay there was no mystery, for of course Mrs. Roosevelt was worried
that her husband might not get the nomination. Still Hick had a
different impression.

In Chicago, two women and one man already were aware of
Eleanor Roosevelt's unhappiness. On the day of the nominating
speeches, a letter from Mrs. Roosevelt had frightened her closest
friends, Nancy Cook and Marion Dickerman; it was they who
shared her weekend hideaway a few miles from the country home
of her formidable mother-in-law, besides working with her at various endeavors. Nan headed the women's division of New York's
Democratic Committee; Marion ran the private school where Eleanor was a part-time teacher. At the convention, apart from whatever duties were required by Nan's job or Marion's post as an
alternate delegate, they both were doing all they could to help the
organizer of Franklin Roosevelt's drive for the nomination. So they
brought Eleanor's letter to Louis Howe.

He had been a political reporter in Albany back when handsome
young Franklin had first entered the state senate. If not for the

unkindness of nature, Louis Howe might have enjoyed a notable political career himself. But he was scrawny and undersized, barely five feet tall, with a head that seemed disproportionately large; the brain it encased had been concentrating since 1911 on the advancement of his "Beloved and Revered Future President." At first Franklin's wife had been hard-pressed to be polite to this rumpled little gnome incessantly dripping cigarette ashes over his clothing and her furniture. During the terrible testing of Franklin's illness, though, she and Louis had become allies—and then friends. Indeed Louis, beneath his wry acceptance of his own ugly exterior, had shown a touching sensitivity to her similar problem, joking with her and constantly encouraging her. There appeared to be a bond between them strong enough to be called love.

Yet by now Louis no longer merely coughed a great deal and sputtered irascibly if something interfered with his grand design. His asthmatic shortness of breath had grown so severe that Nan and Marion worried whether he could survive the steamy heat of pre-air-conditioned Chicago. Frail as he was, they found him on his feet when they arrived at his hotel room bearing Eleanor's letter.

In it—as Marion would relate after a lapse of four decades—Eleanor Roosevelt had poured forth a torrent of anguish at the prospect of having to live in the White House. She "could not live" there, she said. Nan and Marion, seeing Louis pacing tensely because he feared that all of his efforts might suddenly be cancelled by some unexpected defection, felt even more fearful as they handed him the terrible letter.

According to Marion, Louis Howe's pale face darkened as he read the letter, his lips drew into a thin line, and when he had finished reading it, he ripped it into tiny shreds. "You are not to breathe a word of this to anyone, understand?" he ordered. "Not to *anyone*. . . ."

Back at the Albany mansion, the moment it was announced that California had swung into line—giving F.D.R. the required two thirds—bedlam erupted. Cameras flashed, hordes of well-wishers swarmed everywhere, and some of the reporters went looking for Mrs. Roosevelt. They found her in the kitchen, scrambling eggs because her husband had had no dinner.

As Hick stood jotting notes about the lady's pale green chiffon gown, one of those gushy girl reporters she detested chirped above the clamor: "Mrs. Roosevelt, aren't you *thrilled* at the idea of living in the White House?"

Hick could not doubt that Mrs. Roosevelt heard the question. But Mrs. Roosevelt did not answer it. Instead she stared at her questioner with such a forbidding expression that not even the gushiest interviewer could persevere. Watching, Hick felt the scene emblazon itself on her memory. At this instant, as Lorena Hickok became certain that she was regarding a very unhappy woman, her own emotional bondage to Eleanor Roosevelt began.

PART II

"I don't suppose anyone can ever stay so happy . . ."
1932–1936

7. Beginning a Very Special Friendship

Back in the city, Hick suggested to her office that full-time coverage of the wife of the Democratic candidate would be an experiment worth trying because this woman did not merely live in her husband's shadow. However, when the AP decided after about six weeks to accept her advice, Hick turned down the assignment herself. No, she wanted to write about F.D.R. because he was the real story. And there was nothing like a coast-to-coast train trip with a presidential hopeful for quickening the journalistic pulse.

Send a female aboard a campaign special? Well, Hickok had earned it. Let her do the crowd color and other sidelights, the AP's top management decreed; of course, a couple of men from Washington would handle the candidate's speeches. Meanwhile, the third woman to be hired by the agency's New York bureau, among nearly thirty men, was given the candidate's wife. So Katherine Beebe went to the Roosevelt country place in Hyde Park. She wrote a few pieces but her heart was elsewhere. Not for creamed-chicken-and-green-pea luncheons had she come East, and at the beginning of September she quit to marry in California. Anyway—and how could Hick not have known it?—shortly afterward Mrs. Roosevelt herself joined her husband in Arizona.

By then, Hick had given back better than she got. A berth about half a mile forward was what she had been obliged to settle for, because those in charge of the arrangements had balked at wasting on a solitary female any of the double rooms in the press car reserved for representatives of the wire services and the major dailies. Despite the comparative luxury of the men's accommodation, there was a lack of bathing facilities. Soon the porters began burning incense, and Hick sent a personal telegram. When they reached Denver, where they would stay the better part of a day, only Hick had a room awaiting her at the Brown Palace. She bathed first, while half of the press corps meekly lined up outside her door.

The AP team aboard the Roosevelt train consisted of two men from its Washington bureau, plus Hick. One of them would remember more than forty years later that the first time Hick had an opportunity to chat with Mrs. Roosevelt, she returned so excited to the drawing room they were using as an office that he offered an avuncular caution: Don't forget "the usual AP restraint." Perhaps Hick's concern that something like this might happen had been part of her reason for wishing the assignment on Kay Beebe. If so, it would have been just a glimmer of concern because Hick was not noted for her farsightedness.

In fact she went out of her way to resume her acquaintance with Mrs. Roosevelt's secretary. By now Malvina Thompson had been working so regularly at the gubernatorial residence that the governor's children had indelibly tagged her Tommy. Hick was accustomed to being the only woman on most of her assignments, so it had to be more than a yearning for feminine companionship that led her to keep seeking out Tommy in the dining car or late at night after the last speech had been made and the last story of the day had gone off on the wire.

Then one night Hick seized an opportunity that was also fraught with peril. As the train clickety-clacked across the desert, an unexpected blast from the engine whistle reminded Tommy of her father. He had been a locomotive engineer, and the family had lived near the New York Central tracks in the Bronx. Tommy said she had always known when her father was aboard one of the trains that roared past the apartment windows because he would sound three sharp blasts in a private salute. And then Hick, too, started reminiscing.

That much Hick would disclose tersely thirty years later, writing that she and Tommy had talked "about her childhood and mine." But after relating how Mrs. Roosevelt had seemed more approachable than usual a few nights later, Hick added just two sentences: "Tommy was with her and later she told me she and Mrs. Roosevelt had had a long talk that night. She didn't tell me what they talked about, and I didn't ask her." So it can only be assumed that Tommy relayed to Mrs. Roosevelt whatever Hick had told her about her own father.

At any rate, from then on Eleanor Roosevelt treated Lorena Hickok with the special kindness that a woman of her compassion reserved for life's unfortunates. That is not to say she suddenly got over her distaste for personal publicity. But as if she could not bear to inflict any further wound, she forced herself to offer unexpected boons to this particular reporter. Amid the frenzy of the next six weeks, Hick did not stop to examine what was happening.

Everywhere the blare of "Happy Days Are Here Again!" Even in her sleep Hick could not escape the catchy Roosevelt theme song. At whistle stops, parades and rallies beyond counting, it assaulted her ears jubilantly, and yet what she would remember best were the quiet moments: out near Prescott, Arizona, where Mrs. R. had made a point of coming to talk to her, just the two of them, in a parked car; upstate in New York, having toast and coffee together at a small table in *her* hotel room; and a few days later, the magic of the drizzly morning on which she and Mrs. R., alone in the whole world, had stepped out of a borrowed roadster into great gusts of wet wind as they inspected the site of a proposed power dam on the St. Lawrence River.

Also, Hick would never cease grinning at herself, puffing and perspiring, following a miraculously cool Mrs. R. through a Nebraska cornfield. But the lady did get tired—and picked strange places to rest, such as a box seat at the World Series in Chicago, where she placidly slept while Babe Ruth and Lou Gehrig each hit two home runs. That story of Hick's probably got a bigger play than anything else she wrote during the whole campaign, not that she cared as much as she ought to anymore about getting her own name into the papers.

Indeed Hick would have to marvel over her own detachment on meeting Ellie again, that day when she and Tommy had played hooky from the train in San Francisco. Yet Hick had certainly felt far from detached in that smoky hotel corridor up in Boston, keeping the local press entertained till nearly midnight while Mrs. R. stole off to comfort her husband's secretary, Missy LeHand, who had just lost her mother. Nor were Hick's feelings uninvolved on the night when she and Mrs. R., just the two of them, were returning to New York on a regular train that was so crowded they actually had to share a drawing room.

Writing about this occasion thirty years later in her own little book called *Reluctant First Lady,* Hick would recall:

> To my embarrassment, Mrs. Roosevelt insisted on giving me the lower berth and taking for herself the long, narrow couch on the other side of the drawing room.
>
> "I'm longer than you are," she said when I protested. "And," she added with a smile, "not quite so broad!"
>
> It was early, neither of us was sleepy, and so we started talking. It was then she told me that I could thank Tommy for the fact that she had accepted me and permitted me to follow her about.
>
> "She's very fond of you," Mrs. Roosevelt said, "and Tommy is a good judge of people. So I decided you must be all right.
>
> "It was hard for me at first. I was brought up by a very strict grandmother, who thought no lady should ever have stories written about her, except in the society columns.
>
> "To be frank with you, I don't like being interviewed. And that applied especially to you. For Franklin used to tease me about you. He'd say, 'You'd better watch out for that Hickok woman. She's smart.' He wasn't criticizing you in any way—he likes you. He was only teasing me."
>
> She then proceeded to tell me about her own unhappy childhood and girlhood, the tragic death of her father, whom she loved so much, her strict Grandmother Hall and her aunts who called her "the ugly duckling."
>
> "May I write some of that?" I asked her fearfully before we finally said good-night.
>
> "If you like," she said softly. "I trust you."

Thus as Election Day approached Lorena Hickok was already living on two different levels. There was the top layer of the reporter for the Associated Press, covering a story with her usual brash competence. Beneath lay a woman whose feelings had started to interfere with her professional duties, or at least to limit what she told her office and her readers. During the final weeks of the campaign, when Hick was spending nearly every day tagging after Mrs. Roosevelt, her stories usually did no more than describe that lady's hectic round of campaign appearances. "Since she had grown to trust me," Hick would write three decades later, "she left

it to my discretion as to whether or not I should quote her. I rarely
did. . . ."

Those unquoted remarks were mostly personal reflections, for
instance on Eleanor Roosevelt's forty-eighth birthday, the eleventh
of October in 1932. "I'm a middle-aged woman," she mused then.
"It's good to be middle-aged. Things don't matter so much. You
don't take it so hard when things happen to you that you don't
like." Certainly this was no stop-the-press news—and yet it fasci-
nated Hick. She unerringly connected it with the mysterious unhappiness oppressing this woman, and she longed to ask more
questions but she dared not. Even so, the second Hick, primarily a
reporter despite her growing emotional involvement, gave her office no grounds for complaint. On the last Friday of the campaign
she demonstrated her commitment to her work in a memo to her
boss that certainly seemed to take a dispassionate attitude toward
the public figure whose schedule she so breezily described:

> She arrives back Saturday morning and goes with her son,
> Elliott, to some opening of a Sears Roebuck store in Brooklyn.
> Elliott is in the advertising business, and his firm has the ac-
> count. I think I need say no more? I thought I would not cover
> that.
> At noon Saturday Ed Flynn is giving a big Democratic
> women's luncheon and rally in the Bronnix. Anna Dall [the
> Roosevelts' daughter] is going to speak and her mother is
> going up there to hear her. It is my impression that Mrs.
> Roosevelt never before heard Anna make a speech. That one I
> think I had better cover.
> Saturday night is the Madison Square rally. Mrs. Roosevelt
> will of course be there, and I could undoubtedly do a story if
> the night side wants it. I hardly think the story would amount
> to much, however, but I'm willing.
> Sunday she may go to Hyde Park with the Governor or she
> may stay here in town alone to get some rest. I'm not planning
> to see her, but I could call her up and turn out some sort of
> story for AM's if it is wanted.
> Monday morning she teaches and at noon goes to Hyde
> Park to attend that evening the meeting in Poughkeepsie. The
> Governor, you know, always winds up all his campaigns with
> a speech in Poughkeepsie. She will come back to New York on
> the last train that night, to be here for her teaching the next

morning, Election Day. I think it might be a fairish idea for me to stick around with her Monday, don't you?

Tuesday, Election Day, she teaches in the morning, goes to Hyde Park to vote, and returns to New York in time for dinner. She and the Governor will be at the Biltmore that night. I thought I'd leave her alone Tuesday until night.

Wednesday morning, the day after election, school goes on as usual. And she has promised me that, if he is elected, I may go to school with her that morning to get a story. No photographers, though. And I'm the only reporter she'll allow inside that school.

                                                            LAH

By Election Day, though, there was a third level on which Hick had begun to live. This deepest level would remain hidden from the world, and only in private letters between Eleanor Roosevelt and Lorena Hickok would it ever be alluded to; not until ten years after Hick's death would anybody else read these letters. If Hick had not wished this to happen, she could easily have destroyed her cache instead of donating it to the Franklin D. Roosevelt Library at Hyde Park. Or if just the historical sidelights struck her as worth preserving, she could have pursued a task that she did start and then give up—the task of eliminating all of the personal passages before deeding her papers to a branch of the National Archives. During the five and a half years she survived Eleanor Roosevelt, it would also have been possible for her to stipulate a far longer period than a decade after her death before her papers were opened.

Even in her old age, though, Hick could not resist publishing a personal supplement to her previous journalistic coverage of Eleanor Roosevelt on Election Night in 1932. Before any returns could have been expected in Franklin Roosevelt's first race for the presidency, his wife had been the hostess at a buffet supper at the Sixty-fifth Street town house for a large assemblage of relatives and newspaper people who had covered the campaign.

"She greeted us at the door," Hick wrote in *Reluctant First Lady*, "and when I came in, she kissed me and said softly: 'It's good to have you around tonight, Hick.' " Also, that was the first time Hick had seen Mrs. R. in an evening dress, and the change in her appearance was amazing. "The gown she wore was long, with a short train," Hick recalled, "and it was white, made of some soft material like chiffon. Tall and slender and erect, she looked like a queen in it. I decided that she was as some English women are said to be—thcy may look rather dowdy in daytime clothes, but in evening clothes they are beautiful."

Still it was the second Hick, trying to be both a friendly confidante and a conscientious reporter, who appeared at Sixty-fifth Street at half past eight on the morning after the election in which Franklin Roosevelt had decisively defeated Herbert Hoover; F.D.R. had carried forty-two of the forty-eight states. It was the second Hick who accompanied the next First Lady to the nearby Todhunter School for Girls. As they entered a classroom where a current-events lesson had been routinely scheduled, every pupil stood and one of them made a shy little speech about how pleased they were to have the First Lady of the Land as their teacher. "But I haven't changed inside," Mrs. Roosevelt said a bit sadly. "I'm just the same as I was yesterday." Hick went back to her office then to write a short piece before hurrying to Grand Central Station.

Again, it was the second Hick who boarded a train with Mrs. Roosevelt around midday and who sat beside her in an ordinary day coach as Mrs. Roosevelt, gazing occasionally at the cold rain slanting down the window and spattering into the gray Hudson River, murmured, "If I wanted to be selfish, I could wish Franklin had not been elected." It was that Hick who walked through the Albany station with Mrs. Roosevelt after the rain had stopped, then watched Mrs. Roosevelt wave away a waiting cab. "I'm going to walk," she announced, taking a firm grasp on her heavy briefcase. "I need the exercise."

Standing at the entrance to the station, Hick watched Mrs. Roosevelt set out with her long, swinging stride across the plaza toward the steep hill leading a good mile up toward New York's gubernatorial mansion. At last Hick walked back alone into the station, had a sandwich and a cup of coffee, and took the next train to New York City.

Three hours later, first and foremost a reporter, Hick finally tackled the opening installment of a three-part series she had been assigned to write about the wife of the newly elected President. Unhesitatingly, she started:

"If I wanted to be selfish," said Mrs. Franklin D. Roosevelt today, "I could wish that he had not been elected."

The voters settled that matter yesterday, however, and on March 4 Mrs. Roosevelt will acquire the title bestowed upon her so often in the last few months by the toastmasters.

"I suppose they'll call me that," she said, "but there isn't going to be any 'First Lady of the Land.' There is just going to be plain, ordinary Mrs. Roosevelt."

She smiled, but the expression in her eyes was serious.

"I never wanted it," she said softly, "even though people have said my ambition for myself drove him on—even that I had some such idea in the back of my mind when I married him.

"I never wanted to be a president's wife, and I don't want it now. You don't quite believe me, do you? Very likely no one would—except possibly some woman who had had the job. Well, it's true, just the same.

"For him I am deeply and sincerely glad. I wouldn't have had it go otherwise. And now I shall start to work out my own salvation. . . ."

Hick then proceeded with a sympathetic portrait of Eleanor Roosevelt from her girlhood until her reluctant arrival at her new eminence, compressing into just a few thousand words what would not too long afterward become legend: the sad and lonely childhood, the proper young matron stage, the first real stirrings of concern for the underprivileged following involvement in volunteer work during the war; then the polio crisis, the loyal wife's self-effacing efficiency at the Democratic women's division, combined with part-time teaching at the private school of which she was part owner, and editing a magazine called *Babies—Just Babies,* and also being a partner in a furniture workshop at Hyde Park—all of these jobs to earn a little money of her own to give the people and the causes she felt like helping. Yet Hick still found room to say that this human dynamo of a woman calmly did everything else required by her position as the wife of a governor and the mother of five rambunctious young people, the youngest two sons still at prep school, the other two and the daughter already married; nor did she omit Mrs. Roosevelt's fearless car driving, her horseback riding, her incessant knitting of sweaters for three, nearly four grandchildren.

All of this Hick wrote so swiftly that she astonished her male colleague who was doing a similar six-part series on F.D.R. Since he had had to spend a day in the library before he could start writing, he was amazed to see Hick just punching those keys with hardly a look at her notes. "She knew her subject that well," he would marvel four decades later. Actually, though, Hick herself had in a sense collaborated on producing a new sort of political personage.

Not that she and Eleanor Roosevelt could have done this all by themselves. The time was ripe. Undoubtedly the ratification of the Nineteenth Amendment to the Constitution in 1920, granting women the right to vote, had been the prime factor contributing to that ripening. But a redheaded reporter from Omaha had certainly helped the process.

Bess Furman, working for the Omaha *Bee-News,* had done such a fine job of interpreting Al Smith to Middle Westerners in 1928 that the AP Washington bureau had hired her. When Herbert Hoover defeated Smith, Bess Furman undertook to humanize Mrs. Herbert Hoover. It was not easy. Although press photographers were permitted to record the appearance of a chief executive's helpmate on ceremonial occasions, reporters had to be satisfied with brief statements issued through a social secretary.

Mrs. Hoover's only nondomestic interest lay in promoting the national prestige of—the Girl Scouts. So on Christmas Eve, 1930, disguised as an overgrown Scout, the AP's Furman had accompanied a troop invited for holiday festivities. She thereby became the first writer ever to give the nation a firsthand account of a White House Christmas celebration. Her ruse was never exposed, but the following year a small group of reporters was invited to witness the official White House Yuletide. So even if Hick had never written a line about Eleanor Roosevelt, Bess Furman surely would have grasped the same opportunity a few months later—and the only difference, in the long run, would have been in the life of Lorena Hickok.

During the uneasy waiting period between the election and the inauguration, which would not take place until March 4, 1933, Hick fared much better than she had forced herself to think she would. Instead of having to give way immediately to Bess Furman, whom she'd never met but who had several times wired her a few words of congratulation from the Hoover train, Hick was able to sell the office on a compromise. If displacing Bess down in Washington was out of the question, at least Hick could keep Mrs. Roosevelt right up to the day she actually became First Lady.

It made sense. By now every New York City newspaper and wire service had assigned "girls" to cover the unpredictable Mrs. Roosevelt, who really was trying to behave approximately as usual rather than succumb to celebrity. But her firm refusal of Secret Service protection, her attempts to go about her business on foot or aboard a regular city bus, everything she did created a stir—and a story. Hick, though, did not have to hang around with the others outside Mrs. Roosevelt's office at the Democratic Committee to keep track of what the lady was planning. "I was not among them," Hick would explain thirty years later, "for, since we had become very good friends, I always knew her plans in advance, and we would meet somewhere away from her office."

Indeed, quite often Hick was the the only reporter to know what the next First Lady was planning, and she was frequently the only reporter present when Mrs. Roosevelt made some seemingly unscheduled appearance. As far as Mrs. Roosevelt herself was concerned, this arrangement had several advantages. Unaccustomed as she was to being dogged by the press, she found the experience disconcerting and sometimes extremely irritating; but if she were accompanied by Hick, she could truthfully assure her husband that she was not gadding about all by herself. Furthermore, she could count on Hick's discretion—even her protection.

So Hick was useful to Mrs. Roosevelt. On a number of occasions Hick distracted other reporters while Mrs. Roosevelt privately accomplished a few errands. Hick also shared information with her colleagues when Mrs. R. asked her to. It must be remembered that the political importance of publicity was only just beginning to be appreciated then, and various improvisations were being resorted to by those who made the news as well as those who wrote it. Louis Howe, among his other duties, acted as the President-elect's public relations expert, and Howe, at least for the time being, had no objection to Lorena Hickok's favored treatment by the President-elect's wife.

That was because Hick had taken a calculated risk. Early in the campaign she had promised Howe she would write nothing of any moment about Mrs. Roosevelt without showing him her copy before she gave it to her office. But if Hick's cooperation with Howe was unusual, it was not unprecedented at a time when public figures were much less accessible than they would be a few decades later. Within just a few months, Hick would be torn between her loyalty to her office and her inability to distress the President's wife. Right after the election, though, no such conflict seemed to trouble anybody concerned.

As these were months of mounting tension for the nation and for its President-elect, his gubernatorial duties had been more or less handed over to the lieutenant-governor who would be his successor in Albany. So the Roosevelt's gray stone town house on East Sixty-fifth Street was serving as the base from which the New Deal take-over was being put into motion. It was an unusual residence, seemingly twice the width of most of the other five-story homes in this elite neighborhood. But the future President's mother had built identical dwellings for herself and for her son during the century's first decade, behind a single facade in the dignified Georgian style that she admired, and both houses shared the same tastefully ornate front doorway. Inside the vestibule, though, there were two separate doors.

The younger Mrs. Roosevelt's home, conventionally designed by her mother-in-law, derived its special character from her husband. F.D.R.'s ship models adorned the entrance hall, his sailing prints covered virtually every inch of wall space along the sweeping stair-way that curved upward in a semicircle to the drawing room and the library on the second floor. While Franklin Roosevelt conducted his endless conferences behind the closed door of the library, his wife more and more often welcomed her friend Hick in her own comfortable third-floor sitting room.

If Hick felt any professional qualms over the tacit agreement that anything she saw or heard en route to her tea and chocolate cake would not be relayed to her office, she never wrote about them. Instead, even years later, she divulged only a lesser variety of suffering, such as the discomposure she endured on the day she had been invited for lunch along with the President-elect's Aunt Kassie.

At the table, the elderly Mrs. Price Collier chose to tax her niece by marriage about the amount of personal publicity that she was receiving. Hick, already worried lest she commit some gaucherie such as spilling her soup, still felt obliged to defend her friend. It was difficult, she remarked mildly, for a person in Mrs. Roosevelt's position to avoid publicity.

"Nonsense!" Mrs. Collier proclaimed. *"I have never talked to a newspaper reporter in my life!"* Not only did Hick record this proclamation in italics, she went on to note that after nearly choking on her soup she spent the rest of the meal in terror lest it come out in the general conversation that she was a reporter.

More frequently, though, only Tommy witnessed Hick's visits to Sixty-fifth Street, and Hick and Tommy and Mrs. R. enjoyed much hilarity along with their chocolate cake. For Tommy was irreverent enough to tease her boss by referring to her as "the FLOFL," for First Lady of the Land. Soon she would shorten it to FLOL, because she was remarkably efficient; she had even taught herself stenography when her boss had learned to dictate letters. Since she would be accompanying Mrs. R. to Washington, they also talked freely about the impending adventure. And it struck Hick that, apart from Tommy, Mrs. R. seemed to have nobody to whom she could express her own extreme apprehension. So perhaps this loneliness was part of the reason why the White House might appear a prison to her.

Always Hick had felt a special empathy with women who had not been born beautiful. Such women, as she knew only too well herself, were forced to find their own way in the world, and Eleanor Roosevelt had certainly done that. But now her own interests and preferences were going to have to be buried again, and, having worked so hard to nurture them, she would naturally find it particularly hard to suppress them. Still Hick could not be quite satisfied with her analysis. After all, Eleanor Roosevelt had a husband. Plain or not—and in person she was somehow like a magnet, drawing people around her—she had attracted a most exceptional husband. With him, for him, she had been striving for years to help win the very prize he had just captured. Then why, now, should she feel so deeply disturbed? It was a question that often arose in Hick's mind during December and January but she still could not ask it because she feared the loss of Eleanor Roosevelt's trust.

Indeed as the New Year of 1933 arrived, Hick's meetings with Mrs. R. increasingly subordinated duty to friendship. They spent numerous evenings together, not just attending meetings but going to Hick's favorite restaurants and then to some Broadway production. Far more than in Minneapolis, Hick's taste for simple elegance could now be gratified; instead of "having dinner with" Mrs. R., they "dined" together; they went to "the play," instead of just to a theater. But what need could Eleanor Roosevelt have for the friendship of Lorena Hickok?

It always amazed Hick when people seemed to like her. She still thought of herself as a shy person, and among strangers she often took refuge behind a protective glower. Yet there was something about reporting that made it similar to acting. Just as if Hick were playing the role of some character up on a stage, she could approach anybody with perfect aplomb when she could say, "I'm from the Associated Press." Relieved then of every worry over her own appearance and personal failings, she was free to be herself. And that self could be utterly disarming.

"Moddom!" she had been puckishly greeting Mrs. R. nearly every morning on the telephone. For she insisted, despite repeated invitations to be less formal, that no power on earth could ever make her pronounce three simple syllables together as one word. "El-ea-nor," she could barely manage, blushing profusely.

Still if her humor and humility were attractive qualities, to the Eleanor Roosevelt of 1933 Hick increasingly seemed overly modest. Why, it was wonderful for a woman to have achieved such success in a profession like journalism! Frequently she told Hick how much she envied women of real achievement. She said that she herself would never be able to earn her own bread and applesauce.

What about her teaching, Hick would demand. Remember, said Mrs. R., she was part owner of the Todhunter School. Well, said Hick, there were the magazine articles and the speaking. No, said Mrs. R., the only reason anybody ever wanted her to write anything or to say a few words anywhere was because she was Mrs. *Franklin* Roosevelt. Not even her own sons believed that her opinions on any subject were worth listening to. Nobody could possibly care what *Eleanor* Roosevelt had on her mind.

But Eleanor Roosevelt's view of herself was hardly accurate, and the leaders of several organizations such as the Women's Trade Union League were effusive in their appreciation of her efforts on their behalf. Still this was not a personal sort of caring. And Hick's capacity for caring, for feeling, was extraordinary. When the lights came on again in the opera house after an evening of Wagner, Hick would behave as if she were coming out from under anesthesia. Mrs. R. often told Hick how she admired this capacity for feeling deeply. Although such awe embarrassed Hick, she was powerless to dispel it. For it appeared to be nourishing a real affection, and even a sort of dependency. And how could Hick possibly rebuff what she so profoundly craved?

On January 9, 1933, Mrs. R. invited Hick to a private little party celebrating Tommy's forty-first birthday. Although these two working women got on so well, some differences between them could easily be discerned. Tommy was shorter than Hick and more compact, and her most distinctive feature was a perpetual wrinkle in the bridge of her nose, communicating an amiably blunt message: "You'd better get out of my way, or else." Had her family stayed put, she probably would have spent her mature years managing some of the best church suppers ever to be served in the state of Vermont.

As it was, this Yankee from the Bronx had begun working right after she finished high school in what she dryly called a "classy" sweatshop, typing several hundred envelopes a day. Any typographical errors caused a subtraction from her paycheck; she toiled from eight in the morning until seven at night, with twenty minutes off for lunch. If the experience proved her endurance, Malvina had brought to it a prodigious sense of duty that did not escape notice. After she took a job at the Red Cross, the agency received an atypical request: Could it recommend an able typist to help Mrs. Franklin Roosevelt?

That had been early in the 1920's. During the ensuing decade, Malvina had become an avid Democrat and an incessant smoker, neither of which otherwise unlikely eventualities made much impress on the New England granite of her character. Indeed it was a rock-ribbed inner security that most significantly set Tommy apart from Hick.

With two brothers and a sister producing a highly satisfactory assortment of nieces, Tommy had the further ballast of a loving family. Inflexibly cherishing her privacy, she would leave no evidence at all relating to the gradual deterioration of her own marriage; in 1938, when she quietly secured a divorce, one sentence would disclose that a separation of five years had preceded the decree. But if Tommy's husband disappeared from her life with scarcely any public notice, in the same manner another man, a minor governmental official, entered it. And Tommy's sister was so devoted to her that she was moving her own household to Washington when the Roosevelts took up residence there.

Thus Tommy, despite her absolute loyalty to her boss, was by no means a mere appendage. She provided a tartness and a toughness that the Eleanor Roosevelt of 1933 needed even more than she needed secretarial assistance. In effect, Tommy protected her from her own excess of good impulses—so that Tommy's personal approval of Hick had already given Hick an unprecedented opportunity. On closer acquaintance Tommy became even more positive, fracturing her usual reserve to the extent that she wrote to Hick: ". . . though I do not always tell you, I want you to know that I am tremendously fond of you. . . ."

Tommy, addressing "Hick darling," made this avowal in a note of thanks for her birthday gift. Actually, Hick had brought twin presents of a splendid thoughtfulness to the party—identical engagement books, one for Tommy, the other for her boss, bound sumptuously in leather and filled, loose-leaf style, with pages marked off at every half hour from eight in the morning until eight at night. To symbolize the new life opening for both recipients on the fourth of March, Hick had rejected ready-printed pages beginning with the first of January. Instead she had chosen undated pages and, laboriously by hand, she had penned at the top of the first "Saturday, March 4," then "Sunday, March 5," and so on for several months. As needed, she would provide additional leaves. It really was a selfish present, she explained, for it would guarantee that every morning two very busy gals would have to think of her, if only for a second, while they scanned her own jotting of what day it was.

Ten days after the birthday party Tommy once more had occasion to write to Hick, this time thanking her for a welcome outing: "I want you to know that I had a most peaceful time and thoroughly enjoyed myself last evening, and more than enjoyed my drink. My hat is off to your culinary ability as it is to all the other abilities. You were sweet to ask us and I think it was the first evening in which I actually did nothing for many weeks."

But Mrs. R. had been obliged to leave right after dinner, so Tommy had unburdened herself of some apprehensions then. "I certainly made my exit on a very pessimistic note," she admitted ruefully to Hick, and then further confided: ". . . I am feeling a little low about the new job and all that it entails. Don't misunderstand me, I am not regretting or reneging—I would go even if I had to wear Hoover's cast off hair shirt! Things are never as bad as anticipated and the indomitable Mrs. R. will surmount all obstacles and let us follow in the path she cuts. I am a little scared at all the intrigue and double crossing, but if I mind my business perhaps I can get by. This started out to be a note of thanks and ends up being a wail!"

Whatever intrigue may have prompted this, Tommy undoubtedly surmounted it. But from then on—with barely more than a month remaining before the great move—she no longer had time for relaxing with Hick. During those weeks, Mrs. R. and Hick often were alone. Yet there were two ceremonial occasions that starkly foretold their impending separation.

First, Bess Furman came up from Washington for a little luncheon at Sixty-fifth Street that did not merit any public notice, but to Hick it was almost like attending her own funeral. Oh, she carried it off in fine style! No tears, or more than a crooked little smile when Bess fell for the bait that Hick had planted and said, Why of course, it would be perfectly feasible for the wife of the President to hold her own regular press conferences. And she herself would start arranging with the other girls about credentials, ground rules and so forth.

But Bess was smart, Hick could tell. For all of her freckles and smalltown manner, she understood that if Mrs. R. went out of her way to be helpful with a weekly press conference, then Mrs. R. could expect a little kindness in return. At first when Hick had broached the idea, Mrs. R. had shaken her head. Neither Franklin nor Louis would approve, she had protested. They had, though, as Hick had said they would.

The second adventure was, however, even more searing. It was a trip down to Washington, in response to the protocol summons from Mrs. Hoover, inviting her successor to tour the living quarters of the White House for the purpose of planning where to put furniture, and also to afford Mrs. Roosevelt an opportunity to ask any necessary questions about the responsibilities devolving upon a president's wife.

As if Eleanor Roosevelt needed any such instruction! Listening to her talk about her visits to her Uncle Ted and Aunt Edith, Hick had to nod and decide that here was another partial answer. Even as a young woman, this niece of Teddy Roosevelt's must have noticed, and been distressed by, the empty formality that went with life in that fishbowl, as Eleanor Roosevelt bitterly called it. Still, it was not until the morning Hick accompanied Mrs. R. off the midnight sleeper from New York and they boarded a cab to the Mayflower Hotel that Hick realized how much her friend hated Washington.

Looking out the cab window—Mrs. R. had testily spurned the offer of a White House car and a military aide to meet her—she had the same stony expression that had startled Hick the night Franklin Roosevelt had won the nomination. And Mrs. R. was so annoyed when Mayflower flunkies escorted them to the Presidential suite that Hick had to suppress her own bemusement at the grandeur of their accommodations. After breakfast upstairs, Mrs. R. firmly told her husband's cousin who had come to call for her—Warren Delano Robbins was the State Department's chief of protocol—that she would have no need for his limousine as she intended to walk the few blocks to the White House.

"But, Eleanor darling, you can't do that!" he protested.

"Oh, yes I can," she said. "Miss Hickok is walking over with me."

So Hick did walk with her, struggling to keep up. But she still managed to notice that only one passerby, a bright-eyed old lady, seemed to recognize the tall woman striding across Connecticut Avenue. Finally, at the White House gate, Hick mustered a smile of encouragement. Then she stood and watched as Mrs. Roosevelt, unusually erect, strode on alone toward the stately columns that Hick herself had seen only once previously, as a tourist. At the gate, not even realizing then that reporters were routinely admitted to the White House public areas, Hick waited the longest hour of her life. At last the tall figure emerged, and stood while several news photographers snapped her picture. One of these, showing Mrs. R. smiling toward the approaching Hick, would be the favorite portrait that Hick kept with her always, until her sister found it after her death. It was inscribed: "We were only separated by a few yards dear Hick & I wonder which of us felt most oddly!"

Still it hadn't been so bad inside, Mrs. R. told her later. Mrs. Hoover had been very gracious and the head usher, coincidentally named Ike Hoover, who had been at the White House since McKinley's era, had cheered her by welcoming her as "Miss Eleanor." She even talked with some verve about how she would change the functions of various upstairs rooms. Hick, meanwhile, tried not to think of her own loss when the rearranging of those rooms got underway.

Early in February she spent a weekend at Mrs. R.'s cottage a few miles from the big house at Hyde Park. There Hick suddenly discovered that long walks on woodsy trails were one of life's great pleasures. While she and Mrs. R. walked, they talked over the wording of a statement in which Mrs. R. would describe her plans for continuing at least some of her independent activities after she moved to Washington. Back in New York, they went together to a sort of farewell party thrown by the Women's Trade Union League, where they both laughed heartily at good-natured jibes, in song and skit, about Mrs. Roosevelt's impatience when obliged to give pink teas. Although the guest of honor had not intended to speak, one of the skits impelled her laughingly to disclaim any intention of becoming a power behind the President's chair. "There's one thing I won't do," Mrs. Roosevelt said. "I won't meddle in politics."

Then, reflecting the gist of several of her private talks with Hick, she went on: "I do think, however, that there are possibly a great many things which are not purely political in which I may be interested. I hope I shall be able to do a great deal for women. And when one does things for women, of course, one is also helping the men." Amen, Hick felt like murmuring. If there were any contribution she thought she herself might make, it was to encourage statements like this, confidently anticipating a real campaign on behalf of women—for this woman could do it!

And then, around ten at night on the fifteenth of February, Hick was dropped off at the AP office by Mrs. R. They had enjoyed a pleasant dinner together at a little Armenian restaurant Hick liked, before proceeding to a hotel where Mrs. Roosevelt had accepted a bouquet and spoken briefly to some motion-picture executives. Hick planned to write a few paragraphs, then amble over to Grand Central Terminal in time to meet Mrs. R. aboard the midnight sleeper, bound this time for a conference at Cornell University.

As Hick entered the AP news room, the night editor shouted at her, "Where's Mrs. Roosevelt?"

"On her way home in a cab. I just left her."

"Get the hell up there quick!" he ordered. "Some crackpot in Miami just tried to shoot her husband."

So Hick arrived at Sixty-fifth Street only a couple of minutes after Mrs. R., and found her sitting, very pale, while Louis Howe frantically yelled "Operator!" as he tried to get a call through to Florida. Thus far they, too, knew no more than what the office flash had said: that the President-elect, driving away from the yacht where he had been on a fishing trip, had stopped to make a short impromptu speech, when suddenly shots had rung out from the crowd.

But while Hick sat there another phone rang, and it was Franklin Roosevelt himself, calling to reassure his wife that he was all right, and that although Mayor Anton Cermak of Chicago had been hit, it did not seem to be too serious an injury. So the next day, all over the land, there appeared a vivid story giving Mrs. Roosevelt's reaction to the near assassination of her husband. In the Minneapolis *Tribune,* which took a special interest in printing "by Lorena Hickok" on its front page, the headline was:

> Phew! Exclaims
> Mrs. Roosevelt
> as She is Told

The story was a fine example of journalism under pressure—as far as it went. It went up to the point of reporting that, after Mrs. Roosevelt learned the facts by telephone, with barely twenty minutes to catch her train she saw no point in cancelling her own next-day appointment as long as Franklin himself had urged her to carry on as usual. So the future First Lady had hurried off to the station. And Hick was with her.

The next morning in Ithaca there were more stories. On its own, the railroad as a protective measure had decided to detach the car in which Mrs. Roosevelt was riding and treat it as a special train. The Ithaca *Journal-News,* unexpectedly confronting a major story, headlined its welcome: MRS. ROOSEVELT OUTWARDLY CALM ON ARRIVAL HERE FOR ADDRESS AT FARM AND HOME WEEK; EXPRESSES SOLICITUDE FOR WOUNDED MAYOR OF CHICAGO. And in its subhead: "President-Elect's Wife Fails to Permit Miami Shooting to Interfere with Visit—'Such Things Are Apt to Happen,' She Says." More tersely, Hick filed the same information for millions of readers elsewhere.

No, Mrs. Roosevelt would not dream of asking Secret Service protection for herself. She did give her talk as scheduled at Bailey Hall at two o'clock ("The Widening Interests of the Family" was her topic), then she listened to the address of Pearl Buck, the

Pulitzer prize novelist, at three. She also planned to attend the banquet on the campus that night, so she would remain in Ithaca until the following morning.

Still there were personal matters that neither Lorena Hickok nor Eleanor Roosevelt would ever write about, except obliquely. Nobody else had been with them on many occasions since the election; nobody ever can say what had occurred privately before the Cornell visit, or what occurred during it. But it is likely that the friendship between these two women changed in the course of their sojourn there—under the stress of the attempted assassination of Franklin Roosevelt.

Probably Eleanor Roosevelt confided to Hick then about his affair with Lucy Mercer, which, fifteen years later, still tortured her. Furthermore, it appears that as Franklin reached ever closer to *his* goal of the presidency, his wife was increasingly distraught by the prospect of having to bear new constraints on *her* hard-won independence; she even seems to have contemplated leaving her husband. Thus Hick's sympathy, personally and patriotically, would have been overwhelming.

But despite many uncertainties that can never be resolved, one fact must now be recorded. Just a few weeks after returning from Ithaca, on March 4, 1933, when the forty-eight-year-old Eleanor Roosevelt did become the First Lady, she was wearing the same sapphire ring with which an opera singer had rewarded an enthusiastic young reporter many years earlier. And from the White House three days afterward, on Lorena Hickok's fortieth birthday, E.R. wrote to her:

> Hick darling, All day I've thought of you & another birthday I *will* be with you . . . Oh! I want to put my arms around you, I ache to hold you close. Your ring is a great comfort. I look at it & think she does love me or I wouldn't be wearing it!

8. Hick Ceases to Be a Reporter

There are more than two thousand letters from Eleanor Roosevelt to Lorena Hickok at the Franklin D. Roosevelt Library in Hyde Park, along with slightly over a thousand of the letters that Lorena Hickok wrote to Eleanor Roosevelt and then reclaimed. These raise many questions. At this point in Hick's life, it is important to state a few facts about the correspondence.

First, it is incomplete. Hundreds of additional letters, including the bulk of Hick's communications to E.R. in the early 1930's, did not get saved. Furthermore, the two women met often, and spoke on the telephone almost nightly when they were apart. Thus the letters are frequently cryptic; they raise more questions than they answer. Nor is it possible that anybody can do more than guess at the meaning of certain phrases.

So I must stress that I have used many other sources in reconstructing Hick's story, and a full discussion of my basis for every chapter will be found starting on page 335. However, I must repeat here that I have tried to avoid guessing about feelings or occurrences that there is no way of verifying. Although some readers may be disappointed not to find a detailed account describing precisely how Hick or E.R. felt at every stage of their relationship, or precisely what happened between them, the general course of the relationship does emerge clearly in the evidence that is available, more clearly at some stages than others. Throughout, I have aimed to give each reader a fair summary of what I have found, without imposing my own interpretation. Nevertheless, because I have had more opportunity to consider all of the available evidence than most readers will have, I feel that I must give my own answer here to one inevitable question:

What was the relationship symbolized by that sapphire ring?

Of course, in the best of all possible worlds the private behavior of any adults would be only their own concern. Even in this far from perfect world, until quite recently it would have been all but unthinkable to raise such a question involving a woman of Eleanor Roosevelt's stature. Indeed that word—*unthinkable!*—was the reaction of the senior archivists at Hyde Park when they first scanned The Papers of Lorena Hickok. To them, the effusively affectionate passages in numerous letters were the expression of just an intense, if unusually belated, schoolgirl crush.

At least with regard to E.R. herself, this verdict is, I believe, essentially justified. The preponderance of the evidence, and the total context of her life, does support it. Nevertheless, there undoubtedly were nuances of less naïveté in her relationship with Hick; their correspondence contains dozens of passages that offer some grounds for such an assumption. But there are also, it must be added, ample grounds for rejecting the immediate implication of the letter that ended the last chapter. The fact is that no way exists to banish uncertainty because Hick did deposit a mass of ambiguous material where it was bound to be perused. So any quest for the truth must require, step by step, the telling of her own story.

After Hick and Mrs. R. had returned from Ithaca to New York, just two weeks remained before the inauguration. During those weeks, the nation reached a point of unprecedented crisis, with a wave of bank closings casting doubts about the survival of the American system. If Hick suddenly found herself more mindful of the broad picture than she had ever been previously, still she was mainly concerned by the prospect of being separated from the person who had suddenly given meaning to her own life. Indeed both women were now bent on spending every possible moment together.

Ostensibly, Hick was just doing her reportorial duty. But on the Friday they got back from Cornell, Mrs. R. proposed a weekend expedition to Groton, the school in Massachusetts where the two youngest Roosevelt sons were preparing for Harvard. The only problem was that Mrs. R. wanted Hick's company—and yet no publicity. That Hick won a grudging acceptance of this unusual arrangement from her office emerged between the lines of the somewhat belligerent memo she handed in the night preceding their departure:

> In regard to this Groton business:
>
> We are leaving by motor, in her roadster, at dawn tomorrow. I am staying with her at the school. We return Sunday, getting back here at 10 or 11 p.m.
>
> No one except members of the family knows I am going with her. At her request, I have not said how or when she was going. Of course, there is a chance of its slipping out there, but I don't think so. She is cautioning them all. She is not going to see any reporters in Groton.
>
> I believe the understanding is that I don't have to put out anything unless a really good story breaks. About the only really good stories I can think of are: an automobile accident, attempted kidnaping of her, or something of that sort; or a folo from her should anything happen to the Governor or any member of the family. In which case, I naturally would get busy at once and would be in a position to get a good clean beat. She understands that, if anything of the sort happened, I would of course have to get on it.
>
> No reporters are allowed at the school. In taking me with her, she is not telling them I am a reporter. Therefore, I think it would not be a very good idea for the office to try to reach me there unless it is vitally important.
>
> If, for instance, anything should happen to the Governor, we'll know it about as soon as the office does, and, of course, I'll get on it immediately.

In short, Hick was getting a little tired of telling the office what she was doing every second. If there was something they ought to know, she would let them know; otherwise, leave her alone. Which high and mighty attitude she did manage to get away with, for the time being.

Certainly it was nobody else's business that she and the wife of the President-elect had become close friends. Despite the sensationalism that had been driving at least some segments of the press into printing increasingly juicy scandal, by unwritten law most elected officials were still immune to such disrespect except under extraordinary circumstances, and the idea of embarrassing the wife of a national leader had not yet occurred to the journalistic fraternity. Therefore, when a local correspondent in Massachusetts

learned of Mrs. Roosevelt's arrival at Groton that weekend, he sent
The New York Times just two sentences, announcing the fact and
adding only, "She was accompanied by a woman secretary."

Of course, it was mainly the prevailing climate of morality that
prevented the publication of any innuendo about Mrs. Roosevelt
and Hick. So nobody kept track of how often Hick visited Sixty-
fifth Street, or how often Mrs. Roosevelt took refuge from fittings of
inaugural finery at an apartment building a few doors east of the
Beekman Tower Hotel. During the final week of February, Hick
stayed with Mrs. R. in her secluded cottage near the Val-Kill brook,
safely away from the excitement at the big house on the Roosevelt
estate at Hyde Park. The evening of Wednesday, the first of March,
which Mrs. Roosevelt referred to privately as her last night out of
captivity, she dined alone with Hick at Hick's apartment on
Mitchell Place. The following day she boarded the special Roosevelt train for Washington. And Hick was with her.

At least, Hick and Meggie, Mrs. R.'s little black Scottish terrier,
rode together a few cars from the family's own car; amid all of the
last-minute frenzy, it seemed only mildly odd that Mrs. Roosevelt
could not bear entrusting the animal to anybody else. But the real
reason for Hick's trip, the President-elect had been informed, was
that Hick wanted to finish her assignment of so many months with a
blaze of glory on Inauguration Day, by becoming the first reporter
ever to interview a First Lady in the White House. Would that be
all right? But Franklin Roosevelt had his mind otherwise occupied
by such matters as the emergency proclamation he would probably
have to issue shortly after taking his oath, ordering the temporary
closing of every bank in the nation to avert the spread of rioting
among depositors demanding their money. So he appears to have
paid scant attention to this request from his Missis.

Indeed, throughout the ensuing several days, between interludes
of obligatory ceremony, Eleanor Roosevelt and Lorena Hickok
managed to spend a surprising amount of time alone. Just before
the train arrived in Washington, Mrs. R., walking forward to get
Meggie, gave Hick some instructions. Hick therefore appeared in a
taxi at a side entrance to the Mayflower at 7:45 the following morning, and Mrs. Roosevelt slipped out without being observed. First
she told the driver to take them along R Street so she could show
Hick the house where she had been so unhappy fifteen years earlier,
upon discovering her husband's infidelity. But as they approached

it, she saw a large sign on the lawn identifying this property as the former residence of the new President. Shaking her head, she asked the driver to proceed to the Rock Creek Cemetery.

Hick sensed that her companion did not want to talk, and contained her own curiosity. When they reached the cemetery, Mrs. R. directed the driver through a maze of winding roads until they came to a clump of bushes through which Hick spied a large bronze statue. They left the cab to walk around in front of the bronze figure. Then they sat down on a curved stone bench facing it, still without speaking.

It was the figure of a seated woman, considerably larger than life-size, her body enveloped in the folds of a robe extending up over her head, leaving only the face visible. To Hick, as to so many others before and since, the expression on the face of the Saint-Gaudens "Grief"—more usually called the Adams Memorial because Henry Adams had commissioned it in memory of his wife—was incredibly beautiful. As Hick looked at it, she felt that all the sorrow humanity had ever endured was expressed in that face. She could almost feel the hot, stinging unshed tears behind the lowered eyelids. Yet in that expression there was something almost triumphant. There was a woman who had experienced every kind of pain, every kind of suffering known to humankind, and had come out of it serene and compassionate. Hick found herself thinking that whatever bitter unhappiness, whatever agony of body and soul she herself was going through, that woman had also known and would understand.

Mrs. R. clearly felt some of this, too, and when she broke the silence it was to say that during her stormy period, when she had been much younger and not so very wise, sometimes she had been very unhappy and sorry for herself. "When I was feeling that way," she said, "if I could manage it, I'd come out here, alone, and sit and look at that woman. And I'd always come away somehow feeling better."

Later that afternoon of March 3, the phone rang in Hick's hotel room and it was Mrs. R. saying her husband was tied up with hectic conferences in the adjoining sitting room, and the children were all busy. Would Hick come up and have dinner with her? At the Mayflower's side lobby, from which special elevators rose to the Presidential Suite, there were Secret Service men barring the way.

Newspaper reporters hungry for any crumb of information about the banking crisis swarmed helplessly on the other side of the barrier. Since Mrs. Roosevelt had called down to tell the guards she was expecting her friend Miss Hickok, Hick was passed through instantly.

Upstairs, even in Mrs. Roosevelt's room the atmosphere was electric. As the evening wore on, the Roosevelts' twenty-six-year-old son Jimmy came in frequently for a few minutes' respite. So did gaunt little Louis Howe. They reported that all over the country the panic seemed to be growing worse. If either Jimmy or Louis remembered that the Hickok woman worked for the Associated Press, they gave no sign of it. But neither did Hick herself.

At one point, Franklin Roosevelt sent the final draft of his Inaugural Address for his wife to scan before it went to be mimeographed. Mrs. R. read it aloud to Hick. Had such an opportunity been presented to any of the reporters milling in the lobby, there would have ensued a sprint to the nearest telephone and the quick dictation of the scoop of the year. Of course no such opportunity *could* have befallen any working journalist. Even if Hick herself would not be aware of the fact for another few months, her newspaper career actually ended that night—when it never occurred to her to tell her office not only what F.D.R. was going to say the following day, but also who had been advising him and the gist of their advice. Smack in the middle of the biggest story in the world on the night of March 3, 1933, she kept her eyes and ears open, and her mouth shut.

Only later would Hick suffer twinges of guilt because of this professional lapse, and she chose as her father confessor someone she thought would understand because he had once been a newspaperman himself. But Louis Howe, having given up his own career to promote Franklin Roosevelt's, could offer no absolution. Perhaps he was one person who did perceive a new relationship between Eleanor and Hick, although his only comment was equivocal. "A reporter," he dryly told Hick, "should never get too close to the news source."

On the night, and then the early morning, before the inauguration, however, Hick was totally bent on offering comfort, rather than seeking it herself. Not until well after three A.M. did Jimmy, looking half dead with fatigue, come in to announce that everybody had left and "Pa" was going to bed. Then while Mrs. R. went to say goodnight to her husband, Hick slipped off her dress and shoes, put on the dressing gown she had been handed and lay down on one of the twin beds. All of this she would chronicle in the short book that she wrote thirty years afterward, where she recalled dropping off into uneasy slumber before her friend returned.

When they parted the next morning, Hick had a card admitting her to the church across Lafayette Park from the White House where the new First Family would begin the day by seeking divine guidance. Hick sat at the back during the service, then she stood in the crowd outside watching two long, black limousines drive off toward the Capitol. Hick's next steps took her through the White House gate for the first time in her life. "Don't look so worried," Mrs. R. had said at the Mayflower. "Nobody over there is going to bite you."

Indeed Ike Hoover, the head usher, politely escorted her upstairs, as Mrs. R. had promised he would. Yet for all of Hick's newspaper experience, her awe at being in this house, especially under such unbelievable circumstances, made her spine shiver. Besides, it really was cold in the only partly furnished upstairs room to which Ike Hoover delivered her. Besides an enormous mahogany bed, covered with a plain white counterpane, there were two heavy mahogany wardrobe closets that appeared to have been just dropped at random by moving men. On the gray walls, stretching up toward the lofty ceiling, were square and oblong marks showing where pictures had hung. Not a book or knickknack relieved the gloomy, impersonal chill. And Hick felt no warmer when the usher came back with a tall glass of icy orange juice to refresh her while she waited for the limousines to return from the Capitol.

So Hick did not see Franklin Roosevelt jut forth his chin as he intoned in his marvelous voice, "First of all, let me assert my firm belief that the only thing we have to fear is fear itself." Months afterward, she and Mrs. R. would agree that nobody had seemed particularly struck by those words that day, although years later the whole world claimed to remember them. In the excitement and confusion of March 4th, it was enough for Hick that she and Mrs. R. did manage to carry out their interview project. They sat in Mrs. Roosevelt's cheerless new bedroom while Hick nervously sought the First Lady's impressions of the public reaction to her husband's speech. However, so many people interrupted them that finally they had to retreat to a bathroom.

But for all of their intense talk about Franklin's responsibility, and about the tremendous need people felt to have a leader and the tremendous danger that in their desperation they might have chosen the wrong kind of leader, Hick could scarcely hold back her tears. Having finally found happiness, how much harder to be alone again! Why couldn't this woman who loved and needed her be plain Mrs. Joe Doaks? Significantly, neither of them seems to have had the notion that they might be even happier were Hick's friend Miss Jane Doaks. Eleanor Roosevelt, despite the depth of her need that had made her crave overflowing devotion from a new direction, apparently could not imagine herself without a husband and children. And Hick tacitly accepted a peripheral role.

Still E.R.'s dependence on Hick at this crucial juncture should not be minimized. One small measure of Eleanor Roosevelt's emotional state on the day she became the First Lady of the United States reposes among the several thousand boxes of her own papers at the Hyde Park library named for her husband. In the engagement book that Hick had given her, the first page, headed March 4, 1933, has about a dozen entries, such as "parade" and "family dinner" in E.R.'s distinctive scrawl. One appointment at six-thirty in the evening sounds the only personal note: "Said good-bye to Hick."

Hick stayed in Washington through Sunday the fifth, so they had another brief encounter before protocol—and Bess Furman—inexorably separated them. Each tried to soften the parting in her own way, Mrs. R. by renewing her promise about her "diary." No, she simply could not bring herself to keep a journal, but as long as people seemed to want to read about every little sweater she knitted, and as long as she would be writing to Hick every night before she went to bed, she would include a running account of her day's activities in every letter. Then one of these days Hick, who knew her better than anybody and could write better, too, Hick might even want to write her biography.

Hick had to grin at that. Of course, at the beginning she had cherished some such dream because the stories Mrs. R. told her about her own childhood, her parents, the whole vanishing world of footmen and grand tours of Europe, were like a novel. But even if

Hick was beginning to doubt whether she would be able to write a book about E.R.—without violating the trust that had been granted to her, and inadvertently telling something that was too painful or too private—how could she object to any plan that would keep her in close touch with her dear one? So she naturally encouraged the diary idea, which had probably been her own idea a few months back. But she also had prepared herself for the separation more humbly.

In her purse was a little calendar, with one page for each month of this year of 1933 stapled onto a plain cardboard backing. From now on, Hick would use this calendar to keep track of the future in the only way that mattered to her. Around the numerals designating the first five days of March she had already drawn circles as round as the sun; if only subconsciously, she was reminding herself that on these days her sun had shone upon her. It may seem unbelievable to a more sophisticated era that a topflight newspaperwoman—in the week of her fortieth birthday—would behave with such simplicity, but Hick's calendar is a fair reflection of the simple emotion suffusing this relationship. Indeed most people, given just a few dozen personal passages from the early letters between Hick and E.R., would find their tone incredibly schoolgirlish. Of course, even sophisticates reading some of their own letters after a lapse of many years may feel a similar embarrassment. At any rate, on the sixth of March, when Hick had returned to New York, alone, she marked off that date on her calendar with a darkly penciled X.

The next day she received her first letter from the White House. It was written, by hand, on both sides of two large sheets of creamy stationery embossed in gold with the presidential seal. It read:

> Sunday night
> March 5 [1933]
> Hick my dearest, I cannot go to bed tonight without a word to you. I felt a little as though a part of me was leaving tonight, you have grown so much to be a part of my life that it is empty without you even though I'm busy every minute.
>
> These are strange days & very odd to me but I'll remember the [indecipherable word] & try to plan pleasant things & count the days between our times together!
>
> To begin my diary, after you left I went to supper . . .
> . . . Tommy came & we arranged tomorrow's work. At

ten Meggie & I took her to the gate & I thought of you & "Prinz." She seemed very happy & said everyone had a grand time, also that you looked *"stunning"* dressed up! I then went back & devoted ¾ of an hour to talking to Mama, then listened to F.D.R. broadcast, sorted mail & am now preparing for bed. So endeth my first Sunday.

I'll call you tomorrow night & this should reach you Tuesday a.m.

Oh! darling, I hope on the whole you will be happier for my friendship. I felt I had brought you so much discomfort & hardship today & almost more heartache than you could bear & I don't want to make you unhappy—All my love & I shall be saying to you over thought waves in a few minutes

> Goodnight my dear one
> Angels guard thee
> God protect thee
> My love enfold thee
> All the night through.

Always yours
E.R.

Thenceforth, this pattern would continue, with personal passages alternating with the diary portions that, in tone and content, presaged Eleanor Roosevelt's syndicated "My Day" newspaper column, an indirect outgrowth of these nightly communications to Hick. However, Hick also received many small nuggets that for one reason or another would never be given wider circulation, for instance: "Did I tell you that the first day in his office at 3 p.m. F.D.R. found himself alone & with nothing to do. Horrors, nothing like that had happened to him in years. So he reached under the desk & rang all five bells & people ran in from every side to find him calmly demanding 'Something to do!' "

Still, in that first month of the New Deal when a euphoric surge of hope rose among all sectors of the population, as one man with an enormously winning smile grasped the reins of the government, that man's wife and her dearest friend were engrossed mainly by each other. Not until ten minutes past midnight on the sixth of March did Eleanor Roosevelt have the leisure to write to Hick, although, as the letter noted, they had talked on the telephone a few hours earlier. But E.R.'s son Jimmy had been near the phone,

E.R. wrote to Hick, ". . . & I couldn't say je t'aime et je t'adore as I longed to do but always remember I am saying it & that I go to sleep thinking of you & repeating our little saying."

Already on this first Monday apart, they were planning to meet in New York on the following Tuesday. Mrs. R. had previously thought of coming up on Thursday to attend the wedding of one of her former pupils, but she found it possible to rearrange her schedule so that she could see Hick again two days sooner. To Hick, back at work, even a week seemed interminable. Especially on Tuesday the seventh—her fortieth birthday—her pain was almost unendurable. Yet somehow she went through the motions of covering an assignment, of dining with an old friend from Minneapolis, without displaying her abject misery.

Even the nightly phone calls, the daily letters, failed to help much, despite E.R.'s touching efforts. On Tuesday, Hick's birthday, when E.R. attended an afternoon concert where "I thought only of you & wanted you even more than I do as a rule," the new First Lady devoted four hours at night to going through baskets full of the mail from all over the country that had begun descending on her. Then after seeing that all of the inaugural week visitors in the house were off to sleep, at 1:15 A.M., E.R. wrote to Hick that by the end of the week she hoped to have some time to herself. "What shall we read, Hick?" she asked. "You choose first."

And at 12:30 the following night: "Just telephoned you. Oh! it is good to hear your voice, when it sounds right no one can make me so happy!" And the next night: "My pictures are nearly all up & I have you in my sitting room where I can look at you most of my waking hours! I can't kiss you so I kiss your picture goodnight and good morning! Don't laugh! This is the first day I've had no letter & I missed it sadly but it is good discipline. *Now for the diary* . . ." Again, at the end of the seventh page of this letter: "One more day marked off, my dear. My dear, if you meet me may I forget there are other people present or must I behave? I shall want to hug you to death. I can hardly wait! A world of love to you & good night & God bless you 'light of my life.' "

But if Hick had to focus her entire being on the following Tuesday, she knew that E.R. could not really help becoming distracted by all of the excitement around her, all of the not-so-terrible duties and even the pleasures attending her new job. At the first formal

East Room gathering, officially introducing F.D.R. to the foreign ambassadors stationed in Washington, E.R. must have enjoyed herself at least a little, from her own description: ". . . & I walked all around the room & said sweet nothings to them." Besides, that first press conference of hers had been just as successful as Hick had predicted. Indeed E.R.'s warm interest in people of every sort was quickly endearing her not only to those who met her but also to those who merely read about her, again just as Hick had predicted. Constantly, E.R. was being lifted out of herself by interesting strangers, or that horde of high-toned relatives, or countless friends with prior claims.

Furthermore, how could Hick help being aware that the surest way to E.R.'s heart was to let her feel needed? If only her husband could understand that! But no, Hick's own feelings about this man were such a tangle of the positive and the negative that she could not possibly sort them out. To think that less than a year ago he had been just another politician to her, instead of the greatest hero and the meanest ingrate, all wrapped up into one genius at getting his ego flattered. No, what was the use? She could not express what Franklin Roosevelt meant to her, even though the least nuance about his wife now seemed clear to her.

So Hick was not surprised that after less than a week E.R. was already becoming somewhat reconciled to her new job. ". . . I begin to think there may be ways in which I can be useful," E.R. wrote. "I am getting some ideas which I want to talk over with you." Of course Hick understood, and she tried to rejoice for the sake of her darling, she berated herself as an ungrateful wretch, but still during that interminable first week of separation, when other people were basking in the sunshine from which she herself had been banished, she was consumed by jealousy.

If she fought it, she also confessed it. That was why E.R. ended her Wednesday night letter: "I miss you so much & I love you so much & please never apologize. I always know & understand, one does if one cares enough." Then just a week after the inauguration, E.R. of the iron self-control, E.R. who never cried, had to write: "You have a stormier time than I do but I miss you as much I think. I couldn't bear to think of you crying yourself to sleep. Oh! how I wanted to put my arms around you in reality instead of spirit. I went & kissed your photograph instead & the tears were in my eyes. Please keep most of your heart in Washington as long as I'm here for most of mine is with you!'"

Bess Furman, with a fine professional generosity, had refrained from asking to accompany Mrs. Roosevelt on her initial trip to New York as First Lady because, after all, Hick was entitled to have no interference there. It would be a hard enough wrench for good old Hick when she came to Washington the following weekend as a Furman guest at the newspaper women's party and found herself on the sidelines, with no need to jot down any quote or even stop by the office. For Washington was Furman territory, and Bess had already realized what fabulous luck had come her way when Mrs. R. had moved into the White House. A canny woman, she was also aware that to keep on the right side of Mrs. R., a certain amount of generosity to Hick was advisable.

If Bess had not known this previously, she would have learned it this past week. Waiting on the street late Wednesday afternoon while F.D.R. and his wife and son Jimmy had paid a call on Supreme Court Justice Holmes, Bess had thought that Mrs. R. might decide to walk back to the White House. When that happened, Bess had tried to swing into step with her. But that gentle lady could certainly muster a withering stare, which she had just begun to demonstrate, when Bess thought of mentioning a nice note that Hick had sent her about all of the recent Furman wordage. Not only to Bess was a sudden change apparent. ". . . & [I] was almost rude to Miss Furman!" E.R. wrote to Hick that night. "She's nice though & likes you which melted my heart!"

So for three days in New York, it was again Hick who wrote the stories about Mrs. Roosevelt's doings. Compared with the news the First Lady had begun making in Washington—shattering White House precedents by greeting her guests informally and by rearranging the furniture more comfortably—her reappearance on Sixty-fifth Street produced just a few flimsy paragraphs. But Hick could not care. After eight successive X's on her secret calendar, for three days in a row circles like the sun once more symbolized her happiness.

As charted on her calendar, Hick's life up until the beginning of July alternated thus starkly. However, the weekend late in March when she went to Washington again and stayed two nights at the White House—although she was the guest of Bess Furman at the women's press party—required a new combination of sun and shadow: a circle enclosing an X. It takes no great talent at cryptography to discern that during this weekend Hick's exposure to the sun had been limited by other seekers of the same healing rays.

Among Hick's office friends, the trip had only a diverting importance because it produced Hick's anecdote about her discomposure over having to wear, for the first time in her life, a long formal gown. It was black silk and quite handsome. But Mrs. Roosevelt had to give her a private lesson in how to walk with all that silk flapping around her ankles before Hick would consent to attempt a public appearance. Although Hick herself joked about this, she was hiding her real feeling. For among the assorted papers relating to her association with Eleanor Roosevelt that she had already begun hoarding, a fifteen-page fragment poignantly exposes two separate conflicts raging within her.

The most urgent one concerned her journalistic career. By now she had been torn repeatedly between her loyalty to the Associated Press and her loyalty to Eleanor Roosevelt; she had even endured having five dollars subtracted from her pay after she had point-blank refused to query the First Lady about an offhand sarcasm supposing that the repeal of Prohibition would prove well-bred young ladies could hold their gin. Still, if Hick usually managed to cajole her editors into allowing her an unusual freedom, her common sense told her that a clash was inevitable. So this fifteen-page fragment represented her first serious effort to break out of the strait jacket of wire service journalism. At that time, the personal pronoun was forbidden to AP staffers; so-called objective reporting, submerging the first-person reactions of the writer, was the rule except under extraordinary circumstances. Justifiably perceiving her position to be exceptional, but unable to explain why, Hick still attempted an "I" story—"I Spend a Weekend at the White House."

Despite the high degree of craftsmanship in her telling of her adventure, however, what she told was, alas, trite:

> A limousine with a shield on the door had met me at the station. As it turned in from Pennsylvania Avenue the thought came whirling into my mind:
> "The White House! And I'm to spend the weekend here!"
> I felt half choked . . . The tips of my fingers tingled. . . .

But Hick's choked feeling and her tingling fingertips had afflicted her not merely because she found herself crossing a marble corridor that had once borne the stride of Abraham Lincoln. It was what Hick did not say—indeed, could not say—that would have captured any reader's attention. Nor could she have been unaware of this underlying problem herself.

Nobody could have known better than Hick how confining her job had become, so probably her incomplete opus was an attempt to branch out into magazine writing. But even the greater leeway allowed by magazine editors would not solve her problem. For the second and more basic of her interior conflicts had to do with her inability to offend Eleanor Roosevelt in the slightest degree if she could possibly help it.

Already Bess Furman had written various harmless sentences that distressed Hick. In time, Bess would describe the decor of the house on Sixty-fifth Street, with its armadas of sailing ships and imposing silver table settings, in a manner that struck Hick as likely to irritate E.R. But Hick was supersensitive, and not only about E.R.'s reactions.

At one point in her manuscript about her White House visit, Hick's innate honesty forced her to a cruel diagnosis of her own excessive awe: ". . . it must have been a sense of intrusion that made me uncomfortable—a square, stodgy, middle-class personality rudely thrust against a background of rare beauty and dignity, a crudely cut out comic paper doll pasted on a fine old tapestry." Of course, such extreme self-abnegation was uncalled for. If a magic carpet had dropped Lorena Hickok, in the line of duty, into the most exotic of Persian palaces, she could have charmed any sultan not exclusively bent on increasing his harem. Indeed F.D.R. had greeted her with every sign of real pleasure: " 'Why, hello!' A clear, ringing voice addressed me by a nickname. 'Glad to see you!' " Nor was Hick either stodgy or as crude as she depicted herself. Her trouble was that she felt unworthy, and it was her intense feeling of inferiority that poisoned her pleasure in visiting E.R. in the White House.

No such lack of confidence affected her work, though. Toward the end of March a shocking and spectacularly complicated case against one of the nation's leading bankers was being rushed to trial. Charles E. Mitchell, the newly resigned head of New York's powerful National City Bank, was the defendant facing prosecution—technically, for income tax evasion; more broadly, for incredible speculations with other people's money before the '29 crash. An assistant United States attorney named Thomas E. Dewey was pressing the charges. Covering for the Associated Press, Hick tersely kept millions of people informed about these intricate proceedings.

As the actual trial reached its climax, terseness in what she dictated to her office was no longer demanded. The more she wrote, the better her editors liked it because the story was getting extensive front-page play all across the country. At the height of public absorption in the Mitchell drama, Hick had to compose a telegram of great personal importance. Wiring E.R., who was out West, she frugally restricted herself to fifty words: "Thinking of you hard and hoping everything is well with you. Your wire and letter greatly appreciated. Wrote you today but letter very sketchy. Mitchell on stand and I did three thousand words long hand. Bill complimentary.° Made my announcement. No emotional scene so far. My love to you. Hick."

The announcement, as E.R. well knew, was that Hick had finally decided to quit the AP. Undoubtedly she would have left sooner if any of her efforts to get magazine assignments had succeeded, although one part of her rebelled at having to give up "the life," as she liked to describe her journalistic career. It surely was more than just a job to her. Owing to the profession's disdain for ordinary working hours, and its similar attitude toward ordinary mortals, the comradeship it engendered among reporters could be even more appealing than the work itself; without office camaraderie, the first five of Hick's six New York years would have been hideously lonely. At least for the last several months, however, her pain at the thought of leaving this life had been surpassed by other anguish.

Given the strength of her commitment to E.R., Hick's continuing as a reporter was just not possible. Louis Howe had been right: no newspaper person could put private feelings about a major news source above professional responsibility. Had Hick's emotions been less engaged, perhaps she might have survived journalistically merely by telling occasional little white lies. But in her overwrought state, she could not stand being called on the carpet "upstairs" by the AP's general manager because she would not give the

---

° "Bill" was W.W. Chapin of the AP news desk.

office advance notice every time E.R. confidentially told her about some impending expedition. And Hick, knowing that two of the Roosevelt children were having severe marital problems, simply could not bear facing office questions concerning Anna or Elliott.

So she had to get out, but the question was, where. Hick had twenty years of newspaper work behind her now—and she really was just about the top gal reporter in the country, if she said it herself. Yet even if she wanted to work in Podunk, the same kind of problem would arise sooner or later because of her friendship with the President's wife. Besides, she had to be based in New York or Washington so that she and E.R. could meet frequently. Still, who but an editor would, in this Depression, even consider hiring a fat woman of forty whose only working experience was reportorial?

Harry Hopkins! Eleanor Roosevelt, as the wife of New York's governor, had first brought this lanky, irreverent social worker to the attention of F.D.R., and in New York Hopkins had directed an emergency work relief program that was better than anything any other state had tried. Now the same man, transported to the capital, was heading the New Deal's brand new Federal Emergency Relief Administration (FERA).

Never before had the national government undertaken any sort of public welfare program. But with possibly one quarter of the nation's work force unemployed—nobody really knew how many millions were jobless—an emergency program of federally funded, state-operated work projects, supplemented by outright grants to the unemployables, was supposed to be saving hundreds of thousands of families from starving. Half a billion dollars had just been appropriated for this purpose. But helping the helpless had traditionally been overseen by county poor-commissioners, who were often allied with local political bosses. Was the FERA money actually getting to those people who so desperately needed it? Hopkins was a man of as yet unsuspected political shrewdness. He understood that any scandal in the distribution of the new federal largesse, even any rank unfairness or failure to meet real emergencies while milder hardship was assuaged, would boomerang and discredit the whole idea of federal intervention in this area where every state had always gone its own way. So Hopkins was more than receptive to the notion of hiring an expert reporter as his roving chief investigator.

Hick also liked the idea. How could she help liking it when it was presented to her as an enormous patriotic service for which she was uniquely qualified? Nevertheless, after the necessary preliminaries had been accomplished and she learned that the job was hers, her first communication to her new boss disclosed a rather sketchy acquaintance with him. On a sheet of Associated Press stationery, on June 7, 1933, she addressed herself to Harry Hopkins, Esq., Federal Relief Administrator, Washington, D.C., as follows:

Dear Mr. Hopkins:

I hope this reaches you. I've mislaid the address, but in a place as gossipy as Washington you surely ought to be widely enough known by now so that a letter addressed to you simply in care of the Federal Relief Administration should go straight to you.

I resigned on Monday, and the Associated Press asked me to work through the 17th, which would mean that I would report in Washington on Monday, the 19th. Since you said it would make no particular difference when I appeared, I agreed to do so. Now, however, it looks as though the Mitchell trial may last even longer than that . . . I should like, with your permission to offer to see it through. It's such a darned complicated affair, and I am the only one who is thoroughly familiar with it. It would be pretty tough on anyone to be sent down there cold . . .

Suppose we leave it this way. If you think I ought to come down on the 19th, let me know. Otherwise I'll assume I'm at liberty to stay on and finish the trial. Since it is the last newspaper assignment I'll have for a time, I'd like to . . . do as good a job on it as I can.

I'm looking forward to the new job, even though I did feel a little wistful Saturday night at that damned newspaper party. I think it's going to work out in good style, though, and be interesting. As a matter of fact, it's the only thing that has come along since I began contemplating the possibility of getting out of the AP that has really interested me.

If I don't hear from you, I'll be along on the 19th—or a few days thereafter.

Lorena A. Hickok

The only extant photograph of the Hickok family from Lorena's childhood. Lorena is seated at left next to her mother; Ruby is standing near their father. Myrtle is glowering down front. (LORENA HICKOK PAPERS. F.D.R. LIBRARY COLLECTION)

Lorena Hickok's graduation picture in Battle Creek High School yearbook, *The Paean*, Class of 1912.

Alicent Holt, "the most gifted teacher" of Lorena's school days and later her close friend. (FROM THE BATTLE CREEK HIGH SCHOOL YEARBOOK, *The Paean*, 1912)

Lorena with part of her freshman college class at Lawrence University. She is the chin-up female in the bottom row. (LAWRENCE COLLEGE YEARBOOK, 1913)

Lorena Hickok in the 1920's. (KEYSTONE)

Hick and Brad Morison of the Minneapolis *Tribune* playing a 1920's game at a picnic. (COURTESY OF BRADLEY MORISON)

Ella Morse Dickinson and her new husband, Roy, soon after the 1927 elopement of Hick's closest Minneapolis friend. Ellie "left me to marry Roy," Hick would recall to Eleanor Roosevelt. (COURTESY OF NANCY D. ELLIOTT)

Sunday night
March 5th

THE WHITE HOUSE
WASHINGTON

Hick my dearest, — I cannot go to
bed to-night without a word to
you. I felt a little as though a
part of me was leaving to-night.
You have grown so much to be a
part of my life that it is empty
without you even though I'm busy
every minute.

These are strange days & very
odd to me but I'll remember
the days & try to plan pleasant
things & count the days between
our times together!

E.R.'s first letter to Hick from the White House, March 5, 1933. It was written on both sides of two pages of creamy White House stationery with the presidential seal in gold. (See page 119.) (LORENA HICKOK PAPERS, F.D.R. LIBRARY COLLECTION)

"AS WE JOURNEY THROUGH LIFE,
LET US LIVE BY THE WAY"

HOTEL MOORE
—The House of Merit—
CLARION, IOWA
L. W. MOORE, MGR.

HOTEL KERMOORE
—Pride of North Iowa—
EMMETSBURG, IOWA
J. H. MOORE, PROP.

HOTEL HILDRETH
"Welcome to a Busy City"
J. H. MOORE, PROP.

CHARLES CITY, IOWA

My room —
for Two Dollars!
And I suspect
bed bugs!

Tuesday,
November 28th.

Madame!

Now will you please tell me what in the world one is going to do about cases like these?

I just came in from a long talk with the chairman of the county relief committee. He put them up to me — and I pass them on to you, not expecting or asking you for anything except ideas. But

One of the first of Lorena Hickok's letters to Eleanor Roosevelt, which she later retrieved and added to her cache of correspondence. Only a few dozen of Hick's letters to E.R. in the early years of their intimacy are to be found in the Hickok Papers at Hyde Park, but hundreds of L.H. letters written later in the 1930's are included in the collection.

Hick's favorite picture of Eleanor Roosevelt, which was taken after
Mrs. Roosevelt visited Mrs. Hoover at the White House, January 28,
1933. (U.P.I. PHOTO; INSCRIBED COPY COURTESY OF ANNE FARR)

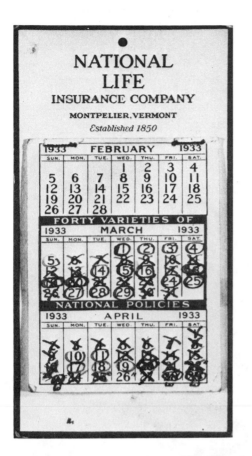

Hick's 1933 calendar keeping track of her reunions with Eleanor Roosevelt. From 1933 to 1935 Hick recorded their every meeting with symbols indicating whether or not their time together was happy and uninterrupted. (LORENA HICKOK PAPERS, F.D.R. LIBRARY COLLECTION)

Eleanor Roosevelt, Lorena Hickok (far right) and two friends they met during their July 1933 summer vacation trip. Hick kept this snapshot. (LORENA HICKOK PAPERS, F.D.R. LIBRARY COLLECTION)

Eleanor Roosevelt on 1933 vacation trip. Presumably Lorena Hickok snapped this photo herself, with the new camera they brought with them. (LORENA HICKOK PAPERS, F.D.R. LIBRARY COLLECTION)

Memento of the one ceremonial day of the 1933 vacation that E.R. and Hick took together: L. A. Taschereau (at left), Prime Minister of the Province of Quebec, officially welcomes them. Lorena Hickok is second from left in back row. (W. B. EDWARDS INC, QUEBEC)

9. The Depression:
On the Road for Harry Hopkins

What with the prolongation of the Mitchell trial and the fruition of another plan that E.R. and Hick had been hatching, it was not until the last day in July of 1933, that one large, nervous but elated woman began investigating the relief situation in the grimy, miserable coal towns of western Pennsylvania.

That other scheme was a vacation that Hick and Mrs. R. had set their hearts on even before the inauguration. It was to be a two-week motor trip, during which just the two of them would leisurely explore the picturesque Gaspé Peninsula of French Canada. But any Roosevelt project apparently contained seeds of grandiosity, and as the summer approached something closer to a month had been scheduled by E.R., although the basic idea of avoiding all fuss and publicity had been retained. As early as April, E.R. had in her own multi-directional way begun to amend their holiday arrangements:

> Hick darling, I hate you to say 'I'm only a reporter.' You are a very good one, and you will some day be as good a journalist as Anne O'Hare McCormick.° Her things are good, but her hold is that she has a reputation and she can get to see important people. She doesn't hesitate to use her friends. She did to get to me and through me to F.D.R. and there is no one you couldn't see! If I take a trip to Mexico will you go with me? We might get some good material. I have an idea even Gaspe may yield some. Wouldn't the AP let you write for a magazine? By the way, can you get off June 17th? F. wants to go off on a cruise from Groton to Marblehead and the next Friday Campobello for the weekend. (This is a secret.) I'll have

° *New York Times* columnist.

> to go if he goes, and, if you can't go, I'll arrange for you
> to take a train from N.Y. to Ellsworth and meet you
> there.

If they both still assumed in April that Hick would remain on the
AP staff during those last two weeks in June that they were supposed to spend together, E.R. was already showing signs of needing
a respite just as much as Hick. "Sometimes I think I am the Washington 'Merry-Go-Round!' " she wrote. That syndicated column by
Drew Pearson and Robert S. Allen was hardly her favorite reading,
but it was her son Elliott's break with his wife that most distressed
E.R. At first her letters to Hick took a sorrowfully philosophic attitude toward this blow. "Well, my dear, there will be no misunder-
standings between us," she wrote. Then a succession of painful
scenes not only displayed irreconcilable differences between the
young couple but also reopened old scars on E.R.'s own heart; in
addition, she grieved that her husband's detachment from his children put too heavy a burden on her. "I'd like to run to you," E.R.
wrote to Hick. "I want to lean on you. . . ."

Hick, despite her own floundering, did buoy up her dearest
friend. She recognized in E.R. a phenomenon she had noted often
among women unhappy in their marriages: beneath a surface existence as Mrs. Joe Doaks or even Mrs. F.D.R. there seethed a separate person yearning to be appreciated on her own. So Hick
encouraged E.R. to do more writing, and she spent hours going
over the manuscripts that Tommy forwarded. Hick returned each
first draft with detailed suggestions based on her own journalistic
experience.

Besides such outright assistance, Hick also served as a safety
valve allowing the harmless expression of varied emotion. E.R. confided her gloom to Hick when her son Elliott's wife tried to give
back family pearls, once that divorce became inevitable. Upon attending a ceremony at the Labor Department, E.R. told Hick she
was "very proud" of Frances Perkins, the first woman Cabinet
member, in whom she took a proprietary interest. After a weekend
in New York, E.R. alluded to another aspect of her dependence on
Hick: "By the way, did I leave my sponge in your bathtub? If so,
please bring!" Then before E.R. finally wrote to Elliott, who had
already gone west to start life anew, E.R. sent the first draft of her
letter to Hick, and fervently accepted Hick's amendments. "I love
you on Elliott, and you are just right."

Nevertheless, the marital difficulties not only of Elliott but of her daughter Anna, too, gnawed at her constantly. "I don't seem to be able to shake the feeling of responsibility for Elliott and Anna," E.R. wrote to Hick. "I guess I was a pretty unwise teacher as to how to go about living. Too late to do anything now, however, and I'm rather disgusted with myself. I feel soiled, but you won't understand that."

To Hick, this fastidious reaction could not but seem threatening. How much more demeaned must E.R. sooner or later feel by her relationship with a person like herself? Still E.R. insisted: "You are my rock, and I shall be so glad to see you Sat. night. I need you very much as a refuge just now."

So when they finally did begin their necessarily postponed but miraculously extended holiday on the sixth of July, they both were in a mood to cherish every moment. E.R., driving her own gray roadster, picked Hick up in New York—and, until they arrived back in Washington together on the 28th, they had the time of Hick's life, at least.

Of course the Secret Service had tried to stop them. Since the Lindbergh kidnaping not much more than a year previously had aroused a rash of kidnaping scares, it was put to the President's wife that she could not go off this way with just one female companion. Hick chortled over the notion of anybody trying to kidnap two women, one nearly six feet tall and the other weighing nearly two hundred pounds. Mrs. R. was amused, too. "Where would they hide us?" the First Lady demanded. "They certainly couldn't cram us into the trunk of a car!"

Nevertheless, the Secret Service insisted on issuing a gun to Mrs. Roosevelt. Subsequently she would take shooting lessons from another of her friends, who had formerly been a New York State trooper assigned to the governor's family, and she would keep her gun, unloaded, in the glove compartment of her gray roadster. However, when she called for Hick in New York on July 6, the glove compartment contained only maps and sunburn cream.

For the next twenty-two days the First Lady, accompanied only by another woman, almost anonymously toured a large quadrant of the Northeast and Quebec, stopping mostly at small hotels or certain secluded retreats that, inevitably, had been added to the itinerary. Just as Hick had been obliged to become familiar with a whole new cast of characters upon joining E.R.'s inner circle, so, too, was her acquaintance with various landmarks obligatory.

Hick, try as she did, had not been able to avoid hating some of these rivals practically on sight; others merely made her uncomfortable; a few she liked. It had taken only one weekend at Hyde Park to convince her that the Val-Kill ladies were unbearable. With their nonstop "Eleanor-ing" and their closing of ranks to exclude any competition, they struck her as toadies who had hitched their wagon to the Roosevelt star because they had dreamed all along of being invited to the White House. Since Nan and Marion had befriended *her* friend ten years ago, and had got her involved in schoolteaching and furniture making as well as sharing the cottage near the brook, Hick's ultimatum refusing further contact with them caused problems. But Hick would not stand for being treated the way they treated her, and thus E.R. had just completed a separate, shorter trip with them.

No more than E.R. could endure hurting their feelings could she be less than motherly to Earl Miller. Oh, yes, Hick was sure now! Back during the campaign when they had visited this Adonis of an ex-trooper and his wife, Hick had had to wonder a little: he was so deferential and E.R. seemed almost smitten. Formerly stationed at the Governor's Mansion, still a state employee, he had worried Hick. But well before E.R. forwarded his Mother's Day card, inscribed "Dear Lady" in his childish hand, Hick understood. E.R.'s own sons only tolerated their mother, while this overgrown boy really needed her. So Hick did not mind stopping briefly to visit Earl on this trip.

Then there were the relatives. In the same category as the stately mother of the President, Cousin Susie who summered in Newport could easily have been visited en route, but Hick would not hear of it. On the other hand, Aunt Maude near Portland was delightful, so Hick had agreed to stop there. Anyway, it would be a convenient resting place after a day with one of her own friends from Minneapolis who was appearing in a local summer theater. Before that, naturally a pause on the island of Campobello where Tommy and some of her family were vacationing at the Roosevelt establishment. Also a detour to the camp at which the youngest Roosevelt son, Johnny, was teaching riding this summer.

Still, the first part of the trip was theirs alone, and unutterably happy. E.R. had brought along one of her favorite books, Stephen Vincent Benét's *John Brown's Body*, from which she read aloud at rest periods after lunch and in the evenings. Thus Hick would never forget discovering, during their initial sightseeing among New York's Adirondack peaks, the sunny, high meadow that had once been part of John Brown's farm. And they both, overlooked only by distant mountains, had stood transfixed before a rough gravestone marking the actual spot where the body of the famed abolitionist lay a-mouldering.

There were less exalted moments, too. Although they had expected to stay in Lake Placid that night, on the way there they passed a new little house in the woods marked with the ubiquitous sign of the era: Tourists Welcomed. Years later when Hick wrote *Reluctant First Lady,* she would recall Mrs. Roosevelt suggesting that they stop here because she had always wanted to try one of these places. Their hosts proved to be a nice young couple, very flustered at recognizing one of their guests and very apologetic because the hot-water system had not been fully installed. So there would be hot water for just one bath.

"Well—you're the First Lady, so you get the first bath," Hick remembered saying after they were ensconced in their small but spotless room. Then according to her own account: "In reply, Mrs. Roosevelt started thrusting her long, slender fingers in my direction. I was so ticklish that all she had to do to reduce me to a quivering mass of pulp was to point her fingers at me. She finally consented to take the first bath, however, but she must have taken it cold. For when I turned on the water for mine, it was warm."

Among the other memories that Hick chose to share were Mrs. Roosevelt's intrepid drive, after dark, up a steep, hairpin-curved road to an old hotel atop Mount Mansfield in Vermont, so that they could watch the sunrise the next morning from that vantage point, and Mrs. Roosevelt's amused "My dear, they're all Republicans up here," when Hick had commented on the fact that nobody was bothering them. Apart from one ceremonial day in the city of Quebec, they enjoyed the same welcome lack of attention in Canada.

But when they crossed back into Maine, to their embarrassment as well as disgust they found a parade lined up to meet them. As they had been driving with the car's top down, Hick's face was a lotion-smeared sunburned mask; her companion, more immune, merely had a sun-blistered lowerlip, twice normal size. As Mrs. Roosevelt turned onto the flag-draped main street of the village of Presque Isle, she swung the wheel a trifle wide and knocked down a portable traffic stanchion placed to mark the parade's route. Unnerved, she uttered one exasperated syllable.

"Damn!" said Eleanor Roosevelt.

On the night of their return to the White House, the travelers dined informally with the President in his study. During the meal he closely questioned his wife about such matters as the state of mind among Maine's potato farmers. Hick well knew that up in Maine the lady had skimmed just one newspaper and spent only part of one morning chatting with a farmer host plus a few of his neighbors; she was amazed therefore by the comprehensive answers the questions elicited. Madame was a pretty good reporter! But then Madame launched a different topic, telling her husband how funny Hick had looked entering a rural French church with a handkerchief pinned atop her head. This gave Hick the gumption to report the epithet that had marked their reentry into the land that he led. F.D.R. roared.

During the last week of June, while E.R. had been covering part of the same route more ceremoniously with those Val-Kill ladies, Hick had gone down to Washington for "indoctrination" by her new boss. "What I want you to do," said Harry Hopkins, "is to go out around the country and look this thing over. I don't want statistics from you. I don't want the social-worker angle. I just want your own reaction . . . and don't pull your punches."

Hick did not. After just one week in Pennsylvania, where the particularly depressed condition of the mining industry had stirred alarmist rumors of Communist organizing, she typed six pages, single-spaced, downgrading the Red menace but otherwise offering scant consolation. She had listened to everybody from the Governor to "the kickers as they came into the offices of the State Emergency Relief Board," then put it all down succinctly in the form of a letter that she signed "Yours very truly, (and apologetically)" because she thought she had written too much. Hopkins disagreed. Perhaps his enthusiasm for hiring her had been purely politic to start with, but Hopkins soon was reaping unexpected benefits from putting Mrs. Roosevelt's friend on his emergency payroll at a decent if not overly generous six thousand dollars a year. For that woman was a demon for work. She would turn up in a town at nightfall and before the next sundown have the whole scene in her head. And then a couple of days later the whole state picture, clear as if he'd been there himself, would flutter onto his desk.

Yet beyond giving Hopkins himself a fast summary, those letters soon he would ask for wires—were real, not just the what-it-should-be or what-the-Democratic-state-chairman-says-it-is that filtered through all sorts of special prisms before they got to the President. Although Hopkins must have guessed that the gist of her reports was going directly to her special friend in the White House, not for another several decades would anybody know just how much Hick was feeding Mrs. Roosevelt. Still, it suited Harry Hopkins to establish his own direct relationship with his Boss, and, even before Louis Howe made the suggestion, Hopkins was sending copies of the best of Hickok over to the Oval Office. For similar reasons, Hopkins also sent various Hickok summaries to half a dozen or so senators or Cabinet members whose support, on one issue or another, he needed.

That F.D.R. appreciated the Hickok reports, from whatever source, would be duly noted by the first historian of the Roosevelt era, Arthur M. Schlesinger, Jr., in his *The Coming of the New Deal,* when he wrote, "[Roosevelt] liked detailed reports of the kind Lorena Hickok . . . rendered on the situation of people on relief." Then Schlesinger quoted one of Roosevelt's secretaries, Grace Tully: "It was not unusual to hear him predicate an entire line of reasoning upon a statement that 'my Missis told me so and so.' "

But as for Hick herself—on the road, removed from the intoxicating excitement of those early New Deal months when it seemed that every bright young professor in America had converged on Washington in hopes of being tapped for the President's "Brains Trust"—her own initial elation at being a part of this great tide swiftly evaporated. Instead, a horrendous personal depression descended. For after Pennsylvania she went down to West Virginia where, in August, 1933, one forty-year-old woman who thought she had already seen just about everything during two decades of newspaper work suddenly found a lot that she had missed.

Never before had Hick seen American babies with their bellies distended, their eyes vacant, because for the whole of their short lives they had not had enough to eat. Or tent villages where thin canvas could not keep even the summer wind from shivering the prematurely old bones of American miners' wives. Near a stream called Scott's Run she came upon a gutter along a village street filled with stagnant, filthy water used for drinking, cooking, washing, and everything else imaginable by the inhabitants of ramshackle cabins that most Americans would not have considered fit for pigs. Within these shacks, every night children went to sleep hungry, on piles of bug-infested rags spread on the floor.

Hick saw and heard, too; she would never stop hearing the voice of "Aunt Cora," who was really old and dying of pellagra. After Hick moved down into Kentucky she met Aunt Cora stumbling along a mountain path on bare, gnarled feet. The old woman clutched at Hick's arm with fingers like a skeleton's and pleaded: "Don't forget me, honey! Don't forget me!"

But before that, Hick had already cried out to E.R. with such despair that, during the middle of August, E.R. managed to join her in Morgantown, West Virginia. Then for a week they were driven around together by some of the dedicated Quakers working under the auspices of the American Friends' Service Committee, and it was sharing this eye-opening experience with Hick that persuaded E.R. to make the Quaker-sponsored welfare agency perhaps the main recipient of her private charity over the next several decades.

Among the other fruits of the West Virginia week that E.R. spent with Hick were two projects, one of merely local impact, the second a major chapter in the education of Eleanor Roosevelt. Yet it was not until E.R. returned to her own round of summer hostessing and visit-paying that her impetus for arranging the endowment of a free hospital clinic came in this letter from Hick:

> . . . Oh, this is the damndest state. Not a county or city hospital with a free clinic in the whole state. . . . Over in the next county a woman, mother of eight children, was about to die. Appendicitis. They said she wouldn't live two hours unless they got her into a hospital. "You'll be responsible for those eight children losing their mother if you don't authorize that hospital bill," they told Major Turner [the state relief administrator, a retired National Guard officer].
>
> He couldn't do a damned thing about it. The Federal Relief Administration absolutely forbids payment of hospital bills. Harry Hopkins told Major Turner the $500,-000,000 wouldn't last until the first of October if they started it. And obviously that's true.

Then in a fine example of the epistolary amplitude that characterized both participants in the Roosevelt-Hickok correspondence, Hick went on:

> When I tell the story to Harry Hopkins, he'll probably boil over and be sore as hell at Turner for a moment,

rules or no rules. But, damn it all, Turner couldn't do anything. Do you know that right now, both Wheeling and Mingo County—and Lord only knows how many more places in the state—are absolutely out of relief funds and can't get any more until September 1? Miss Mahoney [another West Virginia relief official] spent her last cent of relief money today on flour and distributed it among her people, as far as it would go. And that's all they get until the end of next week. Moreover, although the state's policy is to provide relief at the rate of $15 a month for a family of five, it's been cut to $10 for a couple of months, for lack of funds. . . .

This is a terribly long letter, but I must tell you one story I heard yesterday. Miss Mahoney went over to the state penitentiary the other day to say goodbye to the warden who is leaving.

"There were a bunch of wets here today," he told her, "trying to get me to say that most of the prisoners were in here on account of prohibition. (Incidentally, the prison which was built for 800 prisoners, has right now 1,986 inmates!)

"Well, I couldn't give them any help along that line," the warden told her. "I had to tell them that 51 per cent of the men in this prison were here for breaking and entering—and they did it because they were hungry."

Then he went on to tell her about a prisoner who had been dismissed just the day before. He described the prisoner as one of the finest men he had ever known. The man had been a tipple foreman in a mine. The mine closed down a couple of years ago . . .

"At first," he told the warden, "my wife would be cheerful. She'd say, 'Well, never mind. Next week you'll get something . . .'

"But finally one Sunday night I came home, after being gone for a week. She just looked at me, and, when I shook my head, I saw her lower lip start to tremble.

"I looked at the baby, playing on the floor. 'How long since she had any milk?' I asked my wife. 'Three days,' she whispered. 'And the rest of you?' I asked. She just shook her head.

"Then—well, something happened inside me, that's all. The lumber company had a store. I went over there and broke in. I filled a basket with things to eat—canned milk, bacon, eggs, bread and butter, coffee, sugar. I took

it home. Neither of us said anything. She didn't ask me
where I got it. We just sat down, with the children, and
had a meal.

"The next morning of course it was discovered that the
store had been robbed. So I just went over and told 'em
I'd done it—and why. Well, they sent me here.

"Now I'm going back, and I'm sorry, but I'll probably
do the same thing right over again."

If E.R. could not solve all of the woes Hick poured out to her
every night, at least raising money for a hospital clinic among some
of her rich friends gave her a sense of accomplishing something.
But because she had actually seen Scott's Run with Hick she
needed to do more, and E.R. described that open gutter so com-
pellingly to her husband that Louis Howe was ordered into action.
Tearing through red tape, Howe bought two thousand rundown
acres nearby, owned by a family named Arthur; thus was born one
of the most farsighted, or absurd, manifestations of the New Deal
reformist impulse, depending upon the perspective of the observer.

Certainly the whole saga of the homestead communities where
Howe and other F.D.R. aides attempted to resettle jobless rural
families is beyond the scope of this book. Had the program succeeded at Arthurdale and other sites in other states, perhaps it
would have at least partially averted the urban decay of subsequent
decades; but the idea of helping rural families to establish self-
sufficient enclaves, thereby keeping them from migrating to city
slums, was an idea whose time had not yet come. At any rate,
Arthurdale filled a great need for Eleanor Roosevelt herself. When
she had tried to get some assignment from her husband as he was
about to take office, and she had suggested that handling a portion
of his mail would give her a sense of making a real contribution, he
had rebuffed her by saying this would surely seem like interference
to Missy LeHand, his personal secretary who had long been in
charge of his mail. So Arthurdale—widely publicized as Mrs. Roosevelt's pet scheme—provided her with a sort of passport into governmental conference rooms which she used increasingly from then on.
Louis Howe, speaking just about Arthurdale but again displaying
his gift for subtle pronouncement, told Hick, "You really started
something!"

Of course, E.R., even as a private citizen, had been far more
concerned about social problems than Hick had. Like many report-

ers, Hick had focused on whatever story she happened to be covering and, if her emotional reactions tended to be more extreme than those of many of her colleagues, still she had usually behaved more as an observer than an activist. Unlike a good many other underpaid journalists, she did not even care much about politics—until West Virginia. "I don't believe I'll ever feel complacent again in all my life," she wrote to E.R.

Right after Appalachia, though, Hick embarked on a somewhat more relaxing tour of duty in upstate New York and then in Maine. But while the autumn foliage thrilled her, "Bluette" gave her more than merely her job to worry about. Bluette was her own secondhand Chevvy convertible, according to its bill of sale. Actually, E.R. had bought the car under an informal agreement Hick insisted on describing as a mortgage, whereby Hick would repay the cost in monthly installments. Hick needed a car, she had decided, because going from town to town by train, then relying on local relief people to drive her around, had not proved too satisfactory. Besides, after her motor trip to Canada with E.R., Hick concluded that it really was necessary these days to own your own auto for vacations even if you found it a little hard to afford.

Heretofore, Hick's attitude toward her personal finances had been cheerfully similar to Mr. Micawber's, with income apt to be outdistanced by expenditure unless somebody like Ellie out in California or her Aunt Ella in Elgin came to her rescue. But now she knew better, she assured E.R., who was delighted to hear this because the First Lady took pleasure in balancing five separate checking accounts every month—one for her own earnings and charities, the others for housekeeping expenses in her various domiciles. Encouraged by E.R., Hick then made herself a budget which would spread her own new munificence of $230 every two weeks much more than twice as far as her previous salary of approximately half that sum. So not only could she afford the car, according to her own calculations, but she would also religiously send money orders to Aunt Ella, erasing decades of debt, and still meet the monthly bill at the kennel where she had deposited her precious Prinz.

Naturally, doing all of this required some sacrifices, and Hick proposed that as soon as she finished her survey of New York City for Harry Hopkins she would sublet her Mitchell Place apartment, handy as it would be during interludes between her trips. Well, she could always camp with a friend. On the road, she would stay within the government's travel allowance of five dollars a day for herself and five cents a mile for her car. Which left only the weeks she spent in Washington, personally reporting to Hopkins or others. But it would be during these Washington intervals that, instead of merely cherishing letters, she would actually see her dear one. Therefore, despite all sorts of qualms that Hick still had not been able to overcome, she had to agree that their best chance for privacy was upstairs at the White House itself. Thus in the spirit of a martyr, Hick let herself be persuaded to make 1600 Pennsylvania Avenue her own legal address for tax and other official purposes.

Yet there was one problem about Bluette: Hick had never learned to drive. Nevertheless, E.R. had bought the car while Hick was down in Kentucky. Then E.R. had spent two weeks camping on an Adirondack lake with Nan Cook and Earl Miller and a team of dancers Earl knew, a girl called Tiny—more formally Mayris Chaney—and her partner, Eddie. E.R., besides taking shooting lessons from Earl and drying a lot of dishes, also solved Hick's problem while up at Chazy Lake. There was a nice unemployed boy she wanted to hire for Hick, just temporarily, as a chauffeur-teacher. . . .

After about two thousand miles of this unexpectedly useful arrangement, for the young fellow proved to be a good teacher besides being good company, Hick felt able to cope at the wheel, except on hills or in traffic. On her southern trip, come the New Year, she would drive herself, she assured E.R. when they met in New York in the middle of October. A couple of days later, taking turns, they safely navigated Bluette to 1600 Pennsylvania Avenue. There, for a full week on Hick's private calendar, unclouded sun, just round circles, prepared her for the first separation of more than three weeks since Cornell.

Hick left Washington again on October 25, 1933. It would be more than seven weeks before she returned to the White House, seven cold and harrowing weeks back in the middle part of the country where she had some happy memories and also some very sad ones. Even E.R. had agreed that driving to Minnesota, then the Dakotas, where the snow usually started well before Thanksgiving, would not make sense. So Hick departed by train, bent on making the best of her patriotic duty to probe the extent of farmer unrest in the Upper Midwest, where successive years of depressed prices and crop failures had fanned talk of outright rebellion. But almost immediately her emotions began torturing her again. On the first of November she wrote to E.R.: ". . . I'm angry through and through. Almost as angry as I was when I came back from Kentucky. . . ." To the secretary of Harry Hopkins, Hick could still josh. "If your son misbehaves and you want to make him mind, just say to him: 'You do as I say, or I'll send you to Dakota!' " Still, the Siberian weather bothered her less than the people she was meeting, and from Minot in North Dakota, she told Hopkins:

> Into the relief office . . . came today a little middle-aged farmer—skin like leather, heavily callused, grimy hands—incongruously attired in a worn light flannel suit of collegiate cut, flashy blue sweater, also worn, belted tan topcoat, and coat to match. These clothes, he explained, belonged to his ·eldest son.
> "They're all we've got now," he said. "We take turns wearing 'em."

At various times Hopkins would have approximately a dozen field investigators doing similar reporting. Lorena Hickok was the first he hired and he had given her the title of chief investigator, which she amply justified. For she gave him no jargon, and practically every paragraph that she wrote leapt to life: "I was told in Bismarck that in the county I visited this afternoon I would find a good deal of unrest—'farm holiday' spirit. I can't say that I did. They seemed almost too patient to me. I went to see one farmer who was supposed to be a chronic kicker. I found him doing the family washing!"

Nevertheless, Hick's own self-confidence, which had rarely faltered during her journalistic days, constantly needed bolstering now. "How funny you are about your reports," E.R. wrote to her. "Of course they are good, absorbingly interesting. F.D.R. told me he wished your letters could be published! He is hard to please and always asks if I've anything to read from you."

The explanation for Hick's new insecurity was, however, easy to find. Suddenly she had no by-lines to prop up her ego, no colleagues to congratulate her on doing a great job. Furthermore, it constantly tore at her pride to be tagged as just Mrs. Roosevelt's friend or traveling companion or secretary or bodyguard. Dammit, she was somebody herself! Thus a clipping from some local weekly that

E.R. sent to her after one of their expeditions together irritated her more than it amused her. This news item started:

> The First Lady of the Land takes her coffee black and makes her lunch on a toasted cheese sandwich, and if it looks particularly "appetizing" tops it off with a piece of apple pie. This much The Progress learns from Mine Host Peter L. Brion who operates the Windmill Restaurant.
>
> Not so, however, with the lady who was Mrs. Roosevelt's traveling companion on her brief visit to Clearwater yesterday, presumably her secretary. This lady, a buxom, businesslike individual whose every move indicated efficiency, started in with a barbecued sandwich, a dish of baked beans, a glass of buttermilk, and wound up with a topper of ice cream on a piece of apple pie and well-creamed coffee for a chaser, with utter disregard for the effect on the girth.
>
> "A lady after my own heart," said Mr. Brion after he had told of the First Lady's lunch. . . .

But the reporter for *The Progress* had a streak of skepticism. Had the proprietor of this local eatery introduced himself to Mrs. Roosevelt? No, she might have resented any such intrusion and, besides, the lady with her "looked capable of very effectively rebuffing impertinence. In fact she looked as though she might pack quite a wallop with either the tongue or the fist so I played safety first." Then how could he be *sure* it *was* Mrs. Roosevelt. "Do I know my own wife?" Pete shot back.

For in spite of the Depression, millions of Americans were still spending fifteen cents or a quarter every week to go to the movies, and the newsreels that were a regular accompaniment to every double feature served almost as effectively as the television of later decades to make Eleanor Roosevelt increasingly recognizable—far more so than any previous First Lady, for several reasons. Most of them were less distinctive in appearance and they stayed home more, where the newsreel cameras had fewer opportunities to film them. Above all, the personality of Mrs. Roosevelt, her vigorous efforts from her first day in the White House to dispense with protocol and to show her concern for the less fortunate, were turning her into a new sort of celebrity. The avalanche of mail and other appeals that had begun descending upon her in March was definitely not melting away. Thus, to Hick's increasing dismay, her own position was becoming increasingly uncomfortable.

When E.R. had arrived in Morgantown, Hick had rejoiced to see her. But practically overnight, people all over the state of West Virginia knew that the wife of the President was in their midst. And Mrs. Roosevelt's friend could no longer go around as a nameless visitor not in any way connected with Washington. When E.R.'s aura persisted after her departure, Hick had tried to joke about it: "I'm being killed with kindness! Tonight I was obliged to drag my considerable bulk over what seemed to me like most of a 750-acre park left to the city of Wheeling by some citizen named Oglebay, who, however public spirited he may have been, certainly had no pity for 185-pound visiting firemen. These jobs belong to F.L. of L's, not to observers for the Federal Emergency Relief Administration."

Thenceforth, Hick had tried hard to remain dissociated from E.R., at least on the job. Knowing from her small-town background just how nosy postal employees and hotel clerks could be, she had sent E.R. a box of cheap stationery headed merely 1600 Pennsylvania Avenue, Washington, for E.R. to use instead of that gold-sealed White House paper when she wrote her nightly letters to Hick out on the road. Only as Hick was leaving a community would she dare to give Western Union a wire addressed to the White House, conveying the names of the hotels where she could be reached during the next few days. But toward the end of November all of Hick's efforts went right down the drain—because the *Literary Digest* printed not only a story about her but also a picture captioned "Gets Facts for White House."

She need not have fretted. The picture was a head and shoulders newspaper photograph, taken about a decade earlier when Hick had attempted to look sophisticated. With a stylish haircut and teardrop earrings, she might again at least somewhat resemble the woman in the magazine—if she went on a crash diet for a couple of months. As it was, her name alone could hardly stir much recognition among the relief crowd way out in Dakota, or even Minnesota.

Nevertheless, Hick did fret about the publicity, and E.R. tried to reassure her. "Darling, I know they bother you to death because you are my friend, but we'll forget it & think only that someday I'll be back in obscurity again & no one will care except ourselves!" Still, the long separation was taking its toll on both of them. Affectionate passages, musings about how they would behave when they finally met upon Hick's return to Washington ten days before

Christmas, again preoccupied E.R., after a period during which her own hectic schedule had apparently distracted her.

And Hick, despite a warming Thanksgiving with the Dillons in Minneapolis, could not help brooding when she was again among strangers. Once more, E.R. sought to reassure her: "I am prouder, dear, to know you than I can ever tell you, and you ought not only to be proud of yourself, but to have all the self-confidence in the world, because anyone who is 'you' after all you've been through need never be afraid of anything or anyone."

It must have helped. From the remote and frozen Minnesota lumbering town of Bemidji, Hick was moved early in December to send E.R. fourteen handwritten pages replete with confident appraisals of various political developments—and with unashamed love. This letter must dispel any doubt about the nature of her own feeling toward E.R. It started:

Dear:
Tonight it's Bemidji, away up in the timber country, not a bad hotel, and one day nearer you. Only eight more days. Twenty-four hours from now it will be only seven more—just a week! I've been trying today to bring back your face—to remember just *how* you look. Funny how even the dearest face will fade away in time. Most clearly I remember your eyes, with a kind of teasing smile in them, and the feeling of that soft spot just northeast of the corner of your mouth against my lips. I wonder what we'll do when we meet—what we'll say. Well— I'm rather proud of us, aren't you? I think we've done rather well.

And then, after over a dozen pages of political and scenic discourse:

Goodnight, dear one. I want to put my arms around you and kiss you at the corner of your mouth. And in a little more than a week now—I shall!

10. Emotional Peaks and Valleys

At least that infernal machine had been removed from the fireplace of Mrs. R.'s sitting room, Hick was happy to notice when she returned to the White House a week before Christmas 1933. The contraption was large and rectangular, with a pan beneath it like the pan under an old-fashioned icebox. Back in June, while Hick had been getting her indoctrination from Harry Hopkins, she had stayed on the day bed here as usual, even though E.R. was out of town.

The weather was hot, so Hick had naturally opened both windows before retiring on the night of her arrival. Indeed it struck her as rather peculiar that somebody had left them shut. Nobody had told her, alas, that the large metal affair was some sort of dehumidifier—and all that she had done was to challenge it to dry the air of the whole steamy city of Washington. Horribly enough, she awoke in the morning to find her slippers afloat like little boats on a sea fully three inches deep. What was worse, the water was seeping under the closed doors into the hall, and into Mrs. R.'s bedroom, and into the bedroom of the President of the United States.

Before breakfast Hick assured Chief Usher Hoover she was moving to a hotel. "You can't do that to me," he said earnestly. If she left, "Miss Eleanor" would never forgive him. Even as he spoke, mops were being brandished; within a few minutes two men were carrying out the sodden rug, which somehow seemed quite dry and unharmed when she returned in the evening. Of course Hick confessed her error in an anguished letter to E.R.—suppose the ceiling of the state dining room right below had been damaged? It had not, and E.R. actually seemed to think the story was funny. So funny that she told it to F.D.R., who christened the contraption "Hick's rugwashing machine."

153

For some time thereafter, whenever Hick had lunch or dinner at the White House the President might raise his head during a conversational lull, then sniff and remark, "It seems to me that Washington is a little less humid than it was." With a significant look he would add, "What do *you* think, Hick?" A few years earlier, when he had been just the governor of New York and she had been one of the AP's top reporters, she had blithely traded quips with him. Now awe, and perhaps other emotions, inhibited her. "I think you are right, Mr. President," she would answer meekly.

During the week before Christmas of 1933, Hick did lose her temper in the White House. Not at the President. It was his wife who had the memorable experience of being in the path of a Hickok hurricane, which blew up when the reality of their reunion did not meet Hick's expectations. After brewing for several days, the storm finally erupted following an evening that E.R. had positively saved for Hick, and then had spent with her daughter Anna.

In this period, Anna was particularly close to her mother. As the eldest child in the family and the only girl, Anna had gone through an especially troubled adolescence; she had been fifteen the year of her father's polio crisis. And she had felt a great sense of grievance when her mother had moved her into a fourth-floor cubbyhole of a bedroom while her sunny downstairs chamber was occupied by Louis Howe. Anna's grandmother did not help matters when she kept telling the child how unfairly she was being treated, and a more mature Anna would admit that she had rushed into marriage at the age of twenty to escape being a constant bone of contention between her mother and her grandmother.

But the marriage had failed. With her two attractive youngsters, "Sisty" and "Buzzy," Anna was living in the White House now while her stockbroker husband remained in New York. That much was common knowledge. But only insiders were aware that the President's daughter had fallen in love with a handsome reporter from Chicago named John Boettiger, who also was unhappily married, and that these two were bent on court proceedings to legalize their love as soon as the political omens regarding the impact of two divorces seemed more propitious. Despite this trauma, for the last several years there had been a growing bond between Anna and her mother.

Twenty-seven and attractive, Anna had already taught her Ma the rudiments of stylish dressing Under the stress of her own impending divorce and remarriage, she had also learned to confide in her mother more than many other daughters might have found possible. This rapport seems to have gone both ways. Thus Anna herself had become well acquainted with Hick.

It appears, too, that Anna looked on Hick as a valuable ally in the defeat of maternal stodginess. Together, they had already accomplished the banishment of those awful hairnets; and when Anna's Ma rented a little apartment two years later, Anna thought Hick's idea of sharing in the presentation of some cocktail and brandy glasses was swell. "Merry Christmas to you, Hick," Anna would write then from New York, "and double the goddams! This goes for J [John Boettiger] too. . . . Wish I could stay in this town instead of taking the midnight to the village. Ho Hum!"

Still Anna's casual acceptance of Hick is of some importance. No matter that Anna approved of cocktails and considered Washington very dull in comparison with New York, it is surely doubtful that she could have approved of a relationship between her mother and Hick such as their private letters may seem to imply. Indeed to the staff at the F.D.R. Library, screening The Papers of Lorena Hickok before opening the collection, the closeness between Anna and her mother at this period provided persuasive evidence that the relationship between E.R. and Hick must have been more naïve than their correspondence suggests.

To these archivists, it was inconceivable that Eleanor Roosevelt could have actively deceived her daughter. Bolstering their opinion, they would cite one passage from a letter that E.R. sent Hick on Christmas Day of 1933. Following Hick's stormy departure from the White House, she had apparently written to Anna herself before she calmed down, and Anna brought Hick's outpouring to her mother, as E.R. informed Hick: "Anna read me part of your letter this morning & she said she hadn't been able to understand it & thought we must have had a fearful fight but I told her no, you were just feeling very low."

It is my own opinion, though, that the next few sentences in the First Lady's Christmas letter to Hick are still more significant. She wrote:

> Darling the love one has for one's children is different &
> not even Anna could be to me what you are. I love her, I

want to protect her, but I know her life must claim her &
I must only touch it where I can help. There is a different with friends of one's own age & with you there is a
much deeper understanding & a quality of companionship not possible with youth.

Companionship. I believe that word is the key to understanding
E.R.'s actual conduct toward Hick. For E.R. not only told Hick
often what a perfect companion she was. E.R. also described Hick
that way to her husband. From Maine during July of 1933, addressing the President of the United States as "Dearest Honey," his wife
had scrawled in the last paragraph of a chatty letter, "It has been a
wonderful trip & Hick is grand to travel with, nothing bothers her,
she isn't afraid, she doesn't get tired & she's always interested."

Complex as E.R. was, I cannot think that she might have written
those words guilefully. Approaching her fiftieth birthday, she still
displayed the artless enjoyment of an ingenuous child whenever she
managed to dissemble even slightly. Indeed she retained other
youthful emotions, too. After Hick's tantrum in the White House,
E.R. abjectly apologized for being at fault herself: ". . . & I went to
sleep saying a little prayer, 'God give me depth enough not to hurt
Hick again.' "

E.R.'s habit of blaming herself even when somebody else might
be more at fault does require stressing. For if E.R.'s relationship
with Hick had fulfilled the intimations of some of their letters, one
must suppose that Hick's hoard would sooner or later contain numerous expressions of guilt. Instead, one finds passages of utter
ingenuousness.

Back at Thanksgiving time, down at Warm Springs with the
whole presidential entourage, E.R. had written to Hick in Minnesota: "I had a little longing (secretly) that F.D.R. might think I'd
like you to be here & insist on your coming to report to him! You
know how one dreams?" E.R. had added then that, although she
knew her wish would not come true, it was nice to think about it.
But after Christmas, E.R. did more than merely think of how nice it
would be to show Hick the former resort down in Georgia where
F.D.R. had created a treatment center for polio victims. The First
Lady obtained the cooperation of the President in reserving the
guest cottage there so that she and Hick could read poetry together

to their hearts' content for three evenings toward the end of February.

It is pertinent to add here that F.D.R.'s explicit sanction of his wife's association with Hick is repeatedly apparent during this period; for all of E.R.'s independent spirit, her letters indicate that she made no trips or even invited any White House guests without consulting her husband first. Still, there is no way of discovering his own assessment of the relationship between Hick and his Missis. The only evidence available regarding this man's private feelings in his mature years suggests that he encouraged his wife to do so much gadding and to acquire her own friends at least partly to keep her from bothering him with the rigor of her morality, politically as well as personally. So it seems hardly conceivable that he suspected any attachment that would have had to be described then as immoral.

In this connection, it must be remembered that if personal letters are among the most reliable kinds of documentary evidence, they can be very misleading, too. During the past four decades, and especially recently, there has been such a change in the social climate that a contemporary reader can scarcely appreciate the prevailing naïveté of the 1930's on the subject of homosexuality. It is therefore more plausible than might at first be apparent that intense yearnings for hugs and kisses might mean no more than that physical urges had been aroused—and probably suppressed. No matter that, in at least some segments of today's society, such a suppression will seem more sad than noble. It must also be remembered that both Lorena Hickok and Eleanor Roosevelt, despite all of the difference in their backgrounds, were children in the reign of Queen Victoria. In the total picture presented by their thousands of letters, there appears an attitude toward sexual adventuring of any type that must seem prudish to a later era priding itself on its enlightenment. Still, it is not easy to put these women into any category.

E.R., anticipating the February weekend down at Warm Springs, wrote to Hick enthusiastically that three days away from the White House would be marvelous because there had been so much company lately. Anybody reading this letter would be led to conclude that E.R.'s reason for making the trip was simply to escape intimate little dinners with seventy-six guests.

And two days later Hick, back on the road again surveying the South for Harry Hopkins, let off a burst of steam to Hopkins's secretary as she was driving through North Carolina en route to meet E.R. in Atlanta. Hick was inflamed because another magazine had just publicized her White House connection. ". . . I bitterly resent the implication that I got this job solely because I was a friend of Mrs. Roosevelt," Hick proclaimed. "I love Mrs. Roosevelt dearly—she is the best friend I have in the world—but sometimes I do wish, for my sake, that she were Mrs. Joe Doaks of Oelwein, Iowa!" For such an implacably truthful person as Hick, how could such a statement to her boss's secretary betoken anything except injured innocence?

And yet, for Lorena Hickok, there was a special reason why the limelight might be excruciating—and why she would curse a blue streak when she read even that innocuous paragraph in the February 19, 1934 issue of *Time*, buried as it was toward the middle of a remarkably unbarbed cover story examining the new phenomenon of Harry Lloyd Hopkins, Professional Giver. It was a winter of extreme cold—in Manhattan the thermometer had recently dropped to fourteen degrees below zero, and other record-breaking lows were being registered nearly everywhere. "Such icy weather found one out of every six inhabitants of the U.S.—20 million people—with no means of obtaining fire or food, except from the public purse," *Time* soberly stated at the outset. There followed a crisp review of the various federal improvisations that were attempting to cope with human misery on such a scale, giving Hopkins such high marks as an innovator and administrator that the article might have been written by his press agent. Only then did the article get around to:

> *Graft*. All this haste in pushing out Federal money has resulted in cases of padded payrolls and political favoritism. . . .
> [Hopkins'] chief field representative and investigator is Miss Lorena Hickok who for eight years worked for the Associated Press. She is a rotund lady with a husky voice, a peremptory manner, baggy clothes. In her day one of the country's best female newshawks, she was assigned to Albany to cover the New York Executive Mansion where she became fast friends with Mrs. Roosevelt. Since then she has gone around a lot with the First Lady, up to New Brunswick and down to Warm

Springs. Last July Mr. Hopkins, who is a great admirer of Mrs. Roosevelt, hired Miss Hickok and now she travels all over the country using her nose-for-news to report on relief conditions. Last week when it was announced that Mrs. Roosevelt planned to visit Puerto Rico in March, it became known that Miss Hickok would also go along to look into Mr. Hopkins' relief work there.

Besides investigators Mr. Hopkins keeps busy a set of accountants. . . .

Two weeks earlier, ending up an eight-page report, Hick had told Hopkins himself: ". . . believe me, the next state administrator who lets out any publicity on me is going to get his head cracked. . . ." Regarding that episode, Hick had further unburdened herself to her boss's secretary, Kathryn Godwin: ". . . I'm so fed up with publicity I want to kick every reporter I see. Which is a bad state for me to get into, since I'll probably be back in the business myself after I get through with this." Referring to *Time*, Hick admitted to Mrs. Godwin, "I suppose I am 'a rotund lady with a husky voice' and 'baggy clothes,' but I honestly don't believe my manner is 'peremptory.'" Then: "—why the Hell CAN'T they leave me alone?"

Ostensibly, Hick's ire was stirred by the crimping of her ability to get unbiased data when she was identified as a Washington snooper. This did hamper her, just as it demolished the self-respect she had laboriously struggled for to be tagged by *Time* as just a has-been reporter who had turned into a satellite of Mrs. Roosevelt. Still, the vehemence of her negative reaction probably had an even deeper foundation.

Hick, if not E.R., was petrified by the prospect of gossip. Back on Election Day of 1932, when she had ridden up to Albany with the newly anointed First Lady, Eleanor Roosevelt had almost defiantly said: "I shall very likely be criticized. I can't help it." Of course Mrs. Roosevelt had been referring then to her intention of continuing as much as possible her own activities on behalf of causes she considered worthy. By her sponsorship of projects like the homestead community at Arthurdale, she was indeed arousing criticism among Republicans as an unladylike meddler. That was sad enough. But if Hick could help it, no smudge of personal scandal was going to tarnish this great lady.

E.R. herself professed not to care what "they" said about her. It did bother her a great deal, though, to have her daughter Anna's private life talked about, and when Louis Howe told the First Lady that the White House press room was buzzing over John Boettiger's divorce it provoked a remarkable little outburst to Hick: "One cannot hide things in this world can one? How lucky you are not a man!" After Hick glumly replied that there was probably some gossip about them anyway, E.R. dismissed Hick's fear with an airy comment that anyway "they" must think the two of them stood separation rather well.

Nevertheless, the belligerence of Hick's new repugnance for the freedom of the press probably did rest on her own particularly painful kind of guilt. E.R., with the unconscious arrogance nurtured by her privileged environment, felt—it must be assumed—that nobody could suspect her of behavior to which she could not sink. Hick, cushioned by no such sense of immunity, also had less confidence in her ability to resist temptation. So it would be almost irrelevant to her whether or not she deserved being punished for acting sinfully; she could not escape the special torture that would-be puritans mete out privately when they become oppressed by the obligation to charge themselves with guilty thoughts.

Again, it is necessary to emphasize, there is no possible way to plumb the precise nature of the relationship between these two women during this period when their letters contained repeated hints of a physical attachment. But it must also be emphasized that, no matter if Hick judged herself inferior to E.R. in every way, as far as worldly experience went Hick was miles ahead. At the very least, she understood that there might be smirks in store for them, even if E.R. could not. Indeed there are numerous effusive passages in E.R.'s letters to Hick that provoke a smug question: Is it possible that, four decades ago, the First Lady of the Land just did not know anything about homosexuality? It is not possible. That among her own acquaintanceship a few attachments were quietly assumed to be of this nature does not necessarily mean she was aware of what other people assumed. But there is more telling evidence.

In one sequence of several letters that she received from Hick, a very sad story is set forth. It is about a rich young woman from Minneapolis, nicknamed "Butter," who in New York City "got mixed up with" a married woman mainly interested in money; Butter, heartbroken upon being personally spurned, committed suicide. From the matter-of-fact way Hick referred to the emotional basis for the young woman's misery, there can be no doubting Hick's own knowledge that the recipient of her letters would instantly grasp what kind of mix-up provoked poor Butter to jump from her hotel window. Furthermore, E.R.'s compassion upon reading three long letters on this subject was expressed in a way suggesting that Hick had confided certain experiences of her own. "Poor dear, I hate you to suffer for your friends," E.R. wrote, "& thro' your own memories as well."

So Hick herself, in 1934, was in a hideously anomalous position. She dreaded compromising a person she practically deified. Yet daily she was receiving letters in the handwriting of her loved one, telling her what her every fiber longed to believe. "Oh! dear one," E.R. wrote a few weeks before Warm Springs, "it is all the little things, tones in your voice, the feel of your hair, gestures, these are the things I think about & long for." And a week later E.R. confided that she often felt rebellious but someday perhaps fate would be kind and let them arrange a life more to their own liking. ". . . For the time being," she added, "we are lucky to have what we have."

What they had in March, 1934, after their weekend at Warm Springs and after Hick had happily spent the final week of February in the White House, was twenty-nine more days together, despite continuous and sometimes very frustrating surveillance by other people.

In 1949 Bess Furman would write a book called *Washington Byline,* providing the most complete account available of the trip that Mrs. Roosevelt took to Puerto Rico and the Virgin Islands in March, 1934. From the Furman standpoint, the expedition had been inspired by her own friendly rival Ruby Black, representing the United Press as well as a string of small papers unable to afford the full-time services of their own Washington correspondent. Actually even the UP had seen no need for employing a woman in its capital bureau until Mrs. Roosevelt had begun holding her press conferences, to which male reporters were not admitted; other news-gathering operations similarly bereft of feminine staff had also been obliged to remedy this lack, as Mrs. R. had intended. Such expansion of female employment possibilities should set a good example in other industries, she lectured "the girls." However, Ruby Black judiciously held onto her free-lance clients, too, among them *La Democracia* of Puerto Rico. It was to drum up stories for this outlet that Ruby had sought to focus the First Lady's attention on the island's problems.

Mrs. R. did not need much urging. "I am going," her announcement of the trip explained, "because ever since the Puerto Rican Children's Feeding Fund was inaugurated by Theodore Roosevelt, I've been interested in the question of what really was the condition of people in Puerto Rico." She did not feel it necessary to mention that a new burgeoning of this interest had coincided with the approach of Hick's forty-first birthday. During all the preliminary discussions of the adventure at the press conferences and the informal luncheons to which Mrs. R. frequently invited several of "the girls," there was plenty else to mull over, inasmuch as Mrs. R. was nothing if not thorough in preparing for the trip. From a friend of hers who was the wife of the Puerto Rican relief administrator, she obtained shocking data about the effect of three generations of economic hardship on this Caribbean outpost of the United States. She also received some cooperation from the actual heads of several government agencies.

But if the baggage for the expedition was laden with statistics—on disease and overpopulation and underemployment—it also included ball gowns and bathing suits; and the breathless pace of their program at every stop would be the real genesis of Mrs. Roosevelt's reputation for indefatigability. All of this was scarcely what Hick had had in mind when she and E.R. had first discussed a birthday trip together. Still, the advance publicity could have been much worse. Hick's old comrades barely mentioned that Mrs. Roosevelt was being accompanied by a former Associated Press correspondent who now kept Harry Hopkins informed about sore spots where relief was most needed, and who would be giving him her own report on the Puerto Rican situation. However, on the night of their departure, Hick's temper began to simmer.

At the last minute, persistent fog forced a change in the plan to fly directly from Washington. Instead, amid much flashing of cameras they boarded a train for Miami around two A.M. Despite the lack of advance warning, noisy groups welcomed them repeatedly along the railroad's route until they finally were wafted aloft above the blue Caribbean. Taking advantage of this airborne respite, E.R.

dashed off a note to her daughter describing the beautifully smooth flight they were having, and she also reported that Hick was bearing all of the fuss fairly well. Hick's only outburst thus far, the First Lady told Anna, had come aboard the train when a conductor asked if he could bring back a timetable to be autographed. As he closed the door of their compartment Hick had said, "I hope he chokes."

If the next eleven days held beautiful moments that Hick would always remember, tropical sunsets and a storybook pink palace such as she had only dreamed of, so much else was spoiled for her by the crowds and "the girls" that well before they returned to Washington she had issued her own ultimatum: never again would she share her dear one the way she had been forced to on this trip.

July was supposed to be entirely their own, and during the next few months of emotional ups and downs that were extreme even for Hick, this prospect served as her only stabilizer. Again she was traveling in the South, which had to be depressing because economic conditions among such a large proportion of the population were so much worse down south than elsewhere. Perhaps E.R.'s realization that Hick was bound to suffer extremely prompted the special warmth of her first letter upon Hick's departure from Washington at the end of March. It got harder to let her go, E.R. wrote, because each time they met they grew closer. "It seems as though you belonged near me," E.R. added, "but even if we lived together we would have to separate sometimes & just now what you are doing is of such value to the country that we ought not to complain, only that doesn't make me miss you less or feel less lonely!"

This theme that Hick's work was so much more important than what E.R. was doing would recur constantly, and it often accompanied a lament with a strikingly contemporary sound. "I've been very much 'Mrs. R.' all day!" she wrote to Hick on a day devoted to receiving one delegation after another, from Girl Scouts to university women. But she added that suddenly she had felt like herself, not like the First Lady, and had said several things the First Lady should not have said; unfortunately she omitted any further description of her spurt of independence. Just as often, though, E.R. would refer to her endless round of seeing people and inspecting projects as her own job; it seemed consoling to her to equate even her ceremonial duties with more usual categories of employment. Still, her conception of Hick's daily endeavor as more worthwhile than her own is not hard to understand, for at this period E.R.'s scope really was quite limited—while Hick's letters exuded the joys and heartbreak of real life in a way that E.R. could not duplicate in the White House.

The contrast was partly a matter of personal outlook. As one small instance, E.R., try as she did, just could not comprehend what it was about food that gave pleasure to other people; before her friendship with Hick, she had regarded those who sought to gratify their palates as dangerously self-indulgent. Indeed this attitude survived in reference to her husband, which may to some extent have accounted for his lack of tenderness toward her. Besides telling everybody, quite mistakenly, that Franklin really did not care what he ate, his wife during his first month in office had enthusiastically told her press conference about the nutritious but cheap Depression meal she had ordered for a White House luncheon. It was to be served as an example to housewives all over the country. The menu planned by her friend Miss Flora Rose of Cornell cost just seven cents a plate and consisted of hot stuffed eggs with tomato sauce, mashed potatoes, prune pudding, bread and coffee. Could it be pure coincidence, a Cornell historian would subsequently wonder, that a few hours after eating this meal the President had signed the bill legalizing the sale of beer?

Even where Hick was involved, E.R. had originally made remarks, and during the early days Hick had valiantly starved herself for E.R.'s sake, losing twenty pounds. E.R. seemed scarcely impressed. "Stick to your diet, lose twenty pounds more & you'll forget you are forty," the First Lady had briskly advised. But now that they were both a year older, E.R.'s reaction was rather different when Hick wrote to her from New Orleans:

> I ended a long day of conferences—pretty gloomy conferences, for New Orleans is apparently, from the commercial viewpoint, just a charming corpse—with dinner at Arnaud's and, it being my last real meal in New Orleans, I made it a memorable one: two gin fizzes, some kind of a marvelous shrimp concoction known as shrimps Arnaud, pompano baked in a paper bag, potatoes souffle, a pint of sauterne, crepes Suzette (I think I'll never have

them anywhere else!) and black coffee. You never tasted such food! What a town for a glutton!

To which E.R. replied: "How I wish I could enjoy food!"

However, the nightmare horror of much of what Hick was telling E.R. outweighed everything else. It must be doubted whether Eleanor Roosevelt had ever heard about degradation such as Hick reported to her, for instance in her letter from Houston touching on a problem they had discussed frequently—the need for special programs to help jobless single women obliged to fend for themselves. From Houston, Hick wrote to her about a conversation with some social workers handling unattached people, including single women. The gist was that so little was being done to provide jobs or even food allowances for the women that many of them were being driven to prostitution, and yet:

> One of the male social workers put on old clothes one night and went down and had himself put through the transient set-up, to see how transients are treated. Several girls accosted him as he walked down the street. To one of them he said:
> "I can't. I have no money."
> "Oh, that's all right," she said wearily. *"It only costs a dime."*

Well, it was one-thirty A.M., Hick went on, and she still had some packing to do before she went to bed. "Oh, my dear, love me a lot!" Hick ended that letter. "I need it!"

Much of what Hick was writing to E.R. also went into her reports to Harry Hopkins. But because the reports included more facts—and more impressions—Hick also sent a carbon to her friend in the White House. Here is how she started her five pages of single-spaced typing to her boss on the night she told E.R., and also Hopkins, about the ten-cent prostitute:

Dear Mr. Hopkins:
At no time previously, since taking this job, have I been quite so discouraged as I am tonight.
Texas is a Godawful mess. . . .

There followed a fact-sprinkled tirade about the selfishness of local political squabblers, and: "In the meantime—God help the unemployed. . . . A case worker in charge of single women told me tonight that she had orders today to cut their weekly food allowance down to 39 CENTS!" This despite passage of a bond issue which, with matching federal funds, could have provided decent allocations.

But not just the relief situation was discouraging. The cornerstone of the New Deal recovery program was the NRA—the National Recovery Administration, setting up machinery for encouraging every industry to create new jobs. In Texas, Hick reported, businessmen just weren't cooperating, and she quoted a local official: "What Roosevelt seems to be trying to do is to put over a Mussolini program in a democracy. It won't work. Businessmen won't follow any such program voluntarily. . . . They're too selfish and too stupid. . . ." Then a particularly ripe Hickokism:

> And honestly, after nearly a year of traveling around this country I'm forced to agree with him. If I were 20 years younger and weighed 75 pounds less, I think I'd start out to be the Joan of Arc of the Fascist movement in the United States.

More thoughtfully, toward the end of this report, Hick discounted the possibility of any effective form of dictatorship in the United States. Everywhere she went, she said, practically everybody seemed to be cheating on the NRA and other programs because "we might as well, for the other fellow will," while "deep down, they'd be, for the most part, perfectly willing to take orders if they knew they HAD to obey them." Even so, it didn't seem likely that either Fascism or Communism would work in America. "If we have to have a dictator," she concluded wearily, "I personally would prefer Roosevelt above anybody else."

Obviously, Hick's strong point was not analysis, and yet in capturing the mood of a community she had few peers. She was like a mirror, flashing back to Washington not only the urgent problems she uncovered but also the dim thinking of well-meaning people harassed by seemingly insoluble dilemmas. Nowhere does her limited grasp of abstract concepts appear more repugnant, though—a few decades after the civil rights movement has made the most blatant forms of racism untenable—than in her reports regarding the preponderance of Negro relief clients in the South. As will be seen, Hick had a personal empathy with individual blacks that was much less condescending than the Northern norm then. But, as she admitted to E.R., she herself could not defend against a charge of racial discrimination her peculiar suggestion that since blacks "could manage to subsist" without relief, the available funds might better be spent raising the pitifully low relief allowances for white wearers of white collars. Perhaps her lapse of judgment is somewhat mitigated by the grinding torture to which she was daily exposed, with no emotional relief except what she got from penning page after page each midnight to the only person, apart from Hopkins' secretary, who even knew where she was most of the time. That person certainly tried to give Hick positive support.

From the White House at two A.M. one April morning, E.R. reassured her: "No, I am always glad you were assigned to me in 1932 & I am glad if you feel the same way." And E.R., two nights later, after visiting the handcrafted-furniture shop in Hyde Park in which she was a partner, elaborated on the dream they both referred to now and then: "One corner cabinet I long to have for our camp or cottage or house, which is it to be? I've always thought of it as in the country but I don't think we've ever decided on the variety of abode nor the furniture. We probably won't argue."

The degree to which they had come to feel their lives entwined was further displayed when Hick arrived in Fort Worth. There the Roosevelts' son Elliott had recently settled with his second wife, already markedly pregnant although his father had not yet met this new daughter-in-law; E.R. had seen her just once briefly, on a flying trip. As E.R.'s emissary, Hick visited the couple, then sent back a long and mostly affirmative report. In this letter, Hick also demonstrated the protective strength that E.R. often said she leaned on, calling Hick her rock and her refuge. "Darling," Hick wrote, "your Sunday night letter *did* sound low . . . I wish I could be there when you feel as you did Sunday night and take you in my arms and hold you close. Well, I'll try to make you happy every minute while I'm there in May."

Actually, E.R.'s Sunday night letter had complained of no worse than a houseful of intrusive company. More seriously, the same plague afflicted 1600 Pennsylvania Avenue when Hick finally returned for their first reunion since Puerto Rico, and she was particularly affected by it herself because she arrived in very shaky condition after a most distressing accident; on a rutted gravel road in Arizona, a skid had wrecked Bluette. Miraculously, Hick had emerged from the overturned convertible unhurt ("Incidentally, sir, you have to have a darned good neck to get away with anything like that," she had written to Hopkins). But instead of finding comfort on her return to Washington, Hick was forced to invent a horrendous new symbol for her private calendar. On it she marked twelve days of May with circles all but blacked out by heavy diagonal lines, undoubtedly signifying that E.R. had been too busy to spend more than an occasional half hour alone with her. Perhaps only subconsciously, Hick seemed to be slanting her last hopes toward July.

Again, E.R. was contrite. In the future they would have years of happy times, she promised, so these bad times would be forgotten. And although July was two months off, when it came they would be together. It helped, too, that upon Hick's departure from Washington she had a happy experience on her job for a change, touring the territory of the New Deal's proudest accomplishment—where an entire depressed region was being transformed by the Tennessee Valley Authority. After all of the misery Hick had been obliged to report, suddenly a geyser of TVA-inspired hope spewed forth:

> Dear Mr. Hopkins:
> A Promised Land, bathed in golden sunlight, is rising out of the gray shadows of want and squalor and wretchedness down here in the Tennessee Valley these days.
> Ten thousand men are at work, building with timber and steel and concrete the New Deal's most magnificent project, creating an empire with potentialities so tremendous and dazzling that they make one gasp. . . .

While the mood lasted, Hick waxed almost as euphoric about a homestead project near Dayton, Ohio. But then her first glimpse of the harvesting of Colorado sugar beets by children eight years old brought a terrible slump again. Hick's misery was aggravated by large headlines in the Denver papers reporting that the President's daughter had arrived in Nevada to begin the six weeks' residency required under that state's most liberal divorce law. Of course Hick had known of Anna's plan, but still she had cherished the fantasy that it could be accomplished without sensational publicity. In this case, although her own suffering should have been only vicarious, she proved her love painfully. "I ought to write a report tonight,"

Hick wrote to E.R. from Denver, "but I've gritted my teeth so much these last two days that the roof of my mouth is all raw."

Nevertheless, it was Hick's forebodings about the trip she and E.R. were planning to take in July that caused her the most distress. From Washington, the First Lady kept blithely suggesting increasingly elaborate itineraries, as if she could not be satisfied unless she combined what ought to be half a dozen separate jaunts into one glorious holiday. She even wanted to go to Banff in the Canadian Rockies, although common sense finally made her substitute Yosemite, so they could spend a few days with Anna at the secluded ranch where she was awaiting her appearance in a Reno court. To Hick, however, it seemed that each new stopover just multiplied the likelihood that they would be spotted.

Originally they had been going to spend two weeks exploring Northern California en route to Oregon; there E.R. would join F.D.R. as he disembarked from a Hawaiian cruise, and would accompany him on an inspection of assorted New Deal projects in the Columbia River Valley while Hick went back to work. But now in practically every letter F.R. proposed new embellishments, like a few days in San Francisco—anonymously!—so that they could stay at the same out-of-the-way hotel where Hick had spent a few months with Ellie, and ride the cable car together, and dine at the kind of wonderful little restaurant she never went to ordinarily.

How could Hick resist such an appeal? Nor could she refuse to begin their expedition of three whole weeks (she would take unpaid leave for the third week) by visiting Ellie herself in the small city near Sacramento where she now lived. E.R., though, was slightly apprehensive about meeting Ellie. "I'll dread that too just a little," she wrote to Hick, "but I know I've got to fit in gradually to your past, meet your friends & like them so there won't be closed doors between us later on."

Thus it was finally arranged that E.R. would fly to Sacramento, then go with Hick for the better part of a week to make Ellie's acquaintance. Not that they could impose on Ellie's hospitality, because the shrinking of her assets since the 1929 crash had forced her and Roy to move into a tiny bungalow where she did her own housework. Still, Ellie joyfully plunged into supplementing her own limited resources by obtaining the use of a cottage on the grounds of a nearby sanatorium in which Hick and Mrs. Roosevelt would be quite comfortable. Also, they would be close enough to share the meals she fixed for Roy and his wonderful daughter, and to spend delightful evenings reading aloud from Ellie's well-thumbed *Oxford Book of English Verse.*

No wonder Hick gritted her teeth! So prone to jealousy herself, she worried herself into a frenzy that E.R. might suffer a similar torture meeting Ellie. Let alone be put off by Ellie's well-meant arrangements. Wouldn't it have been infinitely better for Hick just to spend a few days alone somewhere with Ellie, and without Roy whom she could barely tolerate, before E.R. flew west? Agreeably, Ellie did join Hick on the road about a week in advance of the First Lady's descent. But if Hick felt grateful for this small blessing, she still sent E.R. such a tense letter at the end of June that from the White House E.R. was moved to write as plainly as she could about a difficult topic.

She was so happy that Ellie had met Hick and that the old companionship was still there, E.R. started. "Yes, dear," she went on, "I think you will remember that I once told you I wished you had been happy with a man or that it might still be. I rather think the lack of that relationship does create emotional *in*stability but people do seem to weather it in time & who knows what the future holds. In the meantime Ellie & I will try to do a little stabilizing or at least help you to do it!"

So E.R. did know what Hick was missing. And on another occasion E.R. would blandly tell Hick—in reference to a young woman they both knew who was enamored of a married man—that if the girl was in love, Hick could teach her how to snap out of it. But if E.R. thought that she and Ellie could alleviate Hick's suffering, merely by loving but chaste companionship, E.R. was mistaken. The five days Hick and E.R. spent near Ellie were not too bad; neither was their interlude at the ranch where Anna was staying. But in Sacramento and San Francisco, when reporters found the First Lady, it was awful. Just as in a ridiculous movie, contingents of state troopers mysteriously changed the license plates of Hick's new car to disguise it; reporters caught on anyway. At one point, there was a chase scene straight out of a Keystone Comedy before the trooper chauffeuring them at eighty miles an hour gave up and said the engine might be ruined. Then as E.R. sat knitting, Hick shook her fists at a whole convoy of her former comrades. In the garage of the San Francisco hotel where they left the car overnight, escaping to the anticlimax of a dinner served in their room, souvenir hunters ripped out everything removable—maps, sun glasses, chocolate bars and even the little St. Christopher medal E.R. had given Hick for good luck.

Still, Yosemite was worse. On her own, E.R. had efficiently written to the Chief Ranger, specifying: "Miss Hickok will require a quiet, gentle horse, since she has not ridden for some time." Not since Bowdle, in fact—and the outcome was excruciatingly similar. As the ranger put it when writing later to express the hope that Mrs. Roosevelt would come again: "Tell Miss Hickok that I am wondering if she still dives backwards from her saddle horse into rivers." He had the grace to add "please give her my best regards."

But by that time, Hick had decided against any further expeditions with her dearest friend.

11. Learning to Let Go

After Hick deposited E.R. with the presidential party in Portland, her own solitary drive southward back to California was something like dying, she thought. Such a feeling of remoteness descended that she wondered if she really were still alive, but this turned out to be just a temporary, merciful numbing of her senses. By the time she reached San Francisco again, pain racked her as though her heart actually had broken. Because now she had no more hope of ever being happy—and, not for the first time, the idea of ending it all struck her as the best way out of the whole damned business.

Fortunately, though, little Ellie came to keep her company while she surveyed the relief scene in the Bay area, and it was almost impossible to remain gloomy around her. What a gift dear little Ellie had for making a game out of reading even an ordinary breakfast menu! She also had a total inability to see any flaw in those she loved; she had to, Hick wryly told herself, to be so blooming cheerful about her Roy. Hick therefore had to hide her own misery as best she could, somewhat irascibly toward the end of the week, although she did manage by mail to fool E.R. Just a week after their parting, the First Lady wrote to her:

> Your letter today was a joy . . . but I'm afraid you & I are always going to have times when we ache for each other & yet we are not always going to be happy when we are together. Somehow we must find the things which we can do & do them so that what time we have together is as happy as it can be in an imperfect world!

By then, E.R. was back East, vacationing again, this time with ex-trooper Earl Miller and some others at the Adirondack lakeside camp where she really had little to do but float around in a motor boat or practice her shooting except to sit on the porch and read and knit and meditate serenely. Thus she found herself able to recollect Hick's surly behavior at Yosemite as just a touch of altitude fever, which E.R. gently suggested might be avoided by cutting down on the cigarettes. Also, E.R. had to admit to Hick that she was happy at Chazy Lake and that one reason of course was the place, but there were other reasons which she had been analyzing as she sat knitting. Perhaps the main one was that she felt needed and wanted, E.R. wrote, adding in a sort of aside that probably that was why she enjoyed being with Anna and John. So often with her sons she felt barely tolerated, she confided. What curious creatures women were, she mused.

Curious indeed. Had Hick ever been able to be seriously critical of E.R., this need to feel needed by people like Earl and his dancer friends would surely have been at the top of her list. For it hurt Hick to be linked so often in her darling's thoughts with this simple manchild—although Hick herself had a tendency in the same direction. Back in Texas the previous spring, Hick had ended a long letter to E.R.:

> And now I'm going to bed—to try to dream about you. I never do, but I always have hopes. The nearest I ever came was the night I ate the Mexican dinner. My dream that night was that I was going to marry Earl and that your mother-in-law was simply furious! Isn't that a honey? The truth is, I almost never dream.

Still, if dreaming was a singular occurrence for Hick, her dyspeptic fantasy was singularly revealing. Certainly somewhere in the back of her mind she perceived that to E.R.'s dowager mother-in-law Eleanor's friendship with a coarse woman journalist must be just as repulsive as Eleanor's peculiar adoption of a most unsuitable foster son. Since Hick felt no great fondness for the haughty Sara Delano, who had already endured the indignity of one Earl Miller wedding at Hyde Park, it was hardly surprising that Hick might relish the notion of punishing the old lady by subjecting her to a second and even more distasteful nuptial ceremony.

Yet Hick also had to realize—and repress her realization—that to E.R. herself, Hick and Earl fit, way down deep, in the same category. They were both beneath her. Thus, by being wonderfully kind to them, she was showing how little such worldly considerations as family background mattered to her. Besides, who among E.R.'s own kind could be so bereft as to depend on her the way they did? Much more compassionately, E.R. conveyed this precise thought when she wrote to Hick from Chazy Lake that she always felt Hick and Earl needed her more than anyone else.

Hick certainly did. Despite her brief distraction by Ellie, once she got back on the road her anguish was overwhelming again. But if Hick had a great capacity for suffering, she endeavored to behave as she knew her dear one wished she would. From Bakersfield at the southern end of California's San Joaquin Valley, she began a long letter:

> Dear You:
> Well—another day gone. A long day of driving about seeing things, with the chairman of the county board of supervisors and several relief people. The most interesting thing I saw was the little village of adobe houses built by Allan Hoover. . . .

Then Hick devoted several pages to elaborating a nice bit of irony. Out in the valley, the son of F.D.R.'s well-hated predecessor was, all but anonymously, building a model colony for the migrant workers on the ranch he managed, while right in Bakersfield, just as in thousands of other towns around the country, there was a place everybody called "Hoover City"—a terrible jungle of tents and tar-paper shacks where about a hundred families lived under unspeakable sanitary conditions. "What *are* we going to do with these people?" Hick demanded.

Finally, after communicating her plan to leave for Fresno in the morning, Hick noted that she had been looking at maps, and many, many miles now separated them. "Good night," she wrote, "I hope you are having a happy, restful time at camp—a happier, more peaceful time than you had with me. Oh, I'm bad, my dear, but I love you so, at times life becomes just one long, dreary ache for you. But I'm trying to be happy and contented."

Hick's new sweater was turning out nicely, E.R. wrote from Chazy Lake. And she had ordered a handmade salad bowl sent as a hostess gift to Ellie. In another week, E.R. added, she would be back at Hyde Park, and for the rest of the year, with only an occasional weekend or a few days now and then, she would be just the President's wife again. But she and Hick would still manage to have some quiet and unobserved time together in New York, she promised.

Soon after Hick started eastward in her balky successor to Bluette—this lemon she had christened "Stepchild"—she sent E.R., and Harry Hopkins, an extra six paragraphs headed "California," apparently after some thought on how to broach a sensitive subject. Atypically, in her haste or embarrassment, she slightly garbled the paragraph in which she finally had to explain what she was talking about. She wrote:

A couple of days ago, while I was down in the San Joaquin Valley, several clients and former clients were brought in to tell me about conditions working in the cotton fields. Among them was a woman, rather above the average, who had gone out with her husband into the cotton fields a year ago. They didn't make enough to support themselves even while they were working, but this is another story.

The next morning the case worker who used to visit that family—the woman's husband is back at work now, at least for the time being, and they are off relief—called me up and said the woman wanted to see me, alone. So I went to see her. Faltering, terribly ill at ease at first, she told me [what] she wanted to talk to me about had nearly driven her crazy when she and her husband were on relief and that she knew [it] was one of the worst problems of women whose husbands were out of work.

"It's this thing of having babies," she said. "You've got no protection at all. And there you are, surrounded by young ones you can't support and never knowing when there's going to be another.

"You don't have any money, you see, to buy anything at the drug store. All you have is a grocery order. I've known women to try to sell some of their groceries to get a little money to buy the things needed. But if they catch you at it, they'll take you off relief. Maybe they wouldn't if they really knew what you wanted the money for, but most women don't like to talk about such things to outsiders. You understand, I'm not asking for any help for myself. My husband's working now, and we're all right."

She looked at me timidly.

"I suppose you can say the easiest way would be not to do it," she said. "But it wouldn't be. You don't know what it's like when your husband is out of work. He's gloomy and unhappy all the time. You have no money of course for movies or anything else to take his mind off his troubles—not even street car fare to go to a park. You must try all the time to keep him from going crazy. And many times—well, that's the only way."

It was just about when this report would have reached Hyde Park, where a frantic Labor Day weekend signaled an end to her leisure, that E.R. wrote to Hick, "Mr. Hopkins said today that your reports would be the best history of the depression in future years." E.R. also wrote that her husband had been in rare form at the clambake given by their neighbors, the Morgenthaus. Then E.R. ended this letter with a wish particularly susceptible to misinterpretation. "I wish I could lie down beside you tonight & take you in my arms," she wrote.

It is necessary to add that a flurry of wires from the terrified Hick had disclosed a health emergency, probably aggravated by her miserable state of mind. Thus a digestive disturbance set off after she had drunk a few dippers of water at a desert spring intended only for cattle had been at least briefly confused with typhoid, and E.R.'s solicitude was mainly—albeit rather extravagantly—maternal. Whatever other emotion Hick may have originally aroused, and despite the sporadic flicker of this feeling during the next several years, there can be little doubt that the final sentence of the above letter does not mean what it appears to mean.

Still it must be emphasized again at this crucial juncture that there is no possible way to provide an accurate account of any private meetings between E.R. and Hick. Thus I have not attempted to surmise what had actually happened at Yosemite. Nevertheless, the available evidence does indicate a major turning point in the relationship during July of 1934—and that is why Hick was so miserable.

For in the course of their recent trip, she had somehow come to realize that she could not mean to E.R. what E.R. meant to her. Indeed Hick must have grasped, at last, that E.R.'s emotional need had never been of the same dimension as her own. Of course, it ought to have been clear all along and yet Hick had managed to fool herself. Certainly this was her own fault, because right from

E.R.'s first week in the White House she had told Hick that she loved many other people ". . . & some of them can do things for me probably better than you could." Still Hick had inevitably paid more heed when E.R. said she had never enjoyed being with anyone the way she enjoyed being with Hick.

Nor would Hick ever forget that. In a biographical sketch of Eleanor Roosevelt that she wrote in the 1950's, there is a telling phrase: "[Mrs. Roosevelt] was able to follow a philosophy that she had acquired as a strictly disciplined child—that it is best to pretend you don't want a thing if you cannot have it, even though you may want it very much." Perhaps that does at least partly explain the change in their relationship after their western trip.

But if Hick desperately wished to believe it was only the pressure of prying outsiders that had made E.R. decide on a new course, her own capacity for self-delusion had limits. She knew that she had behaved terribly—shouting or stalking like a wild animal whenever E.R. was recognized—and yet how could she control herself? For she also knew that, even in remote Yosemite, E.R. had *enjoyed* having those rangers dancing attendance; the role of First Lady now gave her more pleasure than pain. Probably not coincidentally, Hick's own little book *Reluctant First Lady* that she wrote in 1962 ends, abruptly, on the last day of their 1934 vacation.

However, in real life if not in the simplified version Hick chose to recount, the tie between these two women did not end in 1934. Being enormously loyal, besides being in love, Hick did her best to meet E.R.'s special requirements—to behave as if nothing had happened, and to bury the "bad" part of her.

She even had a nice experience en route home from California, just before her loathsome week of guzzling paregoric around the clock at a Utah hotel. With E.R., Hick had had some fine moments at that ranch not far from Reno where Anna had been staying. It was owned by people named Dana, the least stuffy social registerites that Hick had ever met; they had actually seemed to like her and had urged her to stop back by herself on her return trip. More than a little hesitantly, she had. "For heaven's sake," E.R. demanded when Hick incredulously reported her warm reception, "why shouldn't they like you for yourself? They are genuine people."

Bill Dana surely was. Although he must have been rich as

Croesus to be retired at barely forty, he reminded Hick of a nice shaggy collie. Every evening before dinner he would pick up a banjo and render the most marvelous cowboy songs, just as if he had never even heard of Wall Street. About Bill's wife Ella, Hick was not so positive; odd, she thought, how many Ellas she seemed to encounter. This one was a striking blonde, bleached not only by the sun, but in dungarees and with humor she managed to make Hick feel more than welcome. Perhaps it was merely that Hick was never at ease with really attractive women; they had too easy a time of it to care much for her company. Anyway, Bill and Ella had both fervently invited her to visit them on Long Island next spring—and she might do that.

But who knew where she'd be next spring? It was entirely possible that she'd be pounding the pavements in search of a newspaper job again, as if anybody would hire her with her special disability of being officially certified by *Time* as a White House hanger-on. Since most publishers tended to be Republican, their editorial pages were starting to treat the Roosevelts pretty roughly. So who would want her? Not even Harry Hopkins, probably, even if she herself could stand another year of this awful grind. Besides, even among good New Dealers, the scrabbling for personal advantage was more than she could stand. Let somebody's cousin see how they liked a steady run of flea-infested hotels and a steady diet of American lard or worse, while practically all the people they talked to every day were either poor slobs on the verge of slitting their throats—or social workers—or goddam selfish businessmen. Lord, she was fed up!

Maybe the whole New Deal push to help people was just a crazy farce; that thought occurred to her when she stopped, on the last leg of this very long trip, at the Kansas State Fair. According to Washington, every county of Kansas fell within "the primary drought area," but here were fruit and grain and cattle beyond belief. To E.R., Hick wrote "You never saw so many new Chevrolets in your life." How come? After all of the drought stories in the papers, and dozens of special directives from Washington? One fellow at the fair who'd been talking to a lot of Kansas farmers gave her the farmers' own idea: "All we need is a little rain!" The humor of it struck her right in the stomach.

"They didn't want to be rehabilitated," Hick wrote to E.R.

"They didn't want to be transplanted. . . . I wonder if we aren't rather losing our perspective."

Upon returning to the White House the last week of September—coming home, as E.R. so appealingly put it—Hick lost her personal perspective again. To be treated as hardly different from any other friend infuriated her. "Hick dearest," E.R. scrawled after one outburst, "I am sorry you were hurt dear, but weren't you a bit hasty? I was back at 6:45 & I lay on the sofa & read from 7:15 to 7:45 which was the time I had planned for you." For E.R. did plan time for her, she assured Hick, although obviously the situation was not the same as it had been, because now Hick was spending a good deal of time in Washington. If it were only a few days, E.R. explained, interrupting the routine would be easier. And then she added:

> You must not think so long of things I say which I really do not mean so seriously. I want you to be happy because I love you & when I've hurt you I am sorry & cross with myself for not thinking ahead & preventing it but I wouldn't give up our times together & our happiness for these little troubles. You have been a brick & don't think I don't know how hard it is.

It was not easy, and yet Hick did simmer down. But since the only assignment Harry Hopkins had for her toward the end of 1934 was to survey and resurvey the Baltimore area, she had the extra aggravation of being in Baltimore when she wanted to be in Washington, and vice versa. From Baltimore Hick complained, with fairly good humor, that when she had eagerly searched the local papers for a report on an E.R. speech, all she could find was a description of what Mrs. Roosevelt had been wearing. Hick's ire rose, though, as she wrote.

"God damn it," she exploded, "none of us ought to be wearing velvet dinner gowns these days. Not when, as the chief attendance officer in the Baltimore public schools said today, 4,000 Baltimore children couldn't go to school in September because they didn't have clothes. As she was saying that, the thought of that new dress of mine and of you in a blue velvet dinner gown—even though you *are* my friend and I love you—irritated me profoundly. . . ."

In reply, E.R. attempted to soothe Hick:

> Darling, if we all stopped wearing velvet dresses, there would be worse times than these are, if you have money you must spend it now, so I don't feel as guilty as you do. Of course if you could give it all where it would do the most good that would be grand but we can't always do that! Don't think me heartless because your vehemence always makes me calm!

Not always. In the last of her intensely emotional letters among the thousands Hick would save, E.R. came closer to expressing herself than in any previous letter. It is cryptic in some respects; it is not even dated, indicating that it had been dashed off and then delivered by her own hand to Hick's room in the White House. But let it speak for itself:

> Hick my darling,
>   That cry of "I want something all my own" is the cry of the heart & I was near to tears last night. You told me once it was hard to let go but I found it was harder to let go & yet hold on. Love so much & yet share. Gosh! I sound horrible but I mean that you taught me more than you know & it brought me happiness & I wish I could bring it to you. I bring you unhappiness & if I didn't think in the end it would make you happier I'd be desperately unhappy for I love you & you've made of me so much more of a person just to be worthy of you—Je t'aime et je t'adore.
>
> E.R.

"To let go & yet hold on." That, whatever else must remain unclear, was E.R.'s own prescription for their future. Hick herself had, in theory at least, the option of saying No, she could not, would not, share her dear one—but how could she face total emptiness again? So this was no practical choice. At any cost, she would have to learn "to let go & yet hold on."

That E.R. could set such an unrealistic course was hardly surprising because at this period of her life—the year in which she turned fifty—such an earnest disdain for moral weakness, such an earnest faith in the perfectability of humankind, still was an important aspect of her personality; it was the basis upon which cynics and Republicans had begun mocking her, and the viciousness of some of those "Eleanor jokes" would be unparalleled. Not that she should have expected to escape a certain amount of more high-minded criticism. As she herself might have put it about somebody else, it *was* quite strange to hear the First Lady giving Sunday night radio talks for which she was paid a handsome sum by a particular manufacturer of cold cream, even if she did use the proceeds of this commercialization of the presidency to support her private charities.

Nevertheless, after two years in the White House Eleanor Roosevelt had already aroused much more positive than negative emotion. The volume of her mail was only one measure. Everywhere she went, the warmth with which she was surrounded proved that her caring about people had been communicated, and in return, millions now cared about her. Engulfed by this new tide of adulation, the shy person beneath her poised facade required less of the private reassurance she had desperately needed upon her husband's nomination. However, the insecure person had by no means disappeared. And for as long as this E.R. needed her, Hick could not feel that her own life offered any alternative to helping her.

To demonstrate her strength of character, Hick at the White House even took up horseback riding—briefly. But after buying proper boots and breeches, she decided that calisthenics made more sense, and she almost managed to touch her toes before a bout of the flu interrupted her campaign for physical fitness. Mentally, however, Hick did persevere in her effort to imitate E.R., as a letter from Baltimore toward the end of November indicated. Upon receiving a mysterious E.R. confession from Warm Springs about an episode she said she was too ashamed of to write details, Hick wrote:

Dearest:

I don't know what you did to Nan [Cook] and the President but I don't believe you behaved *very* badly. Because it simply isn't in you to behave *very* badly. The trouble is, dear, that most of us demand and expect too much of you—and this despite the fact that you really do give more of yourself to your friends than almost anyone else I ever knew. I suspect that at one time or another you've spoiled most of us. You did me. I say all of this perfectly aware that I am the worst of the lot in the business of expecting and asking too much. But, darling, I'm trying not to be that way any more, and—*I'm going to succeed.*

The episode E.R. had felt too ashamed of to describe to Hick involved drinking. As a consequence of the exceptional history in her family—her adored father had died of drink, and several uncles and her only brother were in process of emulating this sad example—E.R. had a particular horror of alcoholic overindulgence. But what had happened at Warm Springs also demonstrated her distaste for the court jesters with whom F.D.R. enjoyed surrounding himself, especially when on holiday. Their guffaws were too much for her the third evening of the Thanksgiving festivity because it seemed to her that her friend Nan was being made the butt of unconscionable merriment, and this member of her Val-Kill partnership was an easy mark.

Short and stocky, with notably protruding blue eyes and a bustling manner, Nan was the kind of good-hearted arranger of everybody and everything who tempted the malice of practical jokers. Two nights in a row, F.D.R. had mixed her a cocktail before dinner, and the drink had loosened her tongue only a little. Then the third night she talked much too much—and didn't someone purposely mix too stiff a potion? Although the President denied it, his wife lost her temper.

Hick finally heard the whole story from Anna, so she was able to offer proper consolation when E.R. returned to Washington. As she herself could hold her liquor, she pointed out, at least she would never cause any trial of this sort for her dear one. Indeed, as the year drew toward its end Hick could take comfort in the fact that her bad impulses no longer tore her so painfully. Now she was giving help the way she yearned to, instead of constantly begging for help herself. That E.R. noticed this change was especially gratifying. On Christmas night she wrote to Hick up in New York, "I do hope the worst is over for you."

12. 1935: Year of Indecision

By 1935, Harry Hopkins had no need of Lorena Hickok to tell him about relief trouble-spots. The Republican proprietors of newspapers all over the country were taking much pleasure in amply publicizing what was wrong with any New Deal program, although their working reporters, most of them paid less than fifty dollars a week, tended to feel very Democratic. In fact, Hick along her travels had enlisted a small corps of strategically located journalists to alert Washington directly when something struck them as potentially an embarrassment—if possible, before the story got printed.

So Hick started to do some serious thinking about her own future. Spending a lot of time between assignments just moping behind the scenes at 1600 Pennsylvania Avenue sooner or later would drive her crazy, even if there were compensations. For a girl from Bowdle, she had certainly acquired an easy manner in ordering her supper sent upstairs; during this past year, she had put her foot down about donning a long dress or suffering the stares of strangers. But she spent more time than she would ever care to confess, angrily pacing alone in E.R.'s sitting room.

It was the same room with tall windows and lofty ceiling in which Hick had interviewed the new First Lady on March 4, 1933. Of course, E.R. had effected a wonderful transformation since then. The huge bed had been moved out, a smaller one installed in the adjoining little room, and easy chairs with bright, cheerful slipcovers, amid dozens of pictures of family and friends, had made a formerly austere setting homey. From E.R.'s desk here, the First Lady could see the Washington Monument, which she found comforting. If there was no important company, E.R. and Hick frequently dined in front of the fireplace. And the day bed in this almost square chamber at the southwest corner of the White House was reserved for Hick's use when she was in Washington; her clothes occupied one of the large wardrobe chests that were the only available closets.

Still Hick could not really enjoy living here, if only because she had scant privacy. Even so, she did like to show off when one of her AP pals came upstairs, by ringing for a few beers. Nor did she find it any sacrifice to cease attending to her own laundry and mending. Mabel Haley, E.R.'s personal maid, was glad to do for Miss Hickok, too. Indeed Miss Hickok and Mabel spent a lot of time gabbing companionably while Mabel went about her chores. From many sources Hick gathered quite a stock of unvarnished vignettes depicting life in the White House the year before Franklin Roosevelt actively sought his second term—all of which Hick scrupulously kept to herself.

It was no secret that he would run again. But the American political climate tends to be particularly murky the year preceding a national election. Thus the question of whether F.D.R. would win a second term by no means elicited a unanimously affirmative answer. If things had seemed definitely better a year ago, now the economic recovery was not so noticeable; and the Old Guard of conservatives was in a position to make plenty of noise. Even the brain-trusters kept muttering that the election outcome would depend on business conditions a year hence, that it would depend on whom the Republicans put up, not to mention innumerable other less crucial variables. Under the circumstances, White House tempers grew edgy—and an odd notion apparently struck the First Lady.

In that White House sheltering two such exceptional individuals as E.R. and F.D.R., two separate sets of satellites revolved, each around its own celestial figure. Of course every generalization has its exception, and during this penultimate year of the New Deal's trial period, his name was Louis Howe. A peculiar coincidence had previously impressed Lorena Hickok. Since initials were personally as well as officially favored by the Roosevelts, in E.R.'s letters to Hick she often mentioned somebody else tersely as L.H.; so E.R. herself must have noticed a possible cause of confusion. Perhaps only subconsciously, E.R. also took it as an omen.

For there were more significant similarities between Louis Howe and Lorena Hickok than just their initials. Both had started on newspapers; both had risen from hardly privileged backgrounds; both were burdened with unprepossessing exteriors for which they compensated with self-mockery and irascibility; no scanting of brains or humor could be alleged about either. In the bargain, both smoked incessantly, Louis to the extent that, by 1935, he was dying of smoke-aggravated lung trouble.

Hick herself could have no illusions about succeeding Louis as practically the only well-used bridge between Franklin Roosevelt and his Missis. She knew her own weak points better than most people, and just opening her mouth in the presence of the President of the United States still terrified her. "Can you imagine *me* calling the President?" she once asked E.R., when a state official out on the road had tried to get her to pick up the telephone for immediate help on some local emergency. Besides, Hick also knew that her first loyalty must always be to E.R. personally. Still, it appears that E.R. herself, patiently bearing with Louis during his final illness, cherished the notion that she might by happy accident have nurtured a successor to Louis.

Oh, not exactly! E.R. could not have borne even a slight defection by Hick in the direction of her husband's camp; any such inching away would have pained her a hundred, a million times more than the gradual, but eventually unmistakable, slide of Harry Hopkins. More importantly, no matter that E.R.'s political sagacity had yet to develop much beyond the primary stage where expert organizing of battalions of envelope-stuffers was her forte, she already was well aware that Hick lacked the toughness for contending with the likes of Jim Farley, F.D.R.'s Postmaster General and the field commander of the impending re-election campaign.

So Hick's role on behalf of the President would have to be peripheral, which would suit everybody concerned. Nevertheless, was it not entirely feasible for Hick to approximate the part that Louis had played—by using her keen eye to discover political danger signals that might otherwise go undetected? This idea of E.R.'s surely showed her own inner tension; although she kept telling Hick she would be happier away from the spotlight, still she kept doing whatever she could to secure her husband's re-election. Hick, less complex herself, already understood that E.R.'s real happiness lay in serving others. So be it. As the emotional pitch of the relationship between Eleanor Roosevelt and Lorena Hickok diminished

month by month, Hick drew what comfort she could from being—
at least remotely—the First Lady's own Louis Howe.

Unquestionably, Hick had to get out of the White House. In
January of 1935, there had been a few good days on her private
calendar but then black lines reappeared, and abscesses in her
mouth began torturing her; she had, of necessity, gone to New York
to see her dentist. It must be noted in passing that Hick, much
bothered by her teeth, had found a woman dentist whose ministrations gave her such a sense of confidence that she would consult
none other. With reason, Hick dreaded a diagnosis at no distant
period condemning her to dentures, and she wanted to put off the
evil day as long as possible. Having achieved one more postpone-
ment, she felt sufficiently cheerful to look up a number of old
friends.

It is not unusual for such renewals of acquaintanceship to stimu-
late musings about might-have-beens, but unfortunately the letter
in which Hick told E.R. what was running through her mind did
not get saved. However, E.R.'s reply strongly suggests that their
intimacy, even at its warmest, had never been of the sort that many
readers of their earlier letters might assume. With her inimitable
mixture of wisdom and wishful thinking, E.R. wrote to Hick:

> Of course you should have had a husband & children &
> it would have made you happy if you loved him & in any
> case it would have satisfied certain cravings & given you
> someone on whom to lavish the love & devotion you
> have to keep down all the time. Yours is a rich nature
> with so much to give that the outlets always seem mea-
> gre. Dear one, I do love you & appreciate the fight you
> make not to make me unhappy, but there is no use trying
> to hide things from me because I know just how you feel!

"Certain cravings." There E.R. had put her finger on Hick's
problem; but if, under various stresses, E.R. still gave some sign of
such cravings herself, their strength had much abated. Now she
usually mentioned just peering at Hick's picture on her desk to
comfort herself when she was feeling bereft. That they would eventually share a cottage somewhere was still the dream E.R. held
forth for their future, after she had blessedly returned to obscurity.
Yet the vision she alluded to, of the two of them peacefully collab-

orating—on some kind of literary project?—had the hazy serenity of dispassionate retirement. No doubt her advancing years were already having a calming effect, for she frequently looked upon the headstrong impulses of youth from the lofty perspective of an old lady, as she had taken to calling herself wryly since her fiftieth birthday the preceding October. Hick, at forty-two, had not yet reached this plateau of greater peace. In search of it, she tried to forget her own frustration by dedicating herself to alleviating the gloom that—for all of E.R.'s talk of not really suffering—still afflicted the President's wife intermittently.

To Hick, E.R. often bemoaned the emptiness of her daily round. On an evening when she was only mildly depressed, she wrote that she had been busy all day seeing people who would probably have done as well without seeing her. And yet a good deal of the time she hardly seemed to mind "the crowds & the telephones & the fawning" anymore, either in the White House or on her travels. After one of her frequent visits to Arthurdale, she even told Hick a little defensively that although she and Nan had had a long day, there had been very little "first lady" about it, just simple and kindly hospitality. Nevertheless, her underlying personal dissatisfaction could still provoke feelings of utter futility.

The preceding spring, upon returning to Hyde Park with her husband for the first time after their winter in Washington, E.R. had humored F.D.R. by riding around the property with him in the specially equipped car he could drive himself; only once in a blue moon did this couple ever dine alone together, or see each other alone except fleetingly. That evening E.R. had written Hick a revealing glimpse of what had gone through her mind during the ride. "I kept thinking of the mess we had made of our young lives here & how strange it was that after all these years I return here as indifferent & uninterested as a stranger." It was to help herself combat this apathy, and the spurts of temper she had a hard time controlling during 1935, that E.R. leaned heavily on Hick.

Even to a First Lady, family upsets had to loom larger than most men can imagine. So an important aspect of Hick's supporting effort was something like family counseling, and there could scarcely be more of a challenge in this line of work than those Roosevelts offered. For Hick had to be ready with sage advice regarding an over-supply of exasperating relatives; also, the family's position

added infinite permutations and combinations to the normal potential for domestic disturbance, sometimes owing to no fault of any
Roosevelt. For instance on one occasion in May, Hick's role required nothing but laughter, although E.R. could barely appreciate
the joke.

The drama had started late one afternoon. While the First Lady
was entertaining her mother-in-law and a bevy of ladies in the
Monroe Room, she was summoned to the telephone to speak to the
son she called Fjr. in her letters to Hick; young Frank and also
Johnny were at Harvard. E.R. realized at once that the boy on the
other end of the line was dead drunk. Although her hearing was not
sufficiently acute for her to be sure the debauched voice pleading
for a check belonged to either of her student sons, the manager of a
Boston hotel positively identified the culprit as Fjr. So she told this
gentleman to have the house detective escort the boy back to
Cambridge. Then she returned to her guests for fifteen minutes
before dashing to the telephone again to call Johnny in Cambridge.
He was instructed to find his brother and telephone a full report as
soon as possible. In the interval, E.R. went for a swim in the White
House pool, where she informed her husband of his namesake's
disgraceful predicament. However, one hour after the first summons, a perfectly sober Franklin junior, interrupting his supper in
crew headquarters, wanted to know what the fuss was all about. It
turned out the hotel manager had been mistaken, that the real
culprit was a young man from a good family in Newton Centre who
had decided under the influence of a few drinks to play a little
trick. Still, E.R. told Hick, the episode had given her more excitement than she wanted for quite a while.

But more serious problems caused more serious eruptions, among
them a small tempest over a remark by her mother-in-law. E.R.
herself had commented one night after dinner, just before going off
to do mail with Tommy, that it would not break her heart if Franklin failed to be re-elected. Later her son James came to tell his
mother that as soon as she had left the room his grandmother
turned to him and said: "Do you think Mother would do anything
to defeat Father? Is that why she stays in politics, just to hurt his
chances of re-election?"

"Now I ask you," E.R. exploded to Hick, "after all these years?"
But there was more on other fronts. Franklin junior was saying that
if his parents did not make more effort to understand him, he might

just as well leave college. And both of E.R.'s student sons kept changing the dates when they would be coming home for weekends, so that their mother repeatedly had to alter her own plans. It was particularly disconcerting when Johnny suddenly announced he would row at Annapolis on the 25th, then come over to Washington, because that was the weekend E.R. and Hick had accepted an invitation to visit Bill and Ella Dana on Long Island.

But if E.R. tried to indicate to Hick that she was really not too distressed by such domestic complications, the next day she admitted she was still "ready to chew everyone's head off!" A touchy situation involving her husband and their eldest son, James, made her "so mad with F.D.R." that she had to keep telling herself, "be calm Mrs. R.!"

Hick, who knew how angry E.R. felt when she thought F.D.R. ignored or otherwise slighted his parental duty, wrote back with such concern as to make E.R. apologize most revealingly a few days later. ". . . I'm sorry I worried you so much," the First Lady wrote. "I know I've got to stick, I know I'll never make an open break & I never tell F.D.R. how I feel—I blow off to you but never tell F.!"

Hick received this letter while she was out in Michigan making a survey expressly authorized by the President on behalf of his new advisory group, the National Emergency Council. Although in Washington she sometimes thought she was no longer needed, now she did not hesitate. A glance at her copy of E.R.'s itinerary for the month made up her mind and she sent off a wire. At the first possible opportunity, probably somewhere in Ohio, she would join E.R. en route. Then in the privacy of a train compartment they would talk over everything bothering the President's wife.

Thus it happened that Hick was along for one of Eleanor Roosevelt's most celebrated departures from the traditional role of the nation's First Lady. Hick had been warned that they would be inspecting a coal mine—"so wear suitable clothes, if you know what is suitable, I confess I am stumped!" However, the mine owner had also been warned, and he had ordered a great clean-up which gave him the confidence to suggest that ordinary street attire would not be sullied by Mrs. Roosevelt's underground tour.

Hick was grateful for that. A huge covey of photographers awaited them at Bellaire in Ohio, primed to snap away at the bizarre picture of the President's wife donning overalls. They shot plenty of pictures anyway, making the day "perfectly horrible," as Hick wrote to the Battle Creek family she had once lived with and whose hospitality she had just enjoyed again after a lapse of several decades. "The trip into the mine might have been interesting," she informed them, "if only ten of us had made it—as it had been planned. But there were *eighty-five* of us, including all the reporters and photographers in the state, apparently, and so we really didn't see much. We finally got aboard a train for Washington at Steubenville, Ohio, late that night, more dead than alive. Terrible crowd at the station, all shoved right up against the train. We were scared stiff for fear someone would get hurt."

With E.R., Hick arrived in Washington the next day in time to go up to the Capitol and hear F.D.R. address Congress. It was a special occasion—no other President had ever delivered a veto message in person—and Hick thought his explanation of why he could not approve immediate payment of two billion dollars in soldier bonuses showed magnificent courage.° Again her mixed emotions about that man interfered with her professional duty of composing a report she knew was destined for his eyes. What a leader he was; it would be tragic for the whole country if the Republicans managed to beat him next year, but what a colossally self-centered man he also was, utterly indifferent to anybody's feelings except his own. So it took her nearly a week to write twelve and a half pages, summarizing his chances for winning voter support the following year in the pivotal industrial but agricultural north-central state of Michigan.

Still, the report was a cogent summary of why the President had lost ground in Michigan, with suggested steps for regaining it by coordinating the administration of various related New Deal programs. Hick succinctly stated that the greatest need was for a better public-relations effort to counteract "the wise-cracking about not shooting Santa Claus." For even though the President had refused to spend two billion dollars on immediate bonus payments, more than four billion would be spent before the next election in a massive effort to create new jobs under the aegis of the new Works

° Although the House of Representatives voted to override the unprecedented in-person veto, it was upheld by the Senate and the bill died.

Progress Administration. Harry Hopkins, still Hick's boss, must have liked what she wrote because he immediately asked her to give him a list of top newsmen who might be willing to come to work on New Deal public relations. As for Hick herself, Hopkins wanted her to start right away on the same sort of broad-gauge survey out in Missouri—nor was she sorry. Not only had she just endured a couple of very bad days at the White House, during which E.R. was so busy that she practically ignored her, but now Hick had a special reason for wishing to stop off again in Michigan where she had recently renewed another old friendship.

Miss Alicent Holt, her teacher at Battle Creek High School long ago, had moved on to Grand Rapids. In that city, Hick had heard that Miss Holt was recuperating from an operation. Hesitantly, Hick had turned up at Miss Holt's hospital room—when the cherry blossoms were out, they would reminisce a year later—and she was astonished to be welcomed not just as a star pupil but also as a most impressively successful person. That Hick should have been surprised by this made E.R. chide her. "You will never learn what a strong personality you have & how much people admire you," she wrote, "but then I like that about you."

If it was providential that Hick had happened to be in Michigan on that occasion, the frequency of her subsequent appearances in Grand Rapids had more to do with her own planning. There were so many bad days on her private calendar during the second half of 1935 that, despite E.R.'s continuing reliance on her, despite the unvarying regularity of their communication by mail when they were apart, Hick must have felt a great emotional gap. It was filled, at least to a certain extent, by Alicent—soon she was signing *her* letters Alix.

Only very occasionally in The Papers of Lorena Hickok at Hyde Park is there any letter bearing the signature "Lorena." Except for 1,050 of the letters she sent E.R. and later reclaimed,° her cache included scarcely any examples of her own letter-writing, for ob-

---

° Apparently Hick retrieved these letters, from among the several thousand she sent E.R., almost haphazardly at various times when she was staying at the White House; some she took at the time she was planning a book on her WPA experiences.

vious reasons. Also, it could not be expected that most of her correspondents would have saved their letters from her; only a couple of dozen, kept by various friends, seem to have survived. Thus the flavor of her other friendships has been preserved mainly in the miscellany of other letters, besides those from E.R., that emerged out of the cartons that Hick herself donated to the F.D.R. Library.

By no means did Hick keep every letter she ever received. From Ellie alone, she got copious outpourings once or twice a week for more than twenty years, and yet Hick put just a thin sheaf of "Hickey Doodles" epistles into her hoard. Almost as if Hick-the-writer were visualizing the problem confronting her eventual biographer, this handful of letters in which Ellie chatters mostly about what books she has been reading personify a warm-hearted woman of playful wit, not as funny to strangers as to her scores of friends. Because Hick was so fair-minded, it is possible, too, that she wanted it on the record that Ellie was happy with her Roy. But what Hick wished to convey by the thicker packet of letters from Alicent Holt that she also included is harder to surmise. Their immediate impact, though, is powerful. Apart from a few letters from Hick's old Aunt Ella, they are the sole evidence that anybody ever called her "Rena."

Only for awhile did she remain Rena, and then she became Carissima. But Alix—less than ten years Rena's senior—was, heart and soul, a teacher. "Do you remember enough of the Latin I once taught you to know what that means?" she had to ask. "Not that I said that to you, I fancy, twenty-five years ago." Still there is more of a pedagogic than a passionate tone to the whole sequence of Sunday night letters from Grand Rapids that Alix mailed Monday after Monday to her very dear one, wherever she happened to be traveling. Of course, that does not preclude the possibility of a more personal relationship during the dozen or so weekends or longer holidays they spent together in the ensuing couple of years. Probably, though, the relationship was just mutually maternal; the letters suggest that each of these childless women alternated in mothering the other.

Certainly Rena brought a new joy into Alicent Holt's quiet life of caring for her aged father, correcting English compositions and entertaining her bridge club. When Rena sent her white roses on her birthday, it was the first time Alix had received such a lovely bouquet. And yet Alix was so implacably schoolmarmish in a nice way—she called herself Aunt Maria when she lectured Rena on too much smoking—that emotional letting-go hardly fits into the picture she guilelessly left of herself long before she died in 1968, three decades after having written these letters that she could not dream would land in the National Archives.

What possessed Hick to deposit them there? Perhaps it was her need to demonstrate that not always did she play a secondary role, that sometimes she—no less than E.R.—could be the beneficent sun shining upon a humble and grateful inferior. But the simile has only a limited application. To Rena, the narrow world of Alix soon lost its charm and, although the letters continued sporadically for many years, their intimacy did not endure.

After San Francisco—and Yosemite—the preceding July, Hick had vowed never again to subject herself to the multiple indignities of an extended trip with E.R., or to vie with rivals at a theoretically secluded summer retreat like Campobello. So as another vacation season approached, Hick was pursuing her inquiry into F.D.R.'s popularity in Missouri, where Boss Tom Prendergast dictatorially ruled the local Democracy. To E.R. at Hyde Park, Hick dispatched a small sermon on the importance of being prepared to make political compromises. E.R. replied: "I know Prendergast & all that situation & hate it, but you are right, one is practical in these circumstances! That is one reason why I couldn't run for office under any circumstances."

At Hyde Park, though, there were compromises of a nonpolitical nature that had to be made, mostly involving the First Lady's mother-in-law. Hick, too, was endeavoring to make the best of her own situation. Since she now had only limited opportunities to be with her dearest friend, she made a special effort not to spoil a single minute when she returned from Missouri at the beginning of July 1935. She and E.R. had a few wonderful days then en route from Washington to Chautauqua in western New York, where the First Lady had been engaged as a speaker.

Indeed they had such a peaceful time that E.R. wished Hick could have stayed with her as she assembled her other cohorts for a full program of picnics and shopping expeditions and nightly readings of *Goodbye, Mr. Chips* at Campobello. Yet by now they both understood that was not practical. Hick, back on the road again, reflected with some humor about the reason:

> The sunset at Campo Sunday night must have been very lovely, and it was nice to think that you wished I was there. You're probably right, though, when you say I'd not be very happy. I'd probably feel like a fifth wheel. Well—never mind, darling! The time will come when it won't matter to me that there are so many others who have priority rights to your interest and affection. Then I daresay we'll all be one nice big happy family (?) You must admit, though, the possibility of its being some-times tough to be the most recent of the people who have any claim on you! I have no seniority rating at all! I'm so very much an outsider. But when the time comes when I don't care so much—or at least not in the *way* I care now—it will be easier. Anyway, I'm glad you're up there and enjoying it. And we'll have our time together later on.

Meanwhile, Hick vented her suppressed emotion in other direc-tions. "God damn it," she exploded later in the same letter, writing about a state official who had expounded a prevalent idea she had a special reason for detesting, "I just wish some of these people who think all unemployed women ought to be delighted to hire them-selves out as maids or scrubwomen had to take a whack at it them-selves. Believe me, Madame, I've *been* a servant—a maid-of-all work, a slavey in a boarding house! I know what it's *like*. People make me sick."

This outburst came as Hick was plumbing the depth of anti-New-Deal sentiment in upstate New York, with particular refer-ence to rumored mass defections among such stalwarts as the large Polish-American community of Buffalo. How good were Hick's re-ports about matters of this sort? Certainly they provided nothing like the precision that the statistical surveys of future decades would routinely make available to every candidate. Perhaps there is no better measure of the distance American politics has traveled than to compare Lorena Hickok—by herself, sipping a beer in a working-class tavern or standing around factory gates—with a bat-tery of computers. Of course, soundings were also reaching F.D.R. from a variety of other sources. But at their best, Hick's reports

were more like what future decades would call position papers,
very clear and probably used to some extent in campaign planning.
Her summary, later that year, of the electoral pitfalls created by
the whole relief situation still offers a more concise précis of a
complicated issue than many a subsequent scholarly work. For instance, here is Lorena Hickok, in 1935, calling attention to a fear-
some possibility:

> I think it is very important that we should make a check . . .
> on what technological advance is actually doing—and going to
> do—to employment in this country. During the last two years
> this has impressed me, almost more than anything else . . . An
> electric crane, throwing twelve Finns on the Minnesota Iron
> Range permanently out of work. A new process in oil refining
> that lays off 35 men, for good. A coal mining operation, near
> Scranton, that used to employ 1,300 men, now employing,
> with improved machinery, less than 500. A hundred men "fi-
> nalled out" of the Studebaker plant in South Bend by a new
> type of automobile body . . .

Thus it was more than likely that the country might have an
economic boom without any material lightening of the relief rolls,
Hick predicted. "We ought to study this thing. . . ." Realistically,
however, Franklin Roosevelt himself had no great need to read
such documents composed by Lorena Hickok; he had plenty of
professors telling him the same thing. But Eleanor Roosevelt did
need the plain, and sometimes unpalatable, facts that Hick provided, for example about a relief administrator in upstate New
York. ". . . He's *got* to be hard-boiled to do this job," Hick wrote to
E.R. ". . . the attitude of the clients is very bad indeed . . . it is most
necessary that we get them out of the 'relief habit' as soon as we
can . . . it isn't the clients' fault that they've acquired that attitude.
It's ours. Too much social work . . . Too much thinking done for
them—instead of giving them what work and what money we could
and letting them work out their own problems. . . ."

Then after a sharp assessment of the politics inevitably behind
the local dispensing of relief funds, and also of the slippage of the
President's popularity for this and other reasons, Hick informed the
First Lady:

> Well—it's all interesting. But damned depressing,
> when you get it fired at you all day and on into the

evening. The most depressing thing about it is that these business men don't seem to have learned anything at all in the last five or six years. Not one damned thing! And more and more I'm sure that Harry Hopkins was dead right when he said, "Don't forget it—this is a war between the 'haves' and the 'have-nots.' " I think the President needs to get out around the country. Only even then—everybody will "yes" him. . . .

In my own small way, I'm as bad as any of the others. He'll turn to me and say, "Am I right, Hick?" I don't always think he is, but I haven't the nerve to say so. Even if he weren't President, intellectually he'd always have the advantage in any argument with me.

Still Hick was not really so humble intellectually. And when she held forth a few days later about the New Deal's basic flaw—its lack of coherence, its constant improvising—E.R., too, found it possible to criticize her husband as an administrator. "I know what you mean about structure," E.R. wrote, "it comes from not thinking things through from the start & building up step by step & I think I can do that better." Then displaying her own tendency to schoolmarmish stricture, E.R. marked down F.D.R.'s main fault decisively. "It's muddy thinking," she wrote.

So many themes echoed and reechoed through Hick's correspondence with E.R. during this indecisive year of 1935. There were still flashes of emotion from E.R., mostly of a wistful nature. "I'd like to be able to give you a kiss & hold you very close darling, but I send you many warm & loving & very tender thoughts instead," she wrote from Campo. "It is a grand criticism . . ." after Hick sent back a manuscript with detailed comments. "Dearest, you can be as tough as you like in your criticisms," a few days later. "I know my tendency to write speeches & Mr. Bye [George Bye, her literary agent; now that she was trying to be a real writer, she had acquired an agent] said just that too. I want to do good work & I want the help which you can give me, no one else is half as good a critic & I'm very grateful to you & don't mind at all."

On Hick's part, there were dreaded "white nights" to gloss over, when sleep would not come. And bad news many days, such as the corruption among Ohio's Democrats, so odoriferous that at the moment "your esteemed husband couldn't be elected dog catcher in

Ohio!" And in West Virginia "I'm going to recommend that we
send in a federal examiner to go over the books of the relief administration—it's that bad." Also more laments because relief
administrators everywhere would not see the futility and wrong-
headedness of treating all unemployed single women as potential
domestic servants.

Thanksgiving in Grand Rapids with Alicent mellowed her somewhat—until she went back to work on a special survey of Michigan's Upper Peninsula. From the small city of Houghton there, the
mercurial Hick dispatched one of the most agitated—and most interesting—of her letters to the White House:

Dearest:

This has been *a day!* Tragic as parts of it have been I
grin in spite of myself. It's so absurd.

I landed in Iron Mountain at 6:30 this morning. Clear
cold weather, with a biting wind from the North. Lots of
snow. Curse had come in the night. Cramps.

Mr. Sweet, the district WPA director, met me at the
station with his chief engineer, and thcy took me out to
the attractive and cozy little log cabin in the pine woods,
where they "batch it." Then they proceeded to cook
breakfast, while I sat around, feeling foolish. Very delicious food. Nice experience.

Then we went out to look at projects. We slithered
and slid over ice, snow and ruts around and up to the top
of a small mountain over a road that eventually is to be
called "Franklin D. Roosevelt Parkway." Up on the top
of this hill, some 200 men were at work, clearing out
underbrush, digging out stumps, working on the roadway
and building a ski jump. It's a magnificent site—you can
see forty miles away on a clear day, and from one spot I
could see eleven lakes. Beautiful pines down the slopes.
Some day, my dear, it will be a very beautiful park.

But—

These men, most of whom had been working since No-
vember 15, hadn't yet received any pay.

Thirty of them—we checked up later and got the exact
number—*had not even brought dinner pails. Because*
there was nothing to bring in them. . .

These people had been taken off relief the day they
went to work for WPA—almost a month ago. Whether

we like it or not, that is what has happened all over this state—and, I suspect, in many others—as the result of our cutting out of federal relief. The states and counties haven't got the money—whether they *should* be able to raise it or not—and it's the poor devil on relief who catches it in the neck. . . But, ye gods, doesn't *anyone* in Washington realize what it means to run into debt when you are trying to support a family on $44 a month, which is what these men are getting?

Listen, dear, these men went to work on November 15. They had been on relief, which was cut off. They had nothing in reserve. I got paid on the 15th and again on the 30th. And I'll be quite ready to cash my next pay check, which will arrive in Detroit early next week.

Well—you can imagine how I felt. We came back to the office and landed with both feet on the disbursing officer. By special dispensation because it is so far from Lansing, they've finally been allowed to set up a district disbursing office in the Upper Peninsula. He promised to get some of the checks out there this afternoon, the rest tomorrow morning.

But I simply couldn't get those 30 men who hadn't even brought any dinner pails because there was nothing to put in them off my mind. Out there in that bitter wind, working on the "Franklin D. Roosevelt Parkway." Neither could Mr. Sweet. Finally, he said, "Aw, hell, let's send some food out there." "You bet," I said. "I'll pay for it." "No, you won't," he said. So he gave a man a ten-dollar bill and told him to load up a car with sandwiches and hot coffee and get out there to that job, and God help him if he ever told where they came from. We're going fifty-fifty on it, whatever it cost.

Of course, the First Lady made several telephone calls in Washington about the WPA pay situation, as Hick had hoped she would. But that was only the first half of Hick's letter that evening, for she went on:

Next adventure!

I wanted to come up here to the copper country—150 miles north of Iron Mountain. I found out that the district director of women's work was driving up this afternoon. In a Plymouth coupe, with her nephew. They invited me to come along. So here I am. One hundred and fifty miles of solid ice—at 40 miles an hour. Over the first 75 miles I'm sure I acquired 50 new gray hairs . . . lady, I was *scared*. Even so, the scenery was lovely. Miles and miles of pines, all covered with soft white snow. An avenue of Christmas trees. Later she told me they all drive that way up here—only most of them faster—that if you know how to do it, it's the safest way to drive on ice, that they do it all winter long, etc. But tomorrow—I go back to Iron Mountain by train, Madame!

Dined with the lady tonight and—oh, God damn this women's work anyway! It seems that up here in Houghton they have a practice house, for training maids, a project dear to the heart of the state director of women's work. The only trouble is . . . that they apparently reached the saturation point on placing the trained maids they had turned out. Houghton has a population of only 16,000. It's the only town up here where anyone has enough money to employ maids, trained or untrained. So, having apparently placed all the maids they could up here, they began shipping them to Detroit and Chicago. I don't know what pay they're getting in Chicago, but one of the WPA engineers says he investigated about one of the girls who went to Chicago, by calling on her family, and found that she was getting *$10 a month!* Why, damn it, the houses of prostitution in Chicago are full of country girls who went to the big city for less than a living wage. It's been that way since the beginning of time. Now *should* I tell that damned fool of a woman down in Lansing, when I see her in Detroit next week, a few of the facts of life? Or *shouldn't* I? Probably not. But I did tell this district woman that, were I in her shoes, I certainly would *not* okay any maid training project for the Upper Peninsula until I knew where I was going to place the maids when I got them trained, and that I certainly would *not* stand for shipping them to the Detroit and Chicago markets for $10 a month.

So—

And now, believe it or not, I'm writing in front of a beautiful, glowing grate fire! This is an old-fashioned hotel, not *too* long on plumbing, but with *fireplaces in the bedrooms!*

And thus endeth the Tenth Day of December, Anno Domini 1935!

13. War—or the World's Fair

Well before the end of that indecisive year of 1935, Hick had confronted a hard question. Could she, if she wanted to, get back into newspaper work? Ever since June, 1933 when she had quit the Associated Press, a part of her had resented giving up her independence, and it irritated her increasingly as the months passed to keep on hearing, or thinking that she was hearing, whispers referring to her powerful White House connection. Some people even had the nerve to ask Hick how it felt when you knew that you couldn't be fired.

So a dozen times she had been ready to hand in her resignation, except that she did have to eat. Strangely, Hick did not seem concerned about whether she would be able to resume reporting with her old enthusiasm after having been hounded by reporters herself; she had never been noted for her ability to anticipate new problems. Instead she brooded over the unlikelihood of finding anybody willing to hire her at this point in history. Approaching her forty-fourth birthday, she was well aware that many employers refused outright these days even to consider job applicants past the age of forty. Still, her main worry was about Eleanor Roosevelt.

If the AP had demanded off-the-record tips regarding the First Lady's plans, surely other potential employers of a reporter who was known to be Mrs. Roosevelt's crony would make similar demands. Unless Hick were prepared to give up all contact with Mrs. R.—and she was *not* ready to do that—how could she look for a newspaper job? Impossible!

This distressing fact of life Hick had been obliged to communicate to E.R. herself, after she had received a particularly ingenuous response to some restless remark of her own. "I do hope you get back in the newspaper business soon!" E.R. wrote to her. "Can't

you forget you ever knew us, tell them you never see me & can't
find out anything?" To which Hick had replied:

> If you got a laugh out of my idea of the possibility of a
> "happy family" at Campo—I was equally amused at your
> idea that I could get a newspaper job, telling them
> I never saw you and didn't know what was going on.
> They'd never believe it, dear—unless I actually did quit
> seeing you. And that would be expecting a good deal of
> me, in New York. Gosh—I'm not prepared to give you up
> *entirely!*

Hick, upon completing another page of that letter on another
subject, with an increasingly scratchy pen, must have read over the
above. Nearly out of ink, she squeezed in—after *"entirely!"*—"(And
I don't believe you would want that, either.)" During the ensuing
year, she would learn how right she was about that afterthought.
But if E.R.'s need for her had to be immensely gratifying, it also
stimulated a different emotion. Hick never during her life would be
able to express this other feeling in words; it was true, as Alix out in
Grand Rapids kept assuring her, that loyalty and generosity were
Hick's outstanding qualities. Thus it was beyond Hick's power to
cast any aspersions on Eleanor Roosevelt. It still seemed miraculous
to her that such a woman liked, let alone loved, her. How could
Hick not feel eternally grateful? And yet, deprived so blithely of
her own profession—of the only legitimate status she had ever
earned—how could she help nourishing, too, a tiny seed of anger?

Toward the end of September in the non-electoral year of 1935,
F.D.R. found it convenient to make a coast-to-coast inspection tour
with all the trappings of a campaign trip, including his wife by his
side. Hick, after a drizzly day on her own, inspecting WPA projects
in Toledo, Ohio, wrote to E.R.: "Can't imagine where you are
tonight. The papers carry practically nothing—and that under the
vague dateline 'Aboard the President's Special Train.' Just the
same, that dateline makes me damned homesick for the business.
Three years ago now I was writing copy under a similar one.
'Aboard the Roosevelt Campaign Train.' Oh, well—"

Then a new idea occurred to Hick. Overseas, Benito Mussolini
had been making alarming speeches about Ethiopia, and reports

that an even larger war might be impending began turning up in the newspapers. Suddenly Hick remembered 1917 when she had burned to be a war correspondent. Why not try it now! Having a friend in the White House might even prove to be a help instead of a hindrance if Lorena Hickok, formerly of the AP, decided to seek a foreign assignment. But E.R. thought she must be joking, or at least she treated the notion semifacetiously. The First Lady jocularly noted that a woman writing about a war would be something new, indeed she herself would be tempted to join Hick—if by chance F.D.R. did not get re-elected next year. However, E.R. thought her husband probably would win another term by a small margin.

On the telephone the next morning Hick made it clear that she was serious, inspiring E.R. to write that same night: ". . . I am so glad you found that your A.P. work was really what you could stand on & now if you could just stop talking about your friendship for me & ignore it I think you would find it's practically forgotten & no one would think of it—I don't think you have to go to Europe in order to do newspaper work tho' I can see why it would be interesting & why you want to go but if you get a job in N.Y. I don't think you need fear their demands for I think they don't need you now to get any story they want."

Which did not solve much. Indeed Hick had begun to suspect that her most logical solution really was to cease being so close to this news source, as Louis Howe had suggested back in 1933. Yet Hick had to wonder if she could face such a self-inflicted torture. At the same time, she kept brooding about Europe, nerving herself to bring up the subject among some of her old newspaper buddies who might be able to help her. One of these was Mark Barron, the AP's Broadway columnist in the old days when she had been trudging back and forth to see Al Smith in the Empire State Building; now Mark was covering the war in Africa. But before she got around to writing to him, early in December E.R. noticed a little item in the Sunday *New York Times*. In case Hick had missed it, E.R. ripped it out and mailed it to her in Michigan:

WAR CORRESPONDENT
FINDS MANY TROUBLES

Poisonous Insects and Heat of
Jibuti Make an 'Insane Country
for Civilized.'

An indication of the life of war correspondents covering the Italo-Ethiopian conflict is given in the following letter sent by Mark Barron, Associated Press reporter, from Jibuti, French Somaliland, to an associate in the New York office at the organization.

"Walk over to that map in the cable department, place your hand roughly over this section of the globe and swear for the everlasting good of your mind, soul, heart and health that 'there is a place in which I'll never be caught dead or alive.'

"Even the optimistic fellow who runs this alleged hotel will go no further than to insist that the climate is 'endurable.' From 5 to 9 in the morning is all right because it's only good and hot. From 9 A.M. to 5 P.M. every thing is closed and you just lie on your bed and gasp for breath. When there is one of those desert sand storms with the heat, you stick your head under a sheet and beg for the mercy of quick suffocation.

"You have continually to shake out your bed, shoes, and clothes to get rid of scorpions and various other poisonous insects I never heard of. I am full of lice and sand fleas. I've had fever every other day with my cholera, typhoid, smallpox and other injections.

"This is really an insane country for anyone who pretends to be civilized. . . ."

Even so, Hick started the New Year of 1936 with a burst of high spirits because Hopkins had decided that she ought to spend some time in New York—and now she had a home of her own again. As of the preceding October, the two-year period for which she had sublet her Mitchell Place apartment had finally ended. She had long since realized that it had been foolish to leave herself with no other headquarters except the White House, but how very foolish it had been did not become evident until she moved back into her own premises on her return from the Midwest. Then she also reclaimed her precious Prinz from the kennel that had been keeping him, and he remembered her; in a few days it was as if they had never been separated. On the third of January, E.R. wrote to her rejoicing in Hick's satisfaction over the apartment and Prinz.

But in less than three weeks, E.R. had to feel hurt because Hick had not sounded as though she would welcome a visit from her during a quick jaunt to the city. Since Hick appeared to be so busy with other friends, would she rather that E.R. did not try to stop by over the weekend? Indeed, staying at Hick's apartment with her was an old pal who was having a difficult time. As E.R. well knew, it was really just one room, although quite a large one. "I am glad Newky is staying with you," E.R. wrote after she did pop in for a few minutes, which was all she'd had in mind anyway, "& you can give her what she needs. You are especially good at helping people who need to blow off & no one should know better than I do."

Hick continued, though, to behave rather stiffly. And E.R. seemed to be trying especially hard to please her, although somehow her efforts kept failing. Around the middle of February, E.R. sent Hick a wire: "IF YOU ARE FREE WOULD YOU CARE TO MEET ME GRAND CENTRAL STATION EIGHT FIFTY TO-NIGHT LOVE." Hick did go to the station. Although by this time the First Lady's arrivals in New York often were accomplished without any publicity, somebody had tipped off the press; since it was an otherwise quiet evening on the news front, a mob of reporters was on the scene. Just what Hick hated most. "Hick darling," E.R. wrote the next day from her apartment—now E.R. had a private little *pied-à-terre* on East Eleventh Street—"I am so very, very sorry. I ought to know it must be alone or not at all & you probably felt I brought you down under false pretenses but I didn't mean to though I did. You were sweet to telephone this morning & I am grateful."

Hick, surveying New York City and nearby parts of New Jersey for Harry Hopkins during this period, seemed more like her old self when her Aunt Ella came in from Illinois. Aunt Ella, of course, was thrilled to tears at being invited with her niece for a weekend at the White House. But in Washington Hick suddenly turned morose again because her dear silly old chatterbox of a relative was assigned to sit at the White House dinner table *right next to* the President of the United States. How could E.R. embarrass Hick this way? Nor did it console Hick that F.D.R. seemed to be enjoying himself just as much as Aunt Ella.

By the end of February, Hick's grumpiness made E.R. plead with her to see a doctor. Hick refused. Doggedly she finished an exhausting three weeks of running around New York City. Out in the most distant reaches of Brooklyn, where it was rumored that a lot of WPA money was being wasted, she found ragamuffin crews chipping ice on an airport runway more diligently than she would have believed, considering that most of the men had holes in the bottoms of their shoes the size of a quarter. "I had on heavy golf shoes and two pairs of wool socks myself—and my feet were cold," she reported to Hopkins.

Despite all of the anti-WPA sniping in the New York newspapers, she further informed him: "On the whole, dammit, it's a good show . . . This is due entirely, I think, to the kind of supervision they have . . . It's so far above the average that there just isn't any comparison! I spent a week out on the projects talking with these fellows—superintendents, foremen, sub-foremen—and I was amazed to find every darned one of them a man experienced in the kind of work that was being done. . . . Apparently not a single sub-foreman, even, sent in by some ward-heeler! These men actually know their jobs. . . . Gosh, if you could just see for yourself the contrast between New York City and Camden [New Jersey] where I was told about one supposed 'engineer' in charge of a project who didn't even know what a culvert was!"

Besides checking up on the amazing absence of political favoritism in the huge WPA operation in the nation's largest city—a happy condition she attributed to New York's feisty Mayor Fiorello La Guardia—Hick also covered the larger issue of F.D.R.'s prospects in the coming election. ". . . If things go on as they are," she wrote, "the President is going to get a tremendous majority out of New York City. Out of the great mass of little people who constitute the real population . . . I believe he'll get at least ten votes out of every twelve." To help her form this opinion, Hick, of necessity, consulted several political reporters.

She also saw a number of her old AP colleagues, including a man who had covered the Lindbergh kidnaping with her and then had left when the Hearst wire service offered him more money. Over a fine lunch, he and Hick bemoaned the inferior coverage the AP had had to rely on following their departures; emboldened by a couple of cocktails, the pair impulsively decided to stop in at the AP news room right after they left the restaurant. Arm in arm they sauntered up to the desk of the AP's executive editor, leered at him amiably, and inquired in chorus: "Do you miss us?"

Hick missed the AP a whole lot more. Perhaps to a greater extent subconsciously than by design, she was trying hard to reassert her independence. In her own writing, Hick often used common phrases so aptly that they lost their triteness; if she had been able to regard her plight dispassionately, she might well have described herself as a moth attempting to fly away from an incredibly brilliant flame. But even though Hick may not have realized what she was doing, her struggle can be clearly discerned between the lines of the letters she and E.R. wrote to each other during the early months of 1936.

In The Papers of Lorena Hickok, the absence of something else is also significant. Ever since March 4, 1933, Hick had been making her daily notations on her purse-sized calendar, using scarcely cryptic symbols to remind herself whether or not she had seen E.R. on any given day and whether the encounter had been happy or otherwise. However, at the start of 1936 Hick apparently decided to cease keeping any such private record; at any rate, only three of the calendars, for 1933, 1934 and 1935 turned up in the cartons that she donated to the F.D.R. Library. Moreover, the correspondence that she did include shows unmistakeably that Hick had resolved to stop changing her own plans whenever E.R. had time for her. It indicates, too, that Hick finally made up her mind about her job after a bad scare in April at the beginning of another trip to the Midwest as an investigator for Hopkins.

Hick was aiming for Ohio, and almost did not make it. Such a weight of fatigue hit her that she stopped and had a blood-sugar test. The doctor's verdict terrified her. No doubt about it, he said, she had diabetes. Henceforth, she would need insulin daily for the rest of her life. Weary as she was, Hick stalked out of his office determined to prove him wrong, and she checked into a hotel where she slept around the clock. The next day she went onto the miserable old diet, not a grain of sugar, or starch either. Yet she stuck to it. By the time she dared to have another test, a nice Czechoslovakian doctor in Youngstown could tell her not to worry about the insulin, if she would stay off sugar.

It had happened before. That it would probably happen again was something Hick did not care to think about, but she told herself firmly that she had better get back on the track if she wanted any more by-lines. So right after Election Day, no matter how the election went, no matter whether she had to go back to writing about ice-cream socials in Battle Creek, she would hand in a letter of resignation. She would stick it out with Hopkins until then, just on the slight chance that her reports might do some good. Gloomily, though, she surmised that nobody except E.R. bothered to read them anymore.

However, what Hick wrote from Youngstown did get read rather widely. There she found a couple of statistics that took her mind off her own troubles—and also stirred up the President of the United States. The whole affair started when Hick gave E.R. new evidence concerning a problem that had already disturbed both of them in other parts of the country. So Hick began one of her nightly letters:

> Youngstown is terribly depressing. The steel mills are running full blast, 80 per cent of capacity—as good as 1929. And yet . . .
>
> In the last three years, I was told, they've spent ten million dollars modernizing those plants, and the result is that in 1936, with the mills operating at 1929 production, they are employing 10,000 fewer men than in 1929!
>
> The whole population is worried, and the pall of smoke that hangs over the Valley—which in the old days would have meant lots of employment and prosperity—is just a big black cloud to those people now. Ninety per cent of the men [on the] WPA used to work in steel . . .
>
> To run these modernized plants, the workers will tell you, the steel companies are going out after college and high school youngsters—and the cream of the crop, at that. The process of turning a steel ingot into a sheet of steel, out of which the body of an automobile can be cut out like a paper doll, can now be performed by three or four bright young men in white shirts, who stand in a little nook away up in a gallery somewhere and press buttons! The same process [used to require] the hard, sweaty labor of a hundred men or more!

When E.R. read this letter to F.D.R., his eyes glinted. And so it came about that newspapers all over the country printed the above paragraphs a few days later. They appeared under the heading "My Day," a syndicated column in which the First Lady was now writing something very much like the diary portions of her early letters to Hick; whether or not Hick had suggested the idea cannot be proved, but she certainly encouraged it. And, in this case, she actually furnished the text. For F.D.R. apparently wanted immediate

publicity on what the brains trust called technological unemployment—and wanted it in simple language, relating to a basic industry where thousands of men had been thrown out of work by
progress. Let the Republicans try blaming *that* on the New Deal.
As E.R. explained to Hick:

> From your Youngstown letter . . . I've written my Mon-
> day piece at Franklin & Roy Howard's suggestion.° If
> you mind, I'm terribly sorry. I wanted to wire for your
> consent but Franklin won't let me. I think he makes me
> to be whipping boy & tho' he can't bring the question
> out he wants it out.

About six weeks later, on June 26, 1936, the Democratic National
Convention, without a single ballot but by acclamation, renomi-
nated Franklin Roosevelt. In the interim Hick had surveyed Minnesota, accompanied by Jeannette Brice, her librarian friend from
her days at the Leamington; more and more, she had been luring
acquaintances to ride along and enliven endless hours that otherwise would have been miserably solitary. E.R. had had no such
problem. On a last preconvention foray southward, the crowds had
been enormous. No question about it, Hot Springs and Little Rock
were for the President, E.R. wrote to Hick. "He purrs like a cat
under the enthusiasm. . . ." As for herself, E.R. wrote that she was
weary of cheering crowds but would like them less if they booed,
although that would be more interesting. Briefly resting at their son
Elliott's ranch, she read the Republican platform and found it "the
same old bunk"; although she hoped the Democrats would produce
a shorter document, "it is foolish to hope it will be less 'bunk-ish!' "
Then back to hectic campaigning, which laid Tommy low: "I can
stand this pace," E.R. added, "but the others break down & even
my head feels odd with the heat!"

That Democratic convention, lacking though it was in the
slightest suspense about who its candidate would be, still produced
one of the great moments of American political history. On the
final night, before a crowd of 105,000 jamming Philadelphia's
Franklin Field, F.D.R. delivered an acceptance speech no one present would ever forget. It was the speech in which he castigated the
"economic royalists" opposing him, and he vibrantly proclaimed:

° Roy Howard was head of the Scripps-Howard newspaper chain and, at that
point, a strong ally of F.D.R.

There is a mysterious cycle in human events. To some generations much is given. Of other generations much is expected.
This generation of Americans has a rendezvous with destiny.

But emotion beyond words bound Franklin Roosevelt and his
vast audience that night. On and on for fifteen minutes, twenty—
the cheering would not stop. At last he left the platform as the
band tried with "Auld Lang Syne" to signal that the convention
was over. Yet it was not. Airily defying his guard of Secret Service,
F.D.R., sitting in an open car with his wife beside him, smiling as
even he had never smiled before, was driven three times around
that floodlit track encircled by tier on tier of awestruck thousands
who clearly felt that they were, that very moment, participating in
a rendezvous with destiny. Even after the car left the field the
audience stood, still under the spell.

"I felt entirely detached," E.R. wrote to Hick the next night, "&
as an onlooker it was a wonderful sight. I think F. *felt* every word of
his speech . . . I'm anxious to hear if you liked it."

For once, Hick was even more detached. From a place called
Lake Breeze Resort Hotel, on the shore of Lake Superior at the
northernmost point in Michigan, Hick wrote on the Saturday night
of F.D.R.'s acceptance speech:

> Dearest:
> At last I've found the perfect place, in all the world, to
> spend a weekend. This is it. A simple, quiet, scrupulously
> clean little hotel . . . Inexpensive. Alicent and I have a
> lovely room, with water lapping against the rocks right
> outside our window, for $1.50 apiece. Very good food . . .
> Only one fly in the ointment of my content. I can't here
> [sic!] the speech tonight. The radio reception away up
> here is so bad that they don't even bother to have radios.

"Are you taking the absent treatment because it helps?" E.R. had
written to Hick a few days earlier. "If so I won't say a word. Otherwise I should say sometimes too much conscience is an unpleasant
thing! Well, dear it is for you to decide for you are the one who
suffers & I just enjoy what I can have & learned long ago to accept
what had to be—"

To Hick, what had to be was an entire summer, unrelieved by
any real holiday, proving at least to herself that she was not just a
parasite who had been put on the government payroll merely be-

cause she had an important friend. And who could tell? After South Dakota in July, Iowa in August, the worst that Europe or even Africa could offer might not seem beyond her. Just to be doing the kind of writing again that she was good at, instead of sweating over these damned reports—what a blessed relief! And wasn't it better to avoid unpleasant scenes in any way she could?

"You are right," E.R. wrote, "that your bad times when we are together are hard on us both but oh! dear why do you have to *feel* in a way which makes you have bad times, we ought to have such good & happy times together. Perhaps we will some day when I am no longer driven & we are both calmer!"

No, Hick would not blame E.R. To avoid bad times for them both, it was so much more sensible for her to stay out on the road, enlightening the First Lady about phenomena she might not otherwise be aware of. For instance from Chicago early in July, where a scorching weekend was somewhat ameliorated by the company of a young male relative of good friends from Minneapolis:

> Tonight we dined at Colisimo's, one of the less lurid night clubs, which is famous chiefly for its Capone connections . . . The inanities of sin! There was one funny thing. They had billed one June St. Clair, "America's most alluring woman." After waiting all evening, we finally saw her. She was fat, forty, very much bleached. Her hair looked like cotton. She bustled about the stage for a few seconds, looking for all the world like a worried, frowsy housewife. Then she stopped in front of the curtain, dropped her dress, which was all she had on, and stood there for a split second—naked and very *un*lovely. We laughed and left.

From Hyde Park, E.R. wrote to Hick that she had spent two hours with F.D.R., Jim Farley, Charley Michelson, Stanley High and Forbes Morgan. All of these men in her husband's inner circle of advisers and money-raisers apparently saw no peculiarity in the presence of the President's wife at the first high-level strategy discussion since the nomination; by now, E.R.'s political acumen was gaining respect, not only because she had been proving herself an apt pupil but also because she had, whether they liked it or not, turned into quite an asset. It was during this campaign that the nasty tide of Eleanor jokes mounted alarmingly, and there had been some thought about keeping her in the background as much as

possible until the election was over. However, a few solo appearances by F.D.R. on the back platform of his special train during preconvention whistle-stopping had changed some minds.
When the crowds started shouting for Eleanor, the politicians conceded that she had become practically as popular as her husband,
at least among those Democrats who didn't mind her inviting colored people to the White House. And if all of her lecturing and
gallivanting irritated some other voters, they were probably the
ones who'd vote anyway for the Republican candidate, Governor
Alf M. Landon of Kansas.

It must be terribly hot in Kansas, E.R. wrote to Hick traversing
Landon's home state. How was her health standing the strain?

"This summer is going very fast," Hick reassured her. "There *has*
been some hard work, some physical discomfort, and the ever-pres-
ent sense of futility . . . And yet—as I'm about to give it up, I realize
what a fascinating job this has been . . . whatever I'm doing a year
from now—if I'm doing anything—I'll look back on this as one grand
summer."

On the whole, Hick informed E.R. at the beginning of August,
the Landon speech she had just heard over the radio in her hotel
lobby had seemed fairly honest and straightforward. But granting
that he was a well-meaning man, better acquainted with the country's problems than most of his supporters, how much could he do?
For his backers were a crowd of men abysmally ignorant of how
bad the situation was in many areas, including the Dakotas. "I get
scared when I think of it," Hick wrote. "Awfully scared."

It was from Aberdeen in South Dakota that Hick was writing.
Under no circumstances could her return here be happy, but under
the conditions prevailing in the fourth summer of the region's worst
drought in history, no wonder she was shaken. Aberdeen that day
was experiencing its twenty-first consecutive day of temperatures
above one hundred. "They were eating their lunch when I got
there," she wrote of a group of local farmers the WPA had put to
work on a water storage project:

> Just bundles of old rags, they were, huddled inside a
> group of old, rackety cars, against the pitiless sun and the
> scorching wind and dust. They looked like the pictures of
> starving Chinese or Mongolians one sometimes sees in

the Sunday rotogravure sections. When they spoke to me
in English, the effect was rather startling. . . .

And in addition to four years of drought, now there were grasshoppers. "You never saw such grasshoppers! Big as bats . . ." The
cattle were dying, the whole landscape was dying—while Landon's
backers talked of eliminating the waste of taxpayer money on the
WPA and other New Deal programs that were keeping millions of
Americans barely alive. "Darling," Hick demanded, "do they still
feel as complacent in Washington about this election as they did?"
And then: "Oh, Lord, so much more is involved than any one man's
future or his ambition."

"I don't think F. is exactly complacent," E.R. wrote back. "I
think he believes it is a stiff fight but he will win out. He does
realize conditions, that I am sure about & I think after the election
. he will fight for things he'd not dare undertake in the past four
years. I feel he should go on & I don't mind personally, dear, for
perhaps I'll be freer when no election lies ahead. Besides, you are
right, personal preferences don't count & I am rarely unhappy."

E.R. wrote from Campobello, where she was relaxing—as much
as she could with her mother-in-law in close proximity—before embarking on the campaign trail: "I have a feeling that the tide is
setting pretty hard against F.D.R. just now but there is time to turn
it. I feel as usual, completely objective & oh! Lord so indifferent!"
Nevertheless, about the mental and physical strain that Hick was
undergoing, E.R.'s feelings were less dispassionate. "I wish I could
send you some of our cool air," she wrote, "or better still that you
could get on a magic carpet & come & share my room tonight, but
you wouldn't enjoy the *days* any more than I do!"

E.R.'s references to her own indifference about the election result stimulated an extraordinary dialogue. From Pierre in drought-
ravaged South Dakota, Hick was inspired to deliver quite a lecture
to the First Lady:

Dearest:
. . . I'm wondering if you—or I—or any other enlightened
person really has any right to be as indifferent about the
outcome of this election as you are. Oh, I know—you

hate it all. The "position." And so do I when I'm with you. I can't even be polite about it. You can. I know that you at least think you would be happier if you were not in Washington. Perhaps you would. And you are disillusioned, being around them too much. A daily dose of Mac and Missy, along with all the fuss and pomp and adulation the man receives will distort anyone's view.°
And you, personally, would like to be free. Well—it all boils down to this: All your personal inclination would be to rejoice in defeat. And, so far as evaluating the President and his administration go—you "can't see the woods for the trees." I think I may have a little better perspective now. I've been out of the mess, more or less, for a couple of months. With all his faults—and the faults of some of the people around him—I still think he is a very great man. His defeat—and I'm awfully afraid he may be defeated—will be a terrible calamity for millions of people in this country. The kind of people *you*, of all people, are supposed to care about. The poor and the lowly. Forgive me if I have offended you. After all, *you* have several times told *me I'm* an egoist!

E.R.'s response came from Hyde Park, where she was girding herself for a couple of days every week at the Democratic Committee headquarters in New York until she began traveling with her husband after Labor Day.

> [Your] letter sounded like an effort to convert me but really my dear I am doing all I can without being accused of trying to run F.D.R. One can be personally indifferent & yet do one's duty. As a matter of fact it is only when one is in oneself very unhappy that one ever thinks about the individual right to the pursuit of happiness. When you reach my age [E.R. was fifty-one that summer] it comes less & less often & I judge that for the moment you are not thinking about it much either . . .
> Let me tell you a secret dear. I know I'll not be happy in Washington nor out of it so the surroundings don't matter much. I'll get on alright anyhow & tho' I'm not sure anyone is very important still I agree that we must make an effort for what is apparently best.

° Mac was Marvin McIntyre, F.D.R.'s appointments secretary; Missy was Marguerite LeHand, F.D.R.'s personal secretary.

Then E.R. had to add a few days later:

> I'm afraid my reasons for thinking I will probably never
> be much happier than I am are different from yours dear.
> You think some one thing could make you happy, I know
> it never does! We are not happy because we don't know
> what would make us happy, we may want something &
> when we have it, it is not what we dreamed it would be,
> the thing lies in oneself!

Because Hick had accused E.R. of undervaluing herself, E.R.
went on:

> . . . I truly don't think that what I do or say makes much
> difference, someone else *could* do equally well what I do.
> Now you or Marty are different.° You have gifts & can
> really get somewhere & I think you both will.

The longest separation since they had known each other was
almost over. By early September Hick was driving eastward, stopping again to see Alicent in Grand Rapids, still uncertain about her
own future. To E.R. she had recently expressed a more decisive
inclination than at any time previously. "I wonder if that Spanish
business *is* going to lead to a European war!" she had mused. "Boy,
if it happens, I'll be tempted to drop everything and go to New
York and try to land a job!" Nevertheless, as General Franco's
forces kept advancing, while Madrid was being bombed, Hick
made her way back to Washington a little behind schedule.

For E.R. had undertaken one more outing, just with Tommy,
before the campaign got into full swing. This First Lady was absolutely incapable of emulating Marie Antoinette in any important
way. However, having never in her life been required to make a
bed, Eleanor Roosevelt—quite in the manner of Versailles royalty
playing shepherdess—had conceived that it would be relaxing to
spend ten days cleaning up the house near Albany where her ex-
trooper friend Earl Miller would soon be bringing his new bride.

Not only sewing and hanging curtains but actual scrubbing
turned out to be required. Tommy, with her own apartment a few
blocks from the White House, sputtered a bit about not really
needing an intensive course in domestic science. But she had
brought along her typewriter because of those "My Day" columns.

° Martha Gellhorn, the future novelist then working for Harry Hopkins.

Since Tommy's employer was just now learning to use a typewriter herself, it was necessary for Tommy to take down every column in shorthand and then provide a neat copy. It went without saying that no telegraph operator in America could be trusted to decipher a handwritten opus by the First Lady, and the columns were due six days every week at the headquarters of Roy Howard's newspaper syndicate.

Hick found it particularly interesting that her friend the columnist was proving to be very popular among newspaper readers. As the syndicate's profit from selling this feature to dailies all over the country must be considerable, the name of Roy Howard now led her own mental list of potential employers. Surely if E.R. said a word on her behalf . . . But Tommy, the invaluable Tommy, had put forward another name—that of Grover Whalen. This dapper gentleman was sometimes called New York City's official greeter because he was usually on hand, with a suitable posy adorning his lapel, when any celebrity came to town. Now he was organizing a project that would require much cooperation, and money, from Washington. As head of the group planning a spectacular World's Fair in 1939, wouldn't he be receptive to hiring a writer who happened to be a close friend of the First Lady?

Hence a portentous contest was shaping up in Hick's mind that September. On her good days, when she awoke telling herself she was *only* forty-three, she felt buoyant as a cork bobbing in the ocean. That diamond sparkle at the crest of the next wave—oh, she could hardly wait to reach it! So of course she'd take the chance and opt for Europe. But then there were mornings when the weight that dragged her down made her think no, it was too late now. Well, somehow in the coming weeks she would have to make a decision.

From E.R.'s standpoint, the choice was easy although she expressed her opinion in her own wonderfully elliptical way: "I'd hate to go to Europe & see a war but if you really want it I'll speak to Roy Howard if you think it would help. Tommy thinks Whalen would give you the N.Y. Fair publicity job. Well, we can talk all these things over." In short, E.R. would much rather have Hick on this side of the Atlantic. Whenever they were separated by more than a few hundred miles, and she could not reach Hick by telephone to say goodnight without feeling dreadfully extravagant, E.R.'s letters constantly mentioned missing her. Of course, E.R.

wanted Hick to be happy, but wouldn't she be ever so much happier in New York, where she had so many friends, and Prinz? And wouldn't it be stimulating to try something new like writing publicity? Of course, E.R. could not possibly realize how lowly a writer of handouts must be in the eyes of an old newspaper person.

Up near Albany, E.R. was finding her own plunge into domesticity unexpectedly wearing; before dinner one evening toward the end of the week she sent Tommy to buy some aspirin. Meanwhile Hick was visiting Battle Creek on the last leg of her journey back to Washington, where she and the First Lady were to have their first reunion in nearly four months. In Battle Creek, Hick found herself obliged to do a little thinking out loud when she accompanied Leta Browning to work one morning.

Leta had become the hostess at Dr. Kellogg's Sanitarium, and she was supposed to ask eminent visitors for their definition of a word that especially interested the Kelloggs. "What is success, Lorena?" Leta inquired. "Why ask me?" this visitor demurred. Because, said Leta, her picture had been in the *Literary Digest,* she had started from the bottom and risen to the White House. So Lorena Hickok, choosing her words carefully, answered: "Success is the ability to live with the greatest amount of peace and contentment, not only for yourself but for those with whom you come into contact, by choice or necessity."

When Hick arrived at the White House, she found Mrs. R. in bed with a temperature of 104 degrees and two doctors plus a couple of nurses hovering over her. Eventually, the diagnosis was intestinal flu, complicated by exhaustion. A full week later, E.R. was still relying on Hick to read aloud to her. During a spare few minutes, Hick dashed off a delayed thank-you note to the Brownings, telling them about Mrs. Roosevelt's illness. "She had us all badly frightened," Hick wrote. "I don't think I had ever realized before quite how much she meant to me—"

E.R.'s first letter to Hick after they resumed their separate ways offered a well-earned reward. All of Hick's fight had been worthwhile, E.R. assured her, because now it was grand to be with her and feel no strain.

Still it was not until six days later that Hick finally made up her mind. On the morning of October 2, 1936, from her apartment in New York, she telephoned E.R. at the Albany hotel where the First Lady was attending a youth conference. The preceding evening E.R. had started a letter to Hick, asking about the new assignment Hick had been expecting to receive for her last trip on the government payroll. ". . . I pray that you are not going far away!" E.R. had written just before putting down her pen upon being interrupted.

By the time she picked up her pen again, she had received Hick's telephone call, and she added:

> A world of love dear one & I'll write Grover Whalen at once.
>
> You peach!
> E.R.

PART III

"I'll be relieved when it's over . . ."
1937–1968

14. Drifting Apart

In that October of 1936, the ground swelled, the bandwagon got rolling, every cliché in the vocabulary of politics pointed toward a landslide victory for F.D.R. "I never have seen . . . such crowds or such enthusiasm," E.R. wrote to Hick as the campaign special pulled out of St. Louis. "If it doesn't mean votes then we are a dissembling people for they answer F.D.R.'s questions with a roar." After signing her initials, she added: "How I hate being a show but I'm doing it so nicely!"

Then because Hick had taxed her again with lacking the proper attitude, E.R. two days later assured her: "Dear, I realize more & more that F.D.R. is a great man & he is nice to me but as a person, I'm a stranger & I don't want to be anything else." That was on the third page of the three and a half pages she scrawled before retiring; other matters of more immediate concern to Hick, and to her, had to be dealt with first. Yes, she had dictated the letter to Grover Whalen, but it had gone to Washington to be addressed. And Hick's report from Philadelphia would certainly be read carefully. "I displayed so much knowledge of the relief situation in Michigan," E.R. added, "that the gentlemen of the state looked astounded & I never let on where I got my information but F. knew & was amused!"

There was also E.R.'s own literary activity to discuss. Right after the convention, she had offhandedly mentioned to Hick that she might try writing something about her girlhood while she accompanied F.D.R. on his autumnal whistle-stopping. Merely to sit and knit between platform appearances would make her nervous, no matter if Hick did find it possible to ride with her; since Hick did not, E.R. had arranged for Earl's friend, that companionable puss Tiny Chaney, to join her along part of the route. Even so, and

221

despite the endless politicking all around her—in which E.R. took a definite interest—by Election Day she had dictated more than a hundred pages of her autobiography.

Hick, knowing her, was hardly startled by the quantity of manuscript that she kept receiving from the campaign special for her own comments and suggestions. But Hick also knew something about writing, so the quality of those pages awed her. At least thus far her friend clearly needed no help from her, although E.R. still wanted reassurance: "I hope you'll think [the latest installment] interesting tho' you may think I dwell too long on the 'little girl' period." She also confided: "I've been honest so far about everything & I dread the grown up years!"

Well. Originally, E.R. had been planning to stop at 1900, when she had turned sixteen. After that, the life story of this First Lady was to have been Hick's responsibility or, more crudely, her meal ticket. Nevertheless, there is no shred of evidence over the next three decades that Lorena Hickok ever expressed resentment over such a casual usurpation of what she had repeatedly been encouraged to consider her own preserve. Instead Hick gave enthusiastic praise to every E.R. chapter. She expressed pride in her friend's emergence as a real writer, and she deprecated her own abilities so convincingly that it would be impossible to suspect her of dissembling. Only somewhere below all of her self-disparagement did that seed of anger slowly sprout.

On the surface Hick displayed intense longing to be employed by Grover Whalen. A few days after F.D.R.'s smashing victory over Landon—this time the President had carried forty-six of the forty-eight states, losing only Maine and Vermont—she finally was summoned for an interview at the World's Fair office in the Empire State Building. Whalen "didn't swoon exactly," Hick wrote to E.R., but as long as he requested a memo about her qualifications, she almost succeeded in blowing her own horn. Besides her twenty years of newspaper work and her three years as a confidential observer for Harry Hopkins, Hick added: "I have also done a little investigating for the President."

Then she worried, not merely about whether she had bragged unbecomingly; she worried because, dammit, she *needed* that hundred dollars a week Whalen had indicated he would be willing to pay. Her nerve endings quivered so painfully that she completely lost her perspective about another small problem. And she sent a long, tense letter to E.R., off lecturing in the Middle West, imploring that a couple of dozen people who had once been kind to Lorena Hickok in Minneapolis might have their hands shaken after E.R.'s address in that city. The problem was that E.R. would be staying with the Dillons, who were Hick's most prominent friends there, and suddenly Hick could not bear the thought that her other friends might think she was turning into a snob. To soothe her, E.R. had them all to tea. Then in Milwaukee the First Lady tried to pacify Hick further by asking her press conference about Edna Ferber's coffee shop. Had she not been told that it no longer existed, E.R. said, she would have managed to get there to find out whether the pastry was still as good as Hick remembered.

Of course, Hick got the job. It would start at the first of the year, in January 1937, when her six weeks of accumulated leave were used up and she officially left the government payroll. The minute she heard from Whalen she sent an elated wire to E.R., and then she plunged into list-making. All right, she told herself, no more page-one stories; she would just be grinding out handouts from now on. But at least she would be able to afford a little better treatment for her poor old body. So at the top of her list, unpleasant and yet necessary, she would take care of her teeth. Also get a maid to clean her apartment regularly. Come spring, a new car. Yes, that was essential—because she was going to be spending her weekends at the most perfect little house-in-the country on the whole face of this earth.

For something good had come, after all, of that horrendous trip with E.R. to San Francisco and Yosemite. Hick, remembering how she had hesitated about returning to the Dana ranch by herself when she was driving eastward alone, had to feel shivery. But thank heaven she *had* stopped and got comfortable enough with Bill, and even Ella, to go out to their place on Long Island the following spring without shaking over what to wear. The trousers and plaid shirt she had picked up out West for her ill-fated horseback ride were really all she needed, and this time it was fun wearing them. Bill's dogs immediately took to her; they must have sniffed Prinz. As for Hick herself, she took to everything out there.

It was like a separate world, a mile and a half through the woods on a dirt road before you came to the cleared area. Then nothing so fancy as lawn, just fields and meadow where "Bossy" or a few horses might be pastured, with here and there more woods, and sandy lanes leading down to the water; other lanes wound toward one or another house nestling out of sight of any of the others, mostly old and unpretentious because they had originally been farm buildings. Hick still had no idea how many houses there were altogether, although by now she knew why such a place of utter peace still existed hardly more than two hours from New York City.

Ella Dana was a Floyd. Her ancestor who had signed the Declaration of Independence and had also served as one of George Washington's generals had, in addition, amassed considerable property along the Great South Bay. Indeed the major north-south route in the vicinity now was the General William Floyd Parkway. And Ella had other connections, too. She had made her debut at a reception given by her cousin, Mrs. J. Pierpont Morgan.

Like E.R., Ella had lost her parents at an early age; she had been brought up by her Grandmother Floyd in the main farmhouse— parts of it dated back to the 1700's—where she and Bill usually stayed when they came east. They had a newer alternative, though. The house in which Bill Dana had been raised was nearer the water, and thus cooler during muggy weather. For Bill and Ella had been the children of neighboring estates which were now united; to Hick their story seemed practically Shakespearean.

Unlike E.R., Ella had been beautiful, headstrong, a tomboy. Yet she decided after her debut to become an actress, which idea so horrified her grandmother that Ella's other notion, of becoming a scientific farmer, seemed harmless by comparison. So Ella had actually enrolled for an agricultural course at the University of Wisconsin back before the World War, when it had not been easy for a woman to gain admission to any such program. Ella's motive had been to provide herself with practical knowledge about soil and fertilizers, which scarcely interested Bill.

For of course they would sooner or later marry. However, only over Grandmother Floyd's dead body, because to her William Shepherd Dana was impossibly common. His family had been nothing until his grandfather had founded a publication called the *Financial Chronicle* and also struck it rich on Wall Street, so that he could build a country seat abutting the Floyd preserve. In the bargain, young Bill Dana was no good. Instead of going to law school, or even working for his grandfather, he just roamed the woods with his dogs—and drank with local fishermen at taverns near the railroad station.

Headstrong as Ella was, she had let her grandmother persuade her to marry a well-bred architect instead—and thereby changed Lorena Hickok's life twenty years later. For as a wedding present Grandmother Floyd had allowed Ella's architect to build a charming white frame replica of the big farmhouse, reduced in every dimension but by no means tiny; here Ella and her first husband had lived, increasingly unhappy, while Bill Dana enlisted as a buck private in the war, married a nurse and took to serious drinking until Ella's husband left the scene. Then Bill gave up the bottle. But Bill and Ella's happy ending had already receded ten years into the past by the time Hick met them. Now if Ella struck Hick as a little too glossy, and a little too restless, for nice shaggy Bill—it was Ella who offered, out of the blue, to fix up the little house so Hick could use it as her very own.

The Little House! But no, Hick stammered, she couldn't accept, she couldn't afford . . . Ella would not listen. Ella insisted that she liked to fix up houses, maybe she should have been an interior decorator, she had plenty of old furniture around and it would give her something to do. Besides, she liked to have people near her who appreciated unspoiled simplicity instead of the cocktail-party atmosphere farther out at the Hamptons, so it was all settled.

Not quite, Hick kept protesting. Still Ella went ahead with her painting and arranging, while an idea struck Hick. By getting a decent-paying job in New York, she really might swing it—if she shared the rent with somebody. Of course, it would have to be someone she could stand having around constantly, and vice versa, which eliminated just about the entire population of the universe. No, there was one person, although it might raise some eyebrows. He would be ideal, though.

Young Howard, twelve years younger than Hick but looking even more of a kid because he was so skinny, had turned up from Minnesota while she had still been with the Associated Press. Naturally she took pity on the poor lad alone in the big city, not that Howard Haycraft needed any real help from her; he had a good job at a firm putting out reference books, and in his quiet way he was such a whiz that she would not be surprised if he ended as the president of the company. Meanwhile, he liked the same music she did, he had a fine record player in his apartment near First Avenue,

and they spent so many Sunday afternoons listening to Wagner or
Mahler that he'd got to be almost like her little brother. In fact, one
summer when Ruby and Julian had taken a cottage at Oak Beach,
she and Howard had shared the adjoining cottage for a week with
no friction whatever; that boy could even bear Ruby's incessant
chatter.

So Hick had brought Howard out to Mastic for a weekend, he
and Bill went sailing two glorious days while she and Ella puttered
domestically, and by Sunday evening it was all set. Depending, of
course, on whether Hick got the World's Fair job, she and Howard
would have the Little House, starting in April of 1937. If Hick had
no idea at all of money, neither did Ella; the rent for this cozy
dream—on its own couple of acres, with three fireplaces and four
bedrooms so that Hick and Howard could each have their own
guests every single weekend, should they wish to—was to be thirty-
five dollars a month. Thus Hick's share would be seventeen dollars
and fifty cents.

To keep her self-respect, Hick thought that in her spare time she
had better do something more elevating than publicity. More accurately, promotion was what her job would be, not that it made
much difference; at any rate, right after Whalen told her she could
come to work in January she ambitiously pledged to E.R. that she,
too, was going to write a book. That gratified E.R. because she was
always encouraging Hick, and envying her gift with words. What,
at last, had Hick determined to write about?

Since E.R. herself seemed to feel that Hick's travels around the
country at the depth of the Depression had given her a unique
experience, why not a book on the *people* Hick had encountered?
Of course, Hick hastily explained, she did not mean any sort of
exposé that could possibly embarrass the President or his wife, or
Harry Hopkins, or anyone connected with the Administration. She
was thinking of little sketches, not fictionalized the way Marty
Gellhorn had done it, but actual chunks from the best of her own
reports depicting the individuals on relief—the much maligned
"chiselers" and "shovel-leaners" among whose ranks, but for the
grace of God, even you or I might have been. An excellent idea,
E.R. replied. She would tell George Bye, her literary agent, to
expect a call from her friend Miss Hickok. Which resulted in Hick's
writing to E.R. some weeks later:

"Good Lord," [Bye] said, "are you always so humble
and unsure of yourself in anything you do?"

"No," I assured him. "I was a darned good reporter
and knew I was."

Still E.R.'s agent did seem to think she *might* have a book in her,
"So—with George Bye leading me by the hand, and with you push-
ing from behind, I *may* write a book!" That was as far as Hick was
willing to commit herself when she undertook to start the project
during her free time before she would finally report to Grover
Whalen on the first Monday of 1937.

Part of that period Hick spent in the White House, while E.R.
continued with her lecture tour. As usual, Hick slept on the day
bed in E.R.'s sitting room, where there was a metal plate riveted
into the mantel stating that Abraham Lincoln had occupied this
chamber during the Civil War years. Hick, lying awake, had often
thought about him pacing up and down through the night, worrying. But on this visit she had further reason for historical reflection
because a sort of office had also been assigned to her, at the First
Lady's request, in the mansion's two-room Lincoln Suite, so named
because the larger room now contained the forbidding-looking bed
in which Lincoln was supposed to have slept. However, it was at a
desk in the adjoining little room that had recently been Louis
Howe's that Hick went through all of the letters she had sent to
E.R. since 1933, seeking quotable extracts. Delving into her own
personal past proved unexpectedly painful.

For E.R., with quite unintentional cruelty, wrote from Chicago
to Hick in Washington that she had thought of her upon reading
about the death of Mme. Schumann-Heink. "Would you like to
wear her ring now," the First Lady blandly asked, "or put it into
safekeeping? I am careful of it but I never want you to feel you
can't do what you want with it!"

This careless blow fell just as Hick was reliving those days when
the ring had meant so much to them both. After a long, dreary,
rainy Sunday alone in the White House, Hick apparently forgave
her, for she wrote to E.R.:

> Today I stumbled into a lot of the early letters written
> while I was still with the AP. Dear, whatever may have
> happened since—whatever may happen in the future—I
> was certainly happy those days, much happier, I believe,

than many people are in all their lives. You gave me that, and I'm deeply grateful. There were other times, too—many, many of them. What do you want me to do with these letters when I have finished? Throw them away?

And then Hick, musing as she wrote, demonstrated that she preferred to harbor no ungenerous thoughts about that autobiography:

In a way, I'd like to keep them, or have them kept somewhere. They constitute a sort of diary, as yours to me probably do, too. They might be of some use when I get around to that biography. What do you think? . . . In a way, I haven't minded reading them so much today, although some of them make me feel a little wistful. I don't suppose anyone can ever stay so happy as I was that first year or so, though. Do you?

Apparently Hick did keep a few dozen of her own letters that contained vivid accounts of some of her experiences as an investigator for Harry Hopkins. Why she also kept a seemingly random sampling of her more personal communications to E.R. cannot be explained, nor can her subsequent retrieval of hundreds of other letters that she wrote to the First Lady. It must be assumed that haphazardly, almost subconsciously, she was attempting to preserve documentary evidence about *her* life, not merely about Eleanor Roosevelt's. Perhaps she had an amorphous idea of someday writing an autobiography herself. Or possibly she just could not bear the loss of all traces of her greatest emotional experience.

Still, if Hick chose to remember "that first year or so" as supremely happy, it was because time had already dimmed those less than joyous moments right after E.R. moved into the White House in March, 1933. Night after night then, Hick, alone in New York, had cried herself to sleep. So the letters that Hick eventually did save testify perhaps more reliably than she herself might have about some aspects of her relationship with E.R. No matter that the correspondence has many gaps, the broad picture is unmistakable; by early December, 1936, when Hick wrote to E.R. about how happy she once had been, the most intensely emotional period of her life had already receded into wistful memory.

In Washington during that last month of 1936, Hick diligently copied excerpts from her letters for the book she was planning then, and she paid a stenographer to help her. She also acquired two memories of lasting satisfaction. She took a whole day off from her research to ride down to Virginia for the funeral of a son of E.R.'s personal maid, Mabel Haley, at a Negro church where she was the only white person among the mourners. But how could she not have gone, when Mabel was always so sweet to her? And she also handed in her formal resignation at the WPA headquarters without the slightest regret; she thought it would have taken the hide of an elephant to stay on, protected by her friend in the White House, while postelection firings were slashing mercilessly throughout the agency.

But back in New York when Hick brought George Bye her sample material for her WPA book, he completely discouraged her. "All he can think of getting out of me," she wrote to E.R., "is some 'dirt' on Harry and the WPA, which of course I'd never give him."

On Christmas Eve, from Washington, E.R. called Hick in New York because Franklin junior up in Cambridge had some painful problem with his nose that was preventing his coming home for the holiday. E.R. was about to board a train so that she, at least, would share his hospital feast. Could Hick possibly join her? A few hours later Hick met her on the train in New York and rode to Boston with her. By now Hick understood that E.R. hated to be alone, although the idea of solitary peace and quiet always seemed appealing to the First Lady. Then Hick rode back to New York on Christmas morning, by herself. But she was used to that. If she could, with this silly job, spare the time to be of some use to E.R.— well, she would try not to complain.

Silly! It turned out to be asinine. When Hick reported for work at the World's Fair office on January 4, 1937, they assigned her, first of all, to run a poster contest among school children. After years of refusing to cover the Girl Scouts, now she was supposed to be something like a glorified Scout leader promoting entries into a competition among artistic tykes all around the country. Celebrating the "trylon and perisphere" that were the futuristic symbols of this disorganized fiasco. According to the Fair's officials, an administration building was being rushed to completion out at the Flushing Meadow site that would allegedly be transformed into a glorious vision in less than two years. But at its temporary head-quarters in the Empire State Building, chaos reigned. Nobody knew who was in charge of what. Yet Hick gathered that besides planning stunts such as the poster nonsense, she was also expected to write stop-the-press publicity releases about her every enterprise. Of course she knew most of these releases would land in newspaper waste baskets. Nevertheless, she did not say much about any of this to E.R.

At least for the first month or so, Hick's nightly letters to the First Lady were mostly optimistic. However, Hick was more prone than most mortals to psychosomatic illness, and after only one week she felt such aches, even if she had no fever, that she stayed home in bed a good part of the second week. Not long after returning she confessed by mail to her old editor in Minneapolis, who promptly dispatched an inimitable Dillon pep talk.

"You were evidently in one of your emotional slumps," he started. "I am not greatly concerned about that, because I know you'll plump out of it. But there are a few things I should say to you . . ." When she had been a reporter, he proceeded, she had got used to writing something and then seeing it in print an hour later with a by-line proving her accomplishment, so she carried over that expectation in the writing of publicity. No wonder she felt disappointed, disgusted and despondent. Publicity was different, he reminded her, because it was one thing to write about the sinking of the *Vestris* and decidedly another to dream up ballyhoo about an event two years in the future.

"If you can bat .333 in the publicity league," Dillon told her, "you'll lead the league by a wide margin. . . . If you can pull stunts for dog derbies etc., you can put Grover and his fair across. You know all this as well as I. In fact you'd be writing almost an identical letter to a friend in your position. Why don't you write a letter to yourself?"

Of course, Tom Dillon was right. Since she wanted the money, she had better get used to being a nobody. Not that every reporter giving up an underpaid profession would have felt quite the same sense of diminishment that afflicted Hick. For if press agentry still had a slightly disreputable aura that harked back to the carnival barkers who were its founders, of late much of the tarnish had been polished away by high-toned practitioners emulating the masterly redeemer of old John D. Rockefeller. Nevertheless, Hick's own ego was so lacking in ballast that she dreadfully missed the stabilizing effect of her former by-lines.

Indeed a peculiar change in her handwriting occurred right after she stifled her hope of becoming a war correspondent. Although graphology is by no means a precise science, even a skeptic must wonder if pure coincidence can account for Hick's new style of forming "I" once she began working at the World's Fair. Previously, she had written the first person pronoun with a fine cursive amplitude: *ℐ* Thenceforth, while the rest of her penmanship remained distinctively rounded, her every reference to herself was reduced to one meek line:

And she did have a new reason for feeling personally insignificant. No matter that she herself had chosen this job in order to retain a close tie with E.R., somehow Hick had expected that when she left the government payroll other people would stop paying much attention to the fact that she was Mrs. Roosevelt's friend. It did not happen. During her first week on the new job, her immediate boss summoned her to his Park Avenue apartment for a party, prefacing his invitation with the detestable remark: "Of course, it isn't so swanky as the White House—"

Certainly Hick had anticipated that she might now and then have to ask a favor of the President's wife. ". . . And if you don't want to do it," she wrote to E.R., "you won't hesitate to say so, will you?" However, she had not bargained on being treated like the Fair's lackey in soliciting petty favors from Washington. Could Mrs. Roosevelt welcome some foreigners Whalen wanted to impress? What about a dinner with the President for Grover? "I'm not disturbed about it," Hick tried to convince E.R., "—so long as they don't ask me to do anything dirty." Then two days later, having telephoned E.R. a list of urgent guests, she attempted to convey a tolerantly amused attitude. "Thanks ever so much for taking care of all those people," she wrote to E.R. "I hate to bother you with them, but since I took the job, and since everybody in the organization apparently knows how I got it—well? I may as well do all I can, within reason, to make everybody happy!"

E.R. herself seemed not to mind Hick's requests. However, the extra flurry of White House activity accompanying the start of her husband's second term—on January 20, because the Constitution had been amended to change the inaugural date—did precipitate a mood similar to, if much less intense than, the First Lady's 1933 trauma. ". . . My sense of four years more beginning bothered me," E.R. wrote. "Why can't someone have this job who'd like it & do something worthwhile with it?"

Hick had learned, though, that E.R. needed only minor assistance these days to cope with staring strangers. "Honey, don't let 'the eyes' get you!" Hick advised. "Just look right over their heads as you've always done." Would that Hick herself could have been similarly composed confronting the lesser demands she was subjected to at her office—but to be considered simply a conduit made her furious. "I guess my trouble is that, even at the ripe age of forty-four, I still have not learned to live comfortably with people," she informed E.R. "I loathe them and despise them, mostly. Pigs!"

As usual, Hick was downgrading herself. Everywhere she went she stimulated strong reactions, and she did repel a portion of the people she encountered. Her exuberance no less than her wrath made them uncomfortable to the extent that they would remember her as gross, coarse, a singularly unattractive woman. Yet the same intensity more often had a different effect, and she enchanted quite an assortment of admirers along her travels. Among these, the Naval Reserve officer who was Grover Whalen's second in command invited her for a drink one afternoon when she had put up a few storm signals, and told her: "You are a true aristocrat, my dear." So Commander Flanagan listened sympathetically to Hick's tale of woe regarding the White House, and he agreed with her that she ought not to be expected to pester her friend there. If Grover made any further requests that she could not feel comfortable about relaying, Hick was to let the Commander know—and he would take the gaff himself.

That left Hick just a silly and irritating job, instead of an impossible one. Since a couple of likely-sounding alternatives all fizzled as soon as she began investigating them—and also since hordes of unemployed people kept pleading for Fair jobs—she really did try to make the best of things at the office. Thanks to the Commander's secretary, Barbara, who struck Hick as a delightful child, she enjoyed lunch hours at least. If only Hick's away-from-the-office existence had been more satisfactory, maybe she might not feel so weary all the time.

Although the city part of her life was less than satisfying, it was certainly busy; no wonder she dragged her feet on her way to work.

There were, first of all, her pals from the AP to catch up with, and several had endless tales of marital distress requiring sympathy from good old Hick. It tore her more, though, to see friends like Matty White, sixty and jobless, so she *had* to find something for him, via Washington. Also, dammit, for that amusing but spineless Julian her sister was still supporting.

At least Hick's theater friends did not expect her to use her pull for them; Jean Dixon, who now had a rich husband, just smiled when E.R. offered to lure F.D.R. to her new play, as if that would help, after it had been panned by the critics. It was through Jean, formerly of a Minneapolis repertory company, that Hick now had quite a theatrical acquaintanceship and went to parties where she met the Fredric Marches or Judith Anderson. One evening, Hick wrote to E.R., "Judy" appeared at her apartment with a bottle of gin and two dachshunds; Hick shut Prinz up in the dressing room so he could not break their backs, ordered sandwiches from the corner drug store, and settled down for a long, sad story about the man in Judy's life. However, Hick had to rue every such encounter—she could not sleep the next morning the way theatrical people could. In order to give Prinz some exercise, then get herself put together properly, she set her alarm to ring at five-thirty, and only rarely did she loll in bed much later than six.

Even so, quite a procession of out-of-towners took advantage of her couch right in the same room as that alarm clock. It was a lifesaver to Carolyn from a St. Louis suburb; she had been a promising reporter back when Hick, too, had been a lot younger, but when Hick looked her up on one of her WPA trips, she was appalled by the change. For Carolyn's husband bored Carolyn to tears—and with three adolescents still depending on her, how could she leave him? After three weeks in New York with Hick, "C" went home much happier.

Then Alicent came for a week. As a Christmas present, Hick had sent Ellie a round-trip ticket. Before she left, Newky arrived from Scranton. The incessant talk got on Hick's nerves, the expense of so many extra theater tickets demolished her budget, and worst of all, she could barely keep up with her ambitious program for being well-groomed.

Shields. That word, as recently as Hick's day, was the bane of every working woman's existence; neither pharmaceutical nor advertising ingenuity had yet solved the problem of perspiration, and the winter wools of the 1930's, the summer linens, were far more susceptible to unremovable stains than later dress materials would be. Thus the constant sewing-in and ripping-out of washable little crescents was necessary, as was similar activity involving removable white collars and cuffs. Plus an amount of ironing, and even button-sewing, that must seem incredible in the age of miracle fabrics and the zipper.

While none of this was new to Hick, she had been spoiled in the White House during recent years by E.R.'s maid, Mabel Haley. Furthermore, she had never cared as much about looking stylish as she did now that she was practically an executive. However, thanks to E.R., Hick had no shortage of expensive-looking outfits. By now E.R. had learned to order the better part of her wardrobe from Milgrim's or from a custom tailor, instead of just grabbing items off the rack at dowdy Arnold Constable's. So Hick, for her birthday and for Christmas, was receiving handwoven fabric in substantial yardage.

Out of this material, E.R.'s tailor created made-to-measure suits or coats or dresses, sending the bill to the White House. E.R. assured Hick it all cost less than Hick thought because there was a special presidential price. Still Hick could not in conscience accept more than one or two new items every spring and fall, along with several hand-me-downs. For despite certain obvious disparities, E.R. had insisted one weekend that Hick try on a velvet dinner gown for which she herself had no further use; marvelously, it needed just a little shortening of the skirt, a little letting out of various seams, to fit Hick perfectly. Thereafter, Hick often wore clothes that had already been worn a few times by the First Lady—and drew increasing solace from them as she actually saw the First Lady less and less frequently.

They did have a fairly good week together in April. On the spur of the moment, after E.R. had sounded particularly weary of lecturing, Hick had suggested a change in their tentative arrangement for a short motor tour along the Gulf Coast. Instead, how would Madame like an absolutely peaceful week—just the two of them—at the Little House on the Dana place? "It may be that you no longer feel that you would enjoy spending that much time alone with me," Hick wrote carefully. "If so, that's alright with me." Meanwhile, though, E.R. had remembered a longing to visit Charleston again, and therefore replied: "Of course I could settle down for a week or a month alone with you & be happy but I really wanted to see Charleston, S.C. with you . . . I'll do what you want but remember my column has to be written every day but Saturday."

So they went to Charleston for a few days in April, 1937, then along the new drive through the Great Smokies in North Carolina. Although the whole scheme had started with Hick's gustatory nostalgia for New Orleans, which E.R. quite forgot about, still the crabmeat in Charleston was delicious and they really weren't bothered *much* on this trip. Indeed, as spring turned into summer Hick began to cherish that week in April beyond any other, because now E.R. was becoming involved in such a multitude of causes that the time she allotted for pleasure necessarily decreased. Also, the people who could help her on some project were necessarily displacing those who could not. "I'd like to have you here this minute," E.R. wrote to Hick, "but I'd be busy if you were so here's goodnight & a kiss." Unquestionably—as Hick herself put it—she and E.R. were drifting apart.

The Little House on the Dana Place. That was the heading on Hick's new stationery, and her weekends there were all that made the summer bearable. Out in the moonlight with Prinz, walking down toward the water on a pebbly path gleaming milky white, it seemed so heavenly that she really did pinch herself to make sure she was not dreaming.

As for the house itself, Ella had performed a small miracle. With a rocking chair here, a braided rug there, she had given every room a feeling of having been somebody's favorite place. Originally Hick had been charmed just by the exterior; at her first glance, she had realized this was no ordinary white frame cottage, despite its conventional green shutters, because porches and gables had seemingly sprouted at random to take advantage of the garden and meadow vistas. And even before Ella had begun her decorating, Hick had been delighted by the colonial feeling of the interior. The kitchen was pine, there were dark oak beams supporting the dining room ceiling; how *could* she have been so lucky? Only after she moved in, though, did the magnitude of the luck that had come her way strike her.

She had her own *library.* It was not a large room, of course, for the whole downstairs of the Little House was hardly bigger than her city apartment. Nevertheless, her library had built-in book-shelves and a fireplace, it was painted the same colonial blue as the library in Ella's house, and Hick loved it more than any other room she had ever seen. Piles of papers and magazines instantly made it homey; the sofa that Ella had provided was perfectly comfortable; with Prinz sleeping at her feet, Hick felt utterly serene as she sat there writing to E.R.

At least, she felt serene intermittently. More often, people spoiled everything, she herself most of all. Who else was to blame, she wearily berated herself, if she was changing more sheets this summer and frying more eggs than even in her days as a boarding-house slavey? Hickok, she told herself, you did not have to invite the whole world. But she did. Or she'd probably—well, she'd probably just go right on waiting for Mr. Whalen to approve her airplane model contest.

Pretty soon even the letters would stop coming, she gloomily thought. "I'm hungry for a glimpse of you," E.R. would write, and yet there was always something that intervened. Even when they did manage to meet, she seemed to have her mind elsewhere. Oh, Hick was not surprised! Probably it was inevitable, but at least she could salvage her pride and do no more weeping. Stiffly taking her cue from E.R., Hick, too, found appointments that prevented her from accepting any invitations.

Finally, in September, Hick summoned up the strength to tell E.R. when they met for dinner that they might as well face reality. They *had* drifted apart, Hick said. But E.R. denied it: "I just take it for granted that can't happen!"

Something else did. Three times in September of 1937 Hick went right from work to East Eleventh Street, and went back to work the next morning from E.R.'s apartment. Euphoric, she made a grand new list. "Rid of the tooth," she wrote to E.R., "I'll start the next phase of repairs on the old body. I'm going on a strictly protein-fat diet for a week. That ought to bring my blood sugar down to normal. Then a moderate diet for a week. Then a blood sugar test. And as soon as I'm rid of the curse, I'll start doing my calisthenics again. It was silly to let myself get into this condition this summer. But somehow—I didn't give a damn. The old mental state is much better, now, however. And I'll be good."

Even so, the tide of other interests pulling E.R. away from her had become too strong to be reversed, and yet neither of these women was able to take any decisive step toward ending the relationship.

Hick lacked the power to do it. Approaching her forty-fifth birthday, she knew that she ought to be thinking seriously about her future or she might be in for a pretty terrible time. With no money and no real family, Lord only knew what would happen to her if she lost this awful job. Financially as well as emotionally, she had been letting herself count on E.R. far more than she should. Unfortunately, though, Hick's self-confidence always ebbed when she was feeling miserable, so she was caught in a vicious circle. On gloomy days she had all she could do to keep from erupting at the slightest provocation, and frankly she didn't even care what happened to her. Then when the weight lifted, when she was happy again with E.R., how could she think about giving up her only happiness?

For there were still moments of great joy. After she and E.R. had their private Christmas celebration on Eleventh Street, Hick soared again—toward the realm of poetry. "We were peaceful and contented and glad to be together," she wrote to E.R. And she loved not only all of her presents but even more E.R.'s sweet thoughtfulness. "Dearest one—still, and always, dearest one—you made me very, very happy, and I thank you."

By now, though, E.R.'s inability to turn her back on Hick was based on a blend of emotions that could not be separated or reversed. Of course she still loved Hick, and she still valued her companionship, even if other friends might be less demanding. Newer feelings affected E.R. possibly more strongly, though. For the praise that her own autobiography had been receiving inevitably increased her sense of responsibility. "You see I think you are a kind of genius," Dorothy Canfield Fisher had written to her. "Out of your personality and position you have created something of first-rate and unique value—not a book or statue or painting—an example." Thus E.R. could scarcely avoid suffering a special kind of pity, and of guilt, because of Hick's plight.

It would have stirred pity in a far less compassionate person to contemplate Hick's helpless struggle. As 1937 ended, she had one of her worst days so far at the office. The details were too tedious to bother E.R. with, but if Hick did not need the money—desperately—she would have quit in a minute. Oh, she knew she ought not to take a ridiculous job so seriously, she should live her life outside and give as little time and thought to the job as possible. And yet:

> I loathe living that way. I want to be interested in my job, dammit, and do it as well as I possibly can. But much of the time that only means being irritated. Oh, my dear, WHY can't I be better adjusted to life? God knows, I try. But about 90 per cent of the time I'm out of step with life and miserable. I'll try not to step out of it—at least not as long as I have enough to live on in fair comfort. And probably, even if I were broke and hungry, physical cowardice would keep me from finding a way out! But it's been a miserably uncomfortable business, most of it, and I'm tired of it and bored with past, present and future.
>
> There, there, Hickok.

Unquestionably, Lorena Hickok had lacked emotional stability back in 1932, and perhaps she would have gone downhill emotionally during the next five years even if she had never met Eleanor Roosevelt. But professionally, Hick had already achieved success by the time she encountered E.R. Possibly she could have retained her sense of achievement, although nobody can be sure. For as things did work out, despite the force of her own personality, she had been caught irresistibly in a moth-and-flame relationship.

At last E.R. must have perceived this. After four years in the White House, at the age of fifty-three she had earned a wide esteem as the most inspiring First Lady in the nation's history, and her best-selling autobiography had brought her a more personal acclaim; even she could no longer doubt that she had far surpassed Hick by any worldly measurement. At any rate, she certainly realized that encouraging Hick to take the job at the World's Fair had been a great mistake. Although Hick herself refused to blame her, E.R. knew better now. "Of course, dear," E.R. told her when Hick protested, "I never meant to hurt you in any way but that is no excuse for having done it." And then E.R. went on, in perhaps the most revealing passage of the entire correspondence:

> It won't help you any but I'll never do to anyone else what I did to you. I'm pulling myself back in all my

contacts now. I've always done it with the children &
why I didn't know I couldn't give you (or anyone else
who wanted & needed what you did) any real food I
can't now understand. Such cruelty & stupidity is unpar-
donable when you reach my age. Heaven knows I hope
in some small & unimportant ways I have made life a
little easier for you but that doesn't compensate.

15. At Least Life Is Not Dull

Occasionally a day went by without a letter from E.R., and after one such lapse there was an interesting little disclosure. E.R. had recently converted the former furniture workshop at Hyde Park into a sprawling cottage of her very own; for reasons she told Hick only in person (and never discussed except privately), she was severing her every connection with Nan Cook and Marion Dickerman. Now that she had a sizable place completely to herself, however, she found it easier to focus her energies more effectively. Following a "terrific" day of entertaining sixty people connected with the National Youth Administration, she wrote to Hick: "How you would hate all this & I don't know whether I like it or not, it has advantages & disadvantages."

So in her fifth year as First Lady, E.R. was finally admitting something Hick—and a lot of other people—had known all along. Even if some aspects of her position were unpleasant, it certainly did have advantages, especially for someone with her gift for inspiring idealistic people. That E.R. was actually enjoying herself more and more was obvious to anyone who just glanced at pictures of her, for photographers no longer froze her into a ludicrous stiffness; sometimes they caught her smiling almost as exuberantly as her husband.

During the next two years, the advantages became still more apparent to her—perhaps, at least partly, because she expected to leave the White House after the next election. While it suited F.D.R. politically to keep everybody else guessing about whether he would try to break the no-third-term tradition, he told his wife—and she told Hick—that he would not run again. Unless, of course, a major war in Europe or Asia forced him to change his mind. Still, in the spring of 1939, despite dark glimmers of what might be in the offing, E.R. sailed through the greatest social test of her First Lady-ship quite cheerfully. On each of those three frantic days when the King and Queen of England were her guests, E.R. did manage to dash off a page or so to Hick:

> ... The Queen reminds me of Queen Victoria! He is nice & doesn't stutter *badly* ... The entertainment went well tonight I think & Marian Anderson was divine. ...
>
> This day is also over & has gone well, even F.D.R. is content. ...

Then, from Hyde Park just before the famous picnic where British royalty was served hot dogs: "Mama is as difficult as usual."

At the New York World's Fair—open right on time, its fountains and its Futurama a smashing success—Hick, too, saw the royalty in spite of herself. The morning before they were due, en route between Washington and Hyde Park, she had been ordered to produce five thousand children overnight, the idea being to use them as buffers for holding back the crowd during welcoming ceremonies. It was an idea that infuriated her. "But the police said that was what had been done in Washington and all through Canada," she wrote to E.R., so she'd had no choice. It hadn't been easy rounding up that many kids for such a purpose. "The Girl Scouts said their girls had taken an awful beating in Washington and wouldn't let me have any. I finally got some Boy Scouts." With whom, in the line of duty, Hick held back surging waves of curious Americans intent on glimpsing the royal couple. To E.R. she wrote:

> He looked tired and bored, I thought, and I didn't blame him. She seemed to be enjoying herself and was rather charming, although she does look a lot like Harriet Akerson whom I never liked.° [There was a lot of shoving by the crowd] and I finally got back to my office about 4:30, sighed, "God damn the King and Queen," and took off my shoes.

There it was in a nutshell. Although these two years had been painful for Hick, they certainly were not dull. Which was impor-

---

° Wife of Hick's old friend George Akerson, who had quit writing politics for the Minneapolis *Tribune* to work for the Republicans in Washington.

tant to her, as she indicated in telling E.R. about a Philharmonic concert she and her young friend Howard had attended: "It was a very nice program of Beethoven and Wagner. But we thought it was a rather dull performance. Barbirolli is too pedantic for me. I like lots of thunder in my Beethoven—and fire in my Wagner."

Money, money, money—if she only had enough Hick knew, a year before the Fair opened, just where and how she'd live. Out at the Little House, winter and summer, for the effect that place had on her was miraculous. Oh, she realized that she still might sink into one of her moods when even Prinz, snoring contentedly on his favorite rug after a good romp in the woods, could not chase the demons of loneliness. But she still could dream that here, or perhaps at Hyde Park, in another few years there would be two of them, busy during the day with their own writing and then reading together in the evening, if not poetry maybe Dickens.

Meanwhile, Hick did not completely lack companionship in the country. Once she stopped bringing company every blooming weekend she began to appreciate the Rosses. Because Clarence had run an auto garage in the village, he did have some American Legion cronies who bored her to distraction; and Annie, retired from teaching grammar school, with her snowy braids hairpinned above her brow did seem at first just another Norman Rockwell old lady who put up beautiful jars of peaches. But now Hick knew why Bill, and even Ella, loved them both.

Without Clarence all of those balky generators that provided electricity for every house on the property would long since have quit humming, not that the Rosses were cherished just because Clarence was so handy. That didn't hurt, though. Whenever anything in any of the houses went wrong, the cry would sound: "Clarence!" The assorted relatives of Bill and Ella who lived on the place, and the odd mix of other people who for one reason or another had been invited to rent or even buy a former barn or old-time tenant cottage, really had nothing in common except their dependence on the same Mr. Fix-It. Of course they paid him—if he would let them. To restore practically a whole roof of wind-ripped shingles, he might accept ten dollars. Yet it was friendship that had originally bound Bill to Clarence; from years of fishing together, such a closeness had grown that it seemed only natural, when Clarence got ready to sell his garage, for him and Annie to move onto the place and become sort of caretakers.

The decrepit house that Clarence had just about rebuilt as their retirement home was only a couple of hundred yards from Hick's house, although the lay of the land was such that she could barely see it from an upstairs window even when the trees were leafless. It was comforting to have them within yelling distance. While she did have a rude sort of special telephone that connected her with some of the other houses on the place, the wiring was prone to break at the first gust of any storm, and she could not possibly afford what it would cost to have a real phone installed. Besides, she liked being unreachable out here; if E.R. *needed* to reach her, she could send a telegram.

But nobody at the office had the address. Hick thought she spent too damn many hours as it was attending to lunatic requests, not that she worked from eight every morning until midnight, as Grover Whalen seemed to expect from his staff. In fact, as soon as they had moved out to the first finished building at Flushing Meadow, she refused to stay at her desk later than eight any evening. For the site was about a half hour closer to Mastic than the Empire State Building had been. Thus, although she still kept her apartment to use when she needed it, almost every night from May through November she drove herself fifty-six miles on her way home. *The Little House was where she lived.*

Tiring as that nightly trip could be, Hick hardly minded it. Along her route she had found a little restaurant in somebody's parlor where the food was good and they had a bookcase filled with yellowing novels by people like Maria Edgeworth, which marvelously distracted her during her solitary suppers. Despite her capacity for self-delusion on the subject of money, Hick also had an uncomfortable capacity to step back a few paces and regard herself with a stranger's eye. So she was aware that anybody else might find her own commuting almost as unbelievable as she found Miss Edgeworth's fiction, if not crazier than anything at her office. What on earth possessed Lorena Hickok, earning only one hundred dollars a week, to aspire to such luxuries as a country house, a car and a very large dog? With no other resources but her salary, by the summer of 1938 she was head over heels in debt.

Although she had restrained her impulse to buy a new car and was still rattling around in arthritic Blue Boy, she owed two women dentists a couple of hundred dollars each, and fifty dollars to the garage that was keeping Blue Boy going. She was also a couple of months behind on both her rent payments, as well as on numerous other bills totalling another several hundred. She even owed ten dollars to the farm stand where she picked up country eggs; quite a substantial arrears, considering that the price of those eggs was thirty-five cents a dozen. "So then—" as she would finally confess to E.R., "for months I've been living, I suppose beyond my income."

Did it somehow console her to know that millionaires had money troubles too? Poor Bill! Hick felt such sympathy for his plight as she told E.R. all about it: back when he'd got his divorce from his first wife, he'd set up a trust fund for her and their daughters. Since that was at the height of the boom, he could easily spare a large sum. But nobody had ever informed him that *he* had to pay income tax on the accumulating interest until the girls were twenty-one. Now an official letter demanded a huge payment, including penalties. Since Bill of all people, the most open and *un*devious man alive, had never had the slightest intention of defrauding the government, couldn't something be done about this?

E.R. instantly replied that Henry—Henry Morgenthau, the Secretary of the Treasury—would look into the matter. Of course E.R. considered the Danas her friends, too, not only from Nevada; she had subsequently invited them for a few White House visits, as she invited so many of the acquaintances she made along her travels, but she and they had the further point in common of appreciating Hick. After watching Hick suffer at a formal dinner in Washington, Bill had been led to remark fondly that she reminded him of a trapped Bengal tiger. And he often greeted her himself with an untrammeled bear hug. Ella, less demonstrative but more perceptive, writing to tell Mrs. Roosevelt what time she and Bill would be arriving for a White House weekend, mentioned that she had lunched in the city with Hick that day; she added, ". . . and her face was as interesting as any face I've ever seen, so alive and strong and sweet too!"

Perhaps Ella's insight that the First Lady would especially like to hear such praise of Hick partly explained Hick's inability ever to feel quite at ease with Ella. At any rate, Hick made a point of waiting until the Danas went off to Nevada before choosing the date for her own summer vacation in 1938. For E.R. had promised that this year she would positively spend one whole week in Mastic, and Hick wanted to make sure there would be no Ella hanging around the Little House then. Still, Hick's amusement at E.R.'s barrage of plan-changing messages as the vacation approached showed a clear advance in her own campaign to attain a calmer mental state. After about the tenth revision, Hick wrote to her: "I'll be awfully glad to see you, dear, *when*ever and *how*ever you come and if you like it here one-tenth as much as I do, I'll be satisfied."

From the evidence of E.R.'s "My Day" columns filed from nearby Patchogue during the last week of July, the stay was delightful. Though the First Lady did not mention her hostess by name, she waxed lyrical about picnics on the beach at Fire Island across the bay and the lovely sunsets reflected in the water. As far as Hick was concerned, a good part of the reason they had such a peaceful time was that E.R. had finally learned to type well enough to dispense with Tommy temporarily. Not that Hick felt any less affection for Tommy; she hugely enjoyed the occasional drink she and E.R.'s secretary managed to have together. But Tommy plus E.R. spelled trouble, Hick had decided. They could not, either of them, be together anywhere more than fifteen minutes without remembering their work. Out came the pad, E.R. began dictating, and Hick, shut out as effectively as if she were on another planet, gritted her teeth.

This time, while they had to go to a crafts show farther out on the island and to dinner one night with some Roosevelt connections, it was only the Rosses who joined most of their little expeditions. They, of course, behaved like the perfect neighbors they were. Now that E.R. for the first time in her life had a plot of green around the Hyde Park cottage she considered her very own, she was actually interested in Annie's wildflower garden; when E.R. especially admired the butterfly weed, Annie dug out a clump for her to transplant. The butterfly weed had survived its move and was growing nicely, E.R. wrote after her return to Hyde Park. Would Hick tell the Rosses the good news?

But for the rest of the summer, E.R. was terribly busy again, since she worked hard even at her relaxing: "I've learned at last to stand on my hands in the shallow end of the pool & put my feet in the air & I see a faint glimmer of hope for learning to dive." In addition, there were throngs of young people associated with the youth groups in which she was taking such an interest. Then her son James suddenly required a serious operation at the Mayo Clinic in Minnesota; even the President went there, despite a mounting crisis across the Atlantic, where Hitler was pressing Czechoslovakia to give up territory that he claimed was rightfully German. Fortunately, James's tumor proved to be benign. A few days after E.R. returned to New York, she and Hick finally got together for lunch.

It was the twenty-first of September, 1938, and it was raining heavily in the city when they left the restaurant. As they separated, Hick said she might not drive out to the country that night unless it cleared up; it did not, and on the radio they said that a hurricane was blowing up the coast. Could that be possible? Florida or Cuba had hurricanes, not Long Island. Hick's first thought was for Prinz: the old boy was kept on a trolley adjoining a kennel that would keep him dry in an ordinary storm. But Bill and Ella were back now from the West, and Bill would surely think of bringing in Prinz.

The next morning, the newspapers scared the life out of Hick. Hundreds dead in New England. Wires down everywhere. Of course she couldn't reach a soul by telephone at Mastic, nor even get through to any nearby town just to get an idea of what had happened. Worried sick, she planned to leave the office early but at five o'clock Grover sent for her. He would! So not till six-thirty did she get started; then she drove like mad, hoping that even if she got stopped for speeding, the cop would understand the circumstances and be lenient.

Soon she had to slow down because there were tree branches partly blocking the road. Nearing the shore, she had to detour and take the long way because a big tree blocked the road completely. From the Mastic railroad station on, as she was driving toward the water, so many trees were down that she stopped counting them. What could their woods be like? She reached the entrance to the property just as dusk turned into darkness, and very slowly proceeded in first gear with branches of fallen trees brushing the top of her car. After about a block, the beam of her headlights showed a huge pine on the ground ahead of her, lying right across the road, the lush green of its needles seeming eerily alive. It was like looking at a person who had just died. She got out of the car to peer around the tree, and the silence stunned her. Not even katydids. Nothing but fallen trees, and she had no flashlight.

Still, her first thought was to go ahead on foot. Then it occurred to her that if anybody in there was dead, or even badly hurt, word might have reached the post office somehow. So she turned back. But they hadn't heard anything in the village of anyone dying on the Dana place. No, they couldn't say about the animals out there.

Hick was desperate. Then Johnny, the young fellow who owned the store that also served as the post office, offered to see if he could get through with his car. Back they went, and Hick parked by the first fallen tree. Johnny got around that one, but a few feet beyond it they were stopped by an oak. A car had been left there; Hick thought it belonged to some cousins of Ella's who had one of the houses back in the woods.

Johnny offered to walk in with Hick. But it was more crawling than walking, nearly a mile and a half of climbing up and scrambling over what seemed like a solid mass of fallen trees. Thinking of all the disasters of one sort or another she had encountered as a reporter, Hick could remember nothing like this. The farther they went, the more hopeless it seemed. If the wind had been so bad here in thick woods, how could anyone have survived out in the open where most of the houses stood?

After about an hour and a half, they came to a tractor. By then they were almost at the Dana house. Someone with a saw had obviously been at work, clearing the road from that end. Stumbling over the litter of small branches still impeding their feet, Hick and Johnny hurried as fast as they could—toward a light, and the sound of a motor running. That turned out to be the generator supplying electricity for Bill and Ella's house.

And there they all were, all alive, even Prinz, who had had a very narrow escape. All camped in the Dana house, which had scarcely been hurt. Except for one house right on the point overlooking the bay, none of the houses had been damaged too severely by the wind. It was flooding from the tidal wave that had done the worst harm—six inches of water all over the Rosses' ground floor. The Little House was not quite as bad, Ella reported.

But the trees! Not one of the beautiful old locusts around the Little House remained standing. Practically every tree near Bill and Ella's gone too. With tears in her eyes, Ella told Hick that now the houses stuck up wholly bare, like the houses in a brand new real-estate development.

Then they were all talking. Bill and Clarence had been out during the worst of it, trying to rescue boats. Meanwhile one of the other men had gone to look for children who might be trying to get home from school. Another practically swam—in boots and oilskins—to rescue animals, getting to Prinz barely in time. Obviously the old boy had been desperately trying to swim, and couldn't with his collar and chain keeping him fixed to his trolley. When Bob reached him, Prinz had almost lost his grip on the kennel door, and was howling weakly.

Hick stayed about an hour that night, collecting messages that everybody wanted to get to people elsewhere. Since she had to be at work the next morning, she gave Prinz a final pat in the Dana kitchen, then crawled her way back to her car amid the deathly silence. Around midnight she made a dozen phone calls from Patchogue, then had to push on because every room there was full, with refugees. An hour later, in Smithtown, she found a shoddy hotel by the railroad tracks where she simply fell onto a bed and slept a few hours. Since that was Friday, she waited until Saturday noon—when she would have the weekend ahead of her—to go out again.

The reality of what had happened hit her then, as she saw the place in daylight. The rest of that day and the next she utterly wore herself out, working along with her maid, whom she had brought with her from the city, to make a start at getting the Little House habitable again. They slept, along with a dozen or so others, in makeshift style at the Danas'. By then everybody had stopped saying how lucky they were, after all; the aftermath of so much ugliness, where there had been only beauty, got on everybody's nerves. Tempers flared. Clarence, ordinarily the best-natured man alive, had a terrible spat with Ella. So not just the rare beauty of the place had been spoiled, but also its idyllic peace.

All of this Hick poured out in a letter Monday, finally telling E.R. why she had not been in touch since their lunch together the Wednesday of the hurricane. And then, wrenched from her near the end of the third long page of typing: "But why is it that as soon as I get to care about or depend on any one or anything it must always be taken away from me? No one will ever know what that place has meant to me."

"Your letter painted a marvelous picture of what I feared had happened," E.R. wrote. "I am relieved that Prinz survived . . . Here the hurricane is eclipsed by the world situation, which kept F.D.R. on edge all the time." Indeed the day before, stepping onto the world stage as Europe hovered at the brink of another great war, he had sent an appeal for peace to all of the potential belligerents. "F. says he has done the last thing he can do & we can all pray something moves Hitler tomorrow," E.R. told Hick. "What a mad man!"

Yet the Munich Agreement on September 30, 1938, only gave in to the "mad man's" demands. While it purchased time for the democracies to build up their armed forces, no thoughtful person could feel that it had bought more than a temporary peace. As late as Christmas of the following year, F.D.R. would still tell his whole family, assembled at the White House, that he would not run again. What would they think of Secretary of State Cordell Hull as his successor? However, it is possible that right after Munich F.D.R.'s wife realized that another term might be unavoidable. Or perhaps it was just Hick's discouragement following the hurricane that made the First Lady broach a new idea to her.

How would Hick like to get into doing publicity for the Democratic National Committee? "If you want to talk to Jim [Farley] about me," Hick replied, "I think it might be a good idea."

Indirectly—"Here's a rather illuminating little story, Madame"— Hick had brought up the subject herself by reporting a conversation she'd had with an office boy at the Fair. When he told her that he had just turned twenty-one, Hick congratulated him and added:

> "Voter, eh?" I said with a grin.
> "Yep, straight Democratic ticket," he replied. Then: "No, I'll amend that. Straight *Roosevelt* ticket."
> "Well, suppose you don't have a chance to vote for Roosevelt?" I asked.
> "Well, then—whoever he says," the kid replied simply.

In her next letter, E.R. reacted just as a political wife should: "I loved the story of your office boy & so will F.D.R." Yet the story illuminated more than the faith of one new voter. No less than this office boy, Hick herself was absolutely committed to F.D.R. politically, no matter what personal reservations she might harbor. Not that Hick thought deeply about any issue—she had thrown up her hands during the fierce controversy over the President's Supreme Court plan at the beginning of his second term, when many good Democrats had been distressed by the idea of tampering with the Constitution just because a few judges had outlawed the NRA. Hick had to agree that it was a bad precedent to appoint new judges as a means of circumventing those already on the bench: suppose another Hoover decided there ought to be thirty more

Supreme Court judges to provide a conservative majority outvoting Roosevelt's twenty? But after everything Hick had seen around the country, she also felt it would be playing right into the Communists' hands to let those "nine old men" kill the WPA, Social Security, every New Deal measure keeping the little people from turning Red. As usual when things got too much for her, Hick took refuge in humor; to E.R. she described her nine remaining molars as her own nine old men.

Nevertheless, E.R. had full confidence in Hick's commitment to the liberal philosophy that the First Lady espoused even more vigorously than her husband. By no means, though, was the Democratic party itself entirely liberal. Its Southern wing had never been comfortable with many of F.D.R.'s ideas, and in Congress it was voting almost solidly with the Republicans. That impressed the chairman of the Democratic National Committee. To Jim Farley, the opinions of Senators mattered more than anything the little people might think; in this, he was no different from most professional politicians who had to muster support from influential party figures as the first step in any campaign. But Farley personally did not care much for the New Deal outlook, and especially for New Dealers like Hopkins who owed nothing at all to the Democratic party. In Farley's book, serving the party was the only way to play the game: unless you were loyal to the party, you should not expect any political reward. By the same token, those who served the party deserved consideration when the plums were being distributed. Nothing under the sun, in Europe or elsewhere, could convince Jim that any man was entitled to more than two terms in the White House. Indeed, as 1940 approached it struck the Democratic chairman that his own long years of loyal service entitled *him* to run for President himself.

Yet Farley did seem to realize his own limitations. With the foreign situation so uncertain, maybe the fact that he had no experience in foreign affairs might count against him. So if the war over there really seemed to threaten American interests, then let Secretary of State Cordell Hull get first place on the ticket; Farley would be satisfied with the second slot. That Hull would be seventy-one in the year of the election hardly concerned him. The fact that Hull had put in a quarter of a century as a Democratic congressman from Tennessee was, to Farley, the main point.

To E.R., it was not. Even if Hitler should somehow cease to

threaten the future of democracy, to her the continuation of New Deal social programs would still be urgently important. If there were a Hull-Farley slate in 1940, she wanted to be sure that liberal programs would not fall by the wayside. From her husband, E.R. had learned something of how politics actually worked. So it struck her that Farley might be encouraged, by having liberals around him, to remember the Roosevelt commitment to liberalism.

However, when E.R. mentioned to her husband her notion about getting Hick onto Farley's staff, the President said he liked the idea but doubted if Jim wanted a liberal Democratic party. More plainly, why should Farley—two years before an election about which he had some definite ideas of his own—want to hire a woman closely associated with Eleanor Roosevelt? Undaunted, E.R. wrote Hick that she would talk to Jim soon and let Hick know how things developed.

Hick happened to be in an unusually placid frame of mind when this letter reached her. "You were a peach to talk to the President about that Democratic Committee job," she wrote back. "Many, many thanks. No, I don't think Jim is interested in a *liberal* Democratic party, but let's hope he has the political acumen to keep it more liberal than the Republican party. In the meantime, I'm in no hurry to make a move but I think the National Committee job might be interesting."

In the three months before E.R. finally got around to seeing Jim, Hick's patience ebbed. If things at the office were no worse than usual, they seemed so because life at Mastic—despite flashes of the old magic—often was very trying. Hick even had a row with the ordinarily lovable Bill, when he shouted that those CCC boys cleaning up the woods were no damned good. Didn't he realize, she shouted back, that unemployed city kids couldn't be expected to be expert lumberjacks? Afterward Hick was ashamed of herself, knowing why Bill had turned so prickly. For the secretary of the treasury himself had reviewed his tax case and said there was nothing he could do. So Bill somehow had to raise the money.

On New Year's Day, 1939, he seemed more like his old self. Very early the next morning, however, Hick telephoned the White House; what she communicated to E.R. was not repeated in their subsequent letters, so it must be assumed that newspaper reports about the sudden death of William S. Dana were accurate. According to these obituary notices, the forty-five-year-old sportsman and rancher had died of a heart attack. At any rate, the insurance company involved found no grounds for refusing to pay his widow, as Hick would tersely inform E.R. several weeks later.

During the funeral Hick stayed upstairs in Bill's room, keeping his dogs quiet; she thought that would have pleased him more than if she stood with the whole village listening to the American Legion bugler sounding taps. Now, she told herself as philosophically as she could, her money problem was solved too. For Ella would be foolish not to move back to the Little House herself.

And then Hick could finally catch up on her bills, although, dammit, she was still going to get the new car this spring, no matter what. Without the Little House, she'd need a car more than ever— to escape from the nerve-wracking Fair at Flushing Meadow. But because E.R. had promised to lend her the difference between Blue Boy's trade-in value and the cost of a new model, Hick finally had to disclose her true financial situation to the First Lady. At least Hick felt that she did when Commander Flanagan surprised her in the middle of January with a ten dollar a week raise, and E.R. urged her to put every penny into a special bank account earmarked for the car. "You are right of course," Hick wrote to her, then in four large pages of single-spaced typing explained why this prudent course was impossible.

The gist was that only Prinz, the Little House and her car made her life worth living.

> Now of course, it would be perfectly reasonable to say it was silly—insane, really—for a woman of forty-five, almost forty-six, without a cent in the world except her salary, without any very promising prospects for a well paid job in the future, etc, etc to try to hang on to these three luxuries. All the sane arguments are on that side, I know. They just can't be answered logically at all. But I'll just have to answer them in my own way. Living—just going on living—simply doesn't mean a God damned thing to me, dear. I'm being perfectly honest when I say I'll be relieved when it's over, provided the actual ending isn't too painful. You are always horrified when I say that I wish it had happened when I had that automobile accident out in Arizona. But I still do. I'd have died happy, as happy as I've ever been in my life . . . But it didn't happen that way, and here I am . . .

Being here, I look about for things to make my stay as pleasant as possible. As I say—I'm not the sort who can get my whole happiness out of doing things for others. It would be nice to be that way, but I'm not. Perhaps, too, I'm leaning too heavily on the house, the car and the dog, but they and the occasional happiness I get out of doing things with and for other people are all I have. Through them I have managed to achieve at least a kind of contentment. I'm not actively unhappy any more, although I have my bad moods—and undoubtedly always shall. But since I'm here and obliged to mingle with other people, it at least makes it more comfortable for them if I am reasonably happy and contented. Up to now those three things have helped to keep me that way. It's undoubtedly in the cards that I shall eventually lose all three. And when that happens—well, I'd never have the courage to MAKE it happen.

E.R. received this letter three weeks after Bill Dana's death, and her compassion for Hick completely overcame any impulse to lecture. Hick, besides listing what she owed, had also appended little charts showing, week by week, how she intended to clear up her indebtedness; until then, the only personal expense on her budget was "New raincoat (badly needed) $20." E.R. went to Abercrombie's that afternoon and sent the finest English raincoat in the store to Hick's apartment. Then she crossed over to the Biltmore, where she had arranged to meet Hick for tea.

They talked, of course, about the Democratic job. For Jim Farley's reputation as a consummate politician was not undeserved. Would he brush off a request from the wife of an immensely popular President? Not Jim! No, he'd taken very kindly to the idea of using Lorena Hickok—and instead of the five hundred a month, plus expenses, that Mrs. Roosevelt had mentioned, he said ten thousand a year should be possible.

However, it somehow took a full year for Jim Farley's bland acceptance of the First Lady's proposal to result in his hiring of Hick. First Farley had to make sure Charley Michelson, that old pro in charge of Democratic publicity, was agreeable. By the middle of February, 1939, Michelson was enthusiastic. Call me Charley, he urged Hick when she went down to Washington to see him. But until Congress adjourned, they couldn't really do anything. Yes, Hick understood. Then after Congress finally quit in the middle of

June, Charley had to go to California. In August when Mrs. Roosevelt prodded Farley, Michelson wired Hick that he was ready for her, except that there was a little problem about the money to pay her. They would have to raise some extra money, he explained, as if a separate fund drive were required; indeed Charley called Hick in the middle of September to tell her they were having trouble raising the money to "finance" her. In October, Hick had to wire Charley because at the Fair they were making up next year's budget and she had to tell them whether she was staying. Sorry, Charley wired back, completely stymied now. E.R. got busy again. In December, Jim told her he thought the job would be all settled by next week. And then it took only another four weeks.

Finally, on the fourteenth of January in the presidential election year of 1940, something must have convinced Jim and Charley that they'd better hire Mrs. Roosevelt's friend. Only then did Charley Michelson wire Miss Lorena Hickok to come to work.

16. The 1940 Presidential Campaign

Naturally, Hick had borne the suspense with her "usual saintly serenity." At least, she loved the phrase when Tom Dillon, ordered onto the wagon following an ulcer attack, used it in a letter to her describing how he was confronting this new vicissitude: Hick adopted it for her own. But if her former boss in Minneapolis had in truth attained a milder disposition, Hick had not. Still, it was not so much her job turmoil—the idiocies of the one she had, the uncertainties of the one she hoped to get—that really upset her. Although all of this was irritating, it was not unbearable. People were.

During the weeks immediately following Bill's death, Ella struck Hick as pathetic, but not in the usual way a bereaved widow stimulated pity. The hypocrisy of her writing to thank E.R. for the White House floral tribute: "When the flowers came from you and the President my heart was almost too full, for Bill was so humble in his own eyes, to me he was the whole world." Hick did not think the latter statement was justified. At any rate, Ella wept a lot; Hick thought she was demanding an unwarranted amount of sympathy. But Ella did not ask Hick to give up the Little House.

Instead Ella said she would feel much worse if Hicky abandoned her. Then Ella took Annie and Clarence to Florida before going out to Nevada for a few months. It was not until Ella came back from the ranch—barely nine months after Bill's death—accompanied by a young cowboy with very blue eyes, that Hick exploded.

On first learning that Ella was planning to bring a male companion back to Mastic with her, Hick broad-mindedly wrote to E.R.: "I'm terribly afraid that the Rosses and Unkie [Ella's aged uncle] may be pretty critical. I'm not. I think anyone in Ella's position should do what she can to gain contentment, if not happiness. Ella

255

is the sort of woman who simply must have a man around waiting on her. Of course I don't have any idea that she is actually living with this cowboy. If she did, she'd be a bigger fool than I think she is. He's years younger than she is."

E.R., off lecturing again, was even more broad-minded: "I'm amused by Ella's cowboy. Why should anyone care?"

Once Ella arrived, though, Hick had to change her mind, because Ella did the damnedest thing: "All the years I've known Bill, he used very often to get his banjo just before or after lunch and dinner and sit on the couch in the living room, strumming on it and singing cowboy songs. Dear old Unkie came in while we were there and I'll be darned if Ella didn't ask that cowboy to play his guitar and sing and asked Unkie to get one of the banjos and play a duet with him. I think the very last time Unkie played the banjo was just before Christmas last winter, when he and Bill were playing them. There sat the cowboy right in the very spot where Bill used to sit . . . Unkie looked so queer, and my eyes filled with tears in spite of myself. It brought Bill back so vividly. How could she do such a thing?"

E.R. agreed that Ella was pathetic but she missed Bill and the very things that had mattered to her in Bill probably had attracted her to this boy. When Hick, with mounting disgust, reported that Ella was giving the cowboy Bill's clothes, and even his guns, E.R. tried to explain that lonely women often behaved foolishly, and that Ella's loneliness had been compounded by a sad fact. For Ella could not help realizing that everybody had loved Bill but did not care as much about her.

Hick's former boss Harry Hopkins similarly offended her sense of propriety. Barely six months after his wife died, the newspapers said a new marriage was in the offing for F.D.R.'s relief director. Hick told E.R. that the story that Hopkins was engaged to an actress depressed her profoundly. "It's not that I would wish to deny him any happiness," she wrote, "but how COULD he forget so quickly?"

Again, E.R. told her:

> Hick darling,
> You don't know much about men, do you? Harry was so happy with Barbara & so he is lonelier than if he hadn't been. Women are sorry for him, they like to be

Eleanor Roosevelt and Lorena Hickok on Caribbean trip, taken on March 7, 1934, Hick's forty-first birthday. In the center is Paul Person, governor of the Virgin Islands. (LORENA HICKOK PAPERS, F.D.R. LIBRARY COLLECTION)

Eleanor Roosevelt and Lorena Hickok on Puerto Rican trip, March
1934. (LORENA HICKOK PAPERS, F.D.R. LIBRARY COLLECTION)

Hick during a weekend respite from her travels in the summer of 1936 at Aunt Ella's Wisconsin lake cabin. (LORENA HICKOK PAPERS, F.D.R. LIBRARY COLLECTION)

Hick with Aunt Ella during July 1936, when Hick visited her at a Wisconsin lake resort. During Lorena's girlhood, Aunt Ella was the only person the troubled child really loved. (LORENA HICKOK PAPERS, F.D.R. LIBRARY COLLECTION)

Back view of Hick's Little House in Mastic, Long Island, her refuge from 1937 until 1955. (LORENA HICKOK PAPERS, F.D.R. LIBRARY COLLECTION)

Lorena Hickok in a pensive mood on the sun porch at the Little House, in the summer of 1937. (LORENA HICKOK PAPERS, F.D.R. LIBRARY COLLECTION)

Ella Dana, around the time that she first made the Little House on her Long Island estate available for Hick's use as a weekend hideaway. (COURTESY OF HELEN BULWINKEL)

Annie and Clarence Ross, Hick's neighbors at her Long Island cottage. (COURTESY OF ANNE FARR)

Bill Dana, sportsman and rancher, with a trophy from one of his traps; he presented Hick with a scarf made from the skins of some red fox he had captured. (COURTESY OF HELEN BULWINKEL)

Hick and her companion, Prinz. (LORENA HICKOK PAPERS, F.D.R. LIBRARY COLLECTION)

VAL-KILL COTTAGE
HYDE PARK, DUTCHESS COUNTY
NEW YORK
TELEPHONE: HYDE PARK 87

Dearest, I am trying the little portable as So
Tommy and Ear l have gone off for a morning
of s hopping.The wretc hed t ing s kips be-
ca use I don't hit right.

There is no news but the weather is glorious,and I've ac tually learned to get breakfast if no one eats anything .

I'm reading a war book whic h doesn't
intend to be horrible and is almost the wor st
Iever read.

[handwritten note]

After Prinz died, Eleanor Roosevelt arranged with her secretary's niece, who bred beautiful
English setters, for the delivery
to the White House of a caramel-
colored puppy named Mr.
Choate. Hick kept the dog at
her Little House on Long Island.
(LORENA HICKOK PAPERS, F.D.R.
LIBRARY COLLECTION)

Eleanor Roosevelt and Lorena
Hickok stopping to see some
local weavers during a trip
through the Great Smoky Mountain National Park in North
Carolina in April 1937. (U.P.I.)

Judge Marion Harron of the U.S. Tax Court, with whom Hick had a special friendship, visiting at Hick's Little House on Long Island. (LORENA HICKOK PAPERS, F.D.R. LIBRARY COLLECTION)

A photograph of Judge Harron, printed with a New York *Herald Tribune* interview which bore the headline, "Judge Marion Harron Suggests Tax Field to Woman Lawyers." (THE NEW YORK HERALD TRIBUNE. LORENA HICKOK PAPERS, F.D.R. LIBRARY COLLECTION)

Hick's sister Ruby (left) and her husband, Julian Claff, with an unidentified mother and baby. The Claffs were childless and very fond of children (COURTESY OF ANNE FARR)

Eleanor Roosevelt emerging from the Minneapolis railroad station with Lorena Hickok's friend Clarissa Dillon, March 30, 1943. (LORENA HICKOK PAPERS, F.D.R. LIBRARY COLLECTION)

Lorena Hickok shortly before she resigned her position as Executive Secretary of the women's division of the Democratic National Committee in March 1945. (TENSCHERT PHOTOS/HISTORICAL FILE, WASHINGTON, D.C., ANKERS CAPITOL)

Hick's good friend, Congresswoman Mary Norton, at the 1944 Democratic Party convention in Chicago. (U.P.I.)

Lorena Hickok toward the end of her life. (LORENA HICKOK PAPERS,
F.D.R. LIBRARY COLLECTION)

seen with men whose names are in the paper & it helps him to forget. He isn't serious. . . .

However, an offhand remark by E.R., involving Hick's own sister Ruby, displayed how thin was the veneer of sophistication overlaying the First Lady's own Victorianism. Hearing that Ruby had just lost her job, E.R. blandly wondered: ". . . Perhaps she will now marry?" Hick felt the sting severely because she was so sensitive to any tinge of moral turpitude. Thus she was always distressed to have to introduce *her* sister as *Mrs.* Claff when they had never bothered to make it legal. Maybe that was the real reason Ruby and Julian got on her nerves, Hick sometimes admitted to herself, because everybody else certainly seemed to enjoy their company.

At any rate, after the death of the doctor Ruby had been working for—and Ruby's discovery that, these days, doctors were hiring only pretty young girls with pink fingernails to work in their offices, at fifteen dollars a week—Hick tried to be philosophical. Maybe Julian actually would stir himself now to find a decent job. Meanwhile, on young Howard Haycraft's advice, Hick told E.R., she was not going to offer financial help to her sister, at least for a couple of weeks. "He feels that if I do, Julian may just settle down on me for life. . . . Howard says Julian has a 'Beloved Vagabond' complex." Then Hick added a very quirky opinion of her own:

> I don't object to Ruby carrying him if she wants to. He is to her, I suppose, what my dog, my car and the place in the country are to me—nice things if you can afford them. . . .

Ruby, more attached to her "Jeeb" than Hick imagined, did not supinely await financial help from her sister. With the widow of the doctor she had worked for, she started a cookie-baking business. Mrs. Roosevelt immediately became their most loyal customer, and as a result the *Herald Tribune*'s woman's page gave them a nice write-up. Of course, Hick also dug into her own purse; glumly she decided that if this drain on her salary continued, she would have to sell her car. However, during December E.R. diligently pulled the strings that got Julian hired to work on the upcoming federal census.

Even so, for the second Christmas in a row Hick bought no presents. That made everything seem so terribly bleak. But ever since

September 1939, when Hitler had marched into Poland, it had been impossible to complain about personal problems. Yet E.R. still pretended it wouldn't be long until she sank back into obscurity, writing to Hick after a peaceful night at her Hyde Park cottage that she hoped the quiet was just a taste of what she would enjoy in the future.

Despite E.R.'s deepening involvement in real issues—testifying, unperturbed, on behalf of her youth congress friends in front of the controversial Dies Committee—she did not neglect Hick. With at least a trace of saintly serenity, Hick expressed the current state of their relationship: "It would be so much better, wouldn't it, if I didn't love you so much, sometimes!" she wrote. "It makes it trying for you, and well, thanks for the dinner and the theater. You are very sweet to me always."

Hick's grumpiness to everybody else would have been much worse, however, without her Little House. During the long months while she was waiting for some definite word from Washington, she went there so often that she all but gave up seeing most of her friends. On the last day of 1939, her pal Commander Flanagan sent for her—and let her have it. "You never do anything but go off to the country to be with that damned dog of yours," he boomed at her. How the hell did she think she'd ever find another job when the Fair ended next autumn? Point-blank, he accused her of just sitting back and letting Mrs. Roosevelt look after her. If Hick had any sense, she'd see that the Democratic Committee job was not going to come through. So she'd better get out and meet people, give cocktail parties. . . .

Of course, Hick explained to E.R., the commander was put out because she'd skipped *his* holiday party, but still he was probably right: ". . . Oh Lord, how *does* one go about using people and selling oneself? . . . I *knew* how to get newspaper jobs. But that was my profession and I had such confidence in myself."

From the White House on January 2, 1940, E.R. retorted: "I could spank the Commander . . ." Although some of what he said was probably good advice, "you never expected anything from me & I've never done anything." Nevertheless, E.R. did see Jim Farley the next day and, just to make sure, she also spoke to Charley Michelson two days later. Then a week before Charley finally wired Hick, E.R. called New York to relay tidings that were only slightly disappointing.

It would be a temporary job, from February first, 1940, through early November—in short, before and during the impending presidential campaign. And all the Democratic Committee could pay, scraping the bottom of the barrel, was a hundred and twenty-five a week, plus expenses. Still, Hick was in no mood to quibble. For the first couple of months she'd be back on the road, which would be fun and also a big help financially. Even though her salary wasn't much more than what she was now making, the travel allowance would allow her to save most, or at least much of it.

It was the money that mattered. Now that she was leaving the Fair, it hadn't been so bad; a couple of times she had proved she still had what it took to cope with real problems. At the crisis when Congress had balked over appropriating federal funds for the U.S. exhibit, nobody but Hickok had figured out how to propitiate Sol Bloom, the holder of the purse strings in the House of Representatives, with a behind-the-scenes apology because he thought Grover had insulted him. Since E.R. was out of town, it had been Hick's own show.

Also, a couple of months before the Fair had opened she had personally foiled a nasty plot hatched by the publicity woman for the national teachers' association. Thanks to Hickok, the annual convention of all those teachers had been scheduled at the nearly completed site. So not only would thousands of them go home and tell their pupils to tell their parents to pack up and swell the attendance figures, but also, because the President was scheduled to address this meeting, the magic words "at the New York World's Fair" would appear in every report of what he said all over the country.

Then the teachers' publicity woman had slyly changed the opening session—at which F.D.R. would be speaking—to Madison Square Garden. So Hick forgot her usual tremors. She picked up her phone, made an appointment and boarded a train for Washington. Then she marched into the White House and *asked the President of the United States a favor.* Why, of course, Hick! As far as F.D.R. was concerned, it didn't matter a bit to him where he made the speech.

Actually, when the first two years of chaos had ended and the Fair finally opened, Hick had rather enjoyed showing visitors around. She particularly liked some of the foreign restaurants. Let the hordes arrive from Minneapolis; she relished every new excuse to sample the heavenly smorgasbord at the Swedish Pavilion. Still, it was time, in February of 1940, for her to re-enter the real world.

"Awfully strong third term sentiment here," Hick wrote to E.R. from Philadelphia. ". . . The Democrats can hope to carry Pennsylvania only if the President runs. . . ." On the stationery of the Warwick—Hick prided herself on knowing where to stay in any city, opting for solid comfort—she was summing up her impressions after her first foray into sounding out voter sentiment for the Democratic National Committee.

That, and not any routine sort of publicity writing, apparently was to be her mission. Hick, with her private smile lurking at the corners of her mouth, had understood Charley Michelson perfectly: he didn't know what the hell else to do with her, so let her write reports that might interest at least the First Lady. No matter; as Hick ordered herself steaks in one town after another, following several lean months of bringing her lunch to Flushing Meadow, she was on top of the world again. "This job is such fun, dear," she wrote to her friend in the White House. "I'm having the time of my life."

Not that Hick's conscience would let her merely eat her way across Middle America. Drawing on her newspaper acquaintanceship as well as the network of union people and local politicians that she had established during her WPA days, she gave Washington more than it had expected. E.R. from her own vantage point, quoted that old pirate Bernard Baruch as feeling that circumstances would close in and make F.D.R. run again. "I groan!" she added. From Ohio, Hick summed up a long evening nearer the grass roots by quoting an Irish ward leader:

> "Lady, the way me and my workers and the folks who live in my neighborhood look at it, a man can spend his whole life in the Senate or the House, and nobody thinks nothing about it. So why can't a real good President have three terms? Anyway, we people don't give a damn what George Washington thought about it. What we're interested in is *today.*"
> So—laugh *that* one off!

In every respect, Hick reacted to the new job as if she were taking a tonic. After a devout Third Termer in Toledo invited her home for dinner, where he put on an unpleasant display of domestic tyranny, she assured E.R. "When I see what some women have to put up with, I certainly can bear my spinsterhood with equanimity." The extent of her recovery did not manifest itself, however, until she reached Minneapolis.

Staying with the Dillons, Hick was whirled into a vortex of family emotion only partly caused by the Old Man's sudden intimation of mortality. In a restaurant a month earlier, he had flabbergasted himself by collapsing just as if he were the type of show-off who would purposely pick a conspicuous place for having a heart attack; but his convalescence could have been more placid had his wife Clarissa been able to stand their only son's prospective mother-in-law. This was serious, Hick explained to E.R., because the Old Man doted on his son—who naturally had to side with his girl. Although Ris realized how foolish and harmful her feuding was, she still could not control herself. While it was a situation that might seem far removed from anything Hick herself had experienced, in her newfound composure she perceived a parallel. Loving the Old Man as she did, she might easily have felt angry with Ris, Hick said, but now she could not blame her because, under the same circumstances, she herself would have behaved just as badly, if not worse.

"Seeing people you love—people you get all wrapped up in—slip away from you is a very terrible experience," Hick told E.R. "And if you are of a certain emotional make-up and not very well disciplined, you just can't seem to help doing the very things that you know will drive them still further away. I think I know something of the agony Ris is going through these days. About all I could do was to listen and tell her as quietly and firmly as possible that she must get control of herself or she will kill the Old Man. But she knew all that before. Poor Ris! "

As for Tom Dillon himself, the wistfulness in his eyes when his son departed with his fiancée after a terribly uneasy family supper was almost enough to make Hick cry. Then a few minutes later, she caught the Old Man in the butler's pantry, pouring himself a good stiff drink. He put his finger up to his lips, and Hick nodded. She followed him out onto the sun porch, where he said quietly:

"You know, at best, Hick, I couldn't expect to live many more years. I'm sixty-two."

"Yes, I guess I understand."

Then Dillon put his arm around her shoulder, and patted her

without any need for further conversation. So it was not, as Hick informed E.R., a merry weekend. Fortunately, though, her job gave her the kind of relief that she had been craving during those three years at the Fair. When E.R. worried that the long hours and so much bus riding would undermine her health again, Hick blithely reassured her:

> It's a strenuous job alright, but don't feel sorry for me. This, my dear, is the way to live. I don't think I've been so happy and absorbed and thoroughly contented since I was covering the Walker-Seabury story for the AP. That was better in only one way—I had complete confidence in myself those days and *knew* I was doing a good job. I am not sure about that part of it now, but I *am* having a grand time. This way of living, completely wrapped up in my work, is something I've been hungry for—for a long time. I hadn't expected to get it out of this job. I had thought of it as a means to an end—getting enough money to pay my debts and keep the Little House. . . . But I find myself completely absorbed by it. . . .
>
> Darling, I'm sorry, but it's all third term. . . .

Even in Indiana, the home state of the Democratic presidential hopeful Paul McNutt, his supporters told Hick privately that they would much rather have the President run again. And although she kept meeting politicians who warmly admired Jim Farley, "I haven't met a soul who thought he could be elected." Under the circumstances, Hick should scarcely have been surprised when E.R. wrote that F.D.R. found what she gave him from Hick's letters *very* interesting.

When Hick returned to Washington in May, it gave her a more personal gratification that her immediate boss had changed his mind about her. In New York, a new daily called *PM* was being started by a group of liberals and somebody had suggested that she apply for a job; although nothing was at all definite, she still felt she ought to let Charley Michelson know she was contemplating leaving. To her intense surprise, he not only asked her to stay on—he outright told her that he had taken her only because he'd had to, but now he'd hate to lose her. It was a grand talk, ending on a personal note. During the next couple of weeks, as Hick told E.R., Michelson would be away himself because of a health problem—

"That gland old gentlemen have trouble with"—and he had been hoping she would write a sheaf of speeches for use at upcoming state conventions during his absence. If she wished, she could do the work on Long Island.

So Hick had a glorious spring, out by sunrise with Prinz and picking dewy white violets before getting down to solid stretches at her desk, composing the speeches Charley wanted about various Department of Agriculture programs. She must have done pretty well at making wads of statistics digestible, because when she went down to Washington again after Charley got back to his desk, he asked her to do the same sort of job on the Army and Navy, too. It took her only a few days to fill her suitcase with more statistics— and then she was back at Mastic, bubbling over to E.R. about the lilacs and wistaria. Without even a radio to remind her of the state of the world.

E.R., visiting her own Hyde Park cottage in the same lovely weather, reacted differently. Although the grounds looked nice, she told Hick, she was ashamed of how little she cared about the place. If she never came there again, it would not matter to her. Of course, this apathy was a symptom of the personal depression she had already suffered twice previously during presidential election years, although Hick did not seem to notice the fact.

". . . I'm sorry you don't get more pleasure out of your cottage," Hick wrote to her. "Perhaps if you had to plan and figure *how* you could have it—if you were never quite sure how long you would have it—it might mean more." Still Hick could not remain testy with E.R. for more than two sentences. "But I do wish you could get half the joy out of it that I get out of this place—and my dog!"

It was during the surpassingly balmy spring of 1940 that the war in Europe stopped being just a distant threat. With lightning speed, Hitler's paratroops overran much of Scandinavia; his tanks rolled through the Low Countries, then rumbled into Paris. Aboard a pitiful armada of bobbing little boats, the British retreated to the defense of their own island. But should they fail on their beaches, and in the air and on the streets of London, how long could the suddenly narrow Atlantic save the United States?

Even under such circumstances, James Aloysius Farley, former town clerk of a hamlet in the lower reaches of the Hudson Valley, felt compelled to teach Franklin Roosevelt a lesson. Nobody could believe that Farley seriously was aiming for the White House; as a party organizer he had no peer, but there were gaps in Jim's experience and in his grasp of larger issues. Still, he apparently intended to pursue his own cause right onto the floor of the Democratic National Convention. Hick, boarding the Liberty Limited for Chicago ten days before that conclave started, could have no idea why Jim was being such a sorehead. She learned, though, much sooner than most people.

At least that train ride was a relief from politics, because the white-haired Charley Michelson regaled a group of the committee's advance guard with some choice anecdotes about his boyhood in the ripsnorting old West. After leaving the Nevada silver-mining country, he had become a top reporter while Hick was still in grade school. Ye gods, she wrote to E.R., this man had covered the trial of the lunatic who shot McKinley! Once they arrived at the Stevens Hotel, though, Hick lost track of the rest of the world. Having grown so fond of Charley, she ran her legs off doing errands for him, trying to spare him after his recent operation. Chicago in July was, not unexpectedly, a steamy cauldron.

But if the mob scenes in the hotel lobbies and all the noise and heat and hysteria were more or less normal for a national political convention, this one differed from every previous one very significantly. Even though the President still had not said a word publicly about whether he was willing to serve another four years, in the light of the world situation how could anybody doubt that he would be the party's candidate again? Yet the prospect of defying tradition and nominating F.D.R. for a third term was extremely unsettling.

Everything seemed topsy-turvy. Already the Republicans had astounded the wise men of both parties by failing to nominate either Governor Dewey of New York or Senator Taft of Ohio. Instead, a complete stranger to politics, a corporation lawyer with liberal leanings who as recently as two years ago had considered himself a Democrat, had somehow captured the top spot on the GOP ticket; for the next several months even Eleanor Roosevelt would have difficulty spelling the name of Wendell Willkie. Only the mysterious quality politicians were still at a loss to describe—the word *charisma* had not yet entered the dictionary of politics—could explain such an incredible choice as F.D.R.'s opponent this year.

To Democrats of the old school, their own convention promised to be just as distressing. While everybody knew that F.D.R. would get nominated, there was no proper machinery for making this happen. Instead, a command post operating with a brash disdain for the sensibilities of party stalwarts was located at the Blackstone. Everybody knew about it and knew that Harry Hopkins was in charge of it. Everybody believed, too, that Hopkins, who had never even attended any previous national convention, was acting under specific instructions from F.D.R. himself.

Resentment grew prodigiously in the steamy heat. To those who put the party first, Farley already was more popular than the President, even if pressure from the Hopkins squadrons of New Deal arm-twisters proved irresistible. When the time came for the casting of ballots, just a few dozen delegates dared to vote for Farley or for "Cactus Jack" Garner, the vice-president around whom other last-ditch anti-Third Termers had rallied. The vote for Roosevelt was 946.

Still, the real hero that evening turned out to be Farley at the rostrum, his bald pate gleaming and tears in his eyes as he gallantly moved to declare Franklin Roosevelt nominated by acclamation. The next day, though, when the Hopkins cohorts began another round of arm-twisting, the mood of the convention turned ominous.

For the party regulars who had swallowed the third term reluctantly now wanted to pick a vice-president with whom they could feel comfortable. But F.D.R.'s own choice was Secretary of Agriculture Henry Wallace, among the least popular of the New Deal loyalists. Suddenly revolution was in the air. Speakers attempting to nominate Wallace were booed so loudly that the presiding officer was forced to call a recess. Leaving the convention hall, Secretary of Labor Frances Perkins telephoned her friend Eleanor Roosevelt. The First Lady consulted her husband, and then agreed to try to calm the rebellious delegates—but only if Jim Farley approved of the idea.

Hick, walking into the committee headquarters soon afterward, saw Jim on the phone. "But I do mean it," he was saying. "We need you—badly." Right after he hung up, he grabbed Hick's arm. "That was Mrs. Roosevelt," he said. "Go and call her back and tell her I mean it. She'll have to come. Things are bad."

So E.R. did fly out in a chartered plane, accompanied only by her son Franklin junior. She specified that she wanted only Jim to meet her at the airport, and she had a private dinner with him. Hick waited for her at the back of the crowded platform, where they sat inconspicuously until a perspiring presiding officer tried to shout the name of the President's wife above the uproarious clamor. Then Hick watched with stabbing pain as the person she loved best in all the world moved forward, tall and very erect, through the haze of dust and tobacco smoke under the glaring lights overhead. Hick feared that the delegates would not even listen to the First Lady. But as Eleanor Roosevelt reached the speaker's stand, she stood calmly and waited. And a miraculous wave of silence spread as she was recognized. In the sudden stillness, she began:

"For many years I have worked under and with Jim Farley, and I think nobody could appreciate more than I do what he has done for the party, what he has given in work and loyalty, and I want to give him here my thanks and devotion." With no prepared text, or even any notes, she then delivered a short, earnest sermon on the subject of responsibility—the awesome responsibility facing any man nominated for the presidency at such a point in history, and the responsibility of every citizen to rise above considerations that were narrow or partisan. When she finished, there was a moment of silence before the organist began softly to play "God Bless America." The cheering started then, and after Mrs. Roosevelt left the platform an orderly convention proceeded to nominate Henry Wallace for the vice-presidency.

". . . I am glad you were satisfied with my job in Chicago," E.R. wrote to Hick the following day. "The 'few words' must have come over the air well from what people tell me. . . ." Satisfied? Hick replied that she felt disgustingly proud of E.R.'s convention triumph. Only long afterwards, though, would she realize that witnessing this extraordinary demonstration had caused a subtle change in her own attitude. During the next several months, Hick was much too busy for introspection—and the first item on her personal agenda was forcing herself to swallow a large dose of disillusion.

For E.R. had to unburden herself to somebody. From Jim Farley she had heard quite a story, not just during their dinner in Chicago but also at a two-hour lunch soon after the convention ended. Although she was supposed to be urging Jim to stay on as Democratic chairman at least through November so that he could again manage F.D.R.'s campaign, after hearing Jim's reasons for refusing, E.R. could not blame him.

Eight years later, when Farley got around to writing his own memoir of his relationship with Franklin Roosevelt, he would relate his grievance to a wider public. In brief, he claimed that F.D.R. had on several occasions said he would not run again and had even encouraged Jim to make the race himself. Astute observers of F.D.R.'s habits would distill from Jim's narration a neat little play on words; F.D.R. had been absolutely truthful when he told Jim he would not *run*, but he never promised not to let himself be *drafted*. As to encouraging Jim's own ambitions, F.D.R. hated to be unpleasant to anybody when it could be avoided; let somebody else shatter good old Jim's impossible fantasy.

Since Eleanor Roosevelt had another source she could consult, however, she was able to give Hick a somewhat more complete account than later historians would find it possible to offer. For she told her husband Jim's bill of particulars alleging that the President had lied to him. "F.D.R. can't understand it & acts hurt & innocent," E.R. informed Hick, "but I don't think he can be quite absolved tho' technically he is probably telling me the truth."

At first, Hick professed to be only slightly disillusioned, taking comfort from the fact that the country was still a democracy not really at the mercy of any man or group of men with their ambitions and vanities. Because she felt that the nation's chances of remaining a democracy were infinitely better with F.D.R. than with Willkie, whose Wall Street backers frightened her, she aimed to forget everything else and work as hard as she could for the President's re-election. "He *must* be reelected, dear," she wrote to E.R.

Zealously, Hick began reading through all of F.D.R.'s speeches since 1933, seeking quotable extracts that might be helpful during the next several months; Charley had asked her to do this while the committee was getting set up in New York for its big push to sell the third term among the country's voters. As though aiming to start by selling the President's wife, after a few days Hick assured E.R.: "If you read the President's speeches and messages to Congress these last seven years, you *do* realize that he has put up a whale of a fight!" E.R. replied that she was glad Hick was so impressed. "The fact that he has been consistent in some things at least can be used!" the First Lady added.

By then, though, Hick's own disillusion had been further fed. Even Charley seemed to be sulking because some aide of Henry Wallace had been rude to him. Nobody appeared to know whether the Hopkins crowd or the National Committee would actually run the campaign. Meanwhile, nothing was being done. Helen Gahagan Douglas, the beautiful actress who had recently begun devoting her amazing energy to the Democratic women's division in California, blew into Washington boiling mad because of a hypocritical Willkie statement to a group of farmers about retaining the present farm policy. How could he say such a thing when his own backers would tar and feather him if he tried it? But Charley wasn't even in the office to snap out a reply to Willkie. On her own, Hick dashed off a statement for Helen Douglas to issue. But who would pay any attention to a woman on the farm program?

It all made Hick brood furiously over what Jim had told E.R., shattering her faith in Jim too. For she had really believed that Jim had been opposing F.D.R. on a matter of principle about the third term, instead of because he was nursing a personal grievance. Jim Farley wanted to be President himself! To E.R., Hick exploded:

> My God, dear—these men are *children,* small quarrelsome children. And we are expecting them to run the nation in a time of awful peril! I think they need someone to give them Hell—the whole gang of them, *both* sides. They don't deserve to win this election if they keep on the way they've been going. . . .

But somehow it all worked out. As usual, E.R. suffered in silence except to Hick: "If F.D.R. wins I'll be glad for him & for the country & if he loses I'll be glad for myself & the kids." After frenzied weeks of worry, on Election Night neither Hick nor Charley could eat any dinner because they felt so tense. When it was time to go to the press headquarters on the Biltmore's mezzanine, Hick was glad she had to keep running from Charley's desk to the tabulators. At least she wasn't just standing around shaking with the jitters because the early returns from Massachusetts were not good. "Those are the towns," Charley said. "Wait until we begin to hear from Boston and the industrial cities."

About one A.M., when the Cleveland *Plain Dealer* conceded, Hick began to relax a little. By about two, it was just a question of how many states F.D.R. would carry, and she went up to the apartment of one of the gals in the women's division, had two stiff drinks of brandy and some bacon and eggs, and went to bed there. When she awoke toward noon, it comforted her that the country had been saved; according to the radio, F.D.R. had won by a margin of five million votes. And Hick did not even care too much that she herself was out of a job.

17. Living at the White House

Out at the Little House, sauntering through the woods with Prinz for the first time in weeks, Hick felt all of her fatigue and worry evaporating. It was like dying and going to heaven, she decided. But if, jobless, she wailed only intermittently, her new-found peace was due to more than her surroundings. Thanks to her vow of frugality upon joining the staff of the Democratic Committee, she had no debts now—and five hundred dollars in the bank. Also, thanks to Charley Michelson, she would very probably be back on the committee's payroll, at least by January, 1941.

This time, E.R. had almost nothing to do with it. Because Hick herself had impressed Charley, he had volunteered, during a quiet moment, that he did not know another woman he'd rather have fill the women's division slot that would open up once the campaign was over. Oh, and what was that? He'd smiled then, shaking his head at Hick's lack of push. Of course he meant the top job as director of the whole female operation. Good Lord, Hick murmured, speechmaking! No, Charley said, they'd actually been thinking of dividing it up so that they could give the title and the speechmaking to Mrs. Charles W. Tillett, the committeewoman from North Carolina, who had family responsibilities and could spend no more than two days a week in Washington. It was the day-to-day running of the national women's program, including the editing of the monthly *Democratic Digest*, that Charley had in mind for Hick. They could call her executive secretary of the women's division, he suggested.

Why not? Since Charley had agreed with Tom Dillon in Minneapolis that the newspaper *PM* would probably fold within a year or two, Hick had more or less rebuffed their job offer. *PM* had too many prima donnas anyway, more interested in being columnists than in covering the news. Nobody seemed to be panting for Hickok to do old-fashioned straight reporting, which she was not even sure she would like anymore, now that she had seen how full of mistakes most fast stories turned out to be. Since she found politics so interesting, why not take Charley up on his offer?

E.R. told her. The job would require patience, E.R. said, endless patience with trivial details and with ladies of no great experience in the world outside their sheltered homes. Did Hick really think she would enjoy working with, and attending tea parties with, an unceasing procession of "little" Democratic women visiting Washington?

After just eight days of being unemployed, Hick informed the First Lady of a compelling reason why impatience or boredom were not likely to afflict her if Ed Flynn, Jim Farley's successor, was willing to hire her. Hick could not, she pointed out, afford to be choosy. "I am forty-seven years old, my dear, and have reached an age where it is very, very difficult for a woman to get a job." Lest there be any doubt about this, Hick referred to a few people she knew from the Fair and to her sister. Although Ruby had remained on the reserve list after finishing her nurses' training at Walter Reed back in '17, even in this new defense emergency the Army had just turned her down. She was too old, they told her—at forty-four.

So E.R. thenceforth supported Hick's candidacy. With such backing, and Charley Michelson's promise to speak to the President himself, Chairman Ed Flynn found no objection to the Tillett-Hickok arrangement. Mrs. Tillett also expressed pleasure at the prospect of having Hick as her day-by-day deputy. Thus within a few weeks after the election it was definite that Hick would get the job as of January 1, 1941.

Meanwhile at Mastic, Hick made an interesting discovery: she could live there cheerfully on two hundred dollars a month. By now her music-loving friend Howard, who liked to spend his weekends sailing, was building a small place of his own closer to the water, but Ella did not want Hick to feel pressed about paying rent: could Hick possibly afford fifty dollars a month? Hick could. Learning from the Rosses, she went "upstreet" to pick up mail only a couple of times a week, saving money on gas. Frequently she ate fresh-caught weakfish with Clarence and Annie, or clams that Clarence had just dug. They played Chinese checkers. Occasionally she took them to Patchogue, about twenty minutes away, for dinner and a movie. Weekends Hick usually had company but, in between, strolling with Prinz, she had ample opportunity for introspection.

The process was stimulated by E.R.'s postelectoral blues, which introduced a new theme this time. A month previously, when she had been too concerned over "Wilkie's" gains in the Gallup Poll to worry about her own age, she had turned fifty-six. But right after she was assured of another tour of duty in the White House, she replied to Hick's commiseration: "No, I don't look forward to the next five years for I will probably be too old for a new job at the end & I dread getting accustomed to 4 more years of easy living but perhaps I can keep from being too dependent on it."

What did she mean by an easy life, Hick demanded, adding:

> I don't know anyone in the world who works harder than you do! And I don't believe you'll ever be too old for a job, either. If you were going to get old, you'd be showing signs of it by now. I don't see any. As a matter of fact, I'd never have believed it possible for a woman to develop after fifty as you have in the last six years. My God, you've learned to do, surpassingly well, two of the most difficult things in the world—to write and to speak. I'd not worry about a "life of ease" if I were you.

Then with a flash of insight, Hick suddenly uncovered something she had hidden even from herself. She had recently read a short biography of the First Lady by Ruby Black of the United Press, and her own train of thought reminded her of it. The first part of the book was just an inferior rehash of what E.R. had written herself, Hick said, but the chapters on E.R.'s White House career were excellent—

> —much better than I could do. My trouble, I suspect, has always been that I've been so much more interested in the *person* than in the *personage*. I resented the personage and fought for years an anguished and losing fight against the development of the *person* into the *personage*. I still prefer the *person*, but I admire and respect the *personage* with all my heart. But all this explains why I shall never write your biography. I can think of only one

other person who undoubtedly felt about this as I have—
or would have felt so, increasingly, had he lived. Louis
Howe.

I must go to market. . . .

"You are wrong about Louis," E.R. corrected Hick: "He always
wanted to 'make' me President when F.D.R. was thro' & insisted he
could do it. You see, he was interested in his power to create per-
sonages more than in a person, tho' I think he probably cared for
me as a person as much as he ever cared for anyone & more than
anyone else has! I filled a need on his part, I imagine! I used to
laugh at him & tell him I had no interest in the job & I still think
the personage is an accident & I only like the part of my life in
which I am a person!"

Louis Howe cared for her more than anyone else has! Of course,
E.R., hurt by the implication that she no longer had a heart, could
not help hurting Hick this way. But since there was a limit, even
now, to the pain that Hick could stand, it was merciful that she
failed to perceive the whole truth about E.R.'s transformation. In
1932 Eleanor Roosevelt had still been so insecure—so angry inside—
that she had needed a Lorena Hickok. Not many people realized
this; Malvina Thompson was one of the few.

But if Tommy had understood Mrs. R.'s dependence on Hick
then, Tommy had always known what a magnificent person her
boss was. Also, Tommy had been among the first to comprehend
that Mrs. R. had gone beyond being just idealistic and intelligent,
and had reached a pinnacle few women in history had ever attained. Tommy could even pinpoint the moment when this had
happened; it was when Mrs. R. had stood up in front of that bunch
of wild kids at the Youth Congress meeting in Washington last
winter—and miraculously quieted them.

However, Eleanor Roosevelt's arrival at this eminence had really
taken two decades. While Louis Howe had undoubtedly done
much to build her self-confidence during the 1920's, she had still
been a nervous speaker and a perfunctory writer when she entered
the White House. As Hick observed, she had grown remarkably
after her fiftieth birthday. In 1935, when she was fifty-one, E.R.
remained subject to such qualms about her own judgment that she
could timorously defer to Hick about the merit of some new book:
"It gives me confidence in my judgment when you corroborate it."

It was within the next several years that she ceased to require so much help.

Then—from Hick's standpoint—the person who was Eleanor Roosevelt all but disappeared. The cruel irony that escaped Hick was that nobody had done more to foster the creation of the esteemed personage who replaced E.R., the person, than Lorena Hickok had; it is even possible to describe her as the catalyst in this transformation. Probably it would have happened anyway. Still, as it did happen, she herself was substantially responsible if the personage could not love or need her as the person had.

On the second of January, 1941, Hick arrived at the White House where she was assigned the same room, oddly enough, that had once been Louis Howe's. It was a small room, with nondescript furniture painted gray; everything else was overshadowed by the heavy marble mantel framing the fireplace, and by the enormous gilt-framed mirror above it. On the walls were dim portraits of an unknown colonial gentleman and of a not particularly distinguished senator. As works of art, these paintings had little to recommend them but Hick would never forget them. For she was to live four years in this room.

E.R. had urged Hick to stay there—originally just until she got settled. Perhaps, E.R. suggested, she could find a little place in Virginia since Hick was so fond of country life. That way she would not mind giving up the Little House on Long Island. But Hick had no intention of giving up the Little House, even though she would not be able to spend much time there for the next couple of years.

Would she prefer a convenient apartment then? Of course E.R. was aware that Washington was getting awfully crowded as national defense spending mounted. It surely was, Hick glumly informed her, and if she paid the kind of rent they were asking she'd never be able to afford keeping her place at Mastic, despite finally having let her lease lapse at 10 Mitchell Place. Well, said E.R. briskly, I suppose you had best live here, after all.

So Louis Howe's little room that was part of the Lincoln Suite at the northwest corner of the White House living quarters became Hick's room. While her residency was not exactly one of the capital's top secrets, few people even among Hick's own circle knew that 1600 Pennsylvania Avenue appeared as her address on her tax returns and later her ration books. Since the Democratic Committee had offices at the Mayflower, Hick let it be generally understood that she had a room at the hotel. With her salary of six thousand a year, she would never have been able to afford living at the Mayflower. Yet this fiction forced her into some devious maneuvers.

When somebody at a party offered to see her home, Hick let herself be delivered to the Mayflower lobby, then headed for the elevators. In a telephone booth she waited until the coast was clear before climbing into a taxi and proceeding to the White House. But she found it nerve-wracking to return from a weekend on Long Island after mob scenes at Washington's Union Station forced the city to institute compulsory cab-sharing. The trouble was that she *couldn't* share a cab because the White House sentry would not allow any stranger except the driver to enter the grounds. It took a couple of fierce arguments with the taxi dispatcher until Hick figured out a solution; thenceforth, she shared a cab to the Mayflower—where they recognized her and let her have a taxi all to herself.

Once she arrived at her destination, Hick had other troubles. Since she was anxious to avoid raising any questions about her presence in the mansion, she had no meal but breakfast there; if Mrs. Roosevelt was at home, they ate together at eight-thirty in the informal family area at one end of the West Hall during the winter, on the South Veranda in warm weather. Otherwise Hick stayed as invisible as possible on her way to and from work. The tiny ushers' office near the elevator became her refuge if anybody else was in sight and, over the four years of her peculiar tenancy, Hick ducked into this hiding place hundreds of times. Only through her own closed door did she hear Winston Churchill's voice; already she knew he must be in the house because she had noticed a tray of bottles, highball glasses and ice in the West Hall as she hastened to her room.

Ordinarily nothing stronger than beer or wine was served except in the President's study, where Hick supposed he might still be mixing predinner cocktails for special guests. But she made a point of staying as ignorant as possible about what was going on around her. Indeed "Lorena Lawrence," that enthusiastic young reporter on the Milwaukee *Sentinel,* would have been bemused by the opportunities from which the mature Lorena purposely retreated. Why did she? It must be remembered that back in Milwaukee, even the fiercely ambitious Lorena had felt a paralyzing awe at the sight of Mrs. Woodrow Wilson.

Despite all the changes a quarter of a century had wrought, Hick's real reason for staying in the White House now was not so different. She herself confessed this a few years later when she wrote in her autobiographical fragment that her money problems were less important than something she never told Mrs. Roosevelt: "I couldn't bear the idea of being in Washington and hardly ever seeing her." And:

> . . . With her schedule as heavy as it was, I was certain that that was the way it would be. Even staying in the house, I used to think I did not see very much of her—but at that I think I fared better than most of her friends, except Tommy, who worked with her every day. When she was in Washington we had breakfast together, and I would stop in her sitting room on my way at night to say goodnight. I usually got in around 10:30 or 11, and at that hour I would find her buried in mail. Sometimes, if she was out when I came in, or had visitors, she would come into my room and sit on the foot of my bed and talk for a little while.

On the other hand, the less Hick saw of F.D.R. the better she liked it. More than her old apprehension in the presence of the President made her keep out of his way; although her room was less than two hundred feet from his, she felt compelled during these tense years to preserve him from the slightest unnecessary encounter. Now his work schedule was horrendous, he never had the leisure for just sitting among family and friends, releasing his great, ringing, musical laugh, so joyous and infectious that everybody else involuntarily laughed too. He gave up his daily swim, he dined usually in his study and stayed there all evening, night after night, week after week. Once when E.R. told her, "Franklin says he never knows when you are in the house!" Hick was pleased.

Yet it was her job that made her especially leery of having her White House domicile publicized. Although most of the newspaper women who covered Mrs. R.'s press conferences were aware of Hick's address, they never mentioned it in their stories; by unspoken pact they would cooperate, as long as Hick did nothing questionable like riding around Washington in an official limousine. This journalistic restraint was only one sign of the feeling of sisterhood that united women more effectively, during the latter period of Eleanor Roosevelt's tenure as First Lady, than some feminists two decades afterward would even suspect.

By acclamation, Mrs. R. had become the leader of an informal network devoted to furthering women's interests. "Our tower of strength," Congresswoman Mary Norton called her. In the support of this tower, no organization was more important than the women's division of the Democratic National Committee, and thus Hick had no need to fear unfriendly barbs from newspaper women who personally were fervent champions of feminine advancement. What Hick did have to fear was a bombardment of appeals from other women all around the country—if they knew at whose table she copiously breakfasted every morning.

Naturally, Democratic objectives comprised the program of the party's feminine offshoot. And yet any reader of Hick's output from her desk at the Mayflower must be reminded of what the president of General Motors once said about his corporation and the nation. If it was good for women, it was good for the party: that summed up the philosophy imbuing Hick's year-round activity. Only the approach of an election stimulated outright partisan organizing. Otherwise the program was rather like that of the League of Women Voters in its emphasis on creating a well-informed feminine electorate and in its efforts to focus attention on such issues as the urgent need for day nurseries so that more women could take jobs in defense industries.

Hick's own credentials as an upholder of the feminine potential had not always been impeccable. Back when she had been traveling for the WPA, she had once mentioned to E.R. that a new acquaintance was unusually capable because this woman thought like a man. Which immediately elicited a verbal spank from E.R.: "I want to take you to task for that phrase 'she has the mind of a man.' Why can't a woman think, be practical & a good business woman & still have a mind of her own?" Even if Hick still had a tendency toward jocular disparagement of females en masse, that kind of joking was almost universal then; "the wimmin" expected it. Nevertheless, she had come a long way in the last few years. And during her first year at the women's division, she came a lot farther with the help of a grand new teacher.

If Mary Teresa Norton had appeared in Washington a few decades earlier—or later—her name might be more familiar; but she flourished during the quarter of this century after the suffrage fight had been won and before a new generation of feminists began making headlines. In her day, though, she did darn well. "Battling Mary," they called her at the Capitol, and they smiled as they said it because even those reactionaries who were her political arch-enemies loved her.

An ample woman, Irish as can be, her chestnut hair already threaded with a few strands of gray, she came to Congress in 1925. Not only was she the first Democratic woman ever elected to the House of Representatives, she was also the first woman to prove that she had what it took to play the game of politics. Although she pinned an orchid to her shoulder whenever she had to make an important speech, Mary Norton was no shrinking violet. Early in her career a colleague sarcastically offered to yield to the *lady* from New Jersey. "I'm not a lady," Mary proclaimed, "I'm a member of Congress and will proceed on that basis."

Despite her propensity for ripe platitude, or maybe because in this respect she differed not at all from most of her male colleagues, Mary had earned bipartisan regard by the time Hick met her. Not the least of the Norton fans was F.D.R. himself. It was hardly surprising that he liked her, because almost everybody did. But the President also understood the importance of being her friend.

In plain truth, Mary Norton had become a power in Congress for the same reason that a large number of Southern gentlemen had; since there weren't enough Republicans in her district to worry about, all she had to do to keep being re-elected regularly was to keep on the right side of one man. But that was easy because she never had to doubt the integrity of Mayor Frank Hague of Jersey City; how she happened to preserve such a high opinion of the epitome of oldtime political bosses would require a separate volume to explain, but as far as Hick was concerned, Mary's loyalty to Hague was marvelous. About a reformer challenging Hague, Mary wrote to Hick: "He is devilish. Spite and revenge are his daily playmates. . . ."

For it was Hague who had had the notion, not long after women got the vote, that the wives of his faithful might like the novelty of having a woman on the ballot. Mary Norton had then been a fifty-year-old widow whose only child had died in infancy; she merely had about a thousand nieces, and a job running a hospital nursery, to occupy her before she went to Washington. Once there, she made New Jersey so proud of her that probably even Hague would not have been able to depose her.

Early in the thirties, by seniority, she had become the first woman chairman of a House committee—the District of Columbia Committee, then the actual governing body for the disenfranchised citizens of the capital. Mary Norton was a good, scrappy "mayor of Washington," but in 1937 something even meatier opened up and she took the chairmanship of the House Labor Committee, which at that point in the New Deal was no less important than Foreign Affairs would be in another few years. And by shrewdly steering some of the major Roosevelt measures onto the House floor, Mrs. Norton had endeared herself to the President.

His wife cherished Mary for other reasons, too. Nobody had raised Mary Norton's feminine consciousness; all by herself, she had figured out that women had better stick together if they ever wanted the same pay scales as men, and more opportunities to use the brains that God had given them. Years ago she had organized a weekly lunch, originally just for the handful of women in Congress, to further such female objectives, and by now she was periodically holding lunchtime seminars attended by women with important jobs all over Washington. A rousing speaker, she willingly went wherever the Democratic women's division thought she might do some good, and that was how she first met Hick.

Only after enjoying Mary's oratory did Hick discover a fascinating coincidence: they shared the same birthday. Mary, of course, was seventeen years older. This became, to Hick and Mary both, a fact of deep significance; already by March 7, 1941, when they spent the first of many birthdays together, the younger and the older had found in each other a relationship they both had missed intensely. Mary treated Hick like a long-lost daughter. And Hick, during her first year in Washington, grew to love Mary far more than she had ever loved her own mother.

If there *were* too many tea parties—when Hick had to curse under her breath as she tried to clutch, simultaneously, gloves, purse, cigarette and also refreshment—there were compensations. Regional conferences in Knoxville and St. Paul and Los Angeles got her out of Washington, and she had fine visits with the Dillons, where things seemed better, as well as with Ellie. By working overtime getting the *Democratic Digest* ready for the printer, she earned repeated three-day weekends out in Mastic, which were becoming especially precious because old Prinz was failing rapidly. In May of 1941, when he stopped eating, she thought she was going to lose him until she got him to take an eggnog with a teaspoonful of brandy. Although that revived him, she had to realize that she had had him thirteen years and he could not last much longer. "We've been through so much together," Hick wrote to E.R. from the Little House, "and he has always been the same loving companion, no matter what happened."

E.R. herself, away so much speaking and inspecting, raised flickers of a private hope in Hick when at the end of the summer she suddenly needed Hick again. Two family crises got her down. Her mother-in-law's death was peaceful, E.R. wrote to Hick from Hyde Park in the first week of September, but putting her brother Hall in the hospital had been difficult. That her husband's mother had succumbed to old age without any protracted invalidism had to be considered a blessing, although the President, like any son, might have some bad moments. The critical condition of E.R.'s brother was, however, a different matter. His disintegration after years of heavy drinking had to bring up very unhappy memories.

When he, too, died, E.R. reverted almost, but not quite, to the person who had once craved Hick's support: "I am so weary that I feel as you sometimes look & yet I know it is because I am letting myself be indifferent inside—you know how I get these moods, they pass, but they are a nuisance!" Yet she remained in a horrid frame of mind for several days. One of these was her fifty-seventh birthday, when Hick wired her: ". . . EACH YEAR I'M PROUDER OF YOU AND LOVE YOU MORE."

It was not really necessary. By now E.R.'s new young friends could distract her, and so could her new interests, especially the Civilian Defense program in which she was deeply involved. Hick had never felt as superfluous, or as weary, as she did when she went up to Long Island for Thanksgiving and a couple of weeks of vacation. But ". . . that old sense of perfect peace and contentment fills my soul," she was able to write to E.R. soon after her arrival. "My God, how I love this spot!"

Then, sitting over a late lunch on Sunday, December the seventh, Hick and her company wondered what Clarence could be running to tell them.

The evening after Pearl Harbor, when Hick arrived back at the White House, the weather was cold, gray and wet. E.R. was away, on a Civilian Defense mission to the West Coast where they were going through terrible air-raid scares. "I seem to have a calming influence," E.R. would write to Hick. As for Hick herself, she came down with the flu. Staying in her room for several days, she was amazed by the silence within the house. Even the Roosevelts' dog, Fala, did not bark. But outside, all day and into the night she could hear a steam shovel at work, digging a trench across the front lawn for a bomb shelter.

When she got up to look out of her window, she saw a machine gun on the roof of the swimming pool, with a soldier standing by. Soon she would discover, but never mention until years later, that if the gun were covered and unattended, it meant that the President was away at Shangri-La, the weekend camp in Maryland, or attending some secret conference. Otherwise, except that she had to be extremely careful about closing the heavy blackout curtains before turning on a light at night, the war did not make much difference in Hick's own life.

Less than three months after Pearl Harbor, however, something else did. Late in February of 1942, writing to E.R. in New York, Hick offhandedly mentioned: "I'm about to dine with Marion Harron."

18. Hick and Judge Harron

The Honorable Marion Janet Harron, ten years younger than Lorena Hickok, was a judge in the United States Tax Court. Since 1936, when she had been just thirty-three, she had been hearing complex cases hinging on fine print in the federal tax laws; she was a serious-minded woman, most people thought. According to *Who's Who*, her progression from Phi Beta Kappa undergraduate through law school at the University of California had been followed by an impressive sequence of banking and governmental positions rarely filled by a female. So her work must have left her little leisure. Numerous acquaintances from the organizations whose meetings she attended knew little more about her than that she lived with her mother in a small house in Chevy Chase, where she enjoyed gardening.

Marion Harron died of cancer in 1972. Thereafter, only a few thick folders of her letters to Lorena Hickok would indicate how funny and playful and intensely emotional a person she also could be. These are, beyond any doubt, love letters. What is mystifying, though, is exactly what Hick intended to convey, regarding Eleanor Roosevelt, when she included them among the contents of those cartons that she donated to the Franklin D. Roosevelt Library.

Certainly E.R. did know about the burgeoning friendship between Hick and Judge Harron. That the friendship warmed to a very close bond could not have been any secret to the First Lady, either; for Judge Harron was practically the only person who ever came to see Hick at the White House, and she came so often that the guards at the gate got to know her well enough to wave her past them without even bothering to ask her for any identification. Also, when the relationship did cool, Hick would inform E.R. of the fact. However, to the question that a liberated society must ask about whether Eleanor Roosevelt understood the degree of intimacy disclosed by Marion Harron's letters, there can be no answer. Nor is it possible to estimate Hick's own commitment to Marion with any precision, because none of her own letters to the judge seem to have survived.

Still, the one-sided correspondence starting in March of 1942, abundantly documents that Marion fell deeply in love with Hick. It suggests, too, that a similar one-sidedness characterized the whole relationship. In her first letter Marion, who was embarking on one of her regular judicial circuits that took her to several other cities, sets the tone by begging Hick not to downgrade herself: ". . . As I view the record, people are greatly in your debt—the score on your side is very high in your devotion to people, in your friendships to people, in your capacity to give others companionship and comfort and warmth. It is my belief that it will come back to you—and is now—in full measure—and please never look upon the future with any fears. The best of life is yet to be for you. Believe that—know it, and count on it! And *never never* let your heart drop down. . . ."

In short, the world-weary Hick, her wry little smile at the corner of her lips, must cease looking upon the past as her only justification, for if she will just allow Marion to coax her into caring again, Marion will make up the sorrow oppressing her. If that did not quite happen, at least Marion revived a spark in Hick; from Long Island, Hick apparently signed herself "Carrie Cuttlefish." Also, during the ensuing three years, Marion learned—no matter that others might not have noted it as clearly as she did—to cease focusing only on the fine print. Among other things, Hick taught her to get her clothes from the same elegant tailor who made up her own birthday presents from E.R., and to let E.R.'s hairdresser give her a less severe coiffure.

At its peak, this new adventure had a zany wartime quality of its own. Judge Harron's office was near the White House, guarded in those days with bayonets. Sometimes the judge found herself unable to concentrate—"Who in tunket cares whether a sale of Treasury stock originally acquired for use as an employees' bonus but never so used results in taxable gain except Cluett, Peabody & Co., *Inc.*—Docket No. 112444?" Then she was apt to dash off a letter to Hick, which she would personally hand a sentry at the White

House gate on her way home. There can be little doubt that such communications made Hick's life more interesting.

For E.R. was continually going off to speak somewhere. "I've been like a pea on a hot shovel since I left on Friday," she wrote to Hick from Nashville in April, 1942. But the First Lady still did not feel that what she was doing had any real importance, as she confided to Hick on Long Island three months later: "F. & I dined alone last night & I took the occasion to suggest I'd like some war work but I doubt if it bears fruit." Nevertheless, this husband and wife's unusual dinner with no other company did precipitate E.R.'s international debut.

F.D.R. decided to send her to beleaguered England; it was to be partly a state visit, partly a morale builder, because American air crews and other troops were now arriving there in such numbers that a certain amount of inter-Allied tension had to be expected. Thus Hick not only acquired a few letters from Buckingham Palace for her collection, but she also reached a new emotional plateau herself:

> Darling:
> I am thrilled about you—and worried.
> Worried over the increased activity of the German bombers over England. Apparently they visited Canterbury right after you were there. No use telling you to be careful—they are probably taking as good care of you as they can, or as you will let them. Anyway it's all on the knees of the Gods. But I can't help worrying.
> I'm thrilled because of the job you are doing. More than anyone else in the world, *you* are holding the British and us together right now. And in your own straightforward, honest way. Oh, I'm *so* proud of you!

Indeed Hick's pride in the personage at this point had begun to outweigh her private feelings for the person. As a result she devoted another long paragraph, in the style of a public relations aide, to an enthusiastic summary of the press and radio response that E.R.'s mission was eliciting back home. "So far only Westbrook Pegler has been nasty . . . You should have heard Ed Murrow on the air from London tonight!" It could hardly have been coincidental that this shift in Hick's attitude occurred as she and Marion were preparing for a long weekend together at Mastic, in anticipation of which Marion wrote to Hick: "Now whatever is not here set down [by] this pen will be forthcoming upon my arrival so don't wonder if I do not quote the *Rubiyat*. All my love darling—and a kiss."

In addition, Hick also had to cope with a sudden and severe storm at her office.

It seemed at first as if she—and the entire women's division of the Democratic National Committee—would be declared an unnecessary luxury. The catch phrase everywhere should have prepared her: Don't you know there's a war on? The rumors relieved Hick, or so she insisted. After all, the war effort was the most important thing in the world, so she leapt to a conclusion.

Even if she weren't too old for the WACS or WAVES, probably she would have failed the physical required by the new women's branches of the Army and Navy. "I'm not much of a militarist anyway," she wrote to E.R. "But I think I could and should try to get into the production end of it." Hickok the Riveter? No, she didn't think she had the endurance for an assembly line; something like personnel work at a war plant would be more likely. A war plant on Long Island, so she could live in the Little House. She even knew a man who had, or used to have, some connection with Sperry Gyroscope there.

The office crisis came to a head following the congressional election of 1942, a disaster for the Democrats. Technically, they retained control of both houses, but a couple of dozen sturdy liberals were beaten. With so many Southern Democrats voting as if they were Republicans, the prospects for legislative sniping at New Deal gains frightened Hick, and yet that did not appear to bother the men of the party hierarchy. Patronage did. How were they going to give jobs to the right people now? And if Congress refused to go along with the party's judicial and other choices, the donors of money for party purposes would balk too. So maybe there wouldn't be any Democratic National Committee for the duration. At the least, the ladies had better pack up and return to their own firesides.

But Gladys Tillett from North Carolina would not credit such nonsense, nor would her tall and angular predecessor from Maine. While Mrs. Tillett and Molly Dewson fought through channels, Lorena Hickok wrote a furious letter to the First Lady over in England. Everybody from the President on down was saying the women of the country had to hold everything together, Hick reminded E.R., and the women's division of the Democratic party had surely been trying. For WHAT, for God's sake? So the men could make deals? It was nothing personal, dammit, she would far rather get away from the muck of Washington into a nice clean war industry, but, she told Eleanor Roosevelt:

> I get so mad I can hardly contain myself. There has got to be a party organization behind the President if we are going to win this peace. But it will have to be the kind of party organization Mrs. Tillett and I believe in and have worked like galley slaves to promote—not the kind the men believe in, the kind that makes the word "politics" stink in the nostrils of the public. Listen, my dear—there will always be political parties in this country as long as we have our present system. They have to be. But Mrs. T. and I are just conceited enough or cocky enough to believe that the only political parties that will survive will be the kind we believe in—political parties based on ideas . . . If our democracy is to survive, it seems to me, we've got to get rid of a lot of damned nonsense . . . We'll have political parties—but they've got to be based on conviction not on hope of jobs or rewards. Maybe that's too idealistic. Well, you will recall that I didn't used to think world peace could ever happen. I've changed my mind. It's got to. And if our system is to survive, we've got to be at least as sincere working for our political ideas as the Nazis are!

It must be remembered that during World War II speeches of this sort were popular. At any rate, while it would be unjustified to claim that Lorena Hickok's tirades to Eleanor Roosevelt in England saved the Democratic party, Hick certainly did stir E.R. to say a few words about saving the women's division on her return to the White House.

So Hick never did apply for a job at Sperry. She was one of that small company, mostly female, who remained on duty at the Mayflower throughout F.D.R.'s third term, holding the Democratic fort there while the armed forces of the United States and its Allies battled democracy's enemies in Europe and Asia.

"Well—all Hell seems to be breaking loose among the gals over this business of getting women on these post-war commissions,"

Hick reported to E.R. in April, 1943. For although victory had by no means been assured, efforts to plan a better world were already being pressed. But the State Department's failure to recognize the importance of feminine participation in the planning had caused eighteen women's organizations in New York to adopt a resolution protesting the absence of women in the U.S. delegations to the impending refugee and food conferences. Of course it would not do for the Democratic women's division to embarrass the Administration in any open way. Therefore Mrs. Tillett wrote privately to one of the President's secretaries, while Hick wrote to the President's wife. A day or so later E.R. saw Under Secretary of State Sumner Welles, who promised to appoint several women as alternate delegates.

During that summer of 1943 E.R. was out of the country almost a month, inspecting and comforting the troops in the Pacific. Although scenic wonders were subsidiary to her real mission as she took repeated trips of this sort, still her horizon kept widening; and so did the gap between her and Hick. E.R., flying over the Amazon, wrote to Hick about an island the size of Switzerland. "Gosh," Hick wrote back wistfully, "I'd like to go to South America sometime." However, E.R.'s schedule on these distant journeys was so crowded that she managed to scrawl a letter to Hick no more than once a week. Even on her domestic travels she no longer attempted a daily note—for they could easily catch up at breakfast when she returned to Washington. Indeed, now it was shop talk that bound them together more than anything else. Political shop talk.

And a political advantage accruing from Hick's residency at the White House had certainly not been overlooked by either of them. Under wartime restrictions the Executive Mansion was, of course, closed to ordinary tourists, even if they defied the difficulties of getting around the country and finding a room in Washington once they arrived. Naturally, women active politically would not wish to be treated as ordinary tourists anyway. In lieu of the less palatable kind of political favors that the men in the party expected, for the women E.R. and Hick cooperated on the serving of tea.

If the out-of-towners were sufficiently important, and if E.R. happened to be at home, the First Lady would personally greet them. Thus Hick had briefed the doormen and the ushers at the White House, lest there be any embarrassment when she turned up shepherding a group of ladies; she was to be greeted formally and asked her name, just as if she had been a stranger. E.R., too, was required to display histrionic ability. "Why, how nice to see you!" she would greet Hick, as though they had not breakfasted together that very morning. Once an usher assisting Hick with her coat murmured to her: "In residence today? Or just a visitor?"

But the White House could be very dreary if E.R. was away. When Hick turned up one Friday evening after the family had left for Hyde Park, the head usher solemnly informed her: "Madame, you are the sole occupant of the White House tonight—with forty-seven men to guard you!" Of course, that was not counting the regular staff. Mabel Haley often stopped by to see her but, as Hick no longer occupied the First Lady's sitting room, the First Lady's personal maid no longer served her, too. Instead Lizzie McDuffie cleaned Hick's room, and Mrs. Mac was one of the most comforting people to have around that Hick had ever known. Mrs. Mac's husband, McDuffie, had been the President's valet until moving to a job over in the Treasury, while she remained on the White House staff; among her other duties, she took care of the President's bedroom. During Hick's bouts with the flu Mrs. Mac borrowed the President's little electric heater daily, and brought it back at night before he returned from his study.

Although Hick would not let Mrs. Mac wait on her much, she loved listening to her talk about her grandmother, who had been a slave, and about her own life before marrying. A graduate of the Hampton Institute, she had taught school as a young woman and traveled about giving dramatic readings. Sometimes Mrs. Mac recited poetry to her, declaiming Oscar Wilde in a thrilling voice. Mrs. Mac also fussed over Hick when a siege of neuritis pained her back and shoulders. "Didn't anybody ever iron you?" Mrs. Mac asked.

Disappearing briefly, she returned with a bath towel and an electric iron, and directed Hick to lie on her stomach. Mrs. Mac spread the towel over her back, then passed the warm iron to and fro, quietly talking of her girlhood days in the old South until Hick felt completely relaxed and drowsy.

During the summer of 1943, the word Hick had been dreading finally came from Mastic. Prinz died in his fifteenth year; it was old age rather than any specific ailment that at last had taken him from

her. Annie and Clarence buried him, wrapped in Hick's old raincoat, right where she had told them to, out back of the Little House
at the beginning of their favorite path through the woods.

Nothing could make up for her loss. But a few weeks later E.R.
arranged with a niece of Tommy's, who bred beautiful English
setters, for the delivery to the White House of a furry caramel
puppy named Mr. Choate. Hick carried him to Long Island the
next morning. Freed from his box he behaved like a bouncing cornflake—or so Hick informed the First Lady. In any case, he kept
Hick so breathless chasing after him that she hardly had time to
miss the reassuring snores of her old companion.

But without Mary Norton—and Marion—Hick's empty feeling on
returning to Washington would have been much worse. Often the
three of them had dinner together. What a time poor Mary was
having with those Southern congressmen who seemed bent on rip-
ping up every legal protection that labor had won under the New
Deal. They made her blood boil! So she was constantly getting her
blood pressure checked and muttering about her B.P., although she
continued to work incredibly long hours for a woman of sixty-
seven. Merely to be around Mary was enough to make Hick forget
that in March she had turned fifty herself, and also to take her mind
off her own aches and pains. As Mary would say, what were friends
for if they couldn't lift you out of the dumps?

It was through Hick that Mary got to know Marion more than
just casually, when the judge began to thaw over their predinner
highballs. Like most of Marion's acquaintances, Mary had noted
that the judge seemed to be an unusually dutiful daughter; now
Mary realized that filial duty was being carried too far. Maternally
deprived as Mary was herself, she shrewdly assessed Marion's basic
problem, which was also the specific impediment to Marion's new
idea of renting her own downtown apartment. "That Mother dame
will never let go of her," Mary wrote to Hick at Mastic. "Poor
Marion!"

Devoutly conventional nonetheless, Mary Norton simply could
not have coped with any homosexual suggestion regarding Hick
and Marion. Several times, the three of them took weekend breaks
together in the Shenandoah country or out at Mastic. On occasions
when just Hick and Marion were away, Mary must have assumed
that the other two behaved no differently in her absence. Once

after Marion returned from a week at the Little House, Mary wrote to Hick from Washington after dining with Marion: "She certainly loves you, the house and Mr. Choate. She is a darling and I wish she had a home in the country with some good man who would appreciate her. It's a darned shame!"

Thus it is difficult to interpret Marion's letters to Hick. Without the shrewd but trustingly moral Mary in the foreground, it would be easier. Because Marion on several occasions reserved a double room at the Hay-Adams Hotel, where Hick was to meet her; and Marion did, despite her mother, eventually rent an apartment in one of Washington's newer apartment buildings. In her letters, Marion frequently urged Hick to consider this place as much her own as she now considered Hick's home on Long Island. Also, Marion's letters to Hick contain passages of a passionate intensity that strongly hint at physical intimacy.

During the last week of 1943 they were together at the Little House, and Marion's adoration of Hick suffuses the three pages she delivered at the White House gate the day after they got back to the capital. "I hope 1944 will be a good year for you, darling," she wrote, "and I hope the Gods will give us many happy hours. Dearest Hick—you have been very good to me and I love you very much—even more."

1944 was, of course, another presidential election year. Once more Hick took some soundings, finding a disquieting amount of anti-fourth-term sentiment. Actually, if it had not been for the war Hick would have agreed that the country would be better off with somebody else; on the rare occasions when she shook hands with F.D.R. these days, that electric vitality was missing. It was like shaking hands with a soft, flabby old man. Indeed it made her feel terribly old herself when E.R., off inspecting the troops again on Hick's fifty-first birthday, by chance wrote to her from Puerto Rico. My God, could it be ten years since their trip there together? From the way Hick felt, though, it might have been ten centuries.

Probably her idea about quitting her job first took root then. Still, she forced herself to go through the motions preceding another campaign, and when the Republicans nominated New York's Governor Thomas E. Dewey, Hick—who had covered one of his first big cases as district attorney—mustered a burst of her former fire. To have that little man with the moustache commanding the crucial stages of the war—let alone striving with giants like Churchill and Stalin to build a just and lasting peace—it was too appalling for Hick to contemplate.

But the Democratic convention in July was pure drudgery this time. It especially irked Hick that the party's new chairman from Missouri had persuaded F.D.R. to dump Wallace on the grounds that he was *too* liberal, and substitute a senator from Bob Hannegan's home state as the candidate for vice-president. E.R. was not pleased either. When a columnist accused F.D.R. of behaving like a dictator on this matter of the vice-presidency, E.R. showed her husband the article, remarking that this expressed her own view about the elevation of Harry Truman. F.D.R. chose to criticize the columnist, as E.R. wrote to Hick in Chicago—and the First Lady added a sharp comment of her own, of which she would have been incapable a few years previously. "F. felt [the columnist] left out the entire point that he, F., didn't want to be a dictator," E.R. wrote. "Hard position when you don't want to be a dictator but want your own way."

Right after the Democratic National Committee moved to New York for the campaign period, Hick lost her temper with Hannegan because he assigned her to a broom closet of an office in the Biltmore Hotel headquarters. He quickly found another room for her. During the next three months Hick should have been in a good mood because she was living on her expense account at the Beekman Towers right next door to her old apartment and she could spend almost every weekend out at Mastic. Instead she grudged every hour she had to be in the city—and by the middle of September she told E.R. not to bother about material for a new spring coat and skirt:

> . . . If my plans work out as I hope they will, I'll be spending a good share of next year down in the country. You see—I realize that I'll have to work the rest of my life. I'm tired—a kind of cumulative fatigue that has been building up for a couple of years. I believe that a good long rest and change would probably prolong my working life by several years. So I'm going to take it. Six months anyway. As a matter of fact, I now have enough ahead to keep me going for a year, maybe—down there. I

don't know just when I'll leave the committee. If we win I probably should stay and help through the Inauguration business . . . I'd thought of staying on possibly—if we win—until March or April.

They did win. Although Dewey carried twelve states, F.D.R. had proved during the last six weeks of a previously listless campaign that he had not lost his political magic. "These Republican leaders have not been content with attacks on me, on my wife, or my sons," he told a Teamsters Union convention late in September. "No, not content with that, they now include my little dog, Fala." By thus deftly ridiculing the anti-Roosevelt theme of his opposition, the President gained his fourth term by a safe, if diminished, margin of the popular vote on November 7, 1944.

Then Hick practically flogged herself through mounting fatigue—until the fourth inauguration of Franklin Roosevelt on January 20, 1945. But her pallor was so alarming that everybody urged her to get some sunshine. In February she spent three weeks in Georgia, visiting one of her most congenial Democratic ladies, a widow who published a country weekly. While Hick was there, E.R. and Mary Norton and Marion Harron reiterated their concern that she really must line up another job before she officially left the Democratic Committee. It was good advice, but Hick was in no mood to take it. Upon her return to Washington, not nearly as rested as she should have been, she resigned. Her coworkers gave her a farewell cocktail party, and when it was over, on March 21, 1945, Hick left a note in E.R.'s room:

Dearest:
    The goodbyes have all been said and presently I shall be on my way out of Washington with two orchids pinned to my shoulder—and wishing that I could live up to the nice things that have been said to me these last few days. With you as an example, I tried awfully hard to do a good job, and, most of the time, I think I honestly did give the women's division the best that was in me. But many times I was irritable and impatient and intolerant. One of the qualities I love most in you is your tolerance, and yet I can be so intolerant if people do not live up to my standards—which have been mostly set by you. It's all very mixed up and inconsistent and makes me very much dissatisfied with myself. And also makes

me feel awkward and inadequate when people say nice things to me—even though I love to hear them and even though, especially now, they mean a lot to me.

I wish I had the words to tell you how grateful I am for your many kindnesses these last four years—and especially for letting me stay here. It did two wonderful things—kept me near you and made it possible for me to hang onto my house, which is so infinitely precious to me. I shall miss you. Yet I shall feel that you are near. After all these years, we could never drift very far apart. You are a very wonderful friend, my dear.

Goodbye and God bless you—

H

19. *Taking Refuge*

For the next three weeks Hick was able to persuade herself that she was feeling better every day. On every previous occasion when her blood sugar had shot up, just behaving herself as far as food was concerned had done the trick; now she had the added mental peace that came of spending day after day polishing her precious Little House. One afternoon as she sat with Annie sewing and watching the sunset, they got to talking about how wonderful it was that they both could have this kind of life they loved so much, doing their housework and trading recipes, walking in the woods and taking little trips to market.

Meanwhile, E.R. wrote that she was extremely busy in Washington but she did enjoy a sunny weekend at Hyde Park after F.D.R.'s return from Yalta; she saw him again just briefly in the White House toward the end of March when he stopped there on his way south for a good rest down in Warm Springs.

And the zenith of Hick's contentment came on the morning of Thursday, April 12, 1945. After finishing her sweeping and dusting she took a big glass of milk and gave Mr. Choate a cookie from the jar that she kept for guests and dogs. Resting a bit before going out to work in her garden, she indulged herself with a long letter to E.R.:

> . . . It's funny—and nice, I think—that I get such a kick out of washing and ironing and cleaning and doing all the things about a house that are to most women such drudgery. I daresay, though, that I shouldn't enjoy it so much if I had had to do it for years and years and raise a family too, or if I had to do it for a living in someone else's home. I know, from experience, how dull *that* can be. Anyway, looking after this little house and keeping it

as neat and attractive as I can is loads of fun and I'm thoroughly enjoying every precious minute of it . . .

The most exciting news of the garden is that the lilacs which Marion had put in for me last fall are apparently going to bloom this year! Also the swamp maple saplings she transplanted from the woods are budding. . . .

When Hick finished her letter she spent an hour or so in the garden before driving upstreet to the post office and to do some other errands. Soon after she returned, Jim Clark, who took care of Ella's animals, ran up to her kitchen door. He had a telephone at his house and sometimes brought her messages. Jim, looking as if he might be ill, blurted: "It's the President. He's dead."

The call had come from Howard Haycraft, now in the Army and stationed in Washington. Having shared the Little House with Hick for several years, he had remembered that she often let the batteries of her radio run down without replacing them. So he thought Hick might not know F.D.R. had been fatally stricken in Warm Springs. According to the radio, it had happened just a few hours ago.

Hick called the White House and got Tommy. E.R. had already left for Warm Springs. Tommy said that, almost the last thing before leaving, Mrs. R. had told her to wire Hick not to try to come. Of course, Hick thought, E.R. even at a time like this was concerned about the blood sugar. So Hick made another call, to the only Roosevelt relative she had ever felt at ease with—dear old Belle, who was Kermit's widow, and they arranged to go to Washington together the following evening.

But around dawn the next morning Hick had second thoughts. As soon as it became a more reasonable hour, she got on the phone again and gave the Warm Springs number. To her surprise, the switchboard answered immediately and a moment later E.R. herself was on the line: "Hick, I don't want you to come. You know what it will be like. And you, of all people, must realize what a load I am carrying now. If you came at this time, you'd be just another worry . . ."

That E.R. could be so frank gave Hick the shivers. It was E.R. the person on the other end of the telephone, telling her that being with Hick would mean a great deal to her when all the furor was over. And Hick, hanging up, felt the stirring amid all of her other emotion of something she hardly dared to label hope. Good Lord, suppose that dream of sharing a cottage together when E.R. left the White House came true, after all!

Possessed by this growing hope, Hick remained at her Little House while the funeral train moved slowly northward, past endless clumps of people weeping or kneeling in prayer. While the flag-draped coffin was borne through the streets of Washington, Hick dug in her warm garden on Long Island. She wandered through the woods with her dog on the morning of the burial service at Hyde Park, and the woods were heartbreakingly beautiful that morning, all burning with the green and rosy fires of spring.

Then, a week later, she went in to the Washington Square apartment in New York that Eleanor Roosevelt had rented when she still thought there would be no third term; it was big enough so that her husband, too, could use it when he retired. Hick was arranging flowers when E.R. and Tommy arrived from the capital.

Incredibly, in just a week the two of them had already supervised the packing of a ten-year accumulation in the White House. Mr. Truman had urged Mrs. Roosevelt not to feel any pressure about moving, but it had helped E.R. to keep busy. At the apartment in New York her mind kept reverting to the even more horrendous job of unpacking at Hyde Park, of settling future plans with the children when all of her four sons in uniform finally received the word at their far-off posts and got leave to come home.

Naturally Hick understood that it would take time. Yet patience had never been her strong point, and in the first week following F.D.R.'s death she had already lost eight pounds. By no means, though, was it only her personal uncertainty that had made her lose all interest in eating, and she preferred to emphasize her concern about the nation's loss when she wrote long letters to E.R. in the period immediately after the President's death. How complacent she had been about the progress of the war, she admitted, and about the outcome of the impending San Francisco conference to set up a new United Nations Organization. "I never realized what implicit faith I had in him until now," Hick admitted, "since he has gone."

> . . . God [Hick went on], he used to be so strong, so vital, so full of energy! I'm glad I didn't see much of him these last four years. I'd rather remember him as I knew him and saw him so often in the thirties. I'll never forget his warm, firm handclasp—the handshake he had, not for the

receiving line, but for his *friends*. The last time I shook hands with him—last September—I was shocked . . . Darling, *sometime* I *may* get straightened out the mixed personal and—shall I say public—feelings I have about you and your family!

About E.R. herself, though, Hick's feelings were much more subtly mixed. Playing the effacingly subordinate role she had practiced so well during recent years, Hick was able to write: "For you and your future I have no worries at all . . . You will find your place—a very active and important place I am sure—and fill it superbly. I'd like to hope that it may be something in which I can help you if only indirectly, from the sidelines."

But then after reminding E.R. that now she was going to be more her own agent, freer to act than she had ever been before, from Hick's heart arose the impassioned pledge: ". . . and as long as we both shall live—I shall be yours to command."

Back in 1933 Hick had written a story for the AP mentioning that the Roosevelts liked their coffee from large mugs, and somebody had sent them a huge blue and white Staffordshire cup capable of holding nearly a pint. Through Hick's various periods of residency in the White House, this cup had always been hers when she and E.R. breakfasted together. Despite everything else on E.R.'s mind the month after she left Washington, she saw to it that the Staffordshire mug was sent to Hick out at Mastic as a permanent memento. Gradually, Hick came to realize that she should not expect much more.

By the middle of May, Hick felt so miserable with a digestive disturbance that her sister Ruby came out to see that she ate properly. It was not too bad, at first, being clucked over by the original mother hen; in fact, now that Julian had found just the right niche and they had quietly got married, Hick could no longer disapprove of them. Julian, running a bookstore on First Avenue for a friend in the Army, wore tweed jackets like a professor. But Ruby, never shutting her mouth, soon had Hick clenching her fists.

Meanwhile, Mary Norton mulled over an idea. When Mrs. R. paid a brief visit to Washington, Mary broached it to her and secured encouragement. Then Mary took pen in hand. "I have always felt that God looks out for people, regardless of religion, who had lived the good life," she wrote to Hick. "You have. Now this is my proposition. I have very little time to digest what is happening at San Francisco [where the United Nations conference was planning for peace while Allied armies kept advancing deeper into Germany]. So it occurred to me that, if it is agreeable to you, you could help me out . . .

"It won't mean much work," Mary continued, "just that you can advise me and give me an outline for speeches about what is going on internationally etc. I can send you plenty of material . . . You know dear, I know what it is to have a mind disturbed about finance. I went through that with my husband who was just as fine and just as proud as you are but it is really foolish . . . When your health is reestablished you will have many opportunities . . . So please let me put you on my payroll . . . strictly between you and me, not another soul will know anything about it. I could put 'Joe Zilch' down for it and it would not be questioned . . . Mrs. R. heartily approved . . . as she is your very best friend and I claim the next place, we know what is good for you. . . ."

How could Hick hurt Mary's feelings? So she signed the enclosed form, with relief and anguish competing to overcome her as she thereby became a part-time research assistant to one of her dearest friends—at the stipend of $1,200 a year. If there was nothing legally wrong about the scheme, Hick still had to feel ashamed and shaken because she had always done anything she could to help her friends, certainly never expecting any pay. In Washington, she had often whipped up speech outlines for Mary without the least thought of money. Well, maybe she would do so again as soon as she felt better. Meanwhile, nobody would be able to say the congresswoman was not getting her money's worth, or rather the taxpayers' money's worth, from her friend on Long Island. And the arrangement surely *would* give Hick a chance to recuperate under less financial pressure.

In truth, Hick's pride had already suffered similarly at numerous points in her past, owing to her lack of fiscal prudence. Ever since 1932 she had striven to give E.R. presents commensurate with E.R.'s gifts to her. It was, of course, impossible; guided by Mabel Haley, Hick had finally learned to provide underclothing that would at least prove useful, supplemented with Christmas decorations and fruit jelly that Annie Ross taught her how to make. Yet the compulsively generous E.R. not only showered a year-round rain of clothing and knickknacks and holiday turkeys upon Hick, she also sent money. "I wish you'd let me help you . . ." To pay a doctor or a maid—the latter no less essential than the former, in E.R.'s frame of reference—the First Lady had continually undertaken well-meaning if misguided subsidizing, accustoming Hick to a higher standard of living than she could possibly afford on her own. To Hick's credit, she had tried to resist, she had protested repeatedly that she must not let herself lean on E.R., she did send back more than a few checks. Hating herself, Hick deposited others.

Thus a pernicious pattern had been established before Hick left Washington in the spring of 1945. Never very farsighted, she could not perceive why her sister Ruby kept making snide remarks that summer about people who had no sense of responsibility. As Hick viewed her own prospects, she was sensibly recouping her strength, living on the money she had put aside; now with Mary's extra little cushion, she might even do some real writing. Anyway, there ought to be a job for her at the New York State Democratic Committee in the autumn. By then, surely she would feel ready to get back into harness. Because her doctor had said that her digestive trouble was nothing but nerves. He had prescribed "jitters pills," which she was obediently swallowing. Moreover, thanks to Marion, she was getting good exercise as well as great satisfaction from her daily toil in her garden.

"It's so much more fun than just having someone do it for you," Hick wrote to E.R. at Hyde Park, where she was still confronting three laundry baskets full of mail daily, and such multitudinous other claims that she doubted whether she could get out to Long Island for a weekend that summer. Judge Harron, though, went too far in the opposite direction as far as Hick's peace of mind was concerned, after Hick wrote to her that a flower had appeared on a bush they had planted together only the preceding fall. This news provoked a most unjudicial outpouring:

Darling—

A peony! You've been hinting about it all along, but I didn't dare dream we were going to have a "blessed event" in our garden. Sweetheart, now that we have found out all about the bees and the flowers, isn't life wonderful! The timing throws me off a bit but I'm not going to worry about it. The catalogue said it happens the second season after. We're just lucky. I guess you knew it all along, planning to be home this spring, taking time away from your work. And I really didn't suspect anything. It's just all I can do to stay here in Washington—but you realize, dear, I have to earn the dough for Vigoro—and your Wheatena. . . .

Confronted thus by more emotion than she could cope with from one correspondent and much less than she wished from another, Hick—despite the vigilance of her sister, and after nearly twenty years of warding off a threat that she dreaded—collapsed in a diabetic coma early in the summer of 1945. To stay alive, she would now have to give herself a daily injection of insulin.

If she avoided stress, her doctor told her, there was still no reason why she could not live a normal life and enjoy a fairly normal diet. Hick took him seriously about avoiding stress. Her first real opportunity to prove that she did came the following month when Marion Harron arrived, laden with parcels containing all manner of wartime scarcities—including a carton of Camels and a fifth of Schenley's. But Hick was allowed a drink a day, and she did not have to give up smoking. It was not that Marion tempted Hick to go off her diet, either. Hick's test during this two-week visit was more privately emotional.

What happened? During those two weeks E.R. herself became concerned at hearing nothing from Hick, but hoped, she wrote, that Hick was too busy enjoying herself to dash off a few lines. Not until another week elapsed, though, did Hick send an explanation of her unusual silence:

Marion has gone, after a pretty stormy visit. The child is not very well, and she is in a nervous and emotional state very similar to mine at her age. [Marion a few days later would mark her forty-second birthday.] I really think that change of life—I don't know how to spell the other word for it—must start, for spinsters, when they are around 40, and that the worst years are from 40 to 45. At least, that was my experience, and Marion seems to be going through the same thing. I feel terribly sorry for her, but there isn't much I can do except tell her that I probably understand a lot better than she thinks I do! And that she will feel better when she gets to be 50! Of

course it makes her very explosive, and this time she got
into a fight with Clarence Ross, which made life a bit
trying for me! And once she got sore at me and packed
up to leave. Thank God, I'm as placid these days as a
cow!

Indeed. But just as Hick had special reason for appreciating what
Marion was going through, E.R.—who just lately had been hearing
about the "jitters pills"—had special reason for sympathizing with
Hick now. "I can well imagine what a time you've had with Marion," she wrote, "but it was bound to happen & at least you know
time makes a difference. I gather your health is fine or you wouldn't
have stayed so placid." Then, although she had not found it possible to get out to Mastic, with hordes of guests at Hyde Park all
summer long, she proposed driving to her apartment in the city
when Hick came in for her next monthly medical checkup.

By late September of 1945, six months had past since Hick's
departure from Washington—in a way, the most eventful six
months of her life. They had seen the arousing, and the dashing, of
her only real hope for her future; they had also seen a health crisis
of lasting severity. When Hick met E.R. in New York that September, it was less than a month after World War II had ended with
the surrender of Japan. In effect, Hick at the age of fifty-two negoti-
ated her own personal surrender.

No more would she even dream of working *with* E.R. Instead,
and not nearly as intimately or importantly as Tommy, now Hick
would work *for* E.R. Doing the same sort of petty research chores
she was doing for Mary Norton. Still, Hick and E.R. both had reasons for not daring to face the future without a protective veil of
one sort or another. Hick's ego by now was so shattered that she
thought she wanted nothing more out of life than simply existing
in peace at the Little House, but to save her last vestige of self-
respect, she kept saying that soon she would feel well enough to see
about that Democratic State Committee job. E.R., for her part,
could not believe that any worthwhile endeavor might remain in
the offing for a woman approaching her sixty-first birthday. "I'm
going to be no leader of thought or action," she told Hick, "but a
homebody in the near future & able to enjoy my friends."

Thus it suited them both to agree that only temporarily would
Hick be doing minor tasks out on Long Island—such as writing
summaries of various documents—for which E.R. would pay her

fifty dollars a month. However, instead of settling down to being a homebody, of course Eleanor Roosevelt rose to new heights after the death of her husband. Appointed by Harry Truman to serve in the American delegation to the United Nations, she became—as Truman himself would aptly put it—the First Lady of the World. And her temporary arrangement with Hick lasted ten years.

Ruby and Jeeb started it. Once when they tried to lure Hick out to a picnic, and she shook her head, they demanded to know why not. Her answer became a Mastic byword. If anybody ever asked what was keeping Hick so busy, a chorus would respond: *She was ironing her dishtowels!* Not that she turned completely reclusive, but during the decade after she left Washington she did retreat in no uncertain terms from the increasing conviviality around her.

Although much of Long Island changed in this period to something like an eastern approximation of Los Angeles, the Dana place remained unspoiled. Nevertheless, more people—at least a couple of dozen of them—were able to enjoy its peace as Ella sold or rented a few acres here, ten acres there. Among the newcomers were Hick's sister and brother-in-law, great friends of Howard Haycraft and his wife, Molly. At first the four of them tried to avoid hurting Hick's feelings by stopping by every weekend. Then one Sunday, as they approached the Little House on foot, they clearly heard a disembodied groan: "God damn it, here they come!"

It turned out that Hick had her own weekend company on the sun porch with her, and everybody had a good laugh—before the intruders retraced their steps. But as the years passed they came less often, and most of the new people never got to know Hick except as a pretty odd old character. In the hot weather she would sit at night reading in front of a window, wearing very little, with a bright light shining down on her. A generation of youngsters who spent their summers on the place learned to expect a quick command from their mothers as they walked or drove past this house after dark: "Look the other way! We're going right by Hick."

Intermittently, she did work a few months at a time at the Democratic State Committee in the city. But if she had to stay at a hotel—when E.R. had people with children in her apartment, or for any other reason could not accommodate her—there went her profits. Also, New York got on her nerves, now that she felt like a stranger there. So she tried to think of something she could write

about in the country to make some money. An emotionally un-
troubled reporter, with her skill at vivid narrative, who had had her
opportunities for first-hand observation, almost surely would have
found a saleable subject—but Hick could not.

Instead she was fooled by the operator of a fly-by-night syndicate
down in Philadelphia. "GAWD LADY YOU CAN WRITE," he
telegraphed Hick when she sent him some old clippings. That she
fell for his line about being able to earn hundreds every month with
hardly any work, showed how far she had come from the shrewd
Hickok who had easily seen through promoters of his ilk; that she
had unnecessarily bothered a few famous women like Bess Truman,
asking if they would mind being interviewed by mail, troubled her
still more. In the low mood this experience engendered, she did not
quibble when Ris Dillon—she and the Old Man had retired to California—forwarded train fare for a Christmas present.

Hick would always be glad she had made this trip, and not just
because she avoided the rigors of another winter out at Mastic. For
she also spent a wonderful few weeks with Ellie, and before that
year was out dear little Ellie died. Then if Hick had to accuse
herself of never having been as loyal as Ellie deserved—Ellie, who
had never neglected writing letters the way Hick sometimes did—
at least they had parted happily. It pleased Hick, too, that she
could keep Ellie's memory constantly alive in another way. Just
when that syndicate mess had begun getting her down, she'd had to
do something she hated: Her dog, the frisky Mr. Choate, had turned
into a troublemaker; trampling flowers was one thing but nipping
children was another, and she had had to get rid of him. Thanks to
a timely check from Mary, Hick replaced him with a placid little
lady of a cocker spaniel named Feathers. After Ellie died, Hick
renamed her pup Muffin because Ellie had so adored her own sweet
Muffin.

Hick also tried to write about Ellie. At least, she wrote an outline
intended for the *Reader's Digest,* which regularly printed profiles of
unsung people who had impressed some contributor as a memorable character. By now, E.R. had a different literary agent—no-non-
ense Nannine Joseph, who got wonderful fees for most of her
clients. Not Hick. Nannine put it kindly, she kept telling Hick she
really was a writer, but much as Hick sweated over her summary of
what she wanted to sell about Ellie, Nannine would not send it to
the magazine. She even gave Hick instructions about how to grasp

an editor's attention, as if Hick were just some beginner trying to get her first story published.

In effect, Hick was. Instead of typing away exuberantly as she used to, now something kept telling her: Don't hurt anybody's feelings, be careful not to give the wrong impression. Tom Dillon—he died, too, not long after Ellie did—would have throttled Hick had he been able to read some of the tedious drivel she composed at Mastic. A proposed magazine piece about the White House, for instance, aimed at simple minds who might appreciate the musings of that mansion's spirit: "I am different from any other house in the whole United States. . . ."

Still, Hick did know how to write, and late in the 1940's she was suddenly inspired as if fate had decreed it. During one of the brief periods she spent working for the State Democratic Committee in New York City, a woman doing an article about Mrs. Roosevelt invited Hick to dinner, to talk about Mrs. R. Heading the UN's Commission on Human Rights, E.R. was now calmly teaching young diplomats how to debate with the Russians. Hick had long since got accustomed to being sought out this way, and she usually offered just a few harmless recollections because she hated to rebuff a working reporter. However this one turned out to have spent part of her childhood in Aberdeen, South Dakota, and even remembered one of the families the young Lorena had worked for. So they sat till after midnight in a Greenwich Village restaurant, and it ended with Hick promising to attempt her own autobiography.

She worked hard for several months, completing four sample chapters plus an outline of the rest and an introduction. According to her new friend, this should be enough to get a contract and an advance payment from a publisher she knew. Hick, with her flimsy self-confidence, raised plenty of doubts, but something about the idea stimulated her. Alone, she had been doing a lot of musing—and maybe she *was* a sort of symbol of what had happened to the country in her lifetime. Like it or not, the golden age of individualism was over; now the greatest good for the greatest number required a certain amount of regimentation. In her foreword, she tried to express her own sense of loss:

> . . . I am pretty certain that, had I been turned loose at the age of fourteen, in the world as it is today here in America, to beat my way around earning a precarious living as an untrained

domestic servant, the welfare agencies, the social workers, the psychiatrists, and the juvenile court would have nabbed me, and I should not have been permitted to work out my own destiny with the aid of generous friends along the way. The chances are that I'd have been sent away somewhere to be trained to be a good servant. Undoubtedly I'd have been better cared for, safer—but think of the fun I'd have missed!

The trouble was that, vividly as Hick wrote about some of her adventures, she failed to make her story moving. For all her detail about her miserable childhood before her mother's death, she skipped right past that crucial incident, leaving the reader baffled. Thus the publisher's verdict: the manuscript lacked the breath of life, but if Miss Hickok cared to try revising it . . .

Actually, Hick was relieved. Just as E.R. had discovered a decade previously, it was difficult to write autobiographically when you could not be wholly honest. Besides this problem, Hick also had an attitude now that was not conducive to producing compelling prose. World-weary, she could scarcely summon the energy to care whether strangers wept or smiled at what she wrote. Symbolically, she expressed how she felt with the two words she typed after the last paragraph of her chapter describing her White House residency. She had left Washington in March of 1945; four years had passed, but to her that was THE END.

Still the fates had not finished with her. How Hick managed to carry on financially after Mary Norton retired from Congress in 1950 cannot be explained, except by E.R.'s frequent rescue operations. The most dramatic—and the saddest—of these occurred as the decade reached its midpoint. Long since, Ella Dana had broken with her cowboy and ceased bleaching her hair; nevertheless, relations between her and Hick did not improve. By now Hick's rent had increased to sixty-five dollars a month, but the figure hardly mattered because Hick was always so far behind in her payments. Harassed over money herself, Ella bore Hick's surly rudeness with increasing distress, until a family Ella had become very fond of—the family of a doctor from the city—found that the house on the property that they had been renting from somebody else would no longer be available to them. Ella could not endure seeing them so disappointed.

Then somebody telephoned Mrs. Roosevelt in Colorado, where she was visiting the ranch of her son Elliott and his new wife. Probably it was Ella. At any rate, right afterward E.R. called Hick—and then her chauffeur, Tubby, at Hyde Park. The following day, on the first of August in 1955, Tubby drove to Mastic to pick up Miss Hickok and her dog and her luggage. Hick was sixty-two then. Never again would she lay eyes on her Little House on Long Island.

20. Hyde Park at Last

During recent years, Hick had already spent the worst of several winters at Hyde Park. Not only had the coal for her furnace in Mastic been a terrible expense, but also she had ceased to enjoy being marooned when it snowed. No matter that E.R. might be in Paris or Geneva or Jerusalem, her Val-Kill cottage was kept open, and having Hick stay there saved E.R. from worrying about her. Besides, E.R. had wanted her to sort through a mountain of old letters.

Still, it was very hard for Hick to come back to Hyde Park as a homeless gypsy. Trying to shut off her pain, Hick did a lot of thinking about Tommy—dead more than two years now. She and Hick had become very close again when Tommy had begun enduring some bad times with her health. Just a year older than Hick, Tommy had actually gone through more harrowing medical crises than Hick had over the decades; a couple of major abdominal operations, besides heart trouble. Considering the tension she had always labored under, her physical deterioration was not surprising, but what amazed Hick was Tommy's mental strength.

Once Tommy had inadvertently put her finger on the difference between them. "My boss is a very big person," Tommy had said, "just about the biggest person in the world. Anything I can do to help her—no matter what—justifies my existence. It's enough for me." And E.R., for her part, appreciated her secretary's deep humility; once E.R. had told Hick how comfortable it was that Tommy never expected attention or entertainment. How Hick wished that she could have been as selfless herself!

On the other hand, considering the dreary pass she had reached, maybe she would have been happier in the long run if she had never gotten friendly with Tommy in '32. Or did her own dreams of

315

glory actually date back to 1928? At any rate, without Tommy she
might still be somebody, and at least she'd have her self-respect if
she were trudging around the city on the kind of tame news assignments befitting a not too energetic sixty-two-year-old spinster. Like
Emma Bugbee of the *Tribune,* still covering Mrs. R.'s incessant
speechmaking in support of the United Nations. For that matter,
E.R. herself had turned seventy on her last birthday.

But nobody, whether person or personage, could match E.R.'s
indomitable spirit. Upon her arrival from the West she briskly took
Hick in hand: clearly, Hick required work and living quarters of
her own. Although the cottage here had twenty rooms, it was usually bursting with grandchildren. Furthermore, Hick and her dog
and her diet would be put off by the hordes that descended for
conferences or other gatherings practically every weekend when
she herself was not abroad. Thus while E.R. besought the assistance
of New York's Governor Averell Harriman in securing a research or
writing position for her friend Miss Hickok, Hick began looking for
a local apartment where E.R. could keep an eye on her until an
Albany job became available.

That was putting the cart before the horse; with no money, how
could Hick move? And unfortunately Governor Harriman found it
impossible to oblige his friend Eleanor, because the civil service
left him no appointive positions suitable for Miss Hickok. So Hick
remained nearly a year at the cottage, while E.R. was there and
while E.R. was, more often, away—until Fala's hostile successor
threatened to kill her Muffin. Then Tubby drove Hick and her dog
just three miles, to the Lakeview Motor Court.

It really was nicer than it sounded, Hick wrote to dear old Mary
Norton. She had her own miniature log cabin, complete with kitch-
enette, and a cute little porch overlooking the lake. But even if that
body of water was also miniature, and reedy—still, the motel cabin
where Hick lived for the next year and a half sat on a small knoll
above Route 9G at the outskirts of Hyde Park; her situation could
have been much worse. Her main problem was that there was nothing within walking distance, except for one store at the traffic light
a few hundred feet to the south. And even if money trouble had not
forced her to give up her car, eye trouble would have anyway. Over
the past several years, spells of virtual blindness had been coming
upon her suddenly; while she had regained her vision each time—as

her doctor assured her she would—after each episode her left eye, in particular, seemed weaker, and she thought it was no longer safe for her to drive. So now she had to depend on E.R.'s chauffeur whenever she wanted to go anywhere.

Archy was his real name, but around town everybody called him Tubby because he weighed 360 pounds. He had once worked for a local builder, so he was well acquainted in the community. Thus his impression of how Hicky (as he referred to her) had first got to know Mrs. Roosevelt surely circulated widely: You see, Hicky was a reporter back when F.D.R. was first running, and on the campaign train she released some news that was supposed to be off-the-record and so she got her butt kicked off the train, and then Mrs. Roosevelt felt awfully sorry for her . . .

At least the same implication that Mrs. R., in an excess of kind-heartedness, was letting this woman take advantage of her, was also murmured by some of the regular guests at Val-Kill. Hick, for her part, had little use for most of them. In that wonderful living room where five people or fifty could feel equally comfortable, Hick never allowed herself to be intimidated. It was enough that she climbed into girdle and appropriate outer garb when she came to visit here, since E.R. disapproved of ladies wearing trousers. Otherwise, as Hick had discovered at Mastic, corduroy breeches and a man's sweatshirt from the Army-Navy store were a helluva lot easier for someone with her shape.

But no matter who else was present, Hick had no hesitancy about lifting her voice—and a very carrying voice it still was—if there were something she wished to ask E.R. at the other end of the room. *"Darling!"* Hick would call out, suddenly silencing all conversation. The director of the F.D.R. Library then, a gentle woman of notable scholarship, could not help cringing slightly at such a display of . . . well, bad taste.

And yet Elizabeth Drewry, more than most others who frequented Val-Kill receptions, appreciated that Lorena Hickok was very efficient and intelligent. Not intellectual, perhaps, but extremely capable as a researcher and a writer. For Hick, finally, under E.R.'s determined prodding, had begun to write books—in her tiny log cabin, and later in the sunny two rooms in the former Episcopal rectory only a block from the village, to which she moved early in 1958. Hick turned out six short biographies for young readers, as the librarians who were the main purveyors of such works liked to describe them.

Hick had already published one similar opus before moving to Hyde Park. Although its cover attributed the authorship of *Ladies of Courage* to Eleanor Roosevelt and Lorena A. Hickok, E.R. herself had insisted that, since Hick had done all of the work, she was entitled to all of the royalties. Of course, it was Mrs. Roosevelt's name that had sold the idea for a collection of profiles of feminine political figures. For a book of this sort it did reasonably well; as an advance payment, Hick received a thousand dollars, and then another three thousand arrived in her mail over the next several years.

But at Mastic it had taken Hick two years to finish *Ladies of Courage*. At Hyde Park, spurred by E.R., Hick worked practically as fast as she had during her AP days; she had always said that she needed a city editor to keep after her. It helped, too, that nononsense Nannine Joseph changed her attitude—because Hick's flair for simple prose neatly fit the requirements of this new field of endeavor. One of Hick's children's books even became something of a best seller.

It was *The Story of Helen Keller*. Thanks to E.R., Hick spent a day visiting this inspiring woman whose triumph over blindness and deafness made her an ideal subject for juvenile literature; nobody had previously secured her cooperation on such a project. Thus a few book clubs with school affiliations swelled the sales of Hick's touching little volume to the extent that suddenly she was self-supporting again. The boost to her ego was tremendous.

Hick's other books included a pair of brief biographies of Franklin Roosevelt, stressing different aspects of his career; both contained forewords by the widow of the late President, commending them. On her own, Hick interested a publisher in a book for teen-age girls relating the career of Anne Sullivan Macy, Helen Keller's gifted teacher. In 1959, at last Hick tried her hand at writing a book called *The Story of Eleanor Roosevelt*, a short volume intended for children around ten years old. Then in 1962, approaching her own seventieth birthday, Hick finally used some of her personal recollections to record a particularly important period in the life of a world-renowned woman nearly seventy-eight. Although Eleanor Roosevelt's health was failing then, it must be assumed that she had approved of the project.

Ostensibly *Reluctant First Lady* was intended for adult readers;

and yet, in style and substance, it bears more resemblance to the unsophisticated fare that was supposed to comprise the literary diet of teenagers as recently as 1962. Nevertheless, the book was interesting—as far as it went. For it was based not only on Hick's own memories, but also on her cache of letters.

As early as 1958, Lorena Hickok had begun donating packets of her letters to the F.D.R. Library. From time to time she added more, until her contributions filled several cartons—all stored beyond the reach of any other researcher, in keeping with the terms of her deed of gift. And yet she also specified that her papers were to be opened for virtually unlimited perusal ten years after her death.

Why did Hick do this? Nothing else throughout her life could have an impact on posterity remotely approaching that of her decision concerning the letters from Eleanor Roosevelt that she had saved over a period of three decades. That itself is the only possible explanation: that Hick could not bear destroying the evidence which would insure some remembrance of her own name.

As she had demonstrated repeatedly, Hick had a great capacity for wishful thinking. Surely she was not a malicious person, but she was capable of nursing grievances to the point of losing any reasonable perspective. Above all, in her youth and her old age, too, her yearning to be "somebody" could not be resisted, or so it appears.

Only a few of her own introspective reflections from her years in Hyde Park have been preserved, and these say outright that she would hate to have strangers invade her privacy. "To Hell with history!" she once wrote to Eleanor Roosevelt's daughter. But by then she herself had already made sure that history could not completely forget her.

In the last few years before Eleanor Roosevelt's death, Hick gave many signs of having at last achieved emotional tranquillity. If she still behaved less than perfectly genteelly, her homage to the personage that E.R. had become certainly seemed to be genuine; she chastised others for making any comment with the slightest negative implication. "Don't say that," she urged, when a mutual friend suggested that the former First Lady had ever disagreed with her husband.

And yet Hick, who had once shivered at the prospect of any gossip about herself and E.R., by her own choice in Hyde Park made such gossip inevitable. Perhaps she did not intend to do so. But her compulsion to secure at least posthumous celebrity circumvented her competing desires for personal respectability and for protecting E.R. from any breath of scandal. It happened over a period of several years.

During those winters before moving to Hyde Park, Hick, on E.R.'s own instructions, had begun going through the letters they had written to each other back in the thirties. This was done in connection with E.R.'s work on the second volume of her autobiography covering the era of her husband's presidency. It seems clear that Hick agreed then to make a typed copy of the entire correspondence, omitting personal passages, and to destroy any handwritten originals that might cause subsequent embarrassment.

But Hick did not get very far with this project. She removed just 129 letters from her own hoard of nearly twenty-five hundred, and replaced them with what a later generation would describe as sanitized copies. Probably she burned another dozen without copying one word of them; these were letters E.R. had sent her before entering the White House. Had Eleanor Roosevelt understood the limited extent of Hick's activity during those winters, it must be assumed that she would have taken more decisive action herself. In any case, somebody did destroy the bulk of the letters Eleanor Roosevelt had received from Lorena Hickok and had kept in her own possession. While this destruction of one side of the correspondence was accomplished, Hick herself was increasingly befriended by a lonely man in ill health who had scarcely any interests apart from his work as curator of the museum sharing the building that housed the F.D.R. Library.

Ray Corry spent hours drinking coffee with Hick at one or another local diner, and his attentive kindness was especially noted after Hick's arthritis made it something of a project to get her in or out of a car. Only a few of Ray Corry's colleagues were aware, however, that from time to time he stopped off at the library director's office following one of his outings with Hick, and delivered another shoebox to be added to those Hickok cartons stored away for future sifting.

The fervency of Corry's archival zeal could not be faulted; whether or not he knew what was in those boxes of Hick's, he realized that his own time for distinguishing himself was limited, and he died within the decade. But Hick, knowing full well what

the boxes contained could have refused to give them up—or reclaimed them. Despite her physical infirmities, there was nothing
at all wrong with her mind. Except, perhaps, an uncontrollable
craving for posthumous fame.

Thus she gave Ray not just E.R. letters, filled with personal as
well as historic nuance, plus more than a thousand of her own
letters to E.R. Those packets also held Alicent Holt letters, Marion
Harron letters, and countless scraps with no possible bearing on the
life of Eleanor Roosevelt. What they did illuminate was the career
of Lorena Hickok herself. Depositing all of this material in the
National Archives might not have been Hick's own idea, but she
surely abetted it.

Despite her extreme reverence for the personage, Hick still did
have subtly mixed feelings about E.R. the person. Her love and
loyalty were indeed severely tested in Hyde Park, where it was
impossible for her not to see the former First Lady's dependence on
another journalist and his wife, and on a refugee doctor and his
wife. Originally, E.R. had become fond of Joe Lash during his days
as an idealistic youth leader in the late 1930's; only after the war
had he gone to work for the New York *Post,* while his wife, Trude,
headed a citizens' committee on children in New York City.
Through Trude, E.R. had come to know and intensely admire Dr.
David Gurewitsch, whose wife, Edna, also entered the inner circle
at Val-Kill. But not merely at close range was Hick's own eclipse
visible. In 1958 Eleanor Roosevelt published the third volume of
her autobiography, entitled *On My Own,* which she chose to dedi-
cate quite fulsomely to "all of those who have worked with me,"
and to her children and close friends. But E.R. then mentioned by
name just her five children, Malvina Thompson, David and Edna
Gurewitsch, and Joe and Trude Lash.

Still the real blow to Hick came less conspicuously, in agate type
on the following page, where her own dearest friend expressed
deep appreciation to a writer who had helped her on the manuscript. "Also I wish to thank those who helped me in minor ways,"
Eleanor Roosevelt added. She then listed two men—"and Miss
Lorena Hickok for some research in the Hyde Park Memorial
Library."

If that were not proof enough of Hick's displacement, more was
to come as Mrs. R.'s mortal failing inevitably began. During the last

two years, while E.R. slowly and then unmistakably was drifting away, Hick increasingly found herself relegated to the sidelines. By now she had new friends in the village who took her marketing, invited her for dinner and applauded gleefully when she served her dog a birthday "cake" of hamburger frosted with cream cheese, topped by a cheese candle. Perhaps Hick's private knowledge about the disposition of her letters cushioned her ego. At the same, her great sorrow was also eased by Anna's daughter Sisty.

No longer an adorable Alice in Wonderland perched upon her own swing under a White House tree, Sisty was now the mother of three beautiful children. Since Hick knew all of the youngsters on her own block—she needed dog-walkers—Sisty often brought her little ones to play there during her visits to Grandmère. Thus Sisty and Hick became quite fond of each other. Indeed it appears that E.R. herself, still thinking of how lonely Hick must be, encouraged a sort of proxy grandmaternal flowering in Hick's heart.

As a result, while E.R. was in the hospital, it was Sisty who thoughtfully kept Hick informed by telephone and wrote marvelous letters to her. The day before E.R.'s seventy-eighth birthday, she herself dictated what would be her last note to Hick. "I'm still horribly weak," she told Hick from her hospital bed, "but as soon as I'm able to hold the phone I'll call you." She knew, Hick was sure, as she herself knew when she read the words, that it would never happen.

On the morning after E.R.'s death, Hick did receive a call from Western Union relaying a telegram to her: "THE FAMILY OF MRS. FRANKLIN D. ROOSEVELT INVITE YOU TO THE CHURCH SERVICE TO BE HELD AT ST. JAMES EPISCOPAL CHURCH . . . AND TO THE INTERMENT SERVICE IN THE ROSE GARDEN. . . ." Because of the limited capacity of the village church, only a few hundred such messages went out. But on November 10, 1962, police lined both sides of Hyde Park's main street for several miles because the mourners at Eleanor Roosevelt's last rites included President Kennedy and Vice-President Johnson, with their wives, and also former Presidents Truman and Eisenhower. Never in history had so many once or future White House residents stood beside each other on any sort of occasion.

Hick chose to say her own farewell privately. After all of the famous people departed, when the police and Secret Service left the village to settle back to normal and Hick finally felt able to keep her composure, she telephoned the Reverend Gordon Kidd. As rector of E.R.'s church, he had also become Mrs. Roosevelt's friend. Although Hick had never been much for organized religion, she liked the Reverend Kidd; he was just the sort of vigorous, white-haired, pink-faced clergyman that she imagined from the novels of Jane Austen. He and his wife, too, had always been very kind to Miss Hickok. It was Mrs. Kidd who had found a woman to take care of her the last time Hick had the flu. Now Hick had another favor to ask.

She wished to put some flowers on Mrs. Roosevelt's grave, but not in daylight because she did not want to be seen. So would the Reverend Kidd be willing to drive her there at an hour when nobody else was around?

It was spooky, he would always remember, turning in at the gate in the pitch blackness. Of course there was a guard who came out, but once he recognized the clergyman he let the car proceed to the parking field. There it was really dark. Although the Reverend Kidd parked as close as possible to the rose garden, they still had to walk along the outer hedge for several hundred feet, hardly able to see a few inches ahead of them. What with her arthritis and bad eyes, Miss Hickok had to give up. The Reverend Kidd took her flowers then—a homemade bouquet, as he remembered, of dried goldenrod and the like that she must have gathered herself. While Miss Hickok waited, he went on alone, barely managing to find the gap in the hedge that was the entrance to the gravesite. There was some sort of railing, he had not expected anything of the sort, so he barked his shin quite painfully. But the Reverend Kidd did make out the shape of the plain white marble slab, at the foot of which he placed Miss Hickok's humble bouquet.

Hick lived five and a half years more, the first several months often in tears. By the following spring, though, she pulled herself together enough to write to some old friends, reporting that she was starting on another book. A biography of Walter Reuther, the labor leader, for teenagers; it was her publisher's idea.

But Hick never finished it. Although she went through spurts of typing notes, her eyes bothered her too much for any sustained work. Whatever her doctor said, she was just about blind in her left eye now, and the right one was not much better. The arthritis was getting worse, too. First she needed a cane and then one of those contraptions called a walker and finally a wheelchair. Through it all, of course, the insulin every day, the regular blood tests, the undercurrent of worry about suddenly going into a coma.

When occasional visitors showed up, Hick could tell they were awfully depressed at what they saw. Strangely, Hick herself did not seem cast down by all her adversity; in fact, quite the contrary. Smiling wryly, she remembered how it had not concerned her personally when the President had got Social Security passed by Congress. Now it came in handy, practically paying her rent. Also, the royalties from her Helen Keller and F.D.R. books were likely to hold up as long as she did. Meanwhile, no matter that other people told her how wonderful a television would be, she did not need to spend the money on it or strain her eyes. She had plenty of entertainment from her radio.

She became a fanatical baseball fan; the Dodgers were her team. Also, she had wonderful companionship from Jenny—the sweet little miniature collie that had been one of E.R.'s last presents to her, after Muffin finally expired. And Hick had her memories.

By herself at her own typewriter, Hick spent hours polishing her will. Every present that E.R. had ever given her, and there were dozens that she had somehow held onto, had to be bequeathed to someone who would appreciate it. To each of the children of her married friends she allotted some item that had originally been a gift from Anna Eleanor Roosevelt; over and over Hick typed that name, cherishing every syllable and recalling the circumstances under which she herself had received this Navajo pottery plate or that autographed copy of *The Oxford Book of English Verse.*

To Sisty, Hick bequeathed several of her most precious possessions, including her dog and the Val-Kill desk and chair that E.R. had given her one Christmas long ago. Hick also passed on to Sisty—now that her own pride was intact again—the monetary bequest that E.R. had provided Hick in her will. Or at least Hick tried to; she had kept this thousand dollars in a separate bank account, which somehow sank to just seven hundred dollars by the time anybody else was aware of her intentions for it.

That happened in 1968. Early in the spring, Hick's doctor had to tell her that some new symptoms were serious. The numbness of her toes—well, circulatory difficulties could have severe repercussions in an old lady who had been on insulin for twenty years. It might be necessary, he said, to amputate. *Both* legs? They would have to wait and see.

At the hospital in Rhinebeck, half an hour north of Hyde Park, after Hick came through the first operation she asked to see her sister. Since Hick's departure from Long Island, there had been scant communication between her and Ruby. But Ruby came, of course—two or three times during the week after that operation—and those two sisters who had squabbled so much in the past parted with love. For Hick did not survive long enough to have to undergo the second operation. Two months after her seventy-fifth birthday, on May 1, 1968, she died.

There was a brief note attached to her will, requesting that the Reverend Kidd be informed of her death. Following her wishes, he arranged for a private cremation at a funeral home in Rhinebeck. Hick had written, "I especially want to avoid any sort of funeral ceremony, with this exception: If the Rev. Gordon L. Kidd is available, I should appreciate it very much if he would go to the crematory chapel and say a brief prayer before the cremation takes place." So in the presence of only the undertaker, the Reverend Kidd conducted a regular Episcopal service.

But somehow nobody noticed what else Hick had written in the typed note she had attached to her will: "The disposal of my ashes is immaterial, although, if it can be done, I should like to have them dug into the soil around growing trees, which may benefit from whatever chemicals the ashes contain." The Dapson Funeral Home, having received no word on the subject, simply stored Lorena Hickok's ashes on a shelf among similar unclaimed remains.

Afterword

At Hyde Park, though, Lorena Hickok was not forgotten. As the tenth anniversary of her death approached, the director of the F.D.R. Library had her cartons brought to the staff workroom. Some of the younger archivists gasped when they saw what emerged. Of course everybody had anticipated that there would be E.R. letters, perhaps as many as a few hundred; instead, amid a jumble of newspaper clippings and other correspondence, there appeared to be a few thousand.

While that was interesting—an unexpected little treasure trove— the procedure for processing acquisitions was routinely followed. At the F.D.R. Library, top-secret documents from World War II are routinely handled, along with private collections of various kinds that become available year after year. So a young archivist was assigned to arrange The Papers of Lorena Hickok in chronological order and to prepare a catalog. Although he scanned every letter, it was not his duty to evaluate the material; what he was seeking, primarily, was any violation of the standard clause in any donor's deed of gift, requiring the removal of material likely to harass or embarrass a living person. In which case, a pink slip noting the date of the document and the general reason for its removal would be inserted at the appropriate place in the folder where the document would otherwise have been filed. Under this provision of Hick's contract, about a dozen letters in the Hickok Papers were removed and replaced by pink slips; it appears that these letters contain some reference to financial or other problems attending one or another divorce in the Roosevelt family.

Lorena Hickok had been informed repeatedly that she had the right to stipulate other restrictions. She could have specified that no material of a personal nature was to be opened until some date in the twenty-first century; she did not. She signed over full discretion on the matter of suppressing any portion of her papers to the National Archives.

During the period when Hick herself had frequented the F.D.R. Library, its director happened to be a woman—a woman who would shake her head decisively, ten years after Hick's death, upon being asked if she would have opened the Hickok Papers. But with a faint smile, Elizabeth Drewry had to add that a lot had occurred since her own retirement. And the archival profession, no less than any other, must reflect the prevailing attitudes of society at large, rather than any immutable standards of its own.

Thus on May 1, 1978, The Papers of Lorena Hickok were opened for unlimited research.

A Personal Note
and Some Acknowledgments

A few days after The Papers of Lorena Hickok were opened at
Hyde Park, it happened that Rosalynn Carter appeared on a TV
show and was introduced as the most active First Lady in the
nation's history. That exasperated Chaucy Bennetts. She is an editor of children's books for whom I had done several biographies of
eminent women, and she asked me if I would do another—of Eleanor Roosevelt. I was elated. Besides having been awed by Mrs. R.
back during my reporting days, I had more recently enjoyed delving into the Roosevelt saga in the course of two literary projects,°
and there was the further attraction that I live not far from Hyde
Park. But in the process of giving myself a short refresher course at
home, I began to feel a little apprehensive because so much had
already been written. When I telephoned the director of the F.D.R.
Library to say I was coming over the next morning, I made a weak
sort of joke to him: Did the world really need another opus on the
same subject? "The fact is," Bill Emerson said, "that we have got in
a lot of new material on Eleanor Roosevelt."

The Papers of Lorena Hickok did sound promising. Still my curiosity was sufficiently mild for me to spend an hour or so browsing
through other catalogs before picking up the catalog labeled
Hickok. It was not just my rereading of Joe Lash that made the
name familiar; "the owl-eyed Miss Hickok," he had called her.†
Years ago, as a wide-eyed reporter for *The New York Times*, I'd
listened with envy when white-haired Emma Bugbee of the *Herald*

° *The Presidents' Mothers* (St. Martin's Press, 1978); and *Franklin Delano Roosevelt* (Abelard-Schuman, 1975), a book for children.

† Joseph P. Lash's *Eleanor and Franklin* (W.W. Norton, 1971); and *Eleanor: The
Years Alone* (W.W. Norton, 1972).

Tribune reminisced about Mrs. R.'s early press conferences. And at some luncheon promoting a worthy cause I'd been extremely impressed when the former First Lady greeted Emma by her first name. Oh, that was nothing, Emma assured me afterward. Lorena Hickok, who had worked for the Associated Press in '32, had become one of Mrs. R.'s closest friends.

In hindsight, I think I expected that The Papers of Lorena Hickok might yield merely a few anecdotes about her famous friend that had not yet been printed, and the first folder in Box 1 nourished this small hope. It contained only two documents, illuminating the origin of this friendship. On the stationery of the Onondaga Hotel in Syracuse, New York, a note in Eleanor Roosevelt's inimitable scrawl, dated October 26, 1932—precisely two weeks before her husband was elected President—invited "Dear Miss Hickok" to drive with her to Elmira the following morning, and also suggested that they might have breakfast together before departing. The second letter, on a sheet of paper imprinted with the emblem of the New York Central Railroad, was written in a blessedly lucid, swift-flowing script, and it said:

> Dear Mrs. Roosevelt:
> About those reporters and cameramen—
> If there are any at the station, I can probably get rid of them without any hard feelings if I tell them you'll see them when you get back from Cambridge. Would that be too awfully bad?
> I know you hate it, but—this is Massachusetts!
> Anyway, I'll do whatever you say.
>
> Hicky

Then I reached for the second folder. It was much thicker, and it held page after page of creamy paper headed THE WHITE HOUSE in gold lettering. "Hick my dearest," I began to read. Probably about an hour later, in something like a classic state of shock, I left my seat in the serene research room where five or six other people were poring over documents, and, in a voice that sounded very strange to my own ears, I asked the library aide on duty if she would call the library's director for me.

William R. Emerson used to teach military history at Yale, but he is no traditional male chauvinist. He listened intently while I read him phrases from several E.R. letters. Taken out of context, he admitted, these did have a shocking impact. When I urged him to imagine a headline splashed across a tabloid front page, he winced. Why, I asked him, why couldn't this collection be locked up again, at least for another several decades? We talked at some length that day before deciding to meet for lunch the following day, when I would bring along my husband, Hal, whose journalistic experience is both longer and broader than my own.

During that lunch the two men did most of the talking. Philosophically. Examining the implications, pro and con, if a branch of the National Archives were to suppress any sort of material against the stated wish of the donor. I must confess that I behaved more emotionally, interrupting them at intervals to say they were missing the point: Eleanor Roosevelt was a great woman, and her effusively affectionate letters should be removed at least until the year 2000. As a result, Bill Emerson promised that he and his senior archivist would "re-review" the entire collection.

That process took a week, which my husband and I spent on Cape Cod. Only out of our hostess's hearing could we talk about those letters, although Bill Emerson had made sure I understood that I was in no way bound to keep silent; the letters had been open when I saw them, so the use I put them to was up to me. But I would not write a word about them, I told Hal. "How are you going to feel when some graduate student tips off the New York *Post?*" he asked me. Wishfully I insisted it would not happen—a way would be found to justify sequestering at least the most ardent letters.

Then the telephone rang while we were still unpacking, and Bill Emerson said that for several reasons it had been decided to leave The Papers of Lorena Hickok just as they were when I had started reading them. Indeed, one of the reasons for deciding against the removal of any of the letters was that the National Archives could not deny any other researcher access to material someone else had already seen. But, I protested, if I agreed never . . . No, of course, this was another real-life version of Catch-22. Furthermore, the removal of any document, by strict professional canon, would have to be recorded on a pink slip in the appropriate folder, and a profusion of pink slips would surely be a red flag to some subsequent researcher.

Most compelling, though, Bill Emerson could not believe there were valid grounds for suppressing this material. I do not know if he consulted any higher authority in arriving at the decision; nor is this the place for an essay on the broad issue raised by Lorena Hickok's gift to the nation. But from my own standpoint as a writer who had happened on Hick's cache, the decision meant something starkly clear. In the five words that one of the Hyde Park staff actually did intone when I sought his advice:

It's going to come out.

Any day, as that summer's tide of assistant professors engulfed the F.D.R. Library, somebody else would begin reading Box 1. In fact, a few other people had already looked at various Hickok boxes. So, I had to ask myself, since the story was bound to be told, how could I not try to tell it as fairly as possible? Although I would much rather avoid publicity myself, of course there were also positive considerations running through my mind. To be confronted by such an opportunity—the Everest of writing, as one of my daughters described it—well, I am not especially brave but I could not live with myself if I turned my back on the adventure. Thus it was with very mixed emotions that I set out, after all, to write *The Life of Lorena Hickok.*

Yes, the reading of those eighteen boxes at Hyde Park was tremendously exhilarating; to keep discovering new facets of an untold story like Hick's is an experience beyond comparison. So were the ensuing expeditions, from Long Island to South Dakota, in quest of further information. Along the way I had much generous help from dozens of people, and ordinarily such assistance would be acknowledged more conspicuously at the front of the resulting book. But this adventure has not lacked trauma. And a number of individuals fervently requested anonymity after I quoted some portions of the Hickok Papers to them. However, with the exception of the staff at the F.D.R. Library and some others with an especially valuable perspective, in whom I confided, only a handful of people knew why a book about Lorena Hickok was occupying me. My own main reason for preserving the mystery was to prevent a flare of innuendo before the whole story could be told. At any rate, many of the people who plumbed their memories when I asked them about Hick must have thought nothing would ever come of my research; and this volume will, I suspect, distress some of them to the extent that they would prefer not to have their own names prominently mentioned. Therefore, more in the interest of establishing the validity of various quotations than to offer the usual sort of acknowledgments, most of my informants will be identified, but only in the source notes about the chapters to which they contributed.

Still—and I wish it had seemed feasible to say so previously—there are other men and women without whose special help I could not have undertaken, let alone completed, this book. My experience of working at the F.D.R. Library did much to renew my faith in federal perfectability; during four months of daily association, everybody I encountered was helpful far beyond what might be anticipated. I suspect this is because Bill Emerson cares about running a good library. His patient and thoughtful interest in the projects occupying other researchers repeatedly impressed me as I sat reading week after week, and I can scarcely express my gratitude for his searching questions, no less than for his perceptive suggestions, regarding my own project. Not so incidentally, day by day I gradually absorbed a deeper understanding of the archival profession, while a similar process with reference to my own task was in some measure occurring. Eventually the inescapable professional imperative that had made Bill Emerson open the Hickok Papers, and keep them open, became more obvious to me. I am still not sure what I would have done, had I been in his position, but that is hardly pertinent; in my position, I can only be grateful for the high level of archival skill with which the entire staff at this library assists visiting researchers. I must especially thank Don Schewe, Frances Seeber, Elizabeth Denier, Sandra Raub, Mark Renovitch and Paul McLaughlin, who aided me in assembling pertinent photographs. Also Emily Williams, in charge of the library's oral history program relating to the life of Eleanor Roosevelt, steered me toward several valuable sources. A former staff member, Ray Geselbracht, who catalogued the Hickok Papers, must be mentioned, too. And to the retired Elizabeth B. Drewry, director of this library during Hick's day, I am enormously indebted, not just for her vivid recollections; when I went to see her at an early stage in my research, she let me talk for hours about my numbing discovery, and I left her feeling that I had made a wonderful friend.

While similar forbearance, as well as wise counsel, from members of my family and some close friends contributed more than I can say, I would rather thank them privately. But I cannot fail to record my gratitude to three whose advice and guidance went far beyond any professional duty: Claire Smith, my literary agent; Eugene Aleinikoff, my lawyer; and Hillel Black, my editor.

Just one more essential paragraph. If I have in any measure met one of the hardest challenges that any writer could face, it is because of the constant support and encouragement and constructive criticism, not to mention the outright research assistance, of my husband. Neither of us could have wished that *The New York Times* would be shut down by a strike in 1978 during a substantial portion of this book's preparation, but had that not happened, the process would have been infinitely more difficult. Thank you for everything, Hal.

D.F.

Notes on Sources

This book is based mainly on the contents of those cartons that Lorena Hickok deposited at the Franklin D. Roosevelt Library in Hyde Park; there her hoarded miscellany has been meticulously put into archival shape as The Papers of Lorena Hickok. The crux of the collection is, of course, its Eleanor Roosevelt–Lorena Hickok correspondence—2,336 letters from ER to LH; 1,024 from LH to ER. Because some readers may be interested in precise figures, I append a chart from the catalog of The Papers of Lorena Hickok:

	ER to LH	LH to ER
1932	1	1
1933	39°	3†
1934	236	20†
1935	231	17†
1936	310	46
1937	293	227
1938	289	195
1939	292	241
1940	213	137
1941	92	50
1942	46	26
1943	44	20
1944	30	20
1945	48	19

° In addition to these holograph letters, there is a typescript copy of excerpts from 129 additional letters, edited by LH.

† Filed separately among LH's papers relating to her work for Harry Hopkins from 1933 through 1936 are parts or the whole of about a dozen other LH to ER letters.

	ER to LH	LH to ER
1946	20	1
1947	18	1
1948	12	–
1949	1	–
1950–1962	102	–‡

Still, all of these ER–LH letters fill only ten of the eighteen boxes in which the LH Papers have been filed, and without the other eight it would have been far more difficult, if not impossible, to tell Hick's own story. Two of the other boxes contain her reports to Harry Hopkins, plus much related material. In the remainder, there are scores of newspaper clippings as well as original copies of some of LH's stories for the Associated Press, office memos and miscellaneous jottings, and also hundreds of letters from other people—most notably, long sequences from Mary Norton and Marion Harron—besides numerous other scraps and manuscripts. These range from, literally, a laundry list (harking back to the Stevens Hotel in Chicago during a Democratic convention) to 105 pages of a professional writer's autobiographical fragment. Consisting of an introduction, an outline, and four sample chapters, this document has been invaluable on many counts. Since LH spoke about her miserable early years to very few people, to discover even simple facts such as her birth date and birthplace would otherwise have posed major problems. Thus my first two chapters rely heavily on the first two chapters of her autobiographical fragment, with corroboration from county records and the recollections of a few confidantes, as the chapter-by-chapter notes that follow will indicate. Similarly, material from her own introduction, setting forth the personal philosophy she had arrived at by 1949, has been incorporated at the appropriate point into my version of her story, as have a few of her anecdotes from her chapters covering the Lindbergh kidnaping and her life in the White House during World War II. Also her outline, summing up her career from 1909 onward in six copious paragraphs and a few other terse ones, gave me dozens of clues that led toward cities where additional data could reasonably be expected. In the same manner, the letters she had saved—from people whose names were totally unfamiliar, no less than from

‡ Among the personal correspondence in The Papers of Eleanor Roosevelt about half a dozen LH letters from this period appear.

ER—provided a multitude of other clues without which essential details about a career that had almost completely faded into obscurity could scarcely have been retrieved.

Nevertheless, the LH Papers taken as a whole certainly raise more questions than they answer. Thus numerous other sources have also been used in the preparation of this book. During the months I spent reading through the eighteen boxes, my husband searched the other and larger Hyde Park collections donated by Harry Hopkins and Eleanor Roosevelt and her daughter Anna Halsted, each of which proved to contain significant LH material. Still, all of this documentation left many questions, not merely about the thirty years the ER–LH association endured, but also about the five years LH survived ER, as well as about the forty years before LH and ER had become close. It was therefore necessary to consult old newspapers and magazines beyond counting, besides practically all of the major and many of the minor memoirs and histories of the Roosevelt era. But for me to reproduce a basic bibliography of this much-written-about period would serve no purpose. The books that proved particularly helpful to me will be listed in the notes concerning the particular chapters where they made some contribution. However, several books of special value should be mentioned here. First of all, Eleanor Roosevelt's own memoirs, *This Is My Story* (Harper & Brothers, 1937) and *This I Remember* (Harper & Brothers, 1949); also Joseph P. Lash's *Eleanor and Franklin* (W.W. Norton & Company, 1971) and *Eleanor: The Years Alone* (W.W. Norton, 1972). In addition, Ishbel Ross's *Ladies of the Press* (Harper & Brothers, 1936) was extremely useful in putting LH's career into its proper perspective, and I shall have more to say about this fine book in the introductory portion to the notes on Chapter Four. Most important of all for my purposes was Lorena Hickok's own small volume *Reluctant First Lady* (Dodd, Mead & Company, 1962); although this made little impression when it was published, in effect it supplements her letters by recounting a sanitized version of her relationship with ER, and I shall be referring to *RFL* frequently in the notes for several chapters.

Even so, it was from people who knew Hick that I gathered much otherwise unavailable information—during a three-week tour of the north central states that my husband and I took in the autumn of 1978, as well as by mail and telephone, and in interviews during several shorter trips. Considering that LH would have been eighty-five had she survived until I began all of this interviewing and corresponding, I could not hope to find many of her contemporaries, and yet I did find a few dozen who could speak from firsthand and sometimes close acquaintanceship. I should add that most of them spoke with a vigor and perspicacity belying any stereotype of the senior citizen. Again, the specific contributions of each will be listed later.

The titles for the three major parts of the book are all quotations from Lorena Hickok. Part I (1893–1932) "I'm going out and make a name for myself . . ." was quoted in a letter to the author from Edna Browning Caldwell, November 9, 1978. Part II (1932–1936) "I don't suppose anyone can ever stay so happy . . ." is from a letter LH wrote to ER December 6, 1936. Part III (1937–1968) "I'll be relieved when it's over . . ." is from another LR–ER letter, dated January 19, 1939.

And now the specific sources for each chapter.

1. SADNESS IN SOUTH DAKOTA

The main source for the period up until the death of LH's mother is the first chapter of the autobiography LH worked on during 1949 at the suggestion of a casual friend; her own title for this was "The Making of an Introvert." With the rest of that abortive manuscript, it is filed in Box 14 of the LH Papers at Hyde Park. A few references to family matters in LH–ER letters when LH was traveling in the Dakotas, or when something else reminded her of her childhood, were helpful, too. In addition, three close friends of LH (who insisted on not being identified) independently recalled hearing her recount various episodes from this period of her life. Hoping to supplement these memories, I spent October 19, 1978, in Bowdle, during which my husband and I read several volumes of back copies of the Bowdle *Pioneer* at the agreeably cluttered office from which the paper is still published; since its original editor had been quite a local booster, its pages yielded much interesting sidelight material, such as "A Short History of Bowdle and Its Business Men" in the 1906 Christmas issue, besides the most valuable "Sad Indeed" quoted from the issue of September 20, 1906, and also several references to LH and her sister Ruby as diligent students and, in LH's case, as a speaker at church functions. Although we found nobody in Bowdle who had known her, just the surrounding landscape on a fine Indian summer day amply corroborated LH's recollection of it.

As to specific facts, quotations or incidents: the dates of her parents' marriage and her birth were recorded in the Walworth County Courthouse in Elkhorn, Wisconsin. The phrase "rise to the White House": Leta Browning to author October 9, 1978. About LH's rape by her father, four people independently recalled hearing LH talk of this; all asked to remain anonymous. Although I would have appreciated further corroboration, I must say that in no instance of a statement by LH of a fact that could be verified more easily, in county or school records or a newspaper, did I discover even a slight deviation from strict honesty. Otherwise, all of the direct quotations in the chapter are from the twenty pages of LH's "The Making of an Introvert."

2. HIRED GIRL

LH's own chapter two (see notes on Chapter One above) provided much more detail about her two years in domestic service than I could use; those years obviously impressed her deeply, which is also apparent from references to this service in the LH–ER letters and from the offering of some of the same anecdotes by LH friends with whom I talked. As to Aberdeen and environs, the local history collection of that city's Alexander Mitchell Library had city directories dating back to LH's sojourn, with ads giving a vivid picture of the community, even if LH did not stay put long enough to get listed at any of her local places of employment. Also helpful in setting the scene was the Dacotah Prairie Museum in Aberdeen, exhibiting photographs, artifacts and furnished rooms from LH's era; still more helpful was the profusely illustrated *Early History of Brown County, South Dakota* (North Plains Press, Aberdeen, S.D., 1970) sold to us there by Helen Bergh, chairman of the Brown County Historical Society.

As to specific incidents and quotations, the material on Aunt Ella comes from LH's chapter one, and there are also several Aunt Ella–LH letters from a later period in the LH Papers. Otherwise, "It appeared that their parents . . ." and all but one of the other quotations come from the twenty-five pages of the second chapter of LH's autobiographical fragment. Details of LH's last encounter with her father came from her own manuscript, but "Send him to the glue factory" was contained in a private communication to author, January 14, 1979. Regarding the original source of "At midnight in his guarded tent . . ." I suspect Byron but can't find it; can you?

3. YEARS OF LONELINESS

As LH's autobiographical manuscript skipped from her youthful arrival in Chicago to her coverage of the Lindbergh kidnaping nearly a quarter of a century later, with only a two-page outline describing what she might have written but never did write about the intervening years, this and the next two chapters required more digging than any of the others covering periods when her acquaintanceship could be more easily identified and traced. But since these early years could hardly have the interest of her later career, I searched mainly for a framework, as it were, from which the later Hick would emerge more clearly. Because LH happened to go to high school and begin her career in Battle Creek, my task in assembling material for this chapter was both immeasurably eased and also made more painful by the fact that a good friend, the writer Gerald Carson, introduced me by mail to a prodigiously willing aide to any literary project involving her city. But Berenice Lowe, a talented amateur historian—whose own multitudinous activities to elevate Battle Creek's renown seemed scarcely to have slowed down since she passed her eightieth birthday some time ago—made no secret of her hope that I would not rake up any unsavory implications concerning Mrs. Roosevelt; and I could not tell her the whole story. Thus not only she, but also the school officials and former LH schoolmates to whom she paved my way, may rue the days they spent assisting me and my husband. Perhaps the trauma will be less severe at the exceptionally well-stocked local history room of Battle Creek's Willard Library, where high-school yearbooks and city directories and reel after microfilm reel of old newspapers were willingly supplied, along with on-the-spot copies of several old pictures.

For the portion of the chapter about LH's college days at Lawrence University in Appleton, Wisconsin, our treatment was similarly of the red-carpet variety; a distinguished alumnus, John Behnke, editor of the biological sciences journal *Bioscience,* had written on our behalf to the university's top administration. Even during homecoming weekend in October, 1978, Vice President Davol H. Meader saw to it that we had access not only to LH's college transcript but also to contemporaneous catalogs and student publications from the university's archives, as well as correspondence between Aunt Ella and the president of Lawrence in those days.

Regarding LH's great interest in Edna Ferber, her autobiographical outline and several references in LH–ER letters were my source.

Now about specific quotations: "hall of knowledge" from Battle Creek High School *Paean,* 1909 edition. "Some of the others thought . . ." Aleen Sleeper to author October 8, 1978. "I remember what she wore . . ." Ruth Kelsey to author October 9, 1978. "Went sort of crazy," LH–ER April 10, 1940. "The most gifted teacher . . ." LH autobiographic outline. "The advantages of city life . . ." and "Average estimates of living expenses . . ." Lawrence University catalog, 1912 edition. LH plans for supporting herself at college, Leta Browning to author October 9, 1978. "We had been living in Dakota . . ." and other excerpts from LH's adventure on horseback, "The Reward of Stuffing," in Lawrence University *Lawrentian* #19, 1913. "Never a handkerchief," Edna Browning Caldwell to author November 9, 1978. "I would say that Miss Hickok . . ." Dr. Samuel Plantz to Ella Ellis May 26, 1913. ". . . Now my dear girlie . . ." Aunt Ella to LH June 1, 1913.

4. FOLLOWING FERBER INTO JOURNALISM

Here the microfilm files of the Battle Creek *Journal* were valuable, although the lack of by-lines prevented any positive identification of early LH journalistic output. On Battle Creek lore, Gerald Carson's *Cornflake Crusade* (Rinehart & Company, 1957) was outstandingly helpful, as was Berenice Bryant Lowe's *Tales of Old Battle Creek* (Albert L. and Louise B. Miller Foundation, Battle Creek, 1976), and also Julian Street's "Michigan Meanderings" in *Collier's* for July 18, 1914.

Concerning LH's 1915–16 sojourn in Milwaukee, no personnel

records survive from the *Sentinel* of her era, nor does the newspaper's library go back that far; but the microfilm collection at the city's Central Library does contain a complete run of papers, and we fed reel after reel through its machines, searching for LH stories—not quite at random, because LH letters to ER and others contained references to what she had covered in Milwaukee, as did her autobiographic outline. In each instance she had mentioned (for example, the Geraldine Farrar story), her own account was borne out by a printed opus "By Lorena Lawrence"; alas, I found no explanation for her alliterative alias. Indeed, except for an effusive paragraph in LH–ER, November 9, 1936, when ER was about to visit Milwaukee, it proved difficult to discern more than a faint flavor of LH's personal life there. By LH's own testimony, though, she aimed to emulate Edna Ferber; thus Ferber's autobiography *A Peculiar Treasure* (Doubleday, Doran & Company, 1939), with lively chapters on her reporting days in Milwaukee about a decade before LH got there, came in most handy, and even *Dawn O'Hara* (Grosset & Dunlap, 1911), the romanticized novel that inspired LH, certainly does contain mouth-watering descriptions of pastry despite its lack of journalistic verisimilitude. More help in that line, albeit about a competing paper, came from *The Milwaukee Journal: The First Eighty Years* by Will C. Conrad, Kathleen Wilson and Dale Wilson (University of Wisconsin Press, 1964); and from *Yesterday's Milwaukee* by Robert W. Wells (E.A. Seemann, Milwaukee, 1976).

As mentioned at the beginning of the Notes on Sources, *Ladies of the Press* by Ishbel Ross has been most useful in a general way; but in addition it also furnished some specific clues supplementing LH's own outline of her journalistic adventures. When Ross was preparing her encyclopedic compendium—still the best history of American women in journalism, at least up until the mid-1930's—she sent detailed questionnaires to all of her living subjects, and evidence that LH filled hers out appears in Ishbel Ross–LH July 31, 1935. Besides picturing LH on the book's flyleaf as one of America's forty most outstanding women journalists from the colonial era to the date of publication, Ross devoted pages 203–09 to LH's career, including details I did not find elsewhere. Still, the book's main value lay in its comprehensive survey of its subject; also useful in placing the professional career of LH in perspective was Marion

Marzolf's *Up From the Footnote: A History of Women Journalists* (Hastings House, 1977).

Now as to specific quotes: "The best advertised little old town . . ." Julian Street's "Michigan Meanderings" in *Collier's* July 18, 1914. "Come on, Edna . . ." and "I'm going out and make a name . . ." Edna Browning Caldwell to author November 9, 1978. "That's where I started to put on weight," LH–ER November 9, 1936. "GERALDINE PROVES . . ." Milwaukee *Sentinel* November 19, 1915. "That dog ruined . . .", "You can tell Miss Farrar . . ." and circumstances surrounding Farrar interview, related by several LH friends but I drew mostly on the version a later LH colleague, Abe Altrowitz, put down in an affectionate obituary in the Minneapolis *Star* May 16, 1968. "Aw, shut up!" Leta Browning to author October 9, 1978. "I clasped the hand of the President . . ." *Sentinel* February 1, 1916. "There goes Mother!" Anne Farr to author September 27, 1978. "Blackmail," LH–ER October 15, 1938 and ER's refusal to see Myrtle, ER–LH April 14, 1940. About LH's notion of going to Russia and her brief sojourn in New York: autobiographic outline, Ross page 206, and Archie Curnan to author September 25, 1978.

5. HICK'S FRONT PAGE DAYS

For the Minneapolis years, when LH became something of a local celebrity, it was still not easy to capture a personality that had flourished a full fifty years previously; even so, three days there were crowded with discoveries. Thanks to Charles Bailey, currently editing the *Tribune* on which LH starred in the 1920's, we quickly found that personnel records from LH's era were no longer available, and that newspaper's library did not contain more than a few later clippings about her. However, we were immediately steered toward the Minnesota Historical Society in nearby St. Paul, where two of us were soon whisking through microfilmed old *Tribunes*, using marvelous machines whereon a button could be pushed to produce an instant copy of a whole page, quite readable with a little help from a magnifying glass. Thus a large number of quarters went into obtaining a representative sampling of LH's printed stories, not only during her eight Minneapolis years but also afterward, when her old boss prominently featured her Associated Press writings.

Again thanks to Chuck Bailey, a copy of Bradley L. Morison's *Sunlight on Your Doorstep: The Minneapolis Tribune's First Hundred Years* (Ross & Haines, Inc., Minneapolis, 1966) filled in the background of LH's *Tribune* period with an expert touch. Anecdotal as well as factual, it also added much to LH's own contributions in many letters to ER about Tom and Ris Dillon, with whom ER stayed on a few Minneapolis visits. Furthermore, Brad Morison, a retired editorial writer for the *Tribune*, turned out to be living nearby, and although we could not make connections for a visit, a long telephone conversation elicited many personal memories as well as those of his wife and sister. Then a letter from him enclosing several snapshots of LH at picnics put me further in his debt. As to LH the sportswriter, Dick Cullum and Charlie Johnson, two alert gentlemen in their eighties who had covered Big Ten football with her, cheerfully reminisced in the course of a splendid dinner at a former speakeasy—or at least its direct successor—that LH herself had often enjoyed.

But the Morisons had not only known LH via the newspaper, they had also known Ella Morse since her childhood. They and others led me to Jeannette W. Brice, a close friend and neighbor of Ellie and Hick at the Leamington Hotel; Mrs. Brice acutely and sensitively contributed a great deal to the Minneapolis chapter, besides allowing me to copy six long letters LH wrote her years afterward. But the kind of factual data about Ellie that only a family member can provide came from Ellie's stepdaughter in California, Nancy D. Elliott, who sent me an affectionate and fact-filled biographic sketch of her stepmother, besides enclosing several snapshots.

Now the quotations. "As I remember Hick . . ." Abe Altrowitz in the Minneapolis *Star* May 16, 1968. "Young man, you must know . . ." Morison's *Sunlight on Your Doorstep* cited above, page 39. "He taught me how to drink," LH autobiographical outline. "Poor little rich girl," Jeannette Brice to author November 7, 1978. "Emotional aberration," Morison, page 41. "Hickey Doodles," Ella M. Dickinson–LH February 9, 1938 and other letters. "I wondered about that," Jeannette Brice to author. "In all the years I knew Hick . . ." private communication to author January 15, 1979. "Resort," Morison, page 41. "Oh, you got off . . ." Jean D. Ely to author

December 9, 1978. "IOWA VILLAGE WAITS . . ." *Tribune* August 7, 1923. "For the body you gave me . . ." Morison, page 39. "Nothing smutty . . ." Morison, page 40. "Now is the winter of Mr. T. Gobbler's . . ." *Tribune* November 18, 1924. "We have met the enemy . . ." and "On his shield . . ." *Tribune* November 16, 1924. "She never stepped on anybody's toes," Charlie Johnson to author October 16, 1978. "Miss Goofer," LH autobiographic outline. "I wake up . . ." Leta Browning to author October 9, 1978. "I remember Hick . . ." James Gray to author December 20, 1978. "The cleverest interviewer . . .", "This woman writer" and "The best job in a newspaper office . . ." Joseph P. Broderick manuscript in LH miscellaneous papers. San Francisco episode, several letters from Nancy D. Elliott to author.

6. SUCCESS IN NEW YORK

Here surfaces the LH whom ER first met in 1928, and thanks to the high standards set by the Associated Press on the matter of crisp writing, together with a remarkable record of longevity, I have been greatly assisted by nearly a dozen of LH's former colleagues as well as by other journalists of my acquaintance. Mainly from various points in Florida, a most welcome rain of letters replete with sharp observation and colorful anecdote began descending after I appealed to Earl Aronson, a former head of AP's Albany bureau; he and Sam Blackman, till the past decade a pillar of the agency's New York headquarters, suggested a few comrades who might have worked more closely with LH than they did, and several who replied suggested other names. In addition, Robert St. John's *This Was My World* (Doubleday & Company, 1953) provided vivid detail on pages 251–313 about what it was like to work for the AP in New York during part of the same period LH was on the staff there. As to LH's short stint on the *Mirror,* for my purposes the back files of that defunct tabloid, at the Newspaper Annex of the New York Public Library, gave me all I needed; LH's reference in LH–ER, January 19, 1938, to the three weeks she had spent in Northampton just ten years earlier, together with the sensational play the *Mirror* gave such a flimsy story, seemed more than ample.

In the area of LH's private life beyond office-related partying, however, I must say that firsthand information was particularly

difficult to find for obvious reasons. One close friend from Minneapolis, who moved to New York around the same time, warmly
defended LH against any imputation of sexual adventures with
women, on the grounds that she herself, moving in a very worldly
milieu, had never seen any sign of such a tendency. Of course this
does not necessarily contradict testimony that the tendency was
given into more anonymously. Because the reluctant account by
the woman I have called Barbara Hanson was so circumstantial, I
felt that I could not exclude it despite the lack of corroboration;
and at least indirect corroboration appears later in LH and ER
letters, notably during the last week of December in 1936.

Professionally only, in this chapter LH herself once again becomes my major source, not merely with her own autobiographical
chapter on the Lindbergh kidnaping but also with a few flashback
sequences in the 176-page book *Reluctant First Lady*, mentioned in
the introductory portion to the Notes on Sources. This is an extraordinary book. In tone and format it resembles several other volumes
for teenagers that she produced toward the end of her life, but she
assured friends it was intended for adult readers. Even in its references to her own encounters with ER before June 1932, and much
more so afterward, the book's ingenuous recital of her life's central
experience must, in anyone who has read the ER–LH correspondence, arouse pity beyond any other emotion. How hard Hick must
have found it to keep silent all those years! Still, as her biographer I
must be thankful that she did get around to writing *Reluctant First
Lady*, because some of what she relates could have come from no
other source. What she does say checks out as absolutely accurate
when it is weighed against *The New York Times* on the sequence of
public events or, at the other extreme, against the hitherto private
ER–LH correspondence, with its frequent spurts of spontaneous
reminiscence. It is, of course, what LH did not write in *RFL* that
would have kept the little book from virtually disappearing—to the
extent that the only copy I could obtain for reference at home
came through the New York State library system from the state's
master library in Albany. Not so incidentally, there is no conflict
between LH's little book and Lash's *Eleanor and Franklin*, for a
good deal of the Lash chapter "I Never Wanted to Be a President's
Wife," including its title, originated with and was credited to LH
although ER–LH letters that were unavailable to Lash might have
altered some subsequent portions of his book.

Now about this chapter's quotations: "Lorena Hickok, by-line sobbie . . ." as noted in the text is from *Variety* August 8, 1928, but almost certainly I would have missed it if LH had not clipped and saved it, thus causing it to land in one of the several folders at Hyde Park filled with her miscellaneous clippings. LH's early encounters with ER from *Reluctant First Lady (RFL)* pages 7–34, with "Eleanor was my brother Ted's favorite . . ." page 11; "The new mistress of the Executive Mansion . . ." page 15; "women's page stuff," page 16; "Isn't it a lovely day?" and "I can see her now . . ." page 23. "A Very Merry Christmas . . ." sample card among LH miscellaneous papers. "She'd open the door . . ." and "She taught me how to bake . . ." Jane Eads Bancroft to author December 8, 1978. "She had absolutely no idea of money . . ." Jeannette Brice to author November 7, 1978. LH's financial reliance on Ellie, Nancy D. Elliott to author May 16, 1979. "I'm going to teach you . . ." "Barbara Hanson" to author November 11, 1978. "You were just so sweet . . ." and two ensuing quotes, "Barbara Hanson" to author November 16, 1978. Material about LH's sister Ruby, who died a few years after LH early in the 1970's, pieced together from numerous LH letters and from Ruby's close friend Anne Farr to author September 27, 1978. "By Paul A. Dana, As Told to . . ." *New York Times* November 14, 1928. General Coxey story and initialed compliment from Tom Dillon, LH miscellaneous papers. "I remember walking up Fifth Avenue . . .", "the Lone Eagle . . ." and "Bill said I could bring you . . ." LH autobiographical manuscript. "That woman is unhappy . . ." *RFL*, page 33, confirmed by Elton Fay to author November 12, 1978. About ER's letter to Chicago, *Invincible Summer*, based on the recollections of Marion Dickerman, by Kenneth S. Davis (Atheneum, 1974) pages 107–8. "Beloved and Revered Future President," *Roosevelt and Howe* by Alfred B. Rollins Jr. (Knopf, 1962) page 53. "You are not to breathe a word . . ." *Invincible Summer*, page 108. "Mrs. Roosevelt, aren't you *thrilled* . . ." *RFL*, unpaged foreword.

7. BEGINNING A VERY SPECIAL FRIENDSHIP

Practically every incident that I have written about in this chapter was recounted in *Reluctant First Lady (RFL)* by LH herself at greater or lesser length. However, from 1932 onward her cache of letters supersedes her own little book as well as numerous other sources, and therefore it is necessary to say a bit more here about some features of this correspondence. Although only two brief, impersonal letters written by ER or LH during the months covered in Chapter Seven are to be found in the LH Papers (both are described in my Personal Note starting on page 329), the collection includes daily letters from ER to LH, except when they were together, and over a hundred LH–ER letters written during the next several years. Not only because both women often wrote copiously, but also because they both did a lot of traveling that reminded them of previous journeys, the later correspondence contains frequent retrospective passages alluding to feelings and events during the 1932 campaign and the early 1933 pre-inaugural period. It is on the basis of several such allusions in subsequent ER letters written at the Cornell guest house with the odd address of 2 The Circle, that I have suggested it as the locale of the unmistakable change in their relationship shown by the comparative formality of the two pre-election jottings, and then the fervency of ER's nightly letters right after the inauguration. I should add here that approximately another two dozen ER–LH letters were probably written between November 1932 and March 1933. LH herself told ER's daughter, Anna, after ER's death that she had burned fifteen letters from Anna's mother meant for her eyes only (LH to Anna Halsted June 9, 1966); and an additional sheaf was found in LH's apartment after her own death by her sister, who destroyed them without sharing their contents, according to Ruby's friend Anne Farr who accompanied her to Hyde Park on that occasion. Possibly these two batches of letters that LH had withheld when she gave so much else to the FDR Library would have made it easier to chart the growth of this relationship. Yet the letters that LH did donate leave no doubt about the basic facts. In addition to the ER–LH correspondence, however, the recollections of practically every LH friend I found also shed some light on LH's general attitude toward ER; about ER's attitude toward LH during the period covered by this chapter, her subsequent letters reveal the various feelings I have attributed to her. Regarding LH's journalistic activities covered in the chapter, again the recollections of her AP friends have supplemented her own hoarded memos, clippings and typed copies of stories; and besides Ishbel Ross's *Ladies of the Press* (see notes for

Chapter Four), Bess Furman's *Washington By-Line* (Knopf, 1949) was also most helpful here. So were back copies of *The New York Times* and Minneapolis *Tribune* for this period.

More specifically now: recollections of LH aboard FDR's campaign train and "the usual AP restraint," Warner B. Ragsdale to author December 13, 1978. Concerning Malvina Thompson and "about her childhood . . ." *RFL* page 38. "Tommy was with her . . ." page 39. LH campaign memories, *RFL* pages 35–51, plus miscellaneous clippings etc. in LH Papers. "To my embarrassment . . ." *RFL* pages 48–9; "Since she had grown to trust me . . ." page 57; "I'm a middle-aged woman . . ." page 44. "She arrives back . . ." original copy of LH typed memo in LH Papers. "She greeted me . . ." *RFL* page 58; "But I haven't changed . . ." page 4; "If I wanted to be selfish . . ." page 1; "I'm going to walk . . ." page 6. "If I wanted to be selfish . . ." LH typed copy of her three-part AP series. "She knew her subject . . ." Gardner Bridge to author November 3, 1978. About Bess Furman and Mrs. Hoover anecdote, Furman's *Washington By-Line;* the specific anecdote on page 58. "Girls," in those days practically the universal term for newspaper women, repeatedly used in *RFL* and in ER letters. "I was not among them . . ." *RFL* page 61. LH agreement with Louis Howe, LH to Malvina Thompson July 23, 1947. "I have never talked . . ." *RFL* page 67. "The FLOFL," several Malvina Thompson to LH letters. "Moddom," LH salutation on some letters to ER, and several friends recollected her inability to use the First Lady's first name, always speaking of her as "Mrs. R.," which LH herself discussed in *RFL* page 118. ER's attitude toward LH, retrospectively in numerous ER–LH letters. "You'd better get out of my way . . ." and biographical details about Malvina Thompson from a typewritten profile headed "Mamie"—another of Tommy's nicknames—by one of her nieces, Eleanor Lund May 25, 1953; when LH tried unsuccessfully to sell an article to the *Reader's Digest* about Tommy after the latter's death, apparently Tommy's niece helped her this way. "Though I do not always . . ." Tommy to LH January 10, 1933; engagement books described in just-cited letter, also referred to frequently in subsequent ER–LH correspondence when LH was often requested to send new pages. "I want you to know . . ." and "I certainly made my exit . . ." Tommy to LH January 19, 1933. Bess Furman luncheon described from her perspective in *Washington By-Line* pages 138–9, and guardedly from

LH's in *RFL* page 68–9. Trip to Washington, *RFL* pages 69–77; "But Eleanor darling . . ." page 73 and "Miss Eleanor," page 75. Photograph with inscription "We were only separated . . ." now in possession of Ruby's friend Anne Farr, thanks to whom a copy appears on page 134 of this book. "There's one thing I won't do . . ." and "I do think . . ." *New York Times* February 4, 1933. LH's guarded account of assassination scare and Cornell visit, *RFL* pages 78–83; "Where's Mrs. Roosevelt . . ." page 79. "Phew! Exclaims Mrs. Roosevelt," Minneapolis *Tribune* February 16, 1933. "MRS. ROOSEVELT OUTWARDLY CALM . . ." Ithaca *Journal-News* February 16, 1933. For personal matters, see introductory section to this chapter's notes. "Hick darling, All day . . ." ER–LH March 7, 1933.

8. HICK CEASES TO BE A REPORTER

Besides the ER–LH correspondence, this chapter also draws on LH memos, clippings and a fifteen-page manuscript fragment about her first weekend visit to the White House, as well as upon *Reluctant First Lady (RFL)*. Again, *The New York Times* and Minneapolis *Tribune* provided background details, supplemented by ER's memoirs and Lash's first volume (see introductory portion to Notes on Sources), and by Ross, cited in notes for Chapter Four, and Furman, mentioned in the Chapter Seven notes.

As to the sources for specific incidents and quotations in Chapter Eight: "In regard to this Groton business . . ." LH Memo to W.W.C. [Chaplin]. "She was accompanied . . ." *NY Times* February 19, 1933. Last night out of captivity, *RFL* page 88. Inaugural events from LH standpoint, *RFL* pages 89–107; "When I was feeling . . ." page 92; "A reporter should never . . ." page 96; "Don't look so worried . . ." page 98. "Said goodbye to Hick," ER's engagement calendars in Papers of ER. "Diary," numerous subsequent ER letters. LH calendar, see picture on page 135. "Hick my dearest," ER–LH March 5, 1933. "Did I tell you . . ." ER–LH undated fragment, presumably March 4, 1933. ". . . & I couldn't say je t'aime . . ." ER–LH March 6, 1933. "I thought only of you . . ." and "What shall we read . . ." ER–LH March 7, 1933. "Just telephoned you. Oh . . ." ER–LH March 8, 1933. "My pictures are . . ." and "One more day marked off . . ." ER–LH March 9, 1933. ". . . & I walked . . ." ER–LH March 11, 1933. LH attitude toward FDR, several later letters retrospectively, also several passages in *RFL*, notably page 116–7. ". . . I begin to think there may be ways . . ." ER–LH March 9, 1933. "I miss you so much . . ." ER–LH March 9, 1933. "You have a stormier time . . ." ER–LH March 11, 1933. ". . . & [I] was almost rude . . ." ER–LH March 8, 1933. General details of LH weekend visit to White House, "A limousine with a shield on the door . . ." and ". . . it must have been a sense of intrusion . . ." LH manuscript fragment dated March 1933. LH decision to quit AP, touched on in *RFL* page 96 and 134–5 and numerous later letters, notably LH to Tommy July 23, 1947. "Thinking of you hard . . ." handwritten draft of LH–ER telegram. "Dear Mr. Hopkins . . ." LH to Harry Hopkins June 7, 1933 in Hopkins Papers.

9. THE DEPRESSION: ON THE ROAD FOR HARRY HOPKINS

The third folder in Box 1 of the LH Papers differs from any other in the ten boxes containing the ER–LH correspondence—in that it contains not actual handwritten ER–LH letters, but a sequence of rather carelessly typed excerpts from 129 ER–LH letters written between the middle of March and the middle of November in 1933. The originals for only two of these letters also appear in the collection. This typescript mystified the FDR Library staff, who had no reason to try to solve the mystery. I believe, though, on the basis of various references in much later LH letters, notably LH to Anna Halsted October 6, 1963 and June 9, 1966, that toward the end of the 1940's LH undertook a project at ER's request. It was to copy over all of the ER–LH letters containing personal passages, eliminating anything likely to cause future embarrassment. There are many reasons for assuming that ER thought the job had been completed; this matter is treated in more detail in the text of my Chapter Twenty as well as the notes for that chapter. Still, it should be mentioned here that most of the ER–LH letters for the period covered in this chapter are merely typed excerpts; also, even the bowdlerized versions do include numerous brief allusions to ER's dependence on LH, which LH seemingly could not force herself to expunge from the record—just as she found it impossible to complete the bowdlerizing job she began. Again, *Reluctant First Lady*

(RFL) expands on the correspondence in this chapter's time span. Also personal recollections of LH in this period were most kindly provided by two of her associates then: Martha Gellhorn, who wrote to me from England January 2, 1979, and Grace F. Tugwell, who reminisced about her travels with LH during a telephone interview from her California home May 14, 1979.

Furthermore, as LH embarks on her employment by Harry Hopkins, the Hyde Park collection of his papers in a major way supplements her own material about this phase of her career. For the Hopkins Papers include frequent correspondence relating to LH's travels, often with Hopkins's secretary, Kathryn Godwin; also it is fascinating to see his scrawled notations on the file copies of her reports, requesting Mrs. Godwin to send duplicates to the President and/or to various other figures in the administration. In the LH Papers, however, there are copies of a few additional reports that somehow did not get filed in Washington, besides a jumble of notes and supporting documents as well as the introduction and other material prepared for LH's abortive book about her WPA experiences (see Chapter Fourteen). Here I must add that I was tempted to reproduce the complete texts of several of the LH reports to Hopkins, which Hopkins himself told ER would be the best history of the Depression in future years (ER–LH September 1, 1934), and yet a personal biography did not seem, after all, the right place for them. As to factual underpinning in recounting LH's government service, for my purposes the best published work was *Harry Hopkins and the New Deal* (R.E. Burdick: Fair Lawn, N.J., 1974) by Paul A. Kurzman.

Now specific sources for this chapter: "Hick darling, I hate you to say . . ." and "Sometimes I think I am . . ." ER–LH April 3, 1933. "Well, my dear, there will be . . ." ER–LH April 4, 1933. "I'd like to run to you . . ." ER–LH April 5, 1933. "Very proud" ER–LH April 25, 1933. "By the way, did I leave . . ." ER–LH April 26, 1933. "I love you on Elliott . . ." ER–LH May 9, 1933. "I don't seem to be able . . ." ER–LH May 27, 1933. "You are my rock . . ." ER–LH May 31, 1933. Details of the Gaspé vacation trip from *RFL* pages 119–34, with "Where would they hide us?" page 120; "Well, you're the First Lady . . ." page 122; "My dear, they're all Republicans . . ." page 123; and "Damn!" page 128. LH's attitude toward other ER friends and family members, numerous LH–ER letters. On LH's new job, "What I want you to do . . ." LH introduction to never-completed book about working for Hopkins. "The kickers . . ." and "Yours very truly . . ." LH–Hopkins August 6, 1933. "[Roosevelt] liked . . ." and "It was not unusual . . ," *The Coming of the New Deal* by Arthur M. Schlesinger (Houghton Mifflin, 1959) page 526. LH described her first months on the new job and ER's trip to West Virginia in *RFL* pages 134–42. "Don't forget me, honey . . ." LH–Hopkins September 6, 1933. "Oh, this is the damnedest state . . ." and "When I tell the story to Harry Hopkins . . ." LH–ER August 23, 1933. ER's interest in Arthurdale, Lash's *Eleanor and Franklin* pages 393–417. "You really started something!" *RFL* page 140. "I don't believe I'll ever feel complacent . . ." LH–ER August 23, 1933.

About LH's financial imprudence, practically everybody who knew her well testified, and the ER–LH correspondence amply documents this LH failing; also the LH Papers include copies of her income tax returns, car deeds and a few dunning letters. Specific material about Bluette has been drawn from several ER letters in the autumn of 1933, plus a little notebook LH kept, documenting mileage and expenses for her every government trip. "At the moment, I'm angry . . ." LH–ER November 1, 1933. "If your son misbehaves . . ." LH to Mrs. Godwin November 9, 1933. "Into the relief office . . ." LH–Hopkins November 1, 1933. "I was told in Bismarck . . ." LH–Hopkins October 30, 1933. "How funny you are . . ." ER–LH September 6, 1933. "The First Lady of the Land . . ." newspaper clipping undated, unidentified as to locale. "I'm being killed with kindness . . ." LH–ER August 25, 1933. *Literary Digest* picture and two paragraphs about LH, issue of November 18, 1933, page 12. "Darling, I know they bother you . . ." ER–LH December 2, 1933. "I am prouder dear . . ." ER–LH November 11, 1933. "Dear: Tonight it's Bemidji . . ." LH–ER December 5, 1933.

10. EMOTIONAL PEAKS AND VALLEYS

In this chapter and the next, the homosexual implications of the ER–LH relationship are finally, and gingerly, touched upon. I have downplayed the question not merely from my personal reluctance to speculate about anybody else's private affairs, let alone Eleanor Roosevelt's, but mainly because after several rereadings of the ER–

LH correspondence I do not believe that either of these women can fairly be placed into the contemporary gay category. Although my scholarly older daughter sent me a large tome on the subject from her university bookstore, it did not help me much. What I did find extremely helpful was a sensitive book about a somewhat similar relationship, also disclosed quite recently upon the opening of a cache of letters—letters written by Mary Emma Woolley, president of Mount Holyoke College from 1901 to 1937, and by Jeannette Marks, chairman of Mount Holyoke's Department of English Literature during much of the same period. Anna Mary Wells, in *Miss Marks and Miss Woolley* (Houghton Mifflin, 1978), provides more than just a moving account of a previously undisclosed emotional attachment between two notable women; she also gives a brief but perceptive overview of the social or cultural setting within which the attachment must be considered. I am most indebted to the author of this fine book for reinforcing my own feeling regarding the unfairness of using contemporary standards to characterize the behavior of women brought up under almost inconceivably different standards. Also I am indebted to her for her discussion of two very pertinent works: Havelock Ellis's analysis of the "borderline" aspect of many female attachments in his section on sexual inversion in Volume I of his *Studies in the Psychology of Sex* (Random House, 1936); and a thoughtful scholarly article about feminine friendships, "The Female World of Love and Ritual: Relations between Women in Nineteenth-Century America," by Carroll Smith-Rosenberg in *Signs: A Journal of Women in Culture and Society*, vol. 1, no. 1, Autumn 1975. I must add that a most loyal alumna of Mount Holyoke who is one of my closest friends called my attention to *Miss Marks and Miss Woolley;* for that and her warm, understanding support I cannot thank Bunny Simon sufficiently. Still, a seemingly less pertinent novel that I serendipitously picked up myself proved perhaps even more valuable. *Maurice* by E.M. Forster (W.W. Norton, 1971) chronicles just such a "pure" affair between two men as the ER–LH correspondence appears to me to exemplify; even if Forster personally deplored the platonic restraint enforced by Maurice's friend Clive, he convincingly depicted a love between two persons of the same sex, transcending friendship, that has definite sexual nuances—and yet stops short of sexual activity. This fictional model was particularly interesting to me because the novel, published comparatively recently, had been written about sixty years earlier, reflecting, as Forster himself put it, the "ignorance and terror" about homosexuality that prevailed in the period when both ER and LH would have formed their opinions, before "familiarity and contempt" superseded the terror. Upon reading those words of Forster's in his 1960 Terminal Note accompanying his novel, I myself felt as if I had discovered the key to interpreting the ER–LH relationship; still I preferred not to speculate along these lines in the text of LH's story.

As to incidents and quotations in this chapter: the dehumidifier episode is from *RFL* pages 143–7, with "You can't do that to me . . ." page 145; "Hick's rugwashing machine" and "What do *you* think . . ." page 147. LH's stormy departure from the White House alluded to in a few ER–LH letters shortly before and on Christmas Day of 1933. Details about ER's daughter from ER's *This Is My Story* pages 336–40, and also from *A Love in Shadow* by John R. Boettiger (W.W. Norton, 1978). I must say here that the latter book by ER's grandson, touchingly recounting his parents' story, proved particularly thought-provoking. For it was precisely during the period when Anna Roosevelt Dall had become passionately involved with a newspaper reporter that Anna's mother and another reporter were also forming a close relationship; but even if the complex nuances suggested by such a strange parallel might tempt a disciple of that theoretical realm of analysis known as psychohistory, I could not believe any such speculation belonged in LH's story. Regarding Anna and LH, references to their compatibility over the years appear in several ER–LH letters, and LH saved a few notes from Anna; in Anna's papers—Anna Halsted was her name for the last two decades of her life—there are a few 1960's LH letters. "Merry Christmas to you, Hick . . ." Anna–LH December 18, 1935. "Anna read me part of your letter . . ." and "Darling the love . . ." ER–LH December 25, 1933. "Dearest Honey" and "It has been a wonderful trip . . ." ER–FDR July 18, 1933. ". . . & I went to sleep . . ." ER–LH December 23, 1933. "I had a little longing . . ." ER–LH December 1, 1933. ". . . I bitterly resent . . ." LH to Mrs. Godwin February 18, 1934. "Such icy weather . . ." and *"Graft.* All this haste . . ." *Time* February 19, 1934, page 11. " . . . Believe me, the next state . . ." LH–Hopkins February 7, 1934. ". . . I'm so fed up . . ." and "I suppose I am a 'rotund lady . . ." LH to Mrs. Godwin February 18, 1934. "I shall very likely be criticized . . ." *RFL* page 3. ER on gossip, ER–LH November 22, 1933 and November 27, 1933, and "One cannot hide things . . ." ER–LH November 22, 1933. LH horror of gossip referred to often by ER. The sad story of "Butter" in successive LH–ER letters Christmas week of 1936; "Poor dear, I hate you to suffer . . ." ER–LH December 30, 1936. "Oh! dear one . . ." ER–LH January 27, 1934. ". . . For the time being . . ." ER–LH February 4, 1934.

On the Puerto Rican trip, Furman's *Washington By-Line* pages 195–204, with "I am going . . ." page 195. "I hope he chokes," ER–Anna March 6, 1934. Rather remarkably, *RFL* carries not a line about Puerto Rico but several ER–LH letters refer to the trip beforehand or retrospectively, and a few LH–ER 1940's letters do so, too. "It seems as though you belonged . . ." ER–LH March 26, 1934. "I've been very much 'Mrs. R.'. . ." ER–LH April 6, 1934. About ER's White House luncheon of hot stuffed eggs, Morris Bishop in *A History of Cornell* (Cornell University Press, 1962) page 481. "Stick to your diet . . ." ER–LH March 11, 1933. "I ended a long day of conferences . . ." LH–ER April 9, 1934. "How I wish I could enjoy . . ." ER–LH April 12, 1934. "One of the male social workers . . ." LH–ER April 11, 1934. "Dear Mr. Hopkins: At no time previously . . ." and several excerpts through "I personally would prefer Roosevelt," LH–Hopkins April 11, 1934. "Could manage to subsist," LH–Hopkins April 13, 1934. "No, I am always glad . . ." ER–LH April 16, 1934. "One corner cabinet . . ." ER–LH April 18, 1934. "Darling, your Sunday night letter . . ." LH–ER April 19, 1934. "Incidentally, sir . . ." LH–Hopkins May 4, 1934. "Dear Mr. Hopkins: A Promised Land . . ." LH–Hopkins June 6, 1934. "I ought to write a report . . ." LH–ER June 15, 1934. "I'll dread that, too . . ." ER–LH February 4, 1934. Details of visit to Ellie, Nancy D. Elliott to author January 29, 1979. "Yes, dear, I think you will remember . . ." ER–LH June 28, 1934. LH's account of July 1934 vacation, *RFL* pages 157–76; "Miss Hickok will require . . ." page 161. "Tell Miss Hickok . . ." Billy Nelson to ER 9/14/35.

11. LEARNING TO LET GO

LH's judgment of herself at this time, as she strove with the intensity of her feeling for ER, is reflected in many of her letters. It is summed up perhaps most explicitly in her letter to ER of August

15, 1934, when she wrote: "Oh, I'm bad, my dear. . ." She expressed similar feelings explicitly or implicitly in several of her surviving letters from the early period of the relationship; the collection includes ninety eight of her letters in the years 1933 through 1936. But there are—nobody can say why—eight hundred LH–ER letters from 1937 through 1940, and the introspective passages in some of these later letters have provided the main basis for my description of her state of mind during the period this chapter covers. Again, as I mentioned in the introductory portion to the notes for the preceding chapter, I chose not to speculate in any detail about private behavior or even intimate feelings; it seems to me that the purposes of history are best served by telling this story with neither fictional nor questionably accurate psychological embellishments. About the fact that the relationship changed after the western trip there can be no doubt, however, even if effusively affectionate passages still appear intermittently in the correspondence.

As to specific references, "Your letter today . . ." ER–LH August 11, 1934. About LH's feelings towards ER's trooper friend, besides several allusions in ER–LH letters, the LH Papers include a small folder of communications, among them a Mother's Day card, addressed to "Dear Lady" by Earl Miller; while these have been filed as if they were intended for LH herself, it seems incontrovertible, from internal evidence, that they had originally been sent to ER, who forwarded them to LH who was, by her own frequent confession, very prone to jealousy. "And now I'm going to bed . . ." LH–ER April 20, 1934. "Dear You . . .", "What *are* we going to do . . ." and "Good night, I hope . . ." LH–ER August 15, 1934. "A couple of days ago . . ." LH–Hopkins August, 1934. "Mr. Hopkins said today . . ." and "I wish I could lie down . . ." ER–LH September 1, 1934. " . . . & some of them can do things . . ." ER–LH March 10, 1933. "[Mrs. Roosevelt] was able . . ." LH in *Ladies of Courage* (G.P. Putnam's Sons, 1954) page 277. About the Danas, several ER–LH references and subsequent correspondence to LH from Ella and Bill Dana. "For heaven's sake . . ." ER–LH August 27, 1934. On LH's nostalgia for newspapering and hope to get back to it, see Chapter Thirteen. "Primary drought area," "You never saw so many . . . ," "All we need . . ." and "They didn't want . . ." LH–ER September 14, 1934. "Hick dearest, I am sorry . . ." and "You must not think . . ." ER–LH October 31, 1934. "God damn it . . ." LH–ER November 2, 1934. "Darling if we all stopped . . ." ER–LH

November 3, 1934. "Hick my darling, That cry . . ." ER–LH undated 1934. About ER, her spontaneous self-revelation in the ER–
LH correspondence plus Lash's *Eleanor and Franklin*. LH's horseback riding referred to by ER several times. "Dearest: I don't know
what you did . . ." LH–ER November 21, 1934. About Nan Cook,
Kenneth Davis's *Invincible Summer* (see notes for Chapter Six) and
Lash page 342; details of Warm Springs episode ER–Anna November 19, 1934. "I do hope the worst . . ." ER–LH December 25,
1934.

12. 1935: YEAR OF INDECISION

Perhaps more than any other, this chapter indicates the range of
issues that both ER and LH touched upon in their private correspondence; practically everything here comes from the LH Papers.
But despite frequent comments by ER or LH on public figures from
Huey Long to Jim Farley, my temptation to dwell at greater length
on political or social issues had to be resisted because it would be
difficult to do so without giving an unjustifiable pretension of importance to LH and her relationship with ER. For, in 1935, ER not
too much less than LH was still involved only peripherally in the
exciting dramas of FDR's first term, as the ER–LH letters amply
document. Nor does it seem to me coincidental, I might add, that
ER's real growth in stature during the next few years coincided
with her ceasing to need in any serious way the woman who is,
after all, the subject of this book.

Now for specific incidents or quotations: LH ordering beer, Jane
Eads Bancroft to author December 8, 1978. About Mabel Haley,
several letters notably LH–ER December 8, 1936 and Mabel Haley
to LH December 16, 1937. Regarding Louis Howe, ER's frequent
use of his initials when referring to him in her letters to LH at first
amused me, until it struck me that, probably only subconsciously,
she must have been associating the two LH's in her own mind. "Of
course you should have had a husband . . ." ER–LH February 1,
1935. ". . . The crowds & the telephones . . ." ER–LH February 15,
1935. "I kept thinking of the mess . . ." ER–LH June 3, 1934. ER's
upset over allegedly drunken son ER–LH May 7, 1935. "Do you
think . . ." and "Now I ask you . . ." ER–LH April 27, 1935. "Ready
to chew . . . ," "so mad with FDR" and "be calm, Mrs. R." ER–LH

April 28, 1935. " . . . I'm sorry I worried you . . ." ER–LH May 2, 1935. About the coal mine visit and "so wear suitable clothes . . ." ER–LH May 7, 1935; other details and "The trip into the mine . . ." from one of the letters Leta Browning very kindly allowed me to copy, LH–Brownings May 29, 1935; in this LH also told of going to hear FDR's "magnificent" speech, then struggling with her report, and she also described with awe his calm demeanor at dinner the day the Supreme Court outlawed the NRA ("He was even able to joke about it a little"). LH's "Confidential Report on Michigan" addressed to Harry Hopkins May 27, 1935 was, according to LH–Hopkins April 17, 1935, undertaken on behalf of the National Emergency Council after an LH talk with the President April 16, 1935; the Michigan report contains "the wisecracking . . . ."

Regarding Alicent Holt, I am indebted to Elaine Dahlman in the personnel office of the Grand Rapids Schools for the information that Miss Holt had been a popular teacher who retired in 1949 and died on May 8, 1968, just a week after LH, although they had apparently lost touch early in the 1950's; LH saved around two hundred letters from her, most of them written 1936-7. "You will never learn . . ." ER–LH May 16, 1935. "Do you remember . . ." Holt–LH May 31, 1936. "I know Prendergast . . ." ER–LH June 15, 1935. "The sunset at Campo . . ." and "God damn it . . ." LH–ER July 31, 1935. "I think it is very important . . ." and "We ought to study this . . ." LH to Aubrey Williams, deputy to Hopkins, October 31, 1935. ". . . He's *got* to be hard-boiled . . ." and "Well—it's all interesting . . ." LH–ER August 7, 1935. "I know what you mean about structure . . ." and "It's muddy thinking," ER–LH September 5, 1935. "I'd like to be able . . ." ER–LH August 25, 1935. "It is a grand criticism . . ." ER–LH September 8, 1935. "Dearest you can be as tough . . ." ER–LH September 14, 1935. "White nights," LH–ER September 9, 1935. "Your esteemed husband . . ." LH–ER September 23, 1935. "I'm going to recommend . . ." LH–ER October 16, 1935. "This has been a day . . ." LH–ER December 10, 1935.

13. WAR—OR THE WORLD'S FAIR

There are numerous references to LH's feelings about her work in LH and ER letters during the 1935-6 time span this chapter covers; but, again, the introspective musings in later letters were even more valuable. Because LH's decision to give up reporting turns out to be a crucial turning point for her, it might be helpful to illustrate the importance of the retrospective passages with a particularly good example. In 1947, when ER was writing the second volume of her autobiography about her White House years, her secretary sent LH the first draft of an episode involving her, eliciting a most revealing reply:

Wednesday, July 23rd [1947]

Dear Tommy:

Many thanks for the preview of what Mrs. R. wrote about me and the first day at the WH.

I hope neither of you will be offended if I say I don't like that sentence "Later I came to realize that in the White House one must not play favorites . . ."

Maybe I'm too sensitive, but the inference one might draw—at least that is how it sounded to me—is that I got that story just because I was a nice, tame, pet reporter.

Tommy, I didn't get that story because I was anybody's pet reporter. Oh, I know a lot of people thought she played favorites—as they later thought she played favorites with Bess [Furman], Geno [Genevieve Forbes Herrick of the Chicago *Tribune* in 1933] etc.

But, dear Tommy, in those days (pardon an old lady her conceit) I was somebody in my own right. I was just about the top gal reporter in the country. It sounds cocky, doesn't it? Well, I was cocky in those days—and I still am when I think about those days. Please forgive me, but I was good, I knew it—and I still know it. God knows, I've had the conceit taken out of me plenty in the years since. Being a newspaper reporter was the only thing I ever was really good at.

I got that story because I earned it . . . [LH proceeded to fill two large pages of single-spaced typing describing her journalistic initiatives regarding ER; and her letter bore results in that the offending sentence was removed from the ER manuscript, with a complimentary paragraph about Lorena Hickok's reportorial reliability substituted.]

More specifically now: "I do hope you get back . . ." ER–LH August 1, 1935. "If you got a laugh . . ." and "And I don't

believe . . ." LH–ER August 7, 1935. "Can't imagine where . . ."
LH–ER September 27, 1935. ER's joking about joining LH as a
war correspondent, ER–LH August 29, 1935. "I am so glad you
found . . ." ER–LH August 30, 1935. "WAR CORRESPONDENT
FINDS . . ." clipping from *New York Times* December 8, 1935
enclosed with ER–LH of same date. ". . . I am glad Newky . . ."
ER–LH January 21, 1936. "IF YOU ARE FREE . . ." ER–LH
telegram February 17, 1936. "Hick darling, I am so very, very
sorry . . ." ER–LH February 18, 1936. Aunt Ella's visit, Ella Ellis to
ER February, 1936. LH's survey of New York City, including "I
had on . . . ", "On the whole . . ." and "If things go as they are . . ."
LH–Hopkins March 2, 1936. "Do you miss us?" LH autobiographical manuscript, chapter on Lindbergh kidnaping. Details of LH's
diabetic flare-up mostly from several Alicent Holt–LH letters in
April and May of 1936. LH decision to quit job implicit in several
later letters. "Youngstown is terribly depressing . . ." LH–ER undated extract from sheaf of similar extracts prepared when LH was
planning to write a book about her WPA experiences. "From your
Youngstown letter . . ." ER–LH May 7, 1936. "He purrs like a
cat . . ." ER–LH June 10, 1936. "The same old bunk" and "it is
foolish to hope . . ." ER–LH June 13, 1936. "I can stand this
pace . . ." ER–LH June 14, 1936. Democratic convention, *New
York Times* June 27 and 28, 1936, also Furman's *Washington By-
Line* pages 245–7. "I felt entirely detached . . ." ER–LH June 28,
1936. "Dearest: At last I've found . . ." LH–ER June 27, 1936. "Are
you taking the absent . . ." ER–LH June 18, 1936. "You are right
that your bad times . . ." ER–LH June 25, 1936. "Tonight we
dined . . ." LH–ER July 11, 1936. About ER's role in the campaign,
Lash pages 445–8. "This summer is going very fast . . ." LH–ER
July 18, 1936. "I get scared . . . ", "They were eating . . ." and
"Darling, do they still feel as complacent . . ." LH–ER July 25,
1936. "I don't think F. is . . ." ER–LH August 2, 1936. "I have a
feeling . . ." ER–LH July 29, 1936. "Dearest . . . I'm wondering if
you . . ." LH–ER July 31, 1936. "[Your] letter sounded . . ." ER–LH
August 3, 1936. "I'm afraid my reasons . . ." and ". . . I truly don't
think . . ." ER–LH August 9, 1936. "I wonder if that Spanish . . ."
LH–ER July 31, 1936. ER's housekeeping bee, several early September ER–LH letters. "I'd hate to go to Europe . . ." ER–LH
September 19, 1936. LH's Battle Creek visit, "What is success?"
and "Success is . . ." Leta Browning to author October 9, 1978.

LH's arrival in Washington and "She had us all badly . . ." LH to
Dear Leta September 21, 1936. ". . . I pray . . ." and "A world of
love . . ." ER–LH October 1, 1936.

14. DRIFTING APART

In the new phase of LH's career starting with this chapter, a full
run of her daily letters to ER offers prolific detail about her
thoughts and feelings, as well as more than anyone could want to
know about her office and domestic trivia; there are still ER letters
almost every day but they become increasingly perfunctory. Fortunately for LH, and for my purposes, a new interest to quite an
extent made up for her personal misery. Concerning her Little
House, in addition to LH's own rhapsodies and about a dozen letters from Ella or Bill Dana, several people uniquely in a position to
add firsthand observation have put me greatly in their debt. On
September 24, 1978, Molly and Howard Haycraft recalled many
episodes from LH's years on Long Island, besides talking at length
about her, and about their close friends Ruby and Julian Claff, LH's
sister and brother-in-law who died early in the 1970's. Through the
Haycrafts, I was led to Anne Farr and the Little House itself; on
September 27 and 28, my husband and I, staying at the beautiful
old home that till five years previously had been the late Ella
Dana's, walked the paths LH had walked so often with her Prinz;
through the courtesy of the New York dentist who now owns LH's
precious hideaway, we toured it, too, and it is still as charming as
LH said it was. Anne Farr also introduced us to Helen E. Bulwinkel, a cousin of Ella's, who allowed me to copy several family
pictures and items from a scrapbook. Furthermore, Mrs. Farr then
and on January 30, 1979 most generously contributed numerous
recollections of her dear friends Ruby and Julian, besides sharing
many pictures and memories dating back to LH's Long Island
Years.

As to specific sources for this chapter: "I have never seen . . ."
and "How I hate . . ." ER–LH October 14, 1936. "Dear I realize . . . ", "I displayed so much knowledge . . ." and "I hope you'll
think . . ." ER–LH October 16, 1936. "Didn't swoon exactly," LH–
ER November 10, 1936. "I have also done . . ." LH to Grover
Whalen November 11, 1936. LH's tense letter to ER about her
Minneapolis friends November 19, 1936 is another instance of a

retrospective bonus; although it was not much use in this chapter, it provided several helpful leads for Chapter Five. About the Dana estate, besides above-mentioned visits and interviews, the *Dictionary of American Biography* entry on General William Floyd was helpful, as was the *New York Times* obituary of William Shepherd Dana January 3, 1939; also Arthur O. Hove, director of the University of Wisconsin's Office of Information Services, confirmed that Ella had registered in 1913 as a "visitor" in the College of Agriculture. On LH's abortive book about her WPA experiences, several letters plus her proposed introduction and supporting documents. "Good Lord, [Bye] said . . ." and "So—with George Bye . . ." LH–ER November 13, 1936. "Would you like to wear her ring . . ." ER–LH November 21, 1936. "Today I stumbled . . ." and "In a way, I'd like to keep them . . ." LH–ER December 6, 1936. "All he can think of getting . . ." LH–ER January 2, 1937. "You were evidently in one of your emotional slumps . . ." and "If you can bat . . ." Tom Dillon to LH February 2, 1937. "Of course, it isn't as swanky . . ." LH–ER January 7, 1937. ". . . And if you don't want to . . ." and "I'm not disturbed about it," LH–ER January 14, 1937. "Thanks ever so much . . ." LH–ER January 17, 1937. ". . . My sense of four years more . . ." ER–LH January 21, 1937. "Honey, don't let the eyes . . ." LH–ER December 28, 1936. "I guess my trouble is . . ." LH–ER July 20, 1937. "You are a true aristocrat . . ." LH–ER January 8, 1938. LH and "Judy," LH–ER February 25, 1937. "It may be that you no longer feel that you would enjoy . . ." LH–ER January 22, 1937. "Of course I could settle down . . ." ER–LH January 23, 1937. "I'd like to have you here . . ." ER–LH May 29, 1937. "I'm hungry for a glimpse . . ." ER–LH July 4, 1937. "I just take it for granted . . ." ER–LH September 9, 1937. "Rid of the tooth . . ." LH–ER September 21, 1937. "We were peaceful . . ." LH–ER December 22, 1937. "You see I think you are a kind of genius . . ." Dorothy Canfield Fisher quoted by Lash, page 433. "I loathe living that way . . ." LH–ER December 28, 1937. "Of course, dear . . ." and "It won't help you any . . ." ER–LH January 19, 1938.

15. AT LEAST LIFE IS NOT DULL

In the period covered by this chapter, the diverging paths of ER and LH are aptly symbolized by LH's overwhelming response to the hurricane on Long Island, while ER has been rapt in the Munich drama overseas. As LH gradually becomes peripheral to the First Lady's life, her own feelings change because she must somehow adjust to a purely subordinate role, and the change is mirrored in their letters. Although it appears that ER still confides in LH when they meet, their correspondence shows much less of a day-to-day involvement with one another. So it is hardly likely, as some people have suggested to me, that ER's relationship with LH precipitated her mysterious break with her Val-Kill partners, which occurred during LH's World's Fair years; a few cryptic references to this break in the ER–LH letters do indicate LH's awareness of ER's reasons for dissolving all ties with Nan Cook and Marion Dickerman, and yet the hints concerning the reasons are too tenuous to bear discussing here.

As to other incidents and quotations: "terrific" and "How you would hate all this . . ." ER–LH October 30, 1937. Regarding the third term issue, ER's letters contain repeated references to her expectation of returning to "obscurity" after 1940. "The Queen reminds me . . ." ER–LH June 8, 1939. "This day is also over . . ." ER–LH June 9, 1939. "Mama is as difficult . . ." ER–LH June 10, 1939. "He looked tired . . ." LH–ER June 12, 1939. "It was a very nice program . . ." LH–ER April 29, 1938. Details about Rosses from Haycrafts and Anne Farr (see notes to Chapter Fourteen). LH life in Mastic, numerous letters. LH financial problems LH–ER January 19, 1939 and many subsequent letters. About the Danas, numerous LH–ER references. ". . . And her face was as interesting . . ." Ella Dana to ER undated. "I'll be awfully glad to see you . . ." LH–ER July 25, 1938. "My Day" last week of July, 1938 included among LH clippings. "I've learned at last . . ." ER–LH August 15, 1938. LH's hurricane letter, including "But why is it . . ." LH–ER September 26, 1938. "Your letter painted . . ." ER–LH September 27, 1938. "F. says . . ." and "What a mad man!" ER–LH September 28, 1938. FDR telling family he won't run and proposing Hull as his successor ER–LH December 23, 1939. "If you want to talk to Jim . . ." LH–ER November 18, 1938. "Here's a rather illuminating little story . . ." LH–ER September 10, 1938. "I loved the story . . ." ER–LH September 13, 1938. About Jim Farley, his own *Jim Farley's Story* (McGraw-Hill, 1948), supplemented as described in notes to Chapter Sixteen. "You were a peach . . ." LH–ER November 22, 1938. Bill Dana obituary *New York Times* January 3, 1939 and Moriches *Tribune* of Center Moriches, N.Y. January 5, 1939. "Now of course . . ." and ensuing two paragraphs LH–ER January 19, 1939. About the Democratic job, numerous ER or LH letters, and telegrams from Charley Michelson.

16. THE 1940 PRESIDENTIAL CAMPAIGN

Since LH was in so many ways as open as a child herself, her attitude toward politics makes for refreshingly simple if unsophisticated judgments about political questions. I was much assisted in my efforts to provide a more rounded account of the 1940 Democratic Convention by my sage old friend Warren Moscow, one of the top political reporters for *The New York Times* during the Roosevelt era; but, of course, any quarrel concerning my necessarily abbreviated version must be with me and not with him, for his *Roosevelt & Willkie* (Prentice-Hall, 1968) is a model of fairminded political writing. James A. Farley's *Jim Farley's Story* (McGraw-Hill, 1948) was also helpful, as mentioned in the notes for Chapter Fifteen; and because LH's own recollections were tapped by Ruby Black of the United Press, her *Eleanor Roosevelt* (Duell, Sloan and Pearce, 1940) was useful, too, although in *Ladies of Courage* by Eleanor Roosevelt and Lorena A. Hickok (see notes for Chapter Twenty) LH covered the same ground herself in her chapter about ER.

Otherwise in this chapter: "usual saintly serenity," quoted in LH–ER January 19, 1939. "When the flowers came . . ." Ella Dana to ER January 10, 1939. "I'm terribly afraid . . ." LH–ER October 5, 1939. "I'm amused . . ." ER–LH October 8, 1939. "All the years . . ." LH–ER October 16, 1939. "It's not that I would wish . . ." LH–ER May 19, 1938. "Hick darling, You don't know much . . ." ER–LH May 21, 1938. ". . . Perhaps she will now marry?" ER–LH May 31, 1938. "He feels that if I do . . ." and "I don't object . . ." LH–ER October 4, 1939. "It would be so much better . . ." LH–ER November 1, 1939. "You never do anything but go off . . ." and ". . . oh, Lord, how . . ." LH–ER December 31, 1939. "I could spank . . ." and "you never expected . . ." ER–LH January 2, 1940. "Awfully strong third term sentiment . . ." LH–ER February 8, 1940. "This job is such fun . . ." LH–ER February 20,

1940. "I groan!" ER–LH February 11, 1940. "Lady, the way . . ." LH–ER February 22, 1940. "When I see . . ." LH–ER February 25, 1940. "Seeing people you love . . ." and "You know, at best . . ." LH–ER April 1, 1940. "It's a strenuous job . . ." LH–ER March 8, 1940. "I haven't met a soul . . ." LH–ER March 11, 1940. "That gland . . ." LH–ER May 24, 1940. ". . . I'm sorry you don't get . . ." LH–ER May 11, 1940. About Charley Michelson, *The Ghost Talks* by Charles Michelson (G.P. Putnam's Sons, 1944) and LH letters. About convention details, see introductory paragraph above. "But I do mean it . . ." *Ladies of Courage* (see notes for Chapter Twenty) page 282. "For many years I have worked . . ." *New York Times* July 20, 1940. ". . . I am glad . . ." ER–LH July 20, 1940. "FDR can't understand . . ." ER–LH August, 1940. "He *must* be re-elected . . ." LH–ER August 2, 1940. "If you read . . ." LH–ER August 5, 1940. "The fact that he has been consistent . . ." ER–LH August 7, 1940. "My God, dear . . ." LH–ER August 7, 1940. "If FDR wins . . ." ER–LH October 22, 1940. "Those are the towns . . ." LH–ER November 7, 1940.

17. LIVING AT THE WHITE HOUSE

The fact that LH lived at the White House from early 1941 through March of 1945 is the obvious explanation for the sharp decrease in the number of letters she and ER exchanged during those years; as the chart at the beginning of the Notes on Sources indicates, the collection includes only ninety-two ER–LH letters in 1941 and fifty LH–ER letters. But there is also a difference in the content of the letters. Written when one or the other was away from Washington, these are no longer daily communications with any notable emotional impact but the letters of old friends whose work keeps them closely associated although otherwise they live mostly separate lives. However, just before LH moved to the capital, when she spent a few months on Long Island, often alone and musing over the past, several of the most revealing letters in the entire collection resulted. Besides the ER–LH letters, though, this chapter also draws on several hundred Mary Norton to LH letters in the LH Papers, as well as on numerous miscellaneous documents relating to LH's period at the women's division of the Democratic

National Committee. The transcript of an oral history interview with one of LH's close associates at the committee, Virginia Rischel, was also helpful; this is one of the first fruits of the FDR Library's comparatively recent undertaking of an oral history project. In addition, LH's autobiographical fragment with its chapter about her White House residency proved extremely useful, despite her extreme reluctance in recounting any but innocuous anecdotes; to some extent this was supplemented by the recollections of a close friend who insisted on not being identified.

As to specific quotations: "little" from ER–LH November 15, 1940, and similar doubts implied by several later letters to LH from Molly Dewson, who had directed the women's division with exceptional ability early in the New Deal and whose strong reservations about LH as her successor soon evaporated. "I am forty-seven . . ." LH–ER November 16, 1940. "No, I don't look forward . . ." ER–LH November 8, 1940. "I don't know anyone . . ." and "—much better than I . . ." LH–ER November 11, 1940. "You are wrong about Louis . . ." ER–LH November 15, 1940. About Tommy's attitude toward her boss, an exceptionally revealing letter of hers to LH July 25, 1940, supplemented by LH to Nannine Joseph February 5, 1954, when LH was attempting to write a magazine article about Tommy after Tommy's death. "It gives me confidence . . ." ER–LH November 5, 1935. "I couldn't bear the idea . . ." and ". . . with her schedule as heavy . . ." and "Franklin says . . ." LH autobiographical manuscript. On Mrs. R.'s feminist network, numerous Mary Norton to LH letters, and Marion Harron to LH April 29, 1945 is especially interesting; "our tower of strength," Norton–LH October 1, 1941. "I want to take you to task . . ." ER–LH May 30, 1934. LH's use of "the wimmin," several friends. On Mary Norton herself, besides several folders of her letters to LH, "Battling Mary Retires" by Margot Gayle in *Independent Woman* for July 1950; biographical article in the *Democratic Digest* for March 1945; and "Profile of a Great Lady" by Esther Van Wagoner Tufty in the *Jersey Journal* August 24, 1946. It should also be mentioned that a carbon copy of Mrs. Norton's unpublished autobiography *Madam Congressman,* which LH helped her with in the 1950's, is included in the LH Papers; although this is disappointing in its lack of personal flavor, it contains a mine of information about Congressional fights of the New Deal era. "I'm not a lady . . ." from "Battling

Mary Retires," cited above. "He is devilish . . ." Norton–LH May 9, 1942. "We've been through so much . . ." LH–ER May 19, 1941. "I am so weary . . ." ER–LH October 8, 1941. "EACH YEAR I'M PROUDER . . ." LH–ER telegram October 11, 1941. ". . . That old sense of perfect peace . . ." LH–ER November 16, 1941. "I seem to have a calming . . ." ER–LH December 13, 1941. "I'm about to dine . . ." LH–ER February 27, 1942.

18. HICK AND JUDGE HARRON

Concerning Marion Harron, in addition to her own scores of long letters to LH, I am indebted to W. Ann Chumbley, clerk of the United States Tax Court, for a copy of the biographical tribute to the judge delivered at memorial services held in a chapel of Washington Cathedral after her death on September 26, 1972; also the obituary in the Washington *Post* September 29, 1972 was helpful, as was "Judge Marion Harron Suggests Tax Field to Women Lawyers" by Margaret Parton in the N.Y. *Herald Tribune* May 8, 1934.

Specifically: ". . . as I view the record . . ." Harron–LH March 22, 1942. "Who in tunket . . ." Harron–LH January 6, 1944. "I've been like a pea . . ." ER–LH April 19, 1942. "F. & I dined alone . . ." ER–LH July 31, 1942. "Darling: I'm thrilled . . ." and "So far only Westbrook Pegler . . ." LH–ER November 1, 1942. "Now whatever is not here set down . . ." Harron–LH November 9, 1942. "I'm not much of a militarist . . ." and "I get so mad . . ." LH–ER October 30, 1942. "Well—all Hell . . ." LH–ER April 23, 1943. "Gosh, I'd like to go . . ." LH–ER March 17, 1944. "Why, how nice . . . ", "In residence . . . ", "Madame, you are . . ." and "Didn't anybody ever iron . . ." LH autobiographic manuscript. On Prinz's death, the LH Papers contain a small folder of communications from a Long Island veterinary doctor, including his handwritten note ("Well it happened this afternoon . . .") informing LH of her dog's death June 30, 1943; and a condolence letter July 1, 1943 from Annie Ross. "That Mother dame . . ." Norton–LH August 30, 1943. "She certainly loves you . . ." Norton–LH May 9, 1945. "I hope 1944 . . ." Harron–LH January 5, 1944. "F. felt [the columnist] . . ." ER–LH July 20, 1944. ". . . If my plans work out . . ." LH–ER September 14, 1944. "Dearest: The goodbyes . . ." LH–ER March 21, 1945.

10. TAKING REFUGE

During the entire decade covered by this chapter, there are fewer ER letters in the LH Papers than during any typical six-month period early in their relationship; as for LH letters, they all but disappear from the collection just about the time she went on ER's payroll, although after several years a smattering of LH–ER letters turn up in ER's own Papers, routinely filed with other miscellaneous personal correspondence. There will be more about this matter of the preservation of many letters and the destruction of others in the notes for Chapter Twenty. Here it is pertinent to add merely that much of this chapter is based on Harron and Norton letters, as well as on communications between LH and other friends or acquaintances, notably Tommy and Mary Dewson, in addition to recollections from people who knew her well.

Specifically: "It's funny—and nice . . ." LH–ER April 12, 1945. "It's the President . . ." LH autobiographic manuscript. Details about LH reaction and "Hick, I don't want you . . ." LH to Molly Dewson May 3, 1945 in the Dewson Papers at Hyde Park; although about LH's unspoken hope I have had to speculate, based on the extremity of her emotional and physical reaction in the weeks following FDR's death and her artless account of her doctor's lecture to her about having nothing wrong with her but nerves (LH–ER May 27, 1945), along with the many references in earlier ER letters to their eventual living together. "I never realized what implicit . . .", "God, he used to be . . .", "For you and your future . . ." and ". . . as long as we both . . ." LH–ER April 13, 1945. "I have always felt . . ." Norton–LH June 9, 1945. "I wish you'd let me help . . ." repeatedly in ER–LH letters. "Jitters pills," LH–ER May 27, 1945. "It's so much more fun . . ." LH–ER May 5, 1945. "Darling—A peony . . ." Harron–LH June 5, 1945. "Marion has gone . . ." LH–ER August 30, 1945. "I can well imagine . . ." ER–LH September 1, 1945. About the financial arrangement between ER and LH, references in several subsequent ER letters to the sending of materials for LH to digest, and in letters from Tommy to LH referring to the sending of a fifty dollar monthly check. "I'm going to be no leader . . ." ER–LH September 29, 1945. About ironing dishtowels and "God damn it . . ." Molly and Howard

Haycraft to author. "Look the other way . . ." Anne Farr to author.
On LH's western trip, miscellaneous correspondence. About LH's
abortive literary efforts, her miscellaneous papers and about a
dozen communications from Nannine Joseph. "I am different from
any other house . . ." LH manuscript fragment. Concerning LH's
autobiography, her papers include not just the manuscript but also
letters from a few friends who read what she wrote, two letters
from the woman who had suggested that she write it, and also a
letter from the publisher who turned it down. ". . . I am pretty
certain . . ." from her foreword to the manuscript. About LH's
departure from Long Island, allusions in a few ER–LH letters early
in August 1955, plus softened versions from a few friends, and
Archy Curnan to author.

20. HYDE PARK AT LAST

Finally, there is no possible way to explain definitely why LH
donated her letters to the FDR Library. In this chapter, I have
advanced what seems to be—based on all that I have learned about
LH—the most likely reason; but some readers may be interested in
more detail than I have given in the text about this crucial issue.
First I must say that documents relating to donations are considered confidential by the National Archives, so I have not had access
to any correspondence or memoranda regarding LH's gift; yet I
have been assured that nothing shedding light on her motive is
included in these closed files. Although LH's contract was signed
before Elizabeth Drewry's appointment as director of the library,
Miss Drewry was in charge at Hyde Park during the period most of
the material was actually handed over; it was her impression that
LH did not seem to anticipate any special interest in her papers.
Indeed the only specific references by LH herself to her disposition
of her papers—and their contents—that I have been able to find are
as ambiguous as they are revealing. These references come in two
letters she wrote after ER's death to ER's daughter Anna—long
letters replete with vintage Hickokisms. The first, dated October 6,
1963, enclosing a touching letter Anna's daughter had sent LH,
suggests that Anna destroy the enclosure after Anna has read it
because "I'd not want strangers pawing over Sisty's letters." Then
LH, quite atypically, makes a pair of extraordinarily misleading

statements: that she had given the FDR Library most of "your Mother's" letters "because that was what she wanted me to do," and that "the people at the Library are going to have conniptions when they . . . find out what I've done to some of your Mother's letters." Years ago, LH adds, "I started to copy them on the typewriter, carefully omitting everything personal, everything about the family!" With her compulsive honesty, though, she does go on:

> But I only started. Never had the time or the eyesight to finish. You know her writing.
> WOW! The Dodgers just won the Series—four games in a row. What pitching! . . .

However, as LH must have known and repressed, ER herself saw to it that personal passages were removed from other correspondence in her own possession. So—assuming that she did urge LH to donate her letters—ER must have believed that the excising of personal material had already been accomplished. But LH certainly knew, no matter that she let baseball interrupt her dwelling on this knowledge, that the job had never been finished. Nevertheless, it must be doubted whether LH had any clear perception of how cleverly she had botched her bowdlerizing. When her cache was eventually unpacked, it was by no means in chronological order, although the great majority of the ER letters were in envelopes with postmarks accurately dating them. Arranging the letters in their proper time sequence, the young archivist assigned to the LH Papers routinely placed two innocuous 1932 communications in the first folder of Box 1, then for all practical purposes led off the collection with seven handwritten letters ER scrawled nightly during her first week in the White House. Next came that typed transcript of 129 edited, or sanitized, letters, followed by hundreds of additional ER letters of gradually diminishing emotional impact, penned with a sometimes hieroglyphic inscrutability. Only a sprinkling of her own letters to ER that she had somehow retrieved appear in the early part of the collection. Thus if LH had destroyed just seven more letters, the impact of her collection would have been substantially lessened. In effect, those seven letters from March 5, 1933 through March 11, 1933 became a signal to subsequent readers of the LH Papers. Nor could the removal of the seven letters by the exercise of archival judgment effectively reduce this impact. For seven successive pink slips right at the beginning of a fairly extensive collection, advertising the suppression of ER letters throughout her first week in the White House, must certainly have stimulated the curiosity of researchers who otherwise might not have been sufficiently interested to plunge into deciphering the contents of folder after folder of presumably just friendly chitchat.

The matter of LH's motive is touched upon more openly in the second of the LH–Anna letters, dated June 9, 1966, which at least to some extent modifies the self-image LH left throughout much of her correspondence with ER. Here resentment does surface, although it is directed not toward ER herself but toward the biographer ER had singled out in her later years; by 1966, nearly four years after ER's death, he was actively at work on the two volumes that would appear early in the next decade. Because this letter is so revealing of LH's tangle of emotions close to the end of her life, here are its pertinent passages:

Dear Anna:

I do want you to know how greatly I enjoyed my visit to the new Wiltwyck last Saturday and how certain I feel that your Mother would have loved it.°

Since she never took herself seriously as "First Lady of the World," but attributed all the honors she received to the fact that she was your Father's widow, I doubt that the big, fancy memorials, with all their elegance and fine speeches, would have had much meaning for her. But Wiltwyck was something different, very, very close to her heart. Those rejected boys, with all their problems, were constantly on her mind. She had something of the same feeling for Israel, but Wiltwyck was more personal.

Since my own relationship with her was purely personal—I was never even on the fringe of her public life—those other things had little meaning for me. It's the difference between the Chandor portrait of her, a very handsome portrait of "the First Lady of the World," and a simple photograph which I have here in my apartment. In the photograph she is smiling slightly—she could smile, as you know, without showing all her teeth—and the expression around her eyes is thoughtful, a little wistful, a little sad, but warm and understanding. That was the Eleanor Roosevelt I knew and loved, for herself.

° A school for delinquent boys, one of ER's major interests in her later years.

Everything last Saturday was exactly as she would have wanted. A good, substantial lunch, with no frills . . . I greatly enjoyed my long, long visit with [a prominent businessman]. He and I became friends of your Mother about the same time, more than thirty years ago. I always knew that she liked him and admired him very much, but I never really talked with him much until last Saturday . . . I'd like to get some of those reminiscences on tape for the FDR Library . . . I'd tell him he could do as I have done—have a written contract with the Library setting a date before which the tapes could not be released to researchers. When I turned over your Mother's letters to them, because she thought I should, I specified that they were not to be released until after we were both dead. But now I think I'll ask for a new contract, providing that they be kept sealed until after all her children are dead.°

Your Mother wasn't always so very discreet in her letters to me. Although the Library people don't know it—they'd have forty conniption fits if they did—I did pull out fifteen and burned them . . . But undoubtedly among the rest—hundreds of them—there are things that would be offensive to you children or hurt you. In any family things happen—disagreements, even quarrels—that are eventually forgotten. So why drag them out while the participants are still around? To her grandchildren and great-grandchildren they would have little meaning.

Joe,† who is certainly thorough, has been after [the businessman] asking if he has any letters from your Mother.

"I told him I didn't," he said calmly, "although I have."

Nobody—but nobody—ever pulled the wool over [the businessman's] eyes. "Just another free-loader" was his comment.

I suggested that he give the letters to the FDR Library and clamp on a release date, as I have done.

Some day—probably years from now—someone will write a fine biography of your Mother. Then, all this material will be

° LH did amend her deed of gift, which had originally called for the opening of her papers right after her own and ER's death; the amendment, in 1966 when ER was already dead, merely specified that the papers should be kept closed for ten years after LH's death.

† Joseph P. Lash

valuable. But it won't be "good old Joe." I'll be damned if he's going to get his hot little hands into my papers.

About other matters covered in Chapter Twenty, miscellaneous correspondence in the LH Papers has been supplemented by several oral history transcripts; particularly helpful were interviews with Maureen Coor, who succeeded Tommy as ER's secretary; with ER's niece Eleanor Wotkyns; and with ER's granddaughter Eleanor Seagraves. Another valuable indication of Roosevelt family feelings toward LH came in *Mother R.: Eleanor Roosevelt's Own Story* by ER's son Elliott and James Brough (G.P. Putnam's Sons, 1977); several paragraphs on page 128 disclose quite a sympathetic attitude toward LH on the part of this maverick among the Roosevelt progeny. Also four lengthy letters that LH wrote at intervals to Jeannette Brice, one of her oldest friends from Minneapolis, verified many factual details during this period, and I am most indebted to Mrs. Brice for allowing me to copy them. Still my conversations with a number of people who had firsthand knowledge of LH in the last years of her life were especially important; among them I must single out Elizabeth Drewry and also the Reverend Gordon L. Kidd, who welcomed my husband and me with great kindness August 14, 1978.

Now for the specific sources: Regarding Tommy, material in the LH Papers relating to LH's unsuccessful attempt to write a *Reader's Digest* article about her. "My boss is . . ." LH to Nannine Joseph February 5, 1954. LH's musings on still being somebody are based on several allusions to her state of mind in Mary Norton to LH letters and on LH–Tommy July 23, 1947. On LH's first year at Val-Kill, several ER–LH letters. About LH being kicked off campaign train, Archy Curnan to author September 25, 1978. Much correspondence relating to *Ladies of Courage* (G.P. Putnam's Sons, 1954) in LH Papers. About LH's other books, the collection includes several Nannine Joseph to LH letters and some miscellaneous correspondence touching upon each of these published works as well as upon other literary projects that never bore fruit. "To Hell with history," LH to Anna Halsted October 6, 1963. About Ray Corry, Elizabeth Drewry to author August 2, 1978. "Also I wish to thank . . ." note on copyright page of *On My Own* by Eleanor Roosevelt (Harper & Brothers, 1958). LH's birthday party for her dog, Eileen DeVries and other Hyde Park friends of

LH. "I'm still horribly weak . . ." quoted by LH to Anna Halsted October 6, 1963. "THE FAMILY OF . . ." unsigned telegram to Miss Lorena Hickok November 8, 1962. LH's private farewell to ER, the Reverend Gordon Kidd to author August 14, 1978. On LH's last years, LH letters to Jeannette Brice, Elizabeth Drewry and others, supplemented by recollections of neighbors and of Anne Farr, who drove LH's sister Ruby to visit LH in the hospital several times. LH's will on file in Dutchess County Courthouse, Pough-keepsie, N.Y. "I especially want . . ." LH's typed note of instructions for cremation, which the Reverend Kidd searched out in his own papers and allowed me to copy. Regarding LH's cremation and the disposition of her ashes, Donald S. Dapson of the Dapson Funeral Home in Rhinebeck.

INDEX

Aberdeen *News,* 32
Adams, Henry, 115
Akerson, George, 241n
Akerson, Harriet, 241
Aleinikoff, Eugene, 333
Allen, Robert S., 138
Altrowitz, Abe, 343, 344
American Friends' Service Committee, 144
Anderson, Judith, 233
Anderson, Marian, 241
Appleton *Crescent,* 43
Appleton Public Library, 45
Aronson, Earl, 345
Arthurdale (homestead community), 146, 159, 187, 353
Associated Press (AP), 65, 71, 75–77, 81–84, 91–93, 99, 108, 116, 124, 126, 162, 200, 202, 205, 225, 233, 305, 318, 330, 336, 345

Babies—Just Babies, 98
Bailey, Charles, 343
Bancroft, Jane Eads, 76, 347, 358
Banking crisis (1933), 114, 116
Barker, Bernice, 61
Barron, Mark, 202, 203
Baruch, Bernard, 268
Battle Creek High School, 40, 41, 130
Battle Creek *Journal,* 47, 341
Battle Creek *News,* 43
Battle Creek Sanitarium, 47–48
"Battling Mary Retires" (Gayle), 367–368
Beebe, Katherine, 91, 92

Beethoven, Ludwig van, 242
Behnke, John, 341
Benét, Stephen Vincent, 140–141
Bennetts, Chaucy, 329
Bergh, Helen, 339
Bioscience, 341
Bishop, Morris, 356
Black, Hillel, 333
Black, Ruby, 161, 162, 280, 365
Blackman, Sam, 345
Bloom, Sol, 267
Boettiger, John, 154, 155, 160, 173
Boettiger, John R., 355
Boston Red Sox, 59
Bowdle High School, 36
Bowdle *Pioneer,* 13, 14, 23, 338
Boy Scouts of America, 241
Brice, Jeannette, 208, 344, 347, 374, 375
Bridge, Gardner, 349
Brion, Peter L., 150
Broderick, Joseph P., 345
Brough, James, 374
Browning, Leta, 47, 48, 67, 216, 339, 341, 343, 345, 359, 361
Browning family, 47, 48
Buck, Daisy, 47
Buck, Pearl, 109–110
Bugbee, Emma, 316, 329–330
Bulwinkel, Helen E., 362
Bye, George, 196, 226, 229

Caldwell, Edna Browning, 48, 338, 341, 343
California, University of, 290

Campobello (Roosevelt summer home), 27, 193, 212
Carson, Gerald, 340, 341
Carter, Rosalynn, 329
Catt, Carrie Chapman, 54
Cermak, Anton, 109
Chaney, Mayris, 148, 221
Chapin, W. W., 126, 126n
Chase, Mary Ellen, 71
Chicago *Tribune*, 360
Chumbley, W. Ann, 368
Churchill, Winston, 283, 299
Cincinnati Reds, 59
Civilian Defense, 288, 289
Claff, Julian, 80–81, 84, 226, 233, 262, 265, 305, 310, 362
Claff, Ruby Hickok, *see* Hickok, Ruby
Clark, Jim, 303
Cleveland *Plain-Dealer*, 277
Collier, Mrs. Price, 101
Collier's, 341, 343
Coming of the New Deal, The (Schlesinger), 143, 353
Commission on Training Camp Activities, 56–57
Communism, 146, 166
Conrad, Will C., 342
Cook, Nancy, 85–86, 140, 148, 181–182, 187, 240, 358, 364
Coor, Maureen, 374
Cornell University, 108, 110, 164
Cornflake Crusade (Carson), 341
Corry, Ray, 320–321, 374
Coxey's Army, 82
Cullum, Dick, 344
Curnan, Archy (Tubby), 314, 316, 317, 343, 370, 374

Dahlman, Elaine, 359
Dakota Farmer, The, 33
Dall, Anna Roosevelt, *see* Roosevelt, Anna
Dall, "Buzzy," 154
Dall, "Sisty," 154, 322, 324
Dana, Ella, 178, 189, 223–226, 242, 244, 246–248, 252, 255–256, 260, 279, 303, 310, 313, 357, 362, 364
Dana, William Shepherd (Bill), 177–178, 189, 223–226, 242, 244, 246–248, 251–253, 255, 256, 260, 357, 362–364

Dapson, Donald S., 375
Dapson Funeral Home, 325, 375
Davis, Kenneth, 358
Dawn O'Hara (Ferber), 43, 342
Del Rio, Dolores, 71
Democracia, La, 162
Democratic Digest, 278, 288, 367
Democratic National Committee, 72, 100, 249, 250, 263, 267, 268, 285, 293, 299
Denier, Elizabeth, 333
Depression (1930's), 84, 127, 226
    Hickok's reports on conditions during, 142–146, 149, 165–167, 174–176, 195–199, 207
DeVries, Eileen, 374
Dewey, Thomas E., 126, 272, 298–300
Dewson, Mary, 369
Dewson, Molly, 293, 367, 369
Dickerman, Marion, 85–86, 140, 240, 347, 364
Dickinson, Roy, 69, 77–78, 131, 169, 170, 172, 192
Dictionary of American Biography, 363
Dies Committee, 266
Dillon, Clarissa, 60, 63, 80, 152, 223, 263, 269, 287, 311, 344
Dillon, Thomas J., 59–60, 65–68, 80, 82, 152, 223, 230, 255, 269–271, 278, 287, 311, 312, 344
Dixon, Jean, 233
Dodd, Mrs., 34
Douglas, Helen Gahagan, 276
Drewry, Elizabeth, 317, 327, 333, 370, 374, 375

Eads, Jane, *see* Bancroft, Jane Eads
Early History of Brown County, South Dakota, 339
Edgeworth, Maria, 243
Eisenhower, Dwight D., 322
Eleanor: The Years Alone (Lash), 6n, 329n, 337
Eleanor and Franklin (Lash), 6n, 329n, 337, 346, 353, 358
Eleanor Roosevelt (Black), 365
Elizabeth, Queen, 241
Elliott, Nancy D., 344, 345, 347, 356
Ellis, Ella (Aunt Ella), 24–25, 27, 31, 38–39, 43, 46, 55–56, 147, 192, 204, 258, 339, 341, 361

Ellis, Havelock, 354
Ely, Jean D., 344–345
Emerson, William R., 329, 330–333

Faber, Hal, 331, 334
Faithfull, Starr, 82
Fala (pet dog), 289, 300, 316
Farley, James A., 185, 210, 249–251, 253, 254, 266, 270–276, 279, 358, 364, 365
Farr, Anne, 343, 347, 348, 350, 362, 364, 370, 375
Farrar, Geraldine, 51–53, 342
Fay, Elton, 85, 347
Federal Emergency Relief Administration (FERA), 127
"Female World of Love and Ritual, The: Relations between Women in Nineteenth-Century America" (Smith-Rosenberg), 354
Ferber, Edna, 43, 49, 50, 80, 341, 342
Financial Chronicle, 224
Fisher, Dorothy Canfield, 237, 363
Flanagan, Commander, 232, 252, 266
Floyd, General William, 363
Floyd, Grandmother, 224
Flu epidemic (1918), 58
Flynn, Ed, 95, 279
Foch, Marshal Ferdinand, 64
Forster, E. M., 354
Franco, General Francisco, 214
Franklin D. Roosevelt Library, 5, 96, 111, 155, 192, 317, 319, 320, 326, 327, 329, 332, 333
Franklin Delano Roosevelt (Faber), 329n
Front Page, The (Hecht and MacArthur), 59
Furman, Bess, 99, 106, 118, 123–125, 161, 349, 356, 360, 361

Garner, John ("Cactus Jack"), 273
Gayle, Margot, 367
Gehrig, Lou, 93
Gellhorn, Martha, 214n, 226, 352
George VI, King, 241
Geselbracht, Ray, 333
Ghost Talks, The (Michelson), 366
Girl Scouts of America, 99, 163, 229, 241
Godwin, Kathryn, 159, 352

Goodbye, Mr. Chips (Hilton), 193
Grange, Red, 66
Gray, James, 345
Great Smoky Mountain National Park, North Carolina, 261
"Grief" (Saint-Gaudens), 115
Groton (secondary school), 112–114
Gurewitsch, Dr. David, 321
Gurewitsch, Edna, 321

Hagedorn, Mrs., 32–33
Hague, Frank, 286
Haley, Mabel, 184, 229, 234, 296, 306, 358
Halsted, Anna, *see* Roosevelt, Anna
Ham, H. L., 64
Hampton Institute, 296
Hannegan, Bob, 299
Hanson, Barbara, 78–79, 346
Harding, Warren G., 64–65
Harriman, Averell, 316
Harron, Marion, 262, 289–301, 303, 308–309, 321, 336, 367, 368, 369
Harry Hopkins and the New Deal (Kurzman), 352
Haycraft, Howard, 225–226, 242, 265, 279, 303, 310, 362, 364, 369–370
Haycraft, Molly, 310, 362, 364, 369–370
Hearst, William Randolph, 70
Hecht, Ben, 59
Herrick, Genevieve Forbes, 360
Hickok, Addison, 13–17, 22–25, 31, 36, 129
Hickok, Anna, 13–17, 19, 21–23, 27, 129
Hickok, Lorena Alice
  with Associated Press, 71–126
  attitude toward Roosevelt (Franklin D.), 122, 157, 185, 190–191, 196, 249–250, 267, 275–276, 284, 298, 304–305
  Battle Creek *Journal* and, 47–48
  books written by
    Ladies of Courage, 318
    Reluctant First Lady, 94, 96–97, 141, 177, 318–319
    The Story of Eleanor Roosevelt, 318
    The Story of Helen Keller, 318

Hickok, Lorena Alice *(Cont.)*
  Dana (Bill) and, 177–178, 189, 223–
    226, 242, 244, 246–248, 251–
    253, 255, 256
  Dana (Ella) and, 178, 189, 223–226,
    242, 244, 246–248, 252, 255–
    256, 279, 303, 310, 313
  Democratic National Committee
    and, 254, 266–277, 279–301
  Dillon (Tom) and, 59–60, 65–68,
    80, 82, 152, 223, 230, 255, 269–
    271, 278, 287, 311, 312, 314
  early love of reading, 17–19, 27
  Ellis and, 24–25, 27, 31, 38–39, 43,
    46, 55–56, 147, 192, 204
  emotional problems of, 67–69, 79,
    153–171, 172, 230, 238
  father and, 14–16, 21–23, 25, 36
  Harron and, 289–301, 303, 308–309
  Haycraft (Howard) and, 225–226,
    242, 265, 279, 303, 310
  Holt and, 42, 191–193, 197, 201,
    209, 214, 233, 321
  Howe and, 184–186
  Hyde Park residency, 315–325
  investigator for Hopkins and
    FERA, 137–199, 207
  the Lindbergh kidnaping and, 82–
    84
  the Little House and, 225–226,
    235–236, 242–248, 251–252,
    266, 271, 278–280, 282, 288,
    297, 298, 302–305, 313–314
  Milwaukee *Sentinel* and, 49–55
  Minneapolis *Tribune* and, 58–69
  Morse and, 61–63, 67–69, 77–79,
    93, 169–170, 172, 174, 192,
    233, 287, 311
  mother and, 14, 21
  New York *Mirror* and, 70–71
  Norton and, 287, 305–306
  plans book on FERA experiences,
    226–229
  publicist for 1939 World's Fair,
    223–254, 267–268
  reports to Hopkins on Depression
    conditions, 142–146, 149, 165–
    167, 174–176, 195–199, 207
  Roosevelt (Eleanor) and
    first impressions of, 72–73, 85, 87
    first interviews with, 73–75
    gifts from, 234, 306–307
    journalistic coverage of, 95–99
    personal letters between, 96,
      110–112, 119–120, 122–123,
      137–138, 152, 155–156, 161,
      163, 165, 167–174, 176, 179–
      182, 186, 191–192, 194, 196,
      200, 209, 227–228, 237–239,
      248, 266, 292, 300–301, 319–
      321
    Puerto Rico and Virgin Islands
      visit, 161–163
    researcher for, 309–310
    trips taken together, 139–142,
      169–171, 193–194, 234–235
    visit to grave of, 322–323
    will of, 324
  Roosevelt's presidential campaign
    (1931), coverage of, 91–95
  Ross (Annie) and, 242, 245, 255,
    280, 297, 302, 306
  Ross (Clarence) and, 242–243, 245,
    247–248, 255, 280, 288, 297,
    309
  Time reference to, 158–159
  White House residency, 148, 282–
    284
  will of, 324
  works as hired girl, 28–39
  writes biographies for children,
    317–319
Hickok, Myrtle, 15, 16, 56, 129
Hickok, Ruby, 15, 16, 18–19, 29, 31,
  36, 55–56, 78, 80–81, 84, 129,
  226, 262, 265, 279, 305, 307,
  310, 325, 343, 347, 348, 350,
  362, 364, 370, 375
High, Stanley, 210
History of Cornell, A (Bishop), 356
Hitler, Adolf, 245, 249, 250–251, 266,
  271
Holmes, Oliver Wendell, 123
Holt, Alicent, 42, 130, 191–193, 197,
  201, 209, 214, 233, 321, 359,
  361
Hoover, Allan, 174
Hoover, Herbert, 71, 74, 81, 97, 99
Hoover, Mrs. Herbert, 99, 106, 107,
  134, 349
Hoover, Ike, 107, 117, 153
Hopkins, Harry, 7, 127–128, 147–149,
  153, 158, 162, 168, 175–179,
  183, 185, 191, 202–206, 214,

226, 228, 229, 250, 256–265, 273, 336, 337, 351, 352, 359
Hickok's reports on Depression conditions to, 142–146, 149, 165–167, 174–176, 195–199, 207
Hove, Arthur O., 363
Howard, Roy, 208, 215
Howe, Louis, 85–86, 100, 106, 108, 116, 126, 143, 146, 154, 160, 184–186, 227, 281, 358
Hull, Cordell, 249, 250, 251
Hyde Park Memorial Library, 321

Independent Woman, 367
Invincible Summer (Davis), 358
Ithaca Journal-News, 109, 350

Jacobs, Helen, 70
Jenny (pet dog), 324
Jersey Journal, 367
Jim Farley's Story (Farley), 364, 365
John Brown's Body (Benét), 140–141
Johnson, Charlie, 344, 345
Johnson, Lyndon B., 322
Joseph, Nannine, 311–312, 318, 367, 370, 374

Kansas State Fair, 178
Keller, Helen, 318, 324
Kellogg, Dr. John Harvey, 216
Kellogg brothers, 47
Kelsey, Ruth, 341
Kennedy, John F., 322
Kidd, Reverend Gordon, 323, 325, 374, 375
Kidd, Mrs. Gordon, 323
Kurzman, Paul A., 352

La Guardia, Fiorello, 205
Ladies of Courage (Roosevelt and Hickok), 318, 357, 365, 366, 374
Ladies of the Press (Ross), 337, 342, 348
Landon, Alf M., 211, 212, 222
Lash, Joseph P., 6, 321, 329, 337, 346, 353, 358, 363, 373–374
Lash, Trude, 321
Lawrence University, 42–43, 46, 130, 340–341
League of Women Voters, 60, 285

LeHand, Marguerite, 93, 146, 213n
Lewis, Sinclair, 69
Lincoln, Abraham, 125, 227
Lindbergh, Charles, 71
Lindbergh kidnaping, 82–84, 139, 205, 336, 340, 346
Literary Digest, 151, 216, 353
Little House, the, 225–226, 235–236, 242–248, 251–252, 259, 260, 261, 266, 271, 278–280, 282, 288, 297, 298, 302–305, 313–314
Long, Huey, 358
Lottie, 26–27, 42
Love in Shadow, A (Boettiger), 355
Lowe, Berenice Bryant, 340, 341
Lund, Eleanor, 349

MacArthur, Charles, 59
McCormick, Anne O'Hare, 137
McDuffie, Lizzie, 296
McIntyre, Marvin, 213n
McKinley, William, 16–17
McLaughlin, Paul, 333
McNutt, Paul, 270
Macy, Anne Sullivan, 318
Madam Congressman (Norton), 367
Mahler, Gustav, 226
Mahoney, Miss, 145
Manville, Mrs. C. B., 55
March, Mr. and Mrs. Fredric, 233
Marie of Roumania, Queen, 64
Marks, Jeannette, 354
Martini's (coffee house), 50, 51
Marzolf, Marion, 342–343
Maurice (Forster), 354
Mayo Clinic, 245
Meader, Davol H., 341
Mercer, Lucy, 57, 110
Michelson, Charley, 210, 253, 254, 266, 268, 270–272, 275–279, 365, 366
"Michigan Meanderings" (Street), 341, 343
Miller, Earl, 140, 148, 172–174, 214, 221, 357
Milwaukee Journal, The: The First Eighty Years (Conrad, Wilson and Wilson), 342
Milwaukee Sentinel, 49, 51, 53, 283, 342, 343
Minneapolis Star, The, 343, 344

Minneapolis *Tribune,* 56, 58, 59, 61,
    64, 66, 67, 109, 131, 241n,
    343–344, 349, 350
Minnesota, University of, 57, 58, 60,
    71
Miss Marks and Miss Woolley (Wells),
    354
Mitchell, Charles E., 125–126, 137
Morgan, Forbes, 210
Morgan, Mrs. J. Pierpont, 224
Morgenthau, Henry, 176, 244
Moriches *Tribune,* 365
Morison, Bradley L., 131, 344
Morse, Ella, 61–63, 67–69, 77–79, 93,
    131, 147, 169–170, 172, 174,
    192, 233, 287, 311, 312, 344
Morse, Grandmother, 61
Moscow, Warren, 365
*Mother R.: Eleanor Roosevelt's Own
    Story* (Elliott Roosevelt and
    Brough), 374
Mount Holyoke College, 354
Mr. Choate (pet dog), 261, 297, 298,
    302, 311
Muffin (pet dog), 311, 316, 324
Munich Agreement, 249
Murrow, Ed, 292
Mussolini, Benito, 166, 201

National Emergency Council, 189
National Recovery Administration
    (NRA), 166, 249
National Youth Administration, 240
Nelson, Billy, 356
New Deal, 120, 146, 168, 169, 178,
    196, 208, 212, 250, 251, 287,
    293, 297
New York *Daily News,* 70
New York *Herald Tribune,* 262, 265,
    316, 329–330, 368
New York *Mirror,* 70, 71, 345
New York *Post,* 321, 331
New York State Democratic Commit-
    tee, 60, 65, 307, 309, 310, 312
New York Times, The, 77, 81, 114,
    202, 329, 334, 346, 347, 349,
    350, 361, 363, 364–365, 366
New York *Tribune,* 56
Norton, Mary Teresa, 263, 285–287,
    297–298, 300, 305–309, 311,
    313, 316, 336, 366, 367–369,
    374
Notre Dame, University of, 66

Omaha *Bee-News,* 99
O'Malley, Mrs., 37–39
On My Own (Roosevelt), 6n, 321, 374
O'Reilly, Mr., 30–31
O'Reilly, Mrs., 28–31
Oxford Book of English Verse, The,
    170, 324

Paderewski, Ignace, 53
Paean, The, 41, 130
Parton, Margaret, 368
Pearson, Drew, 138
Peculiar Treasure, A (Ferber), 342
Pegler, Westbrook, 292
Perkins, Frances, 138, 273
Perry, Oliver Hazard, 66
Person, Paul, 257
Pickford, Mary, 18
Plantz, Dr. Samuel, 46, 341
PM, 270, 278–279
Post, Charles W., 47
Prendergast, Tom, 193
Presidents' Mothers, The (Faber), 329n
Prinz (pet dog), 75–77, 80, 147, 203,
    216, 223, 233, 235, 236, 242,
    246, 247–248, 252, 260, 261,
    271, 278, 280, 288, 296–297,
    368
"Profile of a Great Lady" (Tufty), 367
Progress, The, 150
Prohibition, 124
Puerto Rican Children's Feeding
    Fund, 162

Ragsdale, Warner B., 349
Raub, Sandra, 333
Reader's Digest, 311, 349
Reluctant First Lady (Hickok), 94,
    96–97, 141, 177, 318–319, 337,
    346, 347, 350, 351–352, 356
Renovitch, Mark, 333
Reuther, Walter, 323
Rischel, Virginia, 367
Robbins, Warren Delano, 107
Robinson, Mrs. Douglas, 73
Rockefeller, John D., 230
Rollins, Alfred B., Jr., 347
Roosevelt, Anna, 27, 75, 95, 127, 139,
    154–155, 160, 163, 168–170,
    173, 177, 182, 322, 337, 348,
    351, 355, 370–375
Roosevelt, Anna Hall, 20
Roosevelt, Belle, 303

Roosevelt, Edith, 106
Roosevelt, Eleanor, 5–7, 27, 41–42, 49, 50, 57, 60, 134, 135, 136, 257, 261, 263
  appointed U.N. delegate, 310, 316
  autobiography of, 222, 237, 238
  death and funeral of, 322
  at Democratic National Convention (1940), 273–274
  early marital unhappiness of, 114–115
  Hickok and
    first impressions of, 72–73, 85, 87
    first interviews with, 73–75
    gifts from, 234, 306–307
    journalistic coverage of, 95–99
    personal letters between, 96, 110–112, 119–120, 122–123, 137–138, 152, 155–156, 161, 163, 165, 167–174, 176, 179–182, 186, 191–192, 194, 196, 200, 209, 227–228, 237–239, 248, 266, 292, 300–301, 319–321
    Puerto Rico and Virgin Islands visit, 161–163
    researcher for, 309–310
    trips taken together, 139–142, 169–171, 193–194, 234–235
    visit to grave of, 322–323
    will of, 324
  marriage of, 20
  mother-in-law and, 27, 42, 60, 188, 193, 212, 288
  "My Day" syndicated column, 207, 214–215, 245
  need for personal friendship, 102–110, 118, 281–282
  Norton and, 287
  reluctance to become First Lady, 85–87, 106–107, 232
  Thompson and, 72, 73, 92–93, 102, 104–106, 140, 188, 208, 214–216, 245, 281, 284, 297, 303, 309, 315–316, 321
  visits U.S. troops in Pacific, 295
  visits war-time England, 292
Roosevelt, Elliott, 20, 42, 95, 127, 138–139, 167, 208, 314, 374
Roosevelt, Franklin D., 6, 7, 20, 27, 42, 65, 106, 123, 184, 189, 204, 210, 233, 245, 286, 287, 318, 324
  assassination attempt, 108–110
  Assistant Secretary of the Navy, 48–49
  death of, 303–304
  governor of New York, 74, 85
  Hickok's attitude toward, 122, 157, 185, 190–191, 196, 249–250, 267, 275–276, 284, 298, 304–305
  Howe and, 85–86, 100, 106, 108, 116, 126, 143, 146, 154, 160
  marital infidelities of, 57, 60, 110, 114
  President, 85–87, 97, 101, 116–118, 120, 127, 143, 166, 169, 190, 194–195, 201, 207–208, 209, 222, 240–241, 271–277, 298–300
Roosevelt, Franklin D., Jr., 49, 188–189, 229, 274
Roosevelt, Hall, 288
Roosevelt, James, 27, 116, 120, 123, 188, 189, 245, 246
Roosevelt, John, 188, 189
Roosevelt, Kermit, 303
Roosevelt, Sarah Delano, 27, 42, 60, 173, 188, 193, 212, 288
Roosevelt, Theodore, 17, 19–20, 48, 64, 73, 106, 162
Roosevelt and Howe (Rollins), 347
Roosevelt & Willkie (Moscow), 365
Rose, Flora, 164
Ross, Annie, 242, 245, 255, 260, 280, 297, 302, 306, 368
Ross, Clarence, 242–243, 245, 247–248, 255, 260, 280, 288, 297, 309
Ross, Ishbel, 337, 342, 348
Ruth, Babe, 93

St. John, Robert, 345
Saint-Gaudens, Augustus, 115
Scheider, Frank, 72
Schewe, Don, 333
Schlesinger, Arthur M., Jr., 143, 353
Schumann-Heink, Ernestine, 54, 227
Seagraves, Eleanor, 374
Seeber, Frances, 333
Sharkey, Mrs., 33–34
Signs: A Journal of Women in Culture and Society, 354
Simon, Bunny, 354
Sleeper, Aleen, 341

Smith, Al, 61, 70, 71, 72, 74, 82, 99, 202
Smith, Claire, 333
Smith, Frances St. John, 70
Smith College, 70
Smith-Rosenberg, Carroll, 354
Snyder-Gray murder case, 70
Social Security, 250, 324
Spanish-American War, 17
Sperry Gyroscope (company), 293, 294
Stalin, Joseph, 299
Story of Eleanor Roosevelt, The (Hickok), 318
Story of Helen Keller, The (Hickok), 318
Street, Julian, 341, 343
Studebaker (South Bend plant), 195
Studies in the Psychology of Sex (Ellis), 354
Sunlight on Your Doorstep: The Minneapolis Tribune's First Hundred Years (Morison), 344

Taft, Robert, 272
Tales of Old Battle Creek (Lowe), 341
Taschereau, L. A., 136
Teamsters Union, 300
Tennessee Valley Authority (TVA), 168
This I Remember (Roosevelt), 6n, 337
This Is My Story (Roosevelt), 6n, 337, 355
This Was My World (St. John), 345
Thompson, Malvina, 72, 73, 92–93, 102, 104–106, 138, 140, 188, 208, 214–216, 245, 281, 284, 297, 303, 309, 315–316, 321, 349, 360, 367, 369
Tillett, Gladys, 278, 279, 293–295
Time, 158–159, 178, 355
Todhunter School for Girls, 97, 103
Truman, Bess, 311
Truman, Harry, 299, 304, 310, 322
Tufty, Esther Van Wagoner, 367
Tugwell, Grace F., 352
Tully, Grace, 143
Turner, Major, 144–145

Uncle Tom's Cabin (Stowe), 17–18
United Nations, 304, 310, 316
   Commission on Human Rights, 312
United Press (UP), 161, 280, 365

United States Constitution, Nineteenth Amendment, 99
Up From the Footnote: A History of Women Journalists (Marzolf), 343

Variety, 71
Vestris (steamship), 81, 230

WACS (Women's Army Corps), 293
Wagner, Richard, 226, 242
Walker, Jimmy, 82
Wallace, Henry, 273, 274, 276, 299
Walter Reed Army Hospital, 80
Washington Byline (Furman), 161, 349, 356, 361
Washington *Post,* 368
Watergate, 7
WAVES (Women Appointed for Voluntary Emergency Service), 293
Welch, Mrs., 63
Well of Loneliness, The (Hall), 78
Welles, Sumner, 295
Wells, Anna Mary, 354
Wells, Robert W., 342
Whalen, Grover, 215, 217, 221, 222, 226, 227, 230–232, 236, 243, 246, 267, 362
White, Matty, 233
Who's Who, 290
Wilde, Oscar, 296
Williams, Aubrey, 359
Williams, Emily, 333
Willkie, Wendell, 272, 275, 276, 280
Wills, Helen, 70
Wilson, Dale, 342
Wilson, Edith Bolling, 54–55, 284
Wilson, Kathleen, 342
Wilson, Woodrow, 49, 54–55, 65
Women's Trade Union League, 60, 103, 108
Woolley, Mary Emma, 354
Works Progress Administration (WPA), 190–191, 197–199, 201, 204–205, 207, 211, 212, 229, 233, 250, 268, 285
World's Fair (1939), 215, 241
Wotkyns, Eleanor, 374

Yesterday's Milwaukee (Wells), 342
Youth Congress, 281